## DATE DUE

| NOV 6 2004 | | |
|---|---|---|
| | | |
| | | |
| | | |
| | | |
| | | |
| | | |
| | | |
| | | |
| | | |
| | | |
| | | |
| | | |
| | | |
| | | |
| | | |
| | | |
| | | |
| GAYLORD | | PRINTED IN U.S.A. |

# Saunders Books in Psychology

LEWIS F. PETRINOVICH and ROBERT D. SINGER, *Consulting Editors*

Gorsuch:   *Factor Analysis*

Johnson:   *Aggression in Man and Animals*

Kaufman:   *Introduction to the Study of Human Behavior*

L'Abate and Curtis:   *Teaching the Exceptional Child*

Sattler:   *Assessment of Children's Intelligence*

Singer and Singer:   *Psychological Development in Children*

Skinner:   *Neuroscience—A Laboratory Manual*

Stotland and Canon:   *Social Psychology—A Cognitive Approach*

Wallace:   *Psychology—A Social Science*

Hardyck and Petrinovich:   *Understanding Research in the Social Sciences*

**1976**

**W. B. SAUNDERS COMPANY**

Philadelphia, London, Toronto

# INTRODUCTION TO

# STATISTICS FOR THE BEHAVIORAL SCIENCES

## SECOND EDITION

**CURTIS D. HARDYCK**
*University of California, Berkeley*

**LEWIS F. PETRINOVICH**
*University of California, Riverside*

W. B. Saunders Company:   West Washington Square
Philadelphia, PA  19105

12 Dyott Street
London, WC1A  1DB

833 Oxford Street
Toronto, Ontario M8Z 5T9, Canada

**Library of Congress Cataloging in Publication Data**

Hardyck, Curtis D

Introduction to statistics for the behavioral sciences.

(Saunders books in psychology)

Includes index.

1. Psychometrics.     I. Petrinovich, Lewis F., joint author.
   II. Title.

BF39.H265 1975          150'.1'82          74–21013

ISBN 0–7216–4521–6

Introduction to Statistics for the Behavioral Sciences          ISBN  0–7216–4521–6

Last digit is the print number:     9     8     7     6     5     4     3     2     1

# PREFACE TO THE SECOND EDITION

The mortality rate for introductory statistics texts seems to be rather high. Of the astonishingly large number of texts introduced, relatively few seem to survive to a second edition. We are grateful to the many individuals who used the first edition and found it suitable (despite its many faults) and we hope that this edition will be as well received.

We have attempted to correct some of the problems of the first edition, first among which was a large number of typographical errors. There are few things more infuriating to either instructors or students than books containing trivial but misleading errors. We have made every effort to insure that this edition is as free of errors as possible, and would like to express our gratitude to the many who wrote to us and pointed out some of the errors in the earlier edition.

Several sections have been changed in this edition. The treatment of analysis of variance has been revised extensively (and, in our view, improved), and we have included a discussion of complex analysis of variance. The chapters on regression and correlation have been re-done completely and we believe they also have been improved. In addition, the relationship between regression and analysis of variance is discussed. A chapter on multivariate statistical methods has been added to the book. We have not included computational methods, but have provided a preview of the techniques and methods of multi-variate statistics. We are firmly of the opinion that multivariate methods will come to dominate behavioral science analyses in the future, and that early exposure to the concepts involved in these methods will do no harm but may prove to be quite adequate preparation for advanced courses.

We would like to thank Professor Roy Goldman for reviewing

and commenting on our chapter on multivariate methods, and Edith Lavin, who prepared the final manuscript copy and was of considerable help in our campaign to remove errors.

We are indebted to the Literary Executor of the late Sir Ronald Fisher, F.R.S., to Dr. Frank Yates, F.R.S., and to Oliver and Boyd, Ltd., Edinburgh, for permission to reprint Table A–9 from their book, *Statistical Tables for Biological, Agricultural and Medical Research*.

CURTIS HARDYCK
LEWIS PETRINOVICH

# CONTENTS

## CHAPTER ONE

# INTRODUCTION

It is hard to underestimate the extent to which statistics influence our lives. National political figures worry about public opinion statistics to such an extent that full time pollsters are retained to monitor constantly changes in public opinion. A drop (or rise) in the popularity of the President of the United States is a front page item for most newspapers. Stock market speculators anxiously scan the "Dow-Jones averages" for clues on how to invest. A large manufacturer of processed foods reads a statistical report on the declining birth rate in the United States and decides not to expand a factory preparing canned baby food. A gambler tries out a new system for winning at roulette and discovers (after spending a great deal of money) that his system does not work. Statisticians employed by gambling casinos anticipated his system long ago and adjusted the casino rules to insure that he had, at best, a million to one chance of beating the casino.

Almost everyone living in modern society is surrounded by statistics and has his life affected by decisions that are made on the basis of statistical findings. The advantages gained from at least an elementary understanding of how these decisions are made are justification enough for attempting to understand statistical concepts.

An ability to think in statistical terms and a knowledge of statistical concepts are perhaps the best safeguards a consumer can have against being tricked into making foolish decisions on the basis of advertising slogans calculated to impress (or mislead) a prospective buyer. An enjoyable presentation of the uses and abuses of statistics is given by Darrell Huff in his book *How to Lie with Statistics.** Huff's book is

---

*Huff, Darrell: *How to Lie with Statistics.* New York, Norton, 1954.

recommended to anyone who is curious about the extent to which misuses of statistics exist in our everyday lives.*

## Uses of Statistics in the Behavioral Sciences

Anyone preparing for a career in the behavioral sciences must understand statistical methods in order to comprehend the basic research literature in his field. Almost all conclusions concerning experimental data or survey results are based on statistical tests. If one is to understand how these conclusions are reached and is to be able to critically evaluate them, then it is essential that the logical steps involved in arriving at these conclusions be understood. Individuals in applied fields must have a knowledge of statistical principles to enable them to understand and to evaluate the research reports relevant to their interests. The research worker must have a thorough knowledge of statistics if he is to design experiments and to evaluate the results of such experiments.

In the behavioral sciences data are gathered to resolve questions regarding substantive issues. The experimenter who gathers such data must begin with a careful consideration of the types of statistical methods he will apply to the data, in order that the measurements he makes be in the proper form to permit the intended analysis. On the basis of these statistical analyses the experimenter usually decides whether or not his observed outcomes could reasonably be expected on the basis of chance variability. If he decides that the differences, or the relationships, may have been due to chance he will conclude, essentially, that his experimental manipulations did not result in an effect that could be detected with his procedures and measuring instruments.

## Methods of Teaching Statistics

There have been two primary approaches to teaching statistics. One approach is to present the material in a cook book form. The formulas and the statistics are interpreted for the student much as a recipe in a cook book is interpreted. The student is shown how to

---

*Almost any evening spent watching television will produce examples of the misuse of statistics. Note the next toothpaste, or aspirin, or whatever, advertisement that uses a phrase such as "Out of all dentists surveyed, four out of five recommended brushing with Bilge toothpaste." The number of dentists actually surveyed is not mentioned. The use of the percentage of people in favor of something is a similar gimmick, and equally worthless unless you know the numbers of people entering into the percentages.

take various ingredients (defined by a set of symbols) and how to mix them into a recipe (the formula). If the recipe is followed closely enough, a successful dish (calculation) will be the outcome. This approach has the advantage that almost any student can master at least the basic computational rules. However, even the good student prepared by this teaching method can only plug a set of numbers into formulas and mechanically solve those problems with which he has had some prior experience and instruction. The ability to apply the logic of statistical techniques to problems not previously encountered tends to be lacking in students taught by this approach.

The other conventional approach produces a much better trained individual and certainly improves the student's level of comprehension of statistical methods. At the same time, however, it demands much more of him. Here, the underlying logic of statistical methods is presented by means of mathematical proofs, algebraic demonstrations, and extended abstract accounts. The student is usually assumed to have the mathematical background sufficient to understand such material (a situation that greatly limits the audience to which such a text can be addressed). Alternatively, an attempt can be made to present both the underlying logic and the mathematical bases of statistics in such a way that only the simplest knowledge of algebra is required. In our opinion this is a difficult, if not impossible, task.

We believe that still another approach can be fruitful. Modern computing methods and the availability of digital computers have made it possible to demonstrate by concrete examples what previously could be shown only mathematically. In this text we will demonstrate some basic principles using computer generated examples to demonstrate some principles of modern statistical theory. This approach results in a minimum of mathematical explanation and algebraic derivation, but allows us to present the logic of statistical inference in an easily comprehensible manner.

We are emphasizing the basic logic because an intelligent use of statistical procedures demands more than an inflexible application of a fixed set of procedures. It is necessary to understand statistical logic in order to be able to plan and carry out research; failure to do so may result in data being collected that are worthless because of an inability to understand statistical considerations. Also, the type of statistical methods available to us influences the research problem selected and the manner in which it is approached. If a problem is so complex that we can find no way to untangle it for study, we have to move to a simpler type of problem or try to deal with only limited aspects of the more complex problem. Any researcher who is not aware of these considerations about the basic procedures of statistics is severely limited in what he can accomplish. He will be unable to ask certain kinds of questions and will not be able to understand the answers provided by other research workers.

## Suggestions to the Student

At this point, we would like to make two suggestions to the student who will be using this text. First, we suggest that you keep in mind that statistical theory is a well integrated set of principles and postulates. At times you will be asked to accept certain statements without proof until explanation can proceed to a point where the logic of the statements can be demonstrated. We have adopted this approach rather than attempt to present the entire basis of statistical theory in the initial stages. We will warn you of situations where you are asked to accept something temporarily without proof. Similarly, you will be warned when the relationships among certain concepts might not be clear. You should understand the basic principles of statistical theory and the logic involved in making inferences by the time you finish this book. If you are unwilling to take some things on faith and wish to know the nature of the relationships that are presented to you, the necessary references to obtain a more complete understanding are provided in the text, but this will demand a great deal of effort on your part.

The second consideration involves the differentiation of statistics and pure mathematics. If your experience is similar to that of the majority of students taking a statistics course for the first time, your expectations are probably determined by the courses you have taken in mathematics—whether high school algebra, college algebra, or introductory mathematics. In short, you may expect a simple, exact, and straightforward solution to a problem once you understand the mechanics and rationale by which the solution can be obtained. Unfortunately, statistics is not so simple. Statistical methods require the application of mathematical techniques to problems in the real world (such as the interpretation of data collected in a scientific experiment), and require both the elements of mathematical procedure and that of human judgment. Consequently, you must accept the idea that, after finishing a set of statistical calculations according to a set of prescribed rules, you must exercise a degree of subjective judgment and make reference to arbitrary conventions agreed upon by statisticians in order to interpret your results. This sequence of events will occur over and over again in the material you will encounter in this course. We cannot emphasize too strongly that statistics is a branch of mathematics applied to problems of the real world. If you limit your statistical work to events in which you can be guided by rules or equations, you will find that you are limiting yourself to a clerical or, at most, to a primitive descriptive function.

A primary use of statistical methods in the behavioral sciences is to evaluate the results of experiments and to provide guidelines an experimenter can use to interpret the results. Accordingly, a heavy emphasis is placed on experimentation as well as on the process of interpreting statistics and making inferences on the basis of these statistics. It should be emphasized, however, that statistical methods are of even greater importance when we consider data that have been gathered in natural situations that do not involve the use of experimental methods. Much of what we know about human behavior has been learned from the study of people's attitudes and from what they do in natural situations as opposed to the experimental laboratory. The problems involved in interpreting data obtained in such complex natural situations demand an even greater statistical sophistication than those faced by the laboratory scientist.

## CHAPTER TWO

# FUNDAMENTAL CONCEPTS

In this chapter some of the basic concepts and assumptions of statistical theory will be presented and briefly developed. The topics to be presented follow a logical sequence, although the student must accept some basic premises on faith rather than learning the underlying justification at this time. The material to be presented in this chapter is basic to the understanding of statistical methods and will be referred to time and time again. Consequently, effort spent in understanding the material in this chapter will be well repaid in terms of time and effort saved in later chapters. Three fundamental concepts will be introduced: *random sampling*, the *normal curve*, and *probability*. In addition, some aspects of their interrelationships will be presented.

## Measurements and Observations

Assume that we have a set of *observations* represented by numbers. These *observations* (the term we will use throughout the text to refer to any numerical measurement or score) could represent a variety of things: the heights or weights of people of a certain age and sex; the incomes earned by people in a given profession; or the scores on an examination such as the National Merit Scholarship Examination. Suppose that we have 1000 observations. If we were to take these 1000 numbers and place them on a graph with the values of the numbers arranged from the lowest to the highest along the horizontal axis and the frequency with which they occur along the vertical axis, we would construct a graph such as is shown in Figure 2–1. As a matter of fact, if these numbers represented any of a variety of observations in the real world, we would expect them to be distributed in a shape somewhat similar to the observations in Figure 2–1.

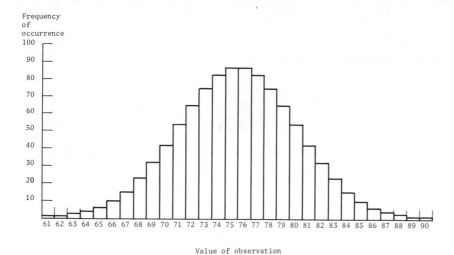

*Figure 2–1.* Normal distribution of 1000 observations.

There may be some skepticism as to whether real observations ever look anything like those in Figure 2–1. Figure 2–2 is a graph of scores on one of the standard tests of intelligence, the Stanford-Binet. Figure 2–3 is a graph of the weight gain of 100 pigs over a period of 20 days. These rather different examples are presented to emphasize

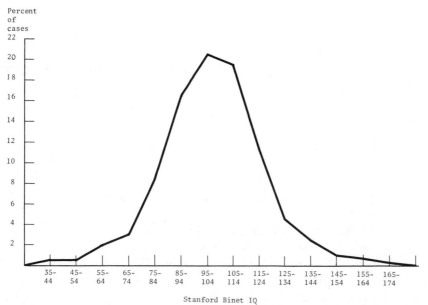

*Figure 2–2.* Stanford-Binet IQ's of 2904 unselected children between the ages of two and eighteen. (From *Measuring Intelligence* by L. M. Terman and M. A. Merrill. Copyright 1937, by Houghton Mifflin Company and reprinted with their permission.)

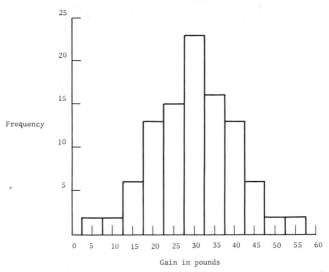

*Figure 2-3.* Graphical representation of gain in weight of 100 pigs over a 20-day period. (Reproduced by permission from *Statistical Methods*, 5th edition, by George W. Snedecor, © 1956 by The Iowa State University Press.)

the point that a wide variety of observations in the real world may be very similar to the demonstration set of 1000 numbers.

## GRAPHICAL METHODS

The conventional method of graphing observations is to represent the values of the observations along the horizontal axis (also called the x axis, or *abscissa*), and the frequency with which observations occur along the vertical axis (also called the y axis, or *ordinate*). Figure 2–1, 2–2, and 2–3 represent three possible variations in graphical representation.

Figures 2–1 and 2–3 are *histograms* (graphical representations in which the height of a bar is used to represent the frequency with which a given value occurs). Figure 2–2 is a *frequency polygon*. In this type of graphical representation points are placed to indicate the frequency of occurrence of given values and these points are then connected by lines. Such a method provides a continuous line enclosing the observations. The basic principle underlying all methods is the same — a change in area or size is used to represent the frequency with which a given value occurs.

Note that Figures 2–1, 2–2, and 2–3 also differ in the arrangement of the values along the horizontal axis. These units are known as *class intervals*. In Figure 2–1, the size of the class interval is 1, for Figure 2–2, the class interval is 10, and for Figure 2–3, the class interval is 5.

What determines the number of class intervals? This is largely arbitrary, since the nature of the scores to be grouped must be taken into consideration. Too fine a grouping destroys the purpose of grouping scores and too coarse a grouping will tend to lose information. In general, 10 to 15 intervals are usually satisfactory. As far as the question of where to start class limits can be answered, one approach is to have the lower limit of each class interval divisible by the class interval, $i$. However, this is a suggestion, not a rule. Note that Figures 2–2 and 2–3 do not use this approach.

In statistical terminology, the class intervals we have used are in terms of working limits. The theoretical limits for the lowest interval of Figure 2–1 are 60.5 to 61.5. This means that the interval theoretically encompasses all values within the range 60.5 to 61.5. Keep in mind that these are the limits in the mathematical sense and that the working limits run from 61 to 62.

## Populations

Examination of Figure 2–1 reveals, first of all, that there is a considerable range of values (from 61 to 90) and that some of these numbers occur much more frequently than do others. If these 1000 numbers represented all the scores of students in a small college on a scholarship examination, we would have what is known in statistics as a *population*. A population, in statistical terminology, is the total number of all possible observations of the same type; all the members of a given class or set of events.

Populations can be defined in a variety of ways; they can be a very small number of things or can be extremely large. For example, the United States census figures define certain characteristics of the entire population of the United States. Within this population another population can exist, e.g., all 36-year-old bald-headed men with one artificial leg. Similarly, all the students at a college at a certain time constitute the population of that college at that time. The population of interest to us may be all the students enrolled in a given university course, which would be a relatively small population. A larger population would be all children between the ages of three and five living within the geographical limits of the city of Stockholm, Sweden. Another population of interest could be all blue-eyed males in the United States, which is a large population. At the extreme our population of interest could be all living human beings on earth.

It is feasible to measure some characteristic of all the members of the population only in such instances as the population of students at a university, those enrolled in a certain university course, or the children between ages three and five living in Stockholm. The other two populations are too large to make such measurement practical.

What are the essential characteristics of the population of numerical observations shown in Figure 2–1? One essential characteristic is the shape of the distribution of the scores when they are graphed, as in Figure 2–1.

For this set of scores, the *distribution* (which is the statistical term for the arrangement of the observations along the scale of measurement) is symmetrical about a central point, tapering off gradually with fewer and fewer observations at the extremes. In appearance, the shape of this distribution somewhat resembles a bell, being very similar in appearance to a distribution known as the *normal curve* (about which much will be said later). Another important characteristic of this distribution is the most representative score—a number used to represent the value of all the observations. One such representative score is the *arithmetic mean*, which is obtained by summing the numerical values of all of the observations and then dividing that sum by the number of observations. For our example, the arithmetic mean would be equal to $75,500/1000 = 75.5$. Still another essential characteristic is the degree of variability—the extent to which the scores scatter or disperse around this most representative score.

## Representativeness of Information: Samples

Of fundamental importance in arriving at a conclusion on the basis of statistical information is the representativeness of the information about the characteristics of the population. If you are fortunate enough to be able to collect information on all the members of a population, then you need have no fear about the representativeness of your information; every possible observation—and thus all information—is present. For example, the Bureau of the Census does not need to worry about whether its statements about the average number of children per family in the total population of the United States are correct, since this information is based on the entire U.S. population; in other words, there is no estimation required. To take another example, if you wish to know how students at a certain college perform on a certain type of national scholarship examination and if you are able to give the test to every student in the college, then you need not be concerned about estimating how well students can do, since you have collected all the information possible. However, in all but a very few types of statistical investigations, measurement of the entire population is not possible. Usually you must settle for some estimate based on testing a few classes or sets of students selected along such lines as academic major, and then you must estimate from their scores how well all the students in the college would be expected to do. In all but a few situations you must settle for some very small estimate of the total population and must make an inference about the characteristics of the total population from the small number of cases actually studied. Those members of the population that are actually tested and on whose results the character-istics of the population can be estimated are known in statistics as a *sample*.

At this point we have defined what is meant in statistics by a population and by a sample. We have also indicated that samples are used to estimate the characteristics of a population under conditions in which not everyone in the population can be measured. If a sample is to accurately represent a population, every member of that population should have an equal chance of being chosen in the sample.

**Table 2–1.** IDENTIFICATION NUMBERS AND TEST SCORES FOR 1000 STUDENTS

| | | | | | |
|---|---|---|---|---|---|
| 000 | 61 | 255 | | 938 | |
| 001 | 62 | ↓ 329 | 73 | ↓ 960 | 83 |
| 002 | 63 | 330 | | 961 | |
| 003 | 63 | ↓ 412 | 74 | ↓ 975 | 84 |
| 004* | | 413 | | 976 | |
| ↓ 007 | 64 | ↓ 499 | 75 | ↓ 985 | 85 |
| 008 | | 500 | | 986 | |
| ↓ 013 | 65 | ↓ 586 | 76 | ↓ 991 | 86 |
| 014 | | 587 | | 992 | |
| ↓ 023 | 66 | ↓ 669 | 77 | ↓ 995 | 87 |
| 024 | | 670 | | 996 | 88 |
| ↓ 038 | 67 | ↓ 744 | 78 | 997 | 88 |
| 039 | | 745 | | 998 | 89 |
| ↓ 061 | 68 | ↓ 809 | 79 | 999 | 90 |
| 062 | | 810 | | | |
| ↓ 093 | 69 | ↓ 863 | 80 | | |
| 094 | | 864 | | | |
| ↓ 135 | 70 | ↓ 905 | 81 | | |
| 136 | | 906 | | | |
| ↓ 189 | 71 | ↓ 937 | 82 | | |
| 190 | | | | | |
| ↓ 254 | 72 | | | | |

*Subjects 004 through 007 all have scores of 64. The same convention applies to all ↓ groupings.

## RANDOM SELECTION

There are certain requirements or rules in statistics that should be observed when obtaining a sample. These requirements serve the same basic function as the rules in certain types of games; they must be followed if you are to be able to complete the game satisfactorily. The first rule to be considered is that of *random selection. Random selection requires that every member of a population have an equal chance of being selected in a sample.*

An example of this procedure can be demonstrated with Figure 2–1. Assume that the distribution of 1000 observations represents the scores of college students on a scholarship examination. In order to draw a random sample from this population, we will arbitrarily assign identification numbers to each student. We will assign the student who received the lowest score (a value of 61) the identification number of 000. The student with the next higher score (62) would have an identification number of 001. Since two students received scores of 63, it does not matter to which one we assign identification number 001 and to which we assign 002. The rest of the identification numbers are assigned such that succeeding numbers are assigned to students with increasingly higher test scores. Table 2–1 is a list of identification numbers and test scores for our entire population of 1000 scores.

When all the subjects in the population have been identified in this fashion, we can draw a random sample. To do this we use the table of random numbers (see Table A–1, p. 277). To select a sample of ten students we enter the table at any point we wish. Since the time needed to draw a random sample by selecting three digits will be considerably less, we will use this option. We will begin at the top of page 280 and read the first three numbers (976), and thus select subject 976 as our first observation for sample 1. Moving down the column to the next three digits, we find the value of 116 and select subject 116. Again, the primary consideration in random selection is to make sure that every subject in the population has an equal chance of being selected.

Five samples of ten observations each that have been sampled from the population of 1000 observations are shown in Table 2–2. The identification numbers of the subjects drawn in each of the five samples are listed. Note that subject 143 appears both in sample 1 and in sample 2. This is not an error; in true random sampling each observation is returned to the population as soon as it is selected. *Thus it is theoretically possible for the same observation to appear in more than one sample or even to appear more than once in the same sample. This method of sampling is called random sampling with replacement.* Usually in actual

**Table 2–2.** IDENTIFICATION NUMBERS AND SCORES FOR FIVE RANDOM SAMPLES DRAWN FROM THE SUBJECTS LISTED IN TABLE 2–1

| | | | | Sample | | | | | |
|---|---|---|---|---|---|---|---|---|---|
| 1 | | 2 | | 3 | | 4 | | 5 | |
| ID# | Score | ID# | Score | ID# | Score | ID# | Score | ID# | Score |
| 143 | 71 | 590 | 77 | 033 | 67 | 719 | 78 | 326 | 73 |
| 942 | 83 | 781 | 79 | 216 | 72 | 869 | 81 | 749 | 79 |
| 071 | 69 | 323 | 73 | 029 | 67 | 515 | 76 | 947 | 83 |
| 416 | 75 | 949 | 83 | 493 | 75 | 117 | 70 | 631 | 77 |
| 234 | 72 | 085 | 69 | 024 | 67 | 904 | 81 | 936 | 82 |
| 421 | 75 | 143 | 71 | 947 | 83 | 969 | 84 | 887 | 81 |
| 420 | 75 | 359 | 74 | 783 | 79 | 854 | 80 | 801 | 79 |
| 967 | 84 | 001 | 61 | 790 | 79 | 244 | 72 | 444 | 75 |
| 238 | 72 | 091 | 69 | 855 | 80 | 763 | 79 | 524 | 76 |
| 580 | 76 | 046 | 68 | 727 | 78 | 982 | 85 | 356 | 74 |

experimentation this requirement is not observed, since each subject is allowed to appear in only one condition. Therefore, the usual sampling procedure is not truly random, but is, rather, random sampling without replacement. This violation of the truly random procedure does affect the chances of subsequent cases being drawn, but if the number of cases in the population is quite large (as is usually true) the effect of non-replacement is so small that it is of no practical significance.

The locations of the observations sampled are shown in Figure 2–4 for the first two samples. The numbers along the baseline indicate the scale values. The dotted rectangles indicate the locations of the observations for sample 1. The black rectangles indicate the locations of the observations for sample 2. As can be seen, the observa-

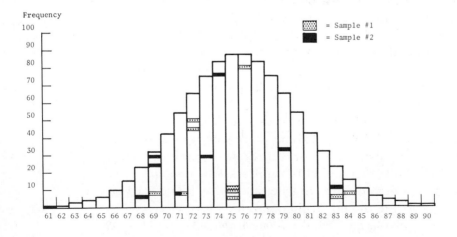

**Figure 2–4.** Location of two sets of sample observations drawn by random selection within a population.

tions are spread throughout the entire population. As is also evident from Figure 2–4, a sample is *not* a miniature replica of a population. Therefore, when decisions about a population are based on a sample, it is necessary to make allowance for the role of chance.

## Arithmetic Mean

As was mentioned earlier, we draw samples in order to make the best possible decision about the characteristics of a population. The average value of a set of observations is one of the things we frequently want to know. For example, one average, the *arithmetic mean*, is calculated by adding up all the observations and dividing that sum by the total number of observations. To determine the arithmetic mean for our total population of 1000 scores, we would add up all the observations and divide this sum by 1000. The sum of our 1000 observations is 75,500. When this sum is divided by 1000, the mean value of 75.5 is obtained. If we could follow this procedure every time we wanted to know the average of a population, sampling would not be necessary. However, in most circumstances we have only samples and must infer from these sample values what the values are for the total population. If we now take the two samples drawn earlier (Table 2–1 and Figure 2–4) and calculate the mean for each set of ten observations, we can compare these values with the population value and observe how close we come to the actual population mean using samples of only ten observations.

For sample 1, the sum of the scores is 752 and the mean is 75.2. For sample 2, the sum is 724 and the mean is 72.4. When we compare these values to the actual population mean of 75.5, we can see that, although neither sample estimates the population mean precisely, we have come quite close using only ten observations. In Figure 2–5 this is shown graphically.

If we look closely at sample 2 we can readily understand why its mean is so low. By chance the lowest observation in the population, 61, was one of the values selected randomly. This value was not balanced by a correspondingly high observation (which would be a value of 90). Therefore, the mean for this sample (72.4) is quite a bit lower than the population mean of 75.5.

## Statistical Inference

When we are drawing different samples from the same population we should be aware that samples vary by chance. On some occa-

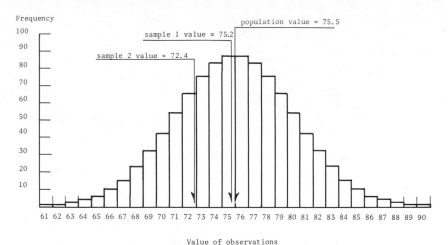

Frequency

population value = 75.5

sample 1 value = 75.2

sample 2 value = 72.4

Value of observations

***Figure 2–5.*** Accuracy of two sample means based on ten observations estimating the mean of a population of 1000 observations.

sions (as with sample 2) an extremely infrequent value in one tail of the distribution will be drawn and will not be balanced by a comparably infrequent value in the other tail. This will result in the sample mean being located away from the population mean and toward the tail from which the infrequent score is drawn. It is possible, under conditions of random sampling, to have many of the observations drawn from only one side of the distribution. For example, all the cases selected could be above the population mean. Such a sample would not provide an accurate estimate of the population mean.

*Using estimates of the characteristics of a population to infer the actual characteristics of the population is the process of statistical inference.* If we do not know the value of the population arithmetic mean, the best estimate we can make is the mean of a sample drawn from the population by random methods. Similarly, the best estimate of the degree of variability of the population scores around the arithmetic mean is the variability of the sample observations around the arithmetic mean of the sample.

The extent to which we can accurately estimate a population *parameter* (the term used to define a statistic calculated on an entire population), such as the arithmetic mean, on the basis of a sample statistic is a function both of random variation and of sample size.

Proper selection of the sample is one of the basic requirements for making a valid statistical inference. If a sample is chosen in such a way that it is not representative of the population, then a quantity calculated from the sample (such as the arithmetic mean) will not be an accurate estimate of the population value. The size of the sample is also extremely important. Although we can make correct inferences about a population from quite small samples, there is a perfect relationship between sample size and accuracy of estimation. In general, *the larger the sample size, the more accurate will be the estimation of the population parameters.*

## Standard Deviation

The index of variability most often used in connection with statistical methods based on the normal curve is called the *standard deviation*. The standard deviation is an expression of the average amount of variability of observations around their arithmetic mean and is one of the essential characteristics of a set of observations. The methods for the computation of the standard deviation will be presented in Chapter 4. At this point it is sufficient to note that it is a quantity that reflects the amount of variability of the observations around the arithmetic mean, and that it has certain properties that make it a valuable tool in statistical inference.

The process of estimating population values and of determining the amount by which these estimates may be in error will be dealt with at considerable length in the remainder of this book. However, before we proceed with the methods of making statistical inferences, some additional basic material must be presented. If the material to be presented is neither intuitively nor logically obvious, you are asked to accept the sequence of events to follow. Hopefully, the logic will be reasonably clear by the end of this chapter.

## THE NORMAL CURVE

To begin, let us review some basic characteristics of the population of 1000 observations that we first presented on page 7. Note that the observations are symmetrical about the mean of 75.5 and that the frequency with which the observations occur decreases as they are located away from the mean. For example, an observation of 75 occurs 87 times out of 1000, while an observation of 89 occurs only once, and an observation of 65 only six times. As you may suspect, these observations were deliberately arranged to have this shape so they would resemble a mathematical entity that is fundamental to statistical inference. This entity is known as the *normal curve*. Figure 2–6 is an illustration of a theoretical normal curve and Figure 2–7 is our population of 1000 observations with the normal curve shown superimposed on it. The equation for the normal curve (which requires a knowledge of calculus to understand) need not concern us here. What is important is that the distributions of many events in the

Frequency
of
occurrence

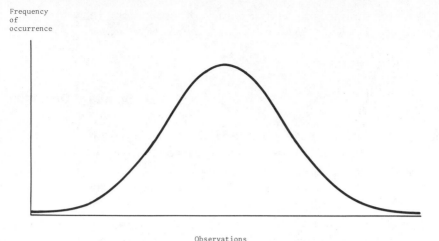

Observations

***Figure 2-6.*** Theoretical normal curve.

real world, if examined in large amounts, are found to have the same basic shape as the normal curve. Our earlier examples (pp. 8–9) were offered as evidence for this point.

Certainly not all things are normally distributed. We would not, for example, expect to give 20 students in a class an exam and find that the scores resembled the normal curve when graphed, but if 1000 students were tested, the distribution of the scores might well resemble the normal curve. However, the fact that large numbers of observations tend to look like the normal curve when graphed is not the most important consideration. Many types of observations never distribute normally. For example, Figure 2–8 is the distribution of the times people arrive for work in the morning. Most people arrive exactly at the scheduled time for work to begin. In this example no one arrives early, and as the minutes go by fewer and fewer people arrive.

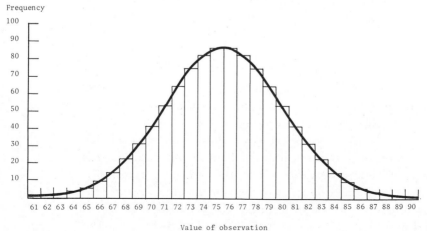

Value of observation

***Figure 2-7***

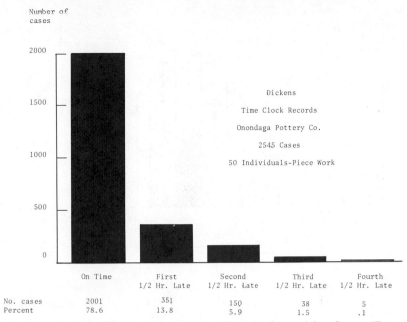

Number of cases

Dickens

Time Clock Records

Onondaga Pottery Co.

2545 Cases

50 Individuals-Piece Work

| | On Time | First 1/2 Hr. Late | Second 1/2 Hr. Late | Third 1/2 Hr. Late | Fourth 1/2 Hr. Late |
|---|---|---|---|---|---|
| No. cases | 2001 | 351 | 150 | 38 | 5 |
| Percent | 78.6 | 13.8 | 5.9 | 1.5 | .1 |

*Figure 2–8.* A distribution of the times people arrive for work in a factory (From Allport, F. H.: The J-Curve Hypothesis of Conforming Behavior. *The Journal of Social Psychology* 5:141–183, 1934).

Observations such as these would never distribute normally, no matter how many thousands of them we accumulate, since the underlying reality is not normally distributed, but if we drew small samples of 30 or more observations from this set of measurements and then calculated the arithmetic mean for each of these samples, we would find that the distribution of sample means would assume a shape very similar to the distribution of the normal curve if we carried the process on long enough. This is one of the fundamental laws of statistical inference. Statistics (such as means) calculated on samples of 30 or more observations will distribute normally even when the population from which they are taken is not distributed normally. Consequently, the properties of the normal curve can be used in problems of statistical inference even when the underlying measurements are not distributed normally.

This can easily be illustrated as in Figure 2–9, which contains two sets of scores. The scores in Figure 2–9 *A* were obtained by using a computer to draw 100 samples of 30 observations each from our population of 1000 normally distributed observations and then to calculate the mean for each sample. The resulting 100 means are graphed on the distribution of the population of scores. These means tend to distribute in a "normal curve" fashion. The mean of these sample means is 75.36, which is quite close to the true population mean of 75.5. The observations in Figure 2–9 *B* were obtained in the

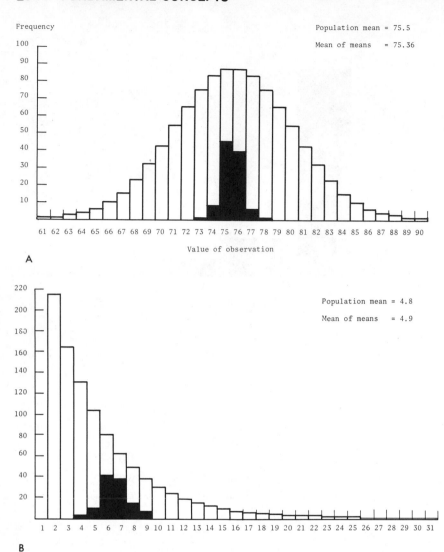

**Figure 2-9.** *A* and *B*, see text for explanation.

same manner, but the population from which they were drawn resembles the distribution based on the times at which people arrive for work, as shown in Figure 2–8. (This is called an exponential distribution.) However, the distribution of means calculated from samples of 30 observations drawn randomly from this population has much the same shape as the distribution of means calculated from the population of normally distributed observations. The mean of these sample means is 4.9. The true population mean is 4.8. Again, the estimate is quite close to the population mean.

USES OF THE NORMAL CURVE.    It might seem reasonable to question just why the normal curve is so important in statistics. The answer is straightforward: the normal curve can serve as a mathematical model for the frequency with which observations in the real world would be expected to occur and, therefore, may be used to estimate the probability of an event occurring or not occurring. For example, look at Figure 2–1 again. Note that certain observations, such as 74 or 76, occur many more times than do observations of 62 or 90. Suppose we were to write these observations on slips of paper and then shake them in a bag until they were completely mixed. (This is essentially what is done when we use a random number table to select a sample.) Suppose you now reach in and draw out one slip of paper. What are your chances of drawing an observation of 74? An observation of 90? Given the circumstances that any observation in the total of 1000 has an equal chance of being selected, the chances of drawing an observation with the value of 74 are better than those of drawing an observation with the value of 90, simply because the value of 74 occurs more often. In statistics the likelihood of selecting a value is referred to as the probability of the occurrence of the value. The normal curve provides us (as you will see in later chapters) with a way to determine the probability with which events occur.

## PROBABILITY

The probability of an event occurring is the likelihood that the event will occur compared to the likelihood that it will not occur. The probability of occurrence of an event is defined as follows: if something can happen in $x$ ways and not happen in $y$ ways, then the probability of $x$ occurring is equal to $\dfrac{x}{x+y}$. This ratio can vary from valules such as .000000001 or less (extremely low probability) to 1.00 (the event *always* happens). If your local weather report stated that the chances of rain in the next 24 hours were three out of ten, then the probability of rain would be $\dfrac{3}{3+7}$ (three chances that it will rain; seven chances that it will not) $= 3/10 = .30$. This will be a sufficient definition of probability for the time being.

To return to a consideration of our population of 1000 observations, we can ask what the probability is of obtaining an observation with the value of 75. Since there are 1000 observations and the value of 75 occurs 87 times, the probability of drawing a value of 75 from this population is equal to 87/1000, which is equal to .087. Similarly, if we wished to know what the probability is of drawing a value of 64, we would divide 4 (the frequency of occurrence of the value of 64) by 1000 to obtain the probability of .004. Thus the probability of drawing a value of 64 is considerably less than the probability of drawing a value of 75.

The probability of an event's occurring or not occurring is directly related to the frequency with which it does occur relative to the number of ways it does not occur. In our example of 1000 observations a value of 90 occurs only once, whereas a value of 74 occurs 84 times. If something can happen only one way out of 1000 and cannot happen 999 ways out of 1000, the probability of its occurring will certainly be less than for an event that can occur in 84 ways and cannot occur in 916 ways.

How does the normal curve enter into the estimation of probability? This will be dealt with in detail in Chapter 5. The calculation of probabilities is not possible unless we can make some assumptions about the underlying distribution of the observations in the population. For now, it is sufficient to say that many different kinds of measurements and observations in the real world do distribute normally (or nearly so) and allow us to use the normal curve to estimate the probability of obtaining given values. The characteristics of the normal curve distribution can be completely specified, and can provide a model for reality that will allow us to determine probabilities. Keep in mind also that the normal curve is useful as a model of reality because calculated statistics such as arithmetic means distribute normally, even if the observations on which they are calculated are not normally distributed.

## Measurement, Scaling, and Statistics

To this point, we have presented what is basically a discussion of the methods used to interpret the meaning of a set of numbers and the calculations based on them. Let us now discuss briefly the process by which differences in quantities are assigned numbers—a process known as *scaling*.

Much of this process involves a good deal of arbitrariness; a way of providing a system to determine relationships. Americans understand height and weight measurements in inches and pounds; the majority of the rest of the world understands it in meters and kilos. One set of measurements is easily convertible into the other and cultural tradition largely determines which is used—an Englishman, for example, can confound most of us by giving his weight in stone.

The above examples are soundly based in reality; height and weight really exist and we can accept intuitively some of the reasons that the terms for measurement developed as they did. However, measurement in the social sciences is a somewhat different problem.

*Figure 2–10*

How do we assign numerical values to a test of intelligence? Is an intelligence test score of 120 twice as good as one of 60? Is a rating on a scale of social status of 4 one more than a rating of 3? One more of what? The process by which the material studied by psychologists, sociologists, and anthropologists is assigned numbers is often quite complex and is a frequently argued topic.

The classification system we will present was originally developed by the psychologist S. S. Stevens* and has achieved such general recognition that we see no reason to deviate from his classification. Stevens divides measurement into four classes or categories, each with its accompanying type of measurement scale: *nominal; ordinal; interval;* and *ratio.* Our presentation will follow Stevens' discussion and we will note where we differ on fundamental points of view.

A *nominal scale* is an arbitrary ordering of numbers to different items, persons, or events. The photograph above of a basketball team forms a nominal scale. This scaling accomplishes nothing except to help you identify a player by his number. No one assumes that No. 44 is twice anything of No. 22; the numbering is arbitrary and a convenience and everyone accepts it as such. A similar convention can be found in public opinion polling, where given racial groups may be polled and for convenience in tabulating, be assigned numerical values such as the following: Caucasian = 1; Negro = 2; Oriental = 3; and Spanish = 4. Here again the numbering is arbitrary and the change in quantities indicates nothing about the relationship of one group to another.

The next type in Stevens' classification is the *ordinal scale.* In the

*Stevens, S. S.: Mathematics, measurement, and psychophysics. *In* S. S. Stevens (Ed.): *Handbook of Experimental Psychology.* New York, John Wiley and Sons, 1951.

ordinal scale changes in numerical value indicate some change in quantity in the item being assigned numbers. Placing things in order is perhaps the best example. For example, suppose that eight children playing together get into an argument about who is the tallest. There is no ruler available, so exact measurements are not possible, but there is a wall and a pencil available. The children stand against the wall and a pencil mark is made indicating who is tallest, who is next, and so forth. The result is an ordinal scale in which all eight children are ordered from the tallest to the shortest, even though there may be very small differences between the heights of some of the children and very large differences between others. The fundamental characteristic of an ordinal scale is that the differences between values on it are not necessarily equal. Table 2–3 provides an illustration of a nominal scale still in use today. This scale was developed in the early 1800's by Admiral Beaufort as a way of ordering

**Table 2–3.** AN ORDINAL SCALE*

*From The Beaufort Scale of Wind Force*

| Beaufort Number | Sea Miles Per Hour (Knots) | Seaman's Description | Effect at Sea |
|---|---|---|---|
| 0 | –1 | Calm | Sea like a mirror. |
| 1 | 1–3 | Light air | Ripples with the appearance of a scale but without foam crests. |
| 2 | 4–6 | Light breeze | Small wavelets, more pronounced; crests have a glassy appearance and do not break. |
| 3 | 7–10 | Gentle breeze | Large wavelets. Crests begin to break. Foam of glassy appearance. Perhaps scattered white horses. |
| 4 | 11–16 | Moderate breeze | Small waves, becoming longer; fairly frequent white horses. |
| 5 | 17–21 | Fresh breeze | Moderate waves, taking a more pronounced long form; many white horses. |
| 6 | 22–27 | Strong breeze | Large waves begin to form; the white foam crests are more extensive everywhere. |
| 7 | 28–33 | Moderate gale (high wind) | Sea heaps up and white foam from breaking waves begins to be blown in streaks. |
| 8 | 34–40 | Fresh gale | Moderately high waves of greater length; edges of crests break into spindrift. |
| 9 | 41–47 | Strong gale | High waves. Sea begins to roll. |
| 10 | 48–55 | Whole gale | Very high waves with long overhanging crests. The surface of the sea takes a white appearance. The rolling of the sea becomes heavy and shocklike. |
| 11 | 56–66 | Storm | The sea is completely covered with long white patches of foam. Everywhere the edges of the wave crests are blown into froth. |
| 12 | 66+ | Hurricane | The air is filled with foam and spray. Sea completely white with driving spray. |

*Note:* The sea mile is 6080 feet, approximately 1.15 land miles.

*Reprinted from Mowat, Farley: *The Serpent's Coil.* Boston, Little, Brown & Co., 1961.

the observations of sailors about wind conditions and as a way to give sailing captains an idea of what might be happening as values on this scale changed. Note that there is an attempt made to keep some sort of equal intervals but there is no absolute way to determine whether the difference between force 4 and force 5 is equal to the difference between force 7 and force 8 — the scale thus serves as an ordering device but not as a precise measurement scale.

The ordinal scale is perhaps the most common type in psychological measurement. For example, a subject answers a personality questionnaire that consists of 175 true-false statements such as "I like repairing electrical appliances." The test is scored and the subject receives a score of 22 on a sub-group of items of a particular type. The score on this sub-group of items is interpreted as a trait score, to indicate how much of a particular personality trait will be ascribed to the respondent. In a test such as this there is no way to insure that all the items are of equal importance as indicators of the presence of this trait. Some items may be of much more importance in separating one group of individuals from people at large; other items may do the same thing but not as effectively. In other words, the items vary as to their effectiveness just as the difference between magnitudes on the Beaufort wind scale may vary from one category to the next.

Ratings such as "social status" are also ordinal scales. Social groups may be ordered by classifying them on a number of measures such as income, years of education, or area of residence. A person with a low income and no formal education might receive a rating of "1" on such a scale while a person with a high income who has graduated from college would be rated as a "4." There is no implication here that the person rated 4 has three more of anything — money, education, or whatever — than the person rated 1. However, the system does serve to order people on such composite dimensions, indicating that the person rated 4 has more income, education, or whatever else is measured than a person rated 1, 2, or 3.

The next kind of scale in Stevens' classification is the *interval scale*. Two kinds of interval scales are shown in Figure 2–11. These scales differ from the previously discussed ordinal scales in that differences between intervals are the same throughout the scale. The difference between 34 and 36 on the Fahrenheit scale is the same as that between 81 and 83, and the differences between 18 and 20 and between 30 and 32 on the Centigrade scale are of the same magnitude. We will not have many occasions to refer to this type of scale since there are almost no measurements in the behavioral sciences that reach the level of equal intervals throughout the scale.

The final type of scale discussed by Stevens is the *ratio scale*. The ratio scale is similar to the interval scale in having equal intervals

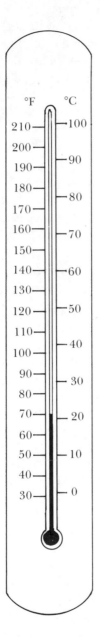

**Figure 2-11.** An interval scale.

throughout its extent and differs from the interval scale only in having a true zero point that indicates the absence of any of that quantity. To obtain a ratio scale with the interval types of scales shown above in temperature measurement, we have to use the Kelvin temperature scale used by physicists, in which zero means the absence of any heat at all. On the Kelvin scale 0° Centigrade and 32° Fahrenheit are equal to 325° Kelvin. Since there are no ratio scales in the behavioral sciences, we will not be concerned further with this problem.

While the types of scales used in the behavioral sciences may be limited, they are of use in further computations. Some writers on the subject of measurement have developed the curious notion that only certain statistical methods are appropriate to certain types of scales — as if the number assigned had some mystical though real physical relationship to the quantity to which it is assigned. There is absolutely no evidence to support this point of view, and it is mentioned here only because some texts and some writers on this topic persist in specifying unnecessary and arbitrary limitations on the uses of certain statistics. A statistic is completely independent of the numbers on which it operates and is totally unconcerned about the nature of the measurement scales to which the numbers are fitted. There is nothing at all to prevent us from calculating an arithmetic mean on the numbers of the basketball players shown in Figure 2–10. The mean as such would be difficult to interpret since the numbers do not refer to any ordered set of terms, but it can be calculated and does represent accurately the average value of the numbers. In general, we are perfectly safe in calculating any statistic we want on any set of measurements that have the properties of an ordinal scale. There is definitive evidence* that statistics calculated on ordinal measurements are just as reliable and meaningful as statistics calculated on interval or ratio scales of measurement.

## SUMMARY

1. The characteristics of a population can be inferred from a sample drawn under true random conditions. In our illustration, we used a sample of 10 observations to estimate the arithmetic mean of a population of 1000 observations and found that we could estimate the population mean with reasonable accuracy.

2. The larger the sample, the more precise the estimate of the population values.

3. Many sets of observations in the real world will distribute in a symmetrical, bell-shaped manner if they include a large enough number of observations.

4. Statistics such as the arithmetic mean, when calculated from random samples, will distribute in a symmetrical, bell-shaped manner even if the population from which they are drawn does not have this distribution.

---

*Baker, B. O., Hardyck, C. D., and Petrinovich, L. F.: Weak measurements vs. strong statistics: An empirical critique of S. S. Stevens' proscriptions on statistics. *Educational and Psychological Measurement, 26*:291–309, 1966.

5. The normal curve is a theoretical mathematical equation that has the same symmetrical bell-shape as do the statistics calculated from random samples.

6. The probability with which an event will occur is defined as the frequency with which it does occur relative to the total number of possible outcomes.

7. The theoretical normal curve can be used as a model of the frequency with which events occur and can be used to estimate the probability with which events occur.

The field of statistics has been described as a body of methods used to make wise decisions in the face of uncertainty. Usually, we are faced with the circumstance that we do not know the characteristics of a population, and on the basis of the evidence available from the sample we want to make an inference regarding the characteristics of the population. We have discussed the fact that if a population is normally distributed we know a great deal about the distribution of its observations relative to one another since we can use the mathematical normal distribution to describe the characteristics of the population in the real world.

In this chapter we have identified the essential elements that characterize a distribution: the nature of the measuring scale, the number of observations, type (or shape) of the distribution, location of the distribution, and variability of the distribution. Since in the real world we usually do not know anything about the "true" population values, the best estimate we can make of these values is on the basis of the sample values we have obtained. The best estimate we can make of the population mean is the obtained sample mean. The best estimate we can make of the population variability is the obtained sample variability. If we can also assume that the population is normally distributed (as many things are) and that the number of cases is extremely large, then we have all of the information we need to estimate the population parameters completely.

The exact nature of the processes by which we estimate population parameters, and the use of statistical procedures to evaluate the result of experiments, are the major concern of the remaining sections of this book.

## EPILOGUE

We have now presented some of the basic steps involved in statistical inference. If you are confused at all, you are urged to reread the chapter. These principles of statistical methods are developed in more detail later and reference will frequently be made to the introduction given in this chapter.

## CHAPTER 3

# THE ESTIMATION OF CENTRAL TENDENCY

In the last chapter, the concept of random sampling was introduced and illustrated. Samples of ten observations were drawn randomly from a population of 1000 observations and the distribution of the samples in the population was shown. If we draw a sample from a population it is because we want to know something about that population. Consequently, we must carry out calculations that will provide us with summary information about the characteristics of that sample.

What we would like is a single number that can be used to represent all the observations in the sample. If this number is to be the sole representative of all the values of the observations, then it should be a value that is near the middle of the sample values or where the sample values are most numerous.

### Statistical Notation

Before we discuss the specific measures of central tendency we should introduce some conventions concerning statistical notation that will be observed throughout this book. Statistical symbols basically are no different from the conventional shorthand expressions used in many branches of life. For example, college students abbreviate references to their courses by saying that they are taking "Econ 104" or "Psych 32." This is basically a shorthand language understood by anyone who has learned what the symbols stand for. The symbols used in statistics are basically the same, and are no more difficult to learn (although it may seem so at first).

The symbol $X$ is used to stand for any observation in a distribution (this is called an observation or "raw score"). Let us use one of our samples of ten observations as an illustration. $X$ may stand for any of those ten observations. $X_1$ is used to symbolize the first observation in the sample, $X_2$ to symbolize the second observation, $X_3$ to symbolize the third observation, and so on through $X_{10}$, which symbolizes the tenth observation. If we want to indicate to someone that the ten observations should be added together to obtain the sum, we can, then, write the following: $X_1 + X_2 + X_3 + X_4 + X_5 + X_6 + X_7 + X_8 + X_9 + X_{10}$. For sample 3 in Chapter 2, Table 2–2 (page 14), this indicates that the following procedure should be carried out: $67 + 72 + 67 + 75 + 67 + 83 + 79 + 79 + 80 + 78$. Since this is a very cumbersome notation, especially with a large number of observations, a simpler way of indicating this is to write $X_1 + X_2 + \ldots + X_{10}$. This notational method is still cumbersome. Therefore, another statistical symbol, the Greek capital letter *sigma* ($\Sigma$), is used to stand for the words "the sum of." Now, we can write the instruction to add all the observations as $\Sigma X$. This instructs us to add together all the observations represented by the letter $X$. In our example this would mean adding the ten observations of the sample together. If we symbolize the observations in another sample by the letter $Y$ we can give instructions to add all the observations symbolized by $Y$ by writing $\Sigma Y$. If the observations in sample 4, Chapter 2, Table 2–2, are symbolized by $Y$, then $\Sigma Y$ equals $78 + 81 + 76 + 70 + 81 + 84 + 80 + 72 + 79 + 85 = 786$. It should be emphasized that any arbitrary symbol can be used to stand for observations. If only one set of observations is involved we prefer the symbol $X$, however.

Another conventional symbol is the letter $N$, which stands for the number of observations. If we wished to instruct someone to take the simple arithmetic average (or mean) of some numbers we could write: $\frac{\Sigma X}{N}$. This indicates that all the observations symbolized by $X$ are to be added together and this sum is to be divided by the number of observations. The result of this computation is the arithmetic mean. Since the arithmetic mean is used so often it has its own symbolic representation, $\bar{X}$.

As you become more familiar with the symbols used, they will look less strange and will begin to take on meanings of their own. They will become intelligible immediately on perceiving them, as are such shorthand abbreviations as "Econ 104," "Psych 32," and similar ones that are immediately understandable without your having to think about the meanings expressed.

## ARITHMETIC MEAN

The arithmetic mean, which was introduced in Chapter 2, is one of the most frequently used measures of central tendency. It takes every observation into account, and is (with certain exceptions) a value that is near the middle of the sample values. It is one of the most common and most useful summary measures in statistics.

The arithmetic mean is a quantity with which you are all familiar. You have all been concerned with whether your grades are above or below "average," with whether a test score was above or below "average" and so forth. To find the arithmetic mean you *sum all the observations and divide that sum by the number of observations*. We can express this statement using statistical notation as follows:

$$\bar{X} = \frac{\sum X}{N}.$$  (3–1)

For our population the sum of the 1000 observations is 75,500. When that sum is divided by the number of observations (1000), the arithmetic mean is found to be 75.5 ($\bar{X} = 75,500/1000 = 75.5$).

### Sample Means as Estimates of the Population Mean

We are seldom able to calculate the arithmetic mean for an entire population since all the observations are not available. In the majority of situations we are limited to gathering samples and attempting to estimate the population mean on the basis of these samples. Often this must be done on the basis of one sample alone. In Chapter 2 five samples of ten observations each were drawn on a random basis and Figure 2–4 (p. 14) was constructed to show the distribution of these observations through the population. We can now ask how accurately these small samples estimate the mean of the population. To do this we perform the same calculations we did to determine the population mean — the observations within each sample are summed and these sums are then divided by the number of observations in each sample. Table 3–1 is the result of these calculations for the five samples of Table 2–2.

In Figure 3–1 these five means are located in the distribution of the population values. Our ability to estimate accurately the population mean on the basis of relatively small samples drawn on a true random basis is really quite good; however, there are occurrences

**Table 3–1.**  The Sum of Observations and the Arithmetic Means for Each of the Five Samples of Ten Observations Each in Table 2–2

|          | 1     | 2     | 3     | 4     | 5     |
|----------|-------|-------|-------|-------|-------|
| $\sum X$ | 752   | 724   | 747   | 786   | 779   |
| $N$      | 10    | 10    | 10    | 10    | 10    |
| $\bar{X}$ | 75.2  | 72.4  | 74.7  | 78.6  | 77.9  |

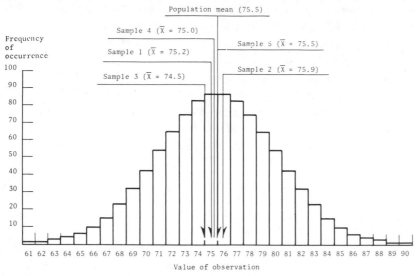

**Figure 3–1.** Relationship of sample means ($N = 10$) to the population mean.

(such as in samples 2 and 4) in which the deviation from the actual population mean is considerable.

At this point it might seem reasonable to ask "if the samples had been larger, would the population mean be estimated more accurately?" The general rule that can be stated in answer to this question is as follows: The larger the sample size in relation to the population size, the greater the precision of the estimate. As an illustration

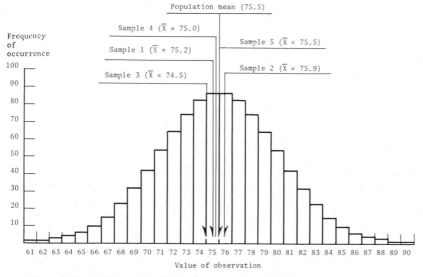

**Figure 3–2.** Relationship of sample means based on 20 observations to the population mean.

of this, consider Table 3–2. This table contains the values for five samples of 20 observations each (exactly twice the size of our original samples). Note that the mean values calculated from these samples deviate much less from the population value than is the case with samples of ten observations each. Whereas the range of sample means ($\bar{X}$'s) with $N = 10$ was from 72.4 to 78.6, the range of sample $\bar{X}$'s with $N = 20$ is only from 74.5 to 75.9, a range of 1.4 as compared to the range of 6.2 for the means based on ten observations. The values of these five means are located in the distribution of the population values in Figure 3–2. If the number of cases in each sample had been less than ten, the variability of the sample $\bar{X}$'s around the population mean would have been even greater.

The likelihood of a less accurate estimate of the population mean based on a single sample is, thus, fairly high with a small sample $N$. Conversely, as the number of cases in each sample increases, the less the variability of the sample $\bar{X}$'s around the population mean, and the less the likelihood of an inaccurate estimate of the population mean based on a single sample. The limiting case, of course, would be reached when the single sample $N$ is so large that it includes all of the cases in the population. In this event, the estimate would *be* the population and there would be *no* error.

Earlier, in discussing our original population of 1000 observations, we mentioned that they tended to follow a symmetrical, somewhat bell-shaped pattern. In Chapter 2 we discussed the relationship between sample means and the population mean. We will now use a computer to draw randomly 100 samples of size 30 (remembering that under true random conditions each observation is returned to the original population as soon as it is selected so that, theoretically, it is possible for one score to be selected over and over again) and will calculate the arithmetic mean for each of the 100 samples. We can graph these values in the same way we graphed the original 1000 population observations. The obtained distribution is shown in Figure 3–3. You can see from Figure 3–3 that our set of 100 $\bar{X}$'s has a very definite relationship to the original population of observations. If we treat the $\bar{X}$'s as observations and average them in turn, we find that the average (or mean of means) is extremely close to the population average. Note also that the distribution of $\bar{X}$'s is very similar in shape to the original population distribution.

Table 3–2. THE SUM OF OBSERVATIONS AND THE ARITHMETIC MEANS FOR EACH OF FIVE SAMPLES OF 20 OBSERVATIONS

| | | | | | |
|---|---|---|---|---|---|
| $\sum X$ | 1504 | 1518 | 1490 | 1500 | 1510 |
| $N$ | 20 | 20 | 20 | 20 | 20 |
| $\bar{X}$ | 75.2 | 75.9 | 74.5 | 75.0 | 75.5 |

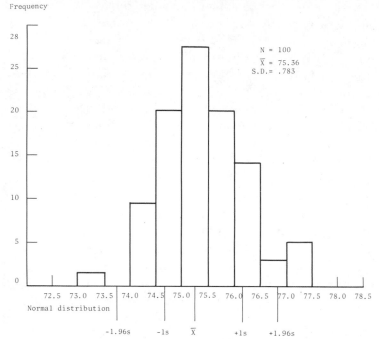

Frequency

N = 100
X̄ = 75.36
S.D.= .783

Normal distribution

-1.96s    -1s    X̄    +1s    +1.96s

***Figure 3–3.*** Distribution of 100 means calculated from samples of 30 observations each randomly selected from a normal population.

> Observations occur with the greatest frequency near the mean and disperse symmetrically about it, with observations at some distance from the mean becoming increasingly less frequent. Note also that when the means are treated as observations the range is much less than in the original population of 1000 observations. The fact that a set of means distributes in this fashion, and that fairly accurate estimates of the population values are possible using sample values, has considerable importance in statistical inference.

## ALGEBRAIC PROPERTIES OF THE MEAN

The value of the mean is one around which all the values of the observations are balanced according to their algebraic weight. The mean, then, is a point in a distribution of values at which the algebraic sum of the deviations from it is zero. Consider the following six values: 60, 61, 62, 64, 65, and 66. The $\Sigma X = 378$, and the $\bar{X} = 378/6 = 63$. We can set the $\bar{X}$ of the values to equal zero and express each of the values in terms of how far it deviates from the mean. (Since the use of numbers to represent quantities is arbitrary this does no violence to reality.) Expressed in this fashion, 60 becomes a $-3$ (60 − 63), 62 becomes a $-2$ (60 − 62), 61 a $-1$, 64 a $+1$ (64 − 63), 65 a $+2$, and 66 a $+3$. If we now add these values we have $(-3) + (-2) + (-1) + (+1) + (+2) + (+3) = 0$.

The deviation of a value from the mean is symbolized as $x$. Thus,

$x = X - \bar{X}$, and the summation, $\Sigma x = 0$. If one of the six values changes $\bar{X}$ cannot remain the same. Assume that the value 66 becomes a 69. If we set $\bar{X} = 63$ as before, our $x = (-3) + (-2) + (-1) + (+1) + (+2) + (+6) = +3$. Since $\bar{X}$ must be the algebraic center of this distribution we must change the value of $\bar{X}$. For this new state of affairs $\Sigma X = 381$; $\frac{\Sigma X}{N} = 63.5$; and $x = (-3.5) + (-2.5) + (-1.5) + (+.5) + (+1.5) + (+5.5) = 0$. Raising the value of 66 to 69 therefore increases $\bar{X}$ to 63.5 and, as it must, $\Sigma X = 0$.

Since each value influences the mean according to its algebraic weight, the value of the mean is strongly influenced by extreme values in one direction that are not balanced by extreme values in the other direction. To return to our original six numbers, assume that the value 66 is changed to a value of 136. Now $\Sigma X = 448$ and $\frac{\Sigma X}{N} = 74.67$. The value of $\bar{X}$ now exceeds the value of all but one extreme value. Obviously, the mean would not be a good quantity to choose to represent the distribution of observations in this instance.

## OTHER MEASURES OF CENTRAL TENDENCY

*Median.* Another measure of central tendency that is often used is the median (Mdn). The median is defined as *a point above which 50 per cent of the observations fall and below which 50 per cent of the observations fall.* Note that unlike the mean, the median is based on the *number of observations*, not on the values of the observations. The median is simple to determine, since one merely has to rank the observations in order of their scale value and then to count the number of observations until the halfway point is reached. The ranking process does not take into account the size of the difference between one value and the next. It is simple to determine the median if an odd number of cases are involved. For example, consider the following five numbers: 7, 12, 1, 98, and 44. To determine the median, the numbers should be arranged in order of magnitude: 1, 7, 12, 44, 98. The median, then, is 12; two observations (1 and 7) fall below the median and two observations (44 and 98) fall above the median. A difficulty arises when there is an even number of observations. Consider the following four values that are arranged in order of increasing magnitude: 14, 15, 17, and 18. The median of these four observations will be the value midway between the second value (15) and the third value (17). There is no observation at that point, so it will be necessary to split the difference between the two values. The total distance between 15 and 17 is two, and half of that distance is one. Therefore, the median is 15 + 1, or 16. This example is illustrated graphically below. Each observation can be considered to occupy an equal amount of space along a continuous scale of values as illustrated.

|  | Median | | | |
|---|---|---|---|---|
| Observation | 1 | 2 | ↓ | 3 | 4 |

| Value | 14 | 15 | 16 | 17 | 18 |
|---|---|---|---|---|---|

The median, then, falls halfway between the two ends of the scale. What is the median of the following four values: 13, 14, 18, and 19? Again, let us diagram the observations on a continuous scale.

| | | | Median | | | |
|---|---|---|---|---|---|---|
| Observation | 1 | 2 | – | ↓ | – | 3 | 4 |

| Value | 13 | 14 | 15 | 16 | 17 | 18 | 19 |
|---|---|---|---|---|---|---|---|

Again, the median will be the scale value halfway between observation 2 (value 14) and observation 3 (value 18). The total distance between 14 and 18 is four, and half of that distance is two. Therefore, the median is $14+2=16$. Even though the value of two of the observations has changed in the second example, the median remains the same since the rank order of the values does not change, and each of the two observations was symmetrically displaced. Let us consider another set of four values: 12, 14, 17, and 18.

| | | | Median | | | |
|---|---|---|---|---|---|---|
| Observation | 1 | – | 2 | – ↓ – | 3 | 4 |

| Value | 12 | 13 | 14 | 15 | 16 | 17 | 18 |
|---|---|---|---|---|---|---|---|

The median will still fall half the distance between observation 2 (value 14) and observation 3 (value 17). Now, the distance between the two observations is three; since one-half of three is 1.5, the median is $14 + 1.5 = 15.5$.

Consider one final set of four values: 13, 14, 15, and 16.

| | Median | | | |
|---|---|---|---|---|
| Observation | 1 | 2 ↓ 3 | 4 |

| Value | 13 | 14 | 15 | 16 |
|---|---|---|---|---|

The median will fall half the distance between observation 2 (value 14) and observation 3 (value 15, as before). This distance is one; one-half of one is 0.5. Therefore the median is 14.5.

In all four of these examples the median falls at a point where no observation occurs. In the last example the median occurred at a point halfway between two whole number values. This can occur even though the original measurements on which the scale of values are based are in terms of whole numbers, since the ranking procedure on which the determination of the median is based considers the number of observations and not the scale of values.

Since the median is based on the order of the observations rather than on their scale values, it is less affected by extreme values in one direction that are not balanced by extreme values in the other direction.

Consider the effect of changing the value of the lowest observation from 13 to 10 in the last set of four values that was presented.

|  | | | | | $\bar{X}$ | Median | |
|---|---|---|---|---|---|---|---|
| Observation | 1 | – | – | – | ↓ 2 | ↓ 3 | 4 |
| Value | 10 | 11 | 12 | 13 | 14 | 15 | 16 |

The median is not affected; it is still 14.5. The mean, however, is now 13.75 (instead of the previous 14.5). If the lowest observation value were changed to 5, the median would still be unaffected, while the mean would now be 12.5. Notice that both of these latter mean values are below all but the lowest observation. Therefore, the mean is not a good measure to use in an instance such as this when we are interested in choosing one representative number to characterize the location of the distribution of values.

The median is also known as the *fiftieth percentile*. Percentiles and percentile ranks are specialized statistics used most frequently in test construction. Since they have little use in statistical inference, computational methods for these measures are not presented in this text.

***Mode.*** One additional measure of central tendency is the mode, which is defined as the value that occurs most frequently. (More precisely, this is the value of the variable at which the concentration of the observations is densest.) In Figure 3–4 *A*, the most frequently occurring observation, and hence the mode, is 15. This distribution has but one mode and would therefore be described as *unimodal*. It is possible, of course, to have more than one mode in a distribution.

Figure 3–4 *B* has two modes; one mode is 13 and the other is 16. It would be described as *bimodal*. This type of distribution often occurs when two samples, each with a different location, are combined into one distribution. (An example of this would be a combined height distribution made up of both men and women. The mean height of the

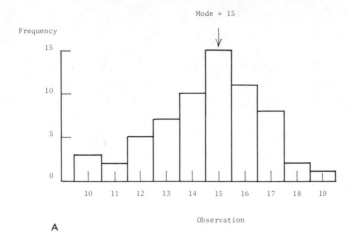

A

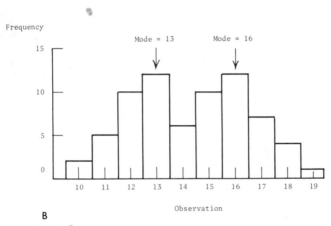

B

**Figure 3–4.** *A*, a unimodal distribution. *B*, a bimodal distribution.

men would be higher than would be the mean height of the women, and a bimodal distribution would probably be the result.) The mode has the advantage of being quick to determine and is a useful descriptive term to characterize the shape of a distribution.

## Skewed Distributions

A distribution of observations is called a skewed distribution if there are cases occurring at the extreme of one tail of the distribution that are not balanced by cases in the other tail. Figure 3–5 *A* is a *negatively skewed distribution* and Figure 3–5 *B* is a *positively skewed distribution*. The term "skew" refers to the direction toward which the tail end of the distribution is extended (and not, it should be noted, to the portion of the distribution at which the majority of observa-

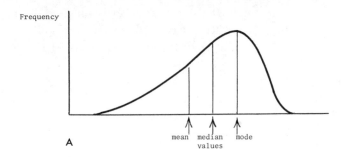

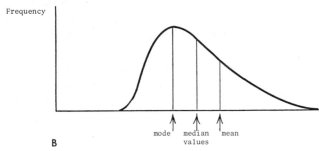

**Figure 3–5.** Skewed distributions. *A*, negative skew. *B*, positive skew.

tions are located). If the elongated tail of the distribution extends in the direction of higher values, then the direction of the skew is *positive;* if the elongated tail extends in the direction of lower values, the direction of the skew is *negative* (see above).

In a skewed distribution the three measures of central tendency always stand in the same relationship, as illustrated in Figure 3–5. The mode will not be affected by the distribution of observations in the tails of the distribution at all. The median will be different, since each observation in one tail that is not balanced by an observation in the other tail will change the median. The mean will be affected the most since each extreme observation influences the mean a great deal.

Therefore, in a positively skewed distribution the mean will be the highest of the three measures of central tendency, the median will be the next highest, and the mode will be the lowest. In a negatively skewed distribution this order will be reversed. Often, it is useful to report both a mean and a median if the distribution is markedly skewed. This gives the reader of these descriptive statistics an estimate of the degree to which the distribution is skewed. If the quantity $\bar{X} - Mdn$ is a positive number the distribution is positively skewed. If the quantity $\bar{X} - Mdn$ is a negative number the distribution is negatively skewed.

If the distribution is unimodal and symmetrical then the three measures of central tendency will all have the same location and only one of them need be reported. If this is the case, the mean is usually the value reported.

## Comparison of the Three Measures of Central Tendency

*Sampling Stability.* One important requirement for any sample statistic used to estimate the value of a population parameter is that the value of the statistic be stable from sample to sample. If we obtain widely varying estimates from sample to sample the conclusions we can draw regarding the true population value must be quite tentative since we have no idea which of the different sample values we should accept as being closest to the population value. The most stable of the three measures of central tendency from the sampling standpoint is the mean. If successive samples are drawn from the same population, the values of the mean will be found to show less variability than the values of either the median or the mode.

The mode is the least satisfactory measure of central tendency from the standpoint of sampling stability. Its location is determined by the observations at one scale value only. Therefore, if the number of observations are nearly equal at several points near the center of the distribution, the movement of only one or two in a distribution of several thousand observations can cause the mode to shift about. The mean would be affected hardly at all by such small shifts of observations in the center of the distribution, while the median would be moved only if the observations crossed from one side of the median to the other.

*Usefulness.* In general, the mean is the most useful measure of central tendency. It is used, in some form, in the sequence of computations involved in most methods of statistical inference. Most inferential methods require the computation of arithmetic sums and means. A few methods of statistical inference involve hypotheses about the median, but these methods are usually not as sensitive as the methods based on the mean, nor are they as adaptable to a wide variety of data. (This issue will be discussed further in Chapter 10.) The mode is practically useless in inferential statistics. Therefore, when the distributions of observations are relatively symmetrical the mean is preferred to both the median and the mode because of its greater usefulness in statistical inference.

The mean also permits a great deal of algebraic flexibility. The mean multiplied by $N$ equals the total sum of the observations, that is,

$\bar{X}(N) = \Sigma X$. Thi algebraic property permits us to perform many operations (and to simplify computational procedures) in ways that would not be possible using either the median or the mode.

*Ease of Computation.* If a frequency distribution is available the mode can be determined with no computation whatsoever. The median is easy to determine for a small number of observations, since this determination is based on ranking and counting. With a large number of observations the median is difficult to determine since the procedure of ranking many numbers is quite laborious. The mean is probably easier to calculate with a large number of observations than is the median since running subtotals can be kept, and the accuracy of the computation thereby can be verified much more easily.

In summary, the method to be preferred depends on the importance of each of these three factors. If a rough, quick measure will suffice and no further inferences are to be made, the mode might be preferred. If a bit more stability is desired, the median might be used instead. If the most stable and useful measure is desired, then the mean should be computed, provided that the distribution is not extremely skewed.

## Abuses of the Average

The average is one of the most frequently abused statistics. First, since there are three "averages" available it is not uncommon for someone desiring to give misleading information to report not the most representative measure of central tendency, but the one most advantageous to the position he wishes to support.

Second, most people have been taught in school to "average" numbers; that is, to calculate the arithmetic mean. Therefore, if one reports the median or the mode, most people untutored in the ways of statistics will assume that the arithmetic mean is being reported if the word "average" is used to identify the statistic.

Third, most people do not appreciate the fact that in badly skewed distributions the mean is inappropriate. For example, in reporting the average income of workers in a particular factory it is possible that of the 100 individuals, 99 of them earn between $5000 and $6000 while one of them (the president of the concern) earns $100,000. Basing an arithmetic average on this distribution could, then, result in an average income that is greater than the income of all but one person. Obviously, the mean is not a good index to use to represent central tendency for this type of distribution. In this example, either the mode or the median would be preferred. If the aim of the president is to avoid raising salaries, however, he might prefer to report the mean, since it bolsters his position.

Another frequent abuse of averages, especially prevalent in advertising, is the use of the phrase "up to." It is often reported that Brand X gives "up to" three times the wear of the average of the four leading competitors. This does *not* mean that Brand X is superior to the other four brands. In fact, it is possible that Brand X is the worst of the lot. The statement is usually interpreted by uncritical readers to mean that an average item of Brand X will be almost three times better than the average item of any of the other four brands. The statement does not say this, however. The statement says no more than that if the very best item produced by Brand X is selected, and if this best item is compared to the average item of the other four, the *best* of X will exceed the *average* of the others. The average of Brand X might be considerably below the average of the other four brands, and the best of Brand X might be far inferior to the best of the other four. This possibility would be enhanced if the quality control for Brand X was quite poor, in fact. Let us assume that the workmen producing Brand X are not trained or supervised adequately. The quality of the product, then, would depend on the workers' own diligence and conscientiousness. The result would probably be a product of considerable variability in quality. However, exceptionally good items would still be expected from Brand X. If these items from the extreme positive tail of the distribution are then compared to the center of the distribution for the other four, the cards are stacked in favor of Brand X.

In general one should always be wary when statistics are presented in order to convince one of the soundness of an advocate's position. Those skilled in misrepresenting reality usually understand that it is easier to convince people using argument based on numerical bases than it is to convince them using arguments based on verbal reasoning alone. Many people uncritically accept false "facts" and inappropriate representations of reality if they are stated quantitatively (especially if they are expressed to four decimal places). The material presented in this chapter should make it possible for you both to accurately represent a distribution of numbers and to interpret such representations.

1. Find the mean for the following sample: $X_1 = 15$; $X_2 = 27$; $X_3 = 12$; $X_4 = 14$; $X_5 = 20$; $X_6 = 18$.

2. a. Find the mean, median, and mode for the following distribution of scores: 2, 18, 9, 5, 5, 25, 4, 5.
   b. Is the distribution skewed? If so, in what direction?

3. a. Compute the mean and the median for the following distribution of scores: $X_1 = 10$; $X_2 = 25$; $X_3 = 9$; $X_4 = 11$; $X_5 = 32$; $X_6 = 12$; $X_7 = 13$; $X_8 = 34$; $X_9 = 14$; $X_{10} = 14$.
   b. For this distribution which of the two measures would be the best representation of central tendency? Why?

4. a. Which measure of central tendency is most affected by the degree of skewness in a frequency distribution? Why?
   b. Which measure of central tendency is least affected by the degree of skewness? Why?

5. One property of the mean is that the sum of the deviations of each observation from the mean must equal _____.
   Write the preceding statement in symbols.

6. The median is also known as the _____ percentile. Why?

7. In a negatively skewed distribution, rank the median, mode, and mean in terms of lowest to highest value.

8. For the following observations prove that $\bar{X}(N) = \Sigma X$: 10, 9, 11, 13, 15, 14, 12, 8.

9. Find the median for the following distribution of scores:

| X | f |
|---|---|
| 30–32 | 1 |
| 27–29 | 2 |
| 24–26 | 4 |
| 21–23 | 6 |
| 18–20 | 4 |
| 15–17 | 2 |
| 12–14 | 1 |
| | $N = 20$ |

10. If you were told that the mean for five students was 80.0 and that the mean for the three (out of the total five) who were men was 82.3, what would be the mean for the two women?

## CHAPTER FOUR

# ESTIMATION OF VARIABILITY

In the last chapter it was stated that the best single descriptive number to characterize the central tendency of a population of observations is the arithmetic mean, provided that the distribution of observations is unimodal and symmetrical. The mean can be estimated fairly precisely on the basis of relatively small samples and is usually the best representative of the individual observations in a symmetrical distribution.

Although the mean conveys considerable information about a population, it constitutes only a partial description of the population's characteristics. It is often as important to know something about the degree of variability of the individual values as it is to know the central location of these values.

An average, itself, tells us nothing about dispersion. In fact, we compute an average in order to see through the variability to the general location of the distribution. Obviously, if you cannot swim you should not decide to wade across a river if you are told only that the average depth of the water is three feet. The average, indeed, might be only three feet, but sometimes you might be in shallow water of only a few inches while at other times you might be in 12 to 20 feet of water. It is important to know something, then, about the dispersion of values around the mean if the distribution is to be described adequately.

The distributions shown in Figure 4–1 all have the same mean, but differ greatly in the manner in which the observations vary around that mean.

The same rules that we used to decide that the mean is the most useful average should apply to the choice of a measure of variability. This measure should summarize the characteristics of all the observations, as does the mean. Similarly, its value should reflect general

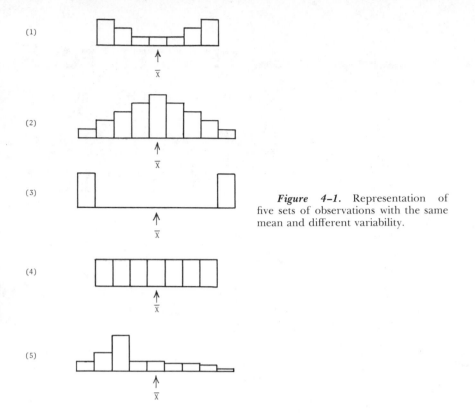

**Figure 4–1.** Representation of five sets of observations with the same mean and different variability.

tendencies for the entire distribution of observations and should not be radically affected by a few extreme values. Also, the measure should permit us to make inferences concerning the variability of the population distribution.

What is needed is another sort of average — one whose value increases as the variability of the observations in the distribution increases. If the mean is the single most efficient description of the location of a set of observations, any estimate of variability we use would do well to use the mean as a base around which the variations in observations are expressed.

One possibility is to subtract the mean from each value and then determine the average of these differences. However, the very nature of the mean makes this impossible. The mean is the algebraic balance point around which all values vary, and it is affected by every observation. The sum of the deviations around the mean, by definition, is zero. This is demonstrated in Table 4–1 where the mean for sample 1 has been subtracted from every observation in the sample and these deviations have been summed. The deviations sum algebraically to zero. In fact, as discussed in Chapter 3, if these values do not equal

**Table 4–1.** DEMONSTRATION OF THE DEVIATIONS OF ALL OBSERVATIONS AROUND A MEAN SUMMING TO ZERO

| Score<br>$X$ | Mean<br>$\bar{X}$ | $X - \bar{X} = x$ | $(X - \bar{X})^2$ |
|---|---|---|---|
| 71 | 75.2 | −4.2 | 17.64 |
| 83 | 75.2 | 7.8 | 60.84 |
| 69 | 75.2 | −6.2 | 38.44 |
| 75 | 75.2 | −.2 | .04 |
| 72 | 75.2 | −3.2 | 10.24 |
| 75 | 75.2 | −.2 | .04 |
| 75 | 75.2 | −.2 | .04 |
| 84 | 75.2 | 8.8 | 77.44 |
| 72 | 75.2 | −3.2 | 10.24 |
| 76 | 75.2 | .8 | .64 |
| 752 | | $\Sigma x = 0.00$ | $\Sigma (X - \bar{X})^2 = 215.60$ |
| | | $\Sigma \lvert x \rvert = 34.8$ | |

zero the value of the mean is incorrect. Obviously, we cannot estimate variability in this manner.

## AVERAGE DEVIATION

There are two solutions for the problem presented above that we can use. One is to subtract the mean from each value and to sum the deviations, disregarding the algebraic signs, and then to divide this sum by the number of cases on which it is based. This gives us a value that is the average amount of deviation regardless of the direction of the deviation. This value is called the *average deviation*. For the scores in Table 4–1 the sum of the deviations when the algebraic signs are ignored (symbolized as $\Sigma \lvert x \rvert$) is 34.8. The average deviation, then, is 34.8/10 or 3.48.

## SUM OF SQUARES

Another solution is to subtract the mean from each value and then to square each of these differences and sum them: $\Sigma (X - \bar{X})^2$. When we do this all the squared differences are positive and as the differences between the mean and the observations increase the sum of these squared differences will increase. This computation is shown for the ten observations in the fourth column of Table 4–1. This quantity is called the *sum of squares*

$$\Sigma (X - \bar{X})^2 = \Sigma x^2 \qquad (4-1)$$

and is symbolized as $\Sigma x^2$. The $\Sigma x^2$ is 215.60 for these ten values. This procedure uses the mean as a reference point, and eliminates minus signs by squaring the deviations. Thus, we have a number whose size increases as the amount of variability increases.

This second solution is the preferred method of representing the degree of variability, although it is not the most intuitively appealing one. It is preferred to the average deviation method because of its usefulness when making inferences based on a normal distribution assumption. If observations are normally distributed, a number of inferences regarding variability can be made using a standard table of the normal distribution and a statistic based on the sum of squares. This provides us with some powerful inferential methods, as we shall see in the next few chapters.

In order to obtain this measure of the variability of observations we divide the sum of the squared deviation values ($\Sigma x^2$) by the number of observations ($N$). This gives us a quantity which is defined as the *variance* and which is symbolized by the square of the lower case Greek letter sigma ($\sigma^2$) when referring to population parameters. The formula for the population variance is

(4-2)
$$\sigma^2 = \frac{\Sigma x^2}{N}$$

The variance is an average expressing the dispersion or scattering of observations around the arithmetic mean. The greater the dispersion of values around the mean, the larger the variance will be. This can be demonstrated by calculating the variance for some of the samples used in earlier examples. The formula for the variance of a sample is

(4-3)
$$\frac{\Sigma(X - \bar{X})^2}{N - 1} = \frac{\Sigma x^2}{N - 1}.$$

We will see the reasons for using $N - 1$ rather than $N$ in a moment. The steps involved in calculating the variance of a sample are as follows:

(1) Calculate the mean. $\bar{X} = \Sigma X/N$.
(2) Subtract the mean from each observation. $x = (X - \bar{X})$.
(3) Square each of the terms obtained in step (2). $x^2 = (X - \bar{X})^2$.
(4) Sum the squared differences. $\Sigma x^2 = \Sigma(X - \bar{X})^2$.
(5) Divide the sum of the squared differences by the number of observations minus one. $\Sigma x^2/(N - 1)$.

## Calculation of The Sum of Squares for The Population of 1000 Observations

In the examples shown in Table 4–2, the sum of squares ($\Sigma x^2$) was calculated by subtracting the mean from each observation,

**Table 4–2.** CALCULATION OF THE VARIANCE

| | | Observations |
|---|---|---|
| | | *Observations* |
| Step 1: | Calculate the mean. | 1 |
| | | 2 |
| | $\bar{X} = \sum X/N = 15/5$ | 3 |
| | | 4 |
| | $\bar{X} = 3$ | 5 |
| | | $\sum X = 15$ |
| | | |
| Step 2: | Subtract the mean from each | $x$ |
| | observation. | $1 - 3 = -2$ |
| | | $2 - 3 = -1$ |
| | | $3 - 3 = \phantom{+}0$ |
| | | $4 - 3 = +1$ |
| | | $5 - 3 = +2$ |
| | | $\sum x = \phantom{+}0$ |
| | | |
| Step 3: | Square each of the differences | $x^2$ |
| | obtained in step 2. | $(-2)^2 = 4$ |
| | | $(-1)^2 = 1$ |
| | | $(0)^2 = 0$ |
| | | $(+1)^2 = 1$ |
| | | $(+2)^2 = 4$ |
| | | |
| Step 4: | Sum the squared differences. | $\sum x^2 = 10$ |
| Step 5: | Divide the sum of the squared differences by $N - 1$. | $s^2 = \dfrac{\sum x^2}{N - 1}$ |
| | | $= 10/4$ |
| | | $= 2.50$ |

squaring the resulting difference, and summing the differences. While this does not present a difficult calculation for small sets of numbers, the process of subtracting the mean from each of 1000 values, then squaring each of the 1000 differences, and, finally, summing the 1000 squared differences is a rather tedious process. There is also a strong likelihood that calculational errors will be made, since the procedure requires such a large number of individual calculations. Fortunately, there are some computational short cuts to obtain the sum of squares that can be done in one operation on an automatic calculator. The "raw score" computational method, which we will use, is algebraically equivalent to the basic formula presented.

To obtain the $\Sigma x^2$ in one machine operation it is necessary to sum the values of the observations, to square each value, and to sum these squares. (See Chapter 1 of the Student Workbook for a description of some standard calculators and for a brief description of the method of operation of each machine.) The square of the summed observations is symbolized by $(\Sigma X)^2$, which is read as "the sum of observations, quantity squared." The sum of the squared observations is symbolized by $\Sigma X^2$. The $\Sigma X^2$ for our original 1000 observations in Table 2–1 equals 5,720,980. To obtain the quantity $(\Sigma X)^2$ we take the original sum of the observations as given on p. 31 in Chapter 3 (75,500) and square it ($75,500^2 = 5,700,250,000$). We now take this $(\Sigma X)^2$ and divide it by the total number of observations ($N$). The general equation for obtaining the sum of squares is

**(4–4)**
$$\Sigma x^2 = \Sigma X^2 - (\Sigma X)^2/N.$$

If we substitute our obtained values for the population into this formula we obtain the following:

$$\Sigma x^2 = 5,720,980 - \frac{5,700,250,000}{1000} = 5,720,980 - 5,700,250$$

$$= 20,730.$$

## Formulas for Population Values and for Statistics

At this point an important notational distinction must be made between *population values* (or parameters) and *sample-based estimates* of these population parameters. When the values under consideration are population parameters, Greek letters are used to symbolize the values. Thus, when we are referring to the variance of a population we use the symbol $\sigma^2$ ("little sigma" squared) to represent it. When the values are obtained samples we usually use lower case English letters to symbolize them. The variance of a sample is represented by the symbol $s^2$. This convention is followed in most statistics texts and will be followed throughout this text. The only exception to this rule is found when referring to the mean. The arithmetic mean of a population will be symbolized by the Greek letter $\mu$ (pronounced "mew"). The arithmetic mean of a sample will be symbolized by $\bar{X}$, however. This convention is extremely useful since it will help to keep clear at all times whether we are referring to hypothetical population values or to the actual sample distributions that we are using to estimate those population values.

Not only does the notational system differ when referring to population parameters as opposed to sample estimates, but the two kinds of values are computed differently in some cases. For the arithmetic mean, no difference is involved between the way the mean $(\bar{X})$ is calculated for a sample and the way the mean $(\mu)$ is calculated for a population. However, when calculating the variance for a sample, we divide our sum of squares $(\Sigma x^2)$ by $N-1$, rather than by $N$ as we would when calculating the variance for a population.

The following definitional formulas have been presented already:

$$\sigma^2 = \sum x^2/N, \qquad \textit{population variance}$$

$$s^2 = \sum x^2/(N-1), \qquad \textit{sample variance}$$

Substituting the necessary values into the equation for the population variance, we have:

$$\sum x^2 = 20{,}730.$$

Dividing 20,730 by 1000:

$$\sigma^2 = \frac{20{,}730}{1000}$$

$$= 20.73.$$

Why do we use different formulas to calculate the population variance and the sample variance? We have seen earlier that it is possible to estimate the mean of a population quite accurately even with relatively small samples. We have also seen that estimates of the mean are seldom extremely inaccurate even though the sample size may be quite small. Unfortunately, the same relationship does not hold for the variance. The variance will be underestimated systematically as the sample size becomes smaller and smaller. For example, if we estimate the population variance on the basis of three samples of $N = 10$ without dividing by $N - 1$ we would obtain the results shown in column 1 of Table 4–3.

If we compare the uncorrected variances for the samples with

Table 4–3. Accuracy of Estimate of the Population Variance from Small Samples ($N = 10$) Without and With an $N - 1$ Correction ($\sigma^2 = 20.73$)

| Sample | 1 $\sum x^2/N$ | 2 $\sum x^2/(N-1)$ |
|---|---|---|
| 1 | $142.68/10 = 14.27$ | $142.68/9 = 15.85$ |
| 2 | $177.63/10 = 17.76$ | $177.63/9 = 19.74$ |
| 3 | $191.23/10 = 19.12$ | $191.23/9 = 21.25$ |

the population variance calculated previously, we can see that the sample variances tend to be systematically smaller than the population variance of 20.73. If we did not use the $N - 1$ correction, we would consistently underestimate the value of the population variance using these sample estimates.

However, if we now correct our estimates by dividing each $\Sigma x^2$ by $N - 1$, as in column 2 of Table 4–3, we can see that our accuracy of estimate is much better. How much would the accuracy of our estimate improve if we were to increase our sample size? In column 1 of Table 4–4 the estimates of the population variance obtained without the $N - 1$ correction for three samples of $N = 40$ are shown. Column 2 contains the same estimate with the $N - 1$ correction. The accuracy of estimate obtained (even without the $N - 1$ correction) is considerably improved over the estimate obtained with samples of only ten observations.

The use of the $N - 1$ correction adjusts the systematic error introduced when small samples are used to estimate the population variance. If we draw a sample of 750 observations and our population is only 1000, the difference in the variance obtained by dividing by 749 instead of 750 is so small that it is not even observable until several decimal places are reached. However, if our sample size is ten, the difference in the values obtained by dividing the sum of squares by 10 in one case and by 9 in the other will be much more substantial, and this difference increases as the number of observations decreases. Therefore, the usual practice is always to use the $N - 1$ correction when using sample values to estimate population parameters.

## Calculation of Sample Variances

We have already calculated the sum of squares for sample 1 (Table 4–1) using formula (4–1), in which we subtract each score from the mean, square that difference, and sum those differences. Now let us use the raw score formula (4–4) to calculate the variance for sample 1.

**Table 4–4.** Accuracy of Estimate of the Population Variance from Samples of 50 Observations Without and With an $N-1$ Correction ($\sigma^2 = 20.73$)

| Sample | 1<br>$\sum x^2/N$ | 2<br>$\sum x^2/(N - 1)$ |
|:---:|:---:|:---:|
| 1 | $1295.39/50 = 25.91$ | $1295.39/49 = 26.44$ |
| 2 | $996.76/50 = 19.94$ | $996.76/49 = 20.34$ |
| 3 | $889.79/50 = 17.80$ | $889.79/49 = 18.16$ |

$$\sum X^2 = 56,766$$
$$(\sum X)^2 = (752)^2 = 565,504$$
$$\sum x^2 = \sum X^2 - (\sum X)^2/N$$
$$= 56,766 - (752)^2/10$$
$$= 56,766 - 565,504/10$$
$$= 56,766 - 56,550.4$$
$$= 215.6$$
$$s^2 = \sum x^2/(N - 1)$$
$$= 215.6/9$$
$$= 23.96.$$

Note that the calculation of the sum of squares with formula (4–4) results in exactly the same value as that obtained with formula (4–1).

The question now arises concerning the use of the variance to indicate the degree of dispersion of the distribution of observations. If we were to pictorially represent the values of sample 1 we would obtain the dispersion about the mean shown in Figure 4–2 A.

Let us compare sample 1 with another of the samples drawn earlier. If we calculate the variance of sample 2, we obtain the result shown in Table 4–5. The variance for sample 2 is larger than that for sample 1. If we graph sample 2 (Figure 4–2 B) in the same manner as we did sample 1 (Figure 4–2 A) and compare the two graphs, we see

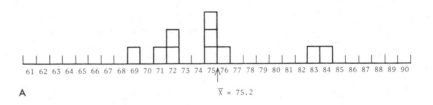

61 62 63 64 65 66 67 68 69 70 71 72 73 74 75 76 77 78 79 80 81 82 83 84 85 86 87 88 89 90

A

$\bar{X} = 75.2$

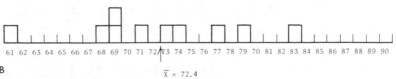

61 62 63 64 65 66 67 68 69 70 71 72 73 74 75 76 77 78 79 70 81 82 83 84 85 86 87 88 89 90

B

$\bar{X} = 72.4$

**Figure 4–2.** A, dispersion of observations for sample 1. B, dispersion of observations for sample 2.

that the observations for sample 2 are more widely dispersed. This greater dispersion is reflected in the larger numerical value of the variance for sample 2 (39.38) as compared to that for sample 1 (23.96).

## STANDARD DEVIATION

The variance, while accurately reflecting the degree of dispersion of a set of observations about the mean, is not stated in units along the baseline of a scale of measurement.

You will recall that, in·calculating the variance, we squared each value to eliminate negative numbers. This insures that the obtained measure of variability (the variance) is a number that becomes larger as the variability of the observations about the mean increases. In doing this we are no longer expressing the observations in their original units. However, if we now take the square root of the variance this will again transform the quantity we use to express variability to the original units. This gives us a number that allows us to specify how far above or below the mean a given value is, and this number is expressed in the same units as the original observations.

This quantity is known as the *standard deviation* (symbolized as $\sigma$ for a population and as $s$ for a sample) and has a number of uses in statistics. Its principal utility lies in the fact that it is a linear measure expressed in units of the original measurements and can be used to describe the position of any observation using a common reference point, the mean. The standard deviation is essentially a mean. It gives positive numbers that increase when variability increases. Since it is a

**Table 4–5.** CALCULATION OF THE VARIANCE FOR SAMPLE 2

| $X$ | $X^2$ | |
|---|---|---|
| 77 | 5929 | |
| 79 | 6241 | |
| 73 | 5329 | $\sum x^2 = \sum X^2 - (\sum X)^2/N$ |
| 83 | 6889 | $= 52{,}772 - (724)^2/10$ |
| 69 | 4761 | $= 52{,}772 - 52{,}417.60$ |
| 71 | 5041 | $= 354.40$ |
| 74 | 5476 | |
| 61 | 3721 | $s^2 = \sum x^2/(N-1)$ |
| 69 | 4761 | $= 354.40/9$ |
| 68 | 4624 | $= 39.38$ |
| $\sum X = 724$ | $\sum X^2 = 52{,}772$ | |

measure of the average amount of variability, the standard deviation (and, of course, the variance) can never be a negative number. You cannot have less than no variability. The basic formula for the variance, formula (4–2), indicates the average amount of variability, based on the squared deviations from the mean. This formula cannot result in a negative number. We obtain the population standard deviation by taking the square root of the population variance. The relationships are as follows:

$$\sigma^2 = \sum x^2/N$$
$$\sigma = \sqrt{\sum x^2/N}$$
$$= \sqrt{20.73}$$
$$= 4.55.$$

Table A–11 may be used to find the square root of 20.73.

Having calculated the standard deviation for the population, we can use the mean and the standard deviation to describe the relative position of any observation in the distribution. For example, since our population standard deviation is 4.55, we know that the value of an observation exactly one standard deviation above the mean is $75.50 + 4.55 = 80.05$. Similarly, we know that any observation two standard deviations above the mean is $75.50 + 9.10 = 84.60$ and an observation three standard deviations above the mean is $75.50 + 13.65 = 89.15$. The same rule applies for values below the mean; an observation two standard deviations below the mean is obtained by subtracting twice the value of the standard deviation from the mean. Therefore, the value of an observation two standard deviations below the mean is $75.50 - 9.10 = 66.40$. Similarly, it is quite possible to find out exactly what value lies 2.58 standard deviations below the mean. To do this we determine what .58 of one standard deviation is. For our present illustration this value is $.58(4.55) = 2.64$. Subtracting $2(4.55) + .58(4.55)$ from the mean will give us the value of the observation lying exactly 2.58 standard deviations below the mean $(75.50 - (9.10 + 2.64) = 75.50 - 11.74 = 63.76)$.

Certain relationships occur for all distributions with the general form of our set of 1000 observations (Chapter 2, Figure 2–1, p. 8). In all normal distributions 68.27 per cent of the values lie between plus or minus one standard deviation; 95.45 per cent lie between plus and minus three standard deviations. The frequency with which an observation is expected to occur in a normal distribution is directly related to how many standard deviations it is from the mean; observations greater than two standard deviations above or below the mean occur much less frequently than do observations within plus and minus one standard deviation. These particular relationships are of considerable importance when we wish to determine the probability of obtaining a certain value, or of obtaining an observation within a certain range of values when selecting at random from a normally distributed population.

## Standard Scores

Having considered the variance and its square root (the standard deviation) as measures of variability, we can introduce a useful descriptive index based on the scale of standard deviations. It is possible to transform the scale of values in which measurements are expressed, and as long as the transformations are linear (that is, they do not alter the relative size of the intervals between individual values), no violence is done to the original scale of measurement. Instead of expressing our observations in raw score units, as we have been doing, we could express them in terms of units of the standard deviation. One convenient way to do this is to let the value of the mean equal zero and then to express each observation in terms of how many standard deviations it is from the mean. If the observation is above the mean it is expressed as a positive number; if it is below the mean it is expressed as a negative number. Observations expressed in this form are known as *standard scores*, symbolized by $z$ and, hence, called *z-scores*.

The formula for transforming a set of observations into standard scores is

**(4–5)**
$$z = \frac{X - \bar{X}}{s}.$$

Thus, the mean is subtracted from each observation and each remainder is divided by the standard deviation. The mean of a set of standard scores will be zero, the standard deviation will be one, and, of course, the variance will be one.

Illustrated in Table 4–6 are the values of sample 1 (Table 2–2) and their transformations into standard scores. If we compute the mean and standard deviation of this set of transformed scores, we find that the mean is indeed zero, since the scores, positive and negative, sum to zero, and zero divided by anything is still zero. The standard deviation and the variance are equal to one because we divided the difference between each score and the mean by the standard deviation of the original set of observations. Since the variance is the square of the standard deviation, it is also one since the square of one is still one.

Figure 4–3 is a graphical representation of these transformations. You can see that none of the basic relationships between the

**Table 4–6.** THE CALCULATION OF STANDARD ($z$) SCORES

| | 1<br>Observations | 2<br>$x$ | 3<br>$z$ |
|---|---|---|---|
| | $X$ | $X - \bar{X}$ | $\dfrac{x}{s}$ |
| Step 1: Calculate the mean and | 69 | −6.20 | −1.2679 |
| standard deviation for the | 71 | −4.20 | −.8589 |
| original observations. (If | 72 | −3.20 | −.6544 |
| calculators are not avaliable, | 72 | −3.20 | −.6544 |
| the squares of the observations | 75 | −.20 | −.0409 |
| may be found in Table A–11.) | 75 | −.20 | −.0409 |
| | 75 | −.20 | −.0409 |
| | 76 | +.80 | +.1636 |
| | 83 | +7.80 | +1.5951 |
| | 84 | +8.80 | +1.7996 |

$$\sum X = 752 \qquad\qquad\qquad .0000$$
$$N = 10 \qquad\qquad\qquad\quad 10$$
$$\bar{X} = 75.20 \qquad\qquad\quad .0000$$
$$\sum X^2 = 56766 \qquad\qquad 9.0164$$
$$(\sum X)^2 = 565504 \qquad\quad .0000$$
$$\frac{(\sum X)^2}{N} = \frac{(565504)}{10}$$
$$= 56550.40 \qquad\qquad .0000$$

$$\sum X^2 - (\sum X)^2/N = \sum x^2$$

| Step 2: Subtract the mean | $= 215.60$ | 9.0164 |
|---|---|---|
| from each value keeping | $s^2 = \sum x^2/(N-1)$ | 1.00 |
| the sign (+ or −) of the | $= 215.60/9$ | |
| numbers. | $= 23.95$ | |
| Step 3: Divide each value in | $s = \sqrt{s^2}$ | 1.00 |
| column 2 by the value of $s$. | $= 4.89$ | |

scores is changed in any way. The only change under such linear transformation is that different numbers are used to represent the scores.

**Transformations of Standard Scores.** A set of standard scores can have any desired value for the mean and the standard deviation. It is necessary only to change the original equation as follows:

$$Z = \frac{X - \bar{X}}{s} s' + \bar{X}', \qquad\qquad (4\text{–}6)$$

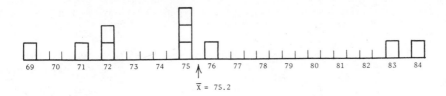

$\bar{X} = 75.2$

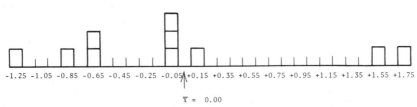

$\bar{X} = 0.00$

***Figure 4–3.*** Relationship of the original observations to the standard ($z$) scores.

where $s'$ is the value you want to establish for the new standard deviation and $\bar{X}'$ is the value you want to establish for the new mean. Table 4–7 illustrates the calculation for a small set of scores; the new mean will be set at 50.00 and the new standard deviation will be set at 10.00.

The new mean of the scores (referred to as Z-scores to distinguish them from z-scores with a mean of zero) is now 50 and the new standard deviation is 10. How was this accomplished? First, we multiplied each of the scores by a constant value (10) and then added another constant value (50). Since the mean of our first set of standard scores was zero, multiplying zero by ten does not affect the mean. Adding 50 to zero does produce a change of 50 in the mean, however. The standard deviation of 1, when multiplied by 10, becomes 10. A score one standard deviation above the mean becomes a 60 when the constant of 50 is then added. A score one standard deviation below the mean becomes a 40, since −1 multiplied by 10 is −10 and 50 added to this is +40. The general rule for transformations of this type can be stated as follows:

1. The addition (or subtraction) of a constant to every score increases (or decreases) the value of any measure of central tendency (mean, median, or mode) by the value of that constant. The addition or subtraction of a constant has no effect on any measure of variability, such as the standard deviation (or the variance).

2. Multiplying (or dividing) every score by a constant has the effect of multiplying (or dividing) every measure of central tendency by the value of that constant. The standard deviation is multiplied

**Table 4–7.** Calculation of Standard Scores with Mean Equal to 50.00 and Standard Deviation Equal to 10.00

| 1 | 2 | 3 | 4 | 5 |
|---|---|---|---|---|
| Scores | $X - \bar{X}$ | $z$ | $(z)(s') + \bar{X}'$ | $Z$ |
| 1 | $-2$ | $-1.26$ | $(-1.26)(10) + 50$ | 37.4 |
| 2 | $-1$ | $-.63$ | $(-.63)(10) + 50$ | 43.7 |
| 3 | $0$ | $.00$ | $(.00)(10) + 50$ | 50.0 |
| 4 | $+1$ | $+.63$ | $(+.63)(10) + 50$ | 56.3 |
| 5 | $+2$ | $+1.26$ | $(+1.26)(10) + 50$ | 62.6 |

$$\sum X = \overline{15} \qquad\qquad 0.000 \qquad\qquad\qquad \overline{250.0}$$

$$N = 5 \qquad\qquad 5 \qquad\qquad\qquad\qquad 5$$

$$\bar{X} = 3 \qquad\qquad .000 \qquad\qquad \bar{X} = \quad 50.00$$

$$\sum X^2 = 55 \qquad\qquad\qquad\qquad \sum X^2 = 12{,}896.90$$

$$(\sum X)^2 = 225 \qquad\qquad\qquad (\sum X)^2 = 62{,}500.00$$

$$(\sum X)^2/N = 225/5 = 45.0 \qquad (\sum X)^2/N = 12{,}500.00$$

$$\sum x^2 = 55 - 45 = 10 \qquad\qquad \sum x^2 = \quad 396.90$$

$$s^2 = 2.50 \qquad\qquad\qquad\qquad s^2 = \quad 99.27$$

$$s = 1.58 \qquad\qquad\qquad\qquad s = \quad 9.96$$

The calculation is identical to that of Table 4–6, until column 4, where each value in column 3 is multiplied by 10 and added to 50. The new values in column 5 are known as $Z$ scores and have a mean of 50 and a standard deviation of 10.

(or divided) by that constant and the variance is multiplied (or divided) by the square of the constant.

Previously, standard score transformations were characterized as being *linear* transformations. This means that no basic characteristics are changed by the transformations except the scale values in which they are expressed; a score one standard deviation above the mean in the original set of observations is still one standard deviation above the mean in the standard score transformation. If we were to transform our population of 1000 observations into standard scores and plot the scores on a graph, this graph would look exactly like the original graph — each score would stand in relation to other scores exactly as it did in the original. The only difference would be that the units expressed on the baseline of the graph would be changed.

Figure 4–4 illustrates two scales of measurement in relation to the normal curve. Scale 1 is in standard deviation units and illustrates

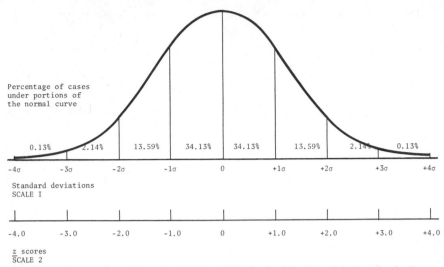

Percentage of cases
under portions of
the normal curve

0.13%   2.14%   13.59%   34.13%   34.13%   13.59%   2.14%   0.13%

-4σ      -3σ      -2σ      -1σ       0       +1σ      +2σ      +3σ      +4σ

Standard deviations
SCALE I

-4.0     -3.0     -2.0     -1.0      0      +1.0     +2.0     +3.0     +4.0

z scores
SCALE 2

**Figure 4–4.** (From Berstein, A. L., *A Handbook of Statistics Solutions for the Be-havioral Sciences.* Copyright 1964 by Holt, Rinehart and Winston, Inc. and reproduced with their permission.)

the percentages of the total area under the normal curve at various standard deviation distances from the mean. Scale 2 illustrates the relationship of standard scores to the standard deviation units in scale 1.

*Use of Standard Scores.* When we use standard scores we are expressing each observation in terms of how far it deviates from the mean in units of the standard deviation. The advantage of this manner of expressing values is that it makes possible the comparison of an individual's standing on one distribution with his standing on another distribution. If we have the distribution of the heights of a group of people and the distribution of the weights of the same people we can, by standard scoring, decide whether or not a given individual is heavier than he is tall, *relative to the appropriate comparison distributions.* Obviously, if an individual is at the mean in height and is one standard score above the mean in weight we know something about his body build, relative to the comparison distribution.

One can also express a value relative to a distribution of observations by using percentiles. However, the advantage of using standard scores is that it is possible to determine a person's standard score knowing only the mean of the distribution, its standard deviation, and the original observation in question. In order to determine a percentile it is necessary to have the entire distribution available.

One further advantage that standard scores have over percentiles is that it is possible to recover the original observation if we know the standard score, as long as the mean and the standard deviation of the distribution are also known. For example, if the mean of a distribution equals 100, the standard deviation equals 10, and a standard score is $-2.5$, we can determine the original value as follows:

$$z = \frac{X - \bar{X}}{s}$$

$$-2.5 = \frac{X - 100}{10}$$

$$-25 = X - 100$$

$$X = 100 - 25$$

$$X = 75.$$

This could also be expressed as follows:                                (4–7)

$$X = zs + \bar{X}$$
$$X = -2.5(10) + 100$$
$$X = 75.$$

## Other Measures of Variability

The two measures of variability we have discussed up to this point, the average deviation and the standard deviation, use the mean as a reference point around which the variability is expressed. The average deviation expresses the variability as the mean of the deviations from the mean, disregarding the algebraic sign of the deviations. The standard deviation expresses the variability as the mean of the squared deviations from the mean, and is preferred because of its relation to the normal curve. In some instances, such as those in which there are badly skewed distributions, a mean is a misleading statistic, and the median is preferred as a measure of central tendency. Similarly, if the distribution of scores is incomplete at either end because, for example, the extremes are reported as open categories, a mean cannot be determined and we must use a median. In such instances it will not be appropriate to use either the average deviation or the standard deviation, and some measure appropriate for use with medians is necessary.

*Semi-interquartile Range.*   The measure of variability used most frequently in instances in which a mean cannot be used, or, when we have only the median (the fiftieth percentile) available as a measure of central tendency, is the *semi-interquartile range*. The semi-interquartile range is defined as follows:

$$\frac{Q_3 - Q_1}{2},$$                                (4–8)

where $Q_3$ is the third quartile (which is the seventy-fifth percentile, below which 75 per cent of the scores lie), and $Q_1$ is the first quartile (which is the twenty-fifth percentile, below which 25 per cent of the scores lie).

This measure tells us the range of the values that include one-half of the middle 50 per cent of the observations. This measure is purely descriptive since percentiles have little function in inferential statistics.

The semi-interquartile range is often used to indicate the direction and the amount of skew in a distribution. If $Q_3 - Q_2$ (the fiftieth percentile) is equal to $Q_2 - Q_1$, then the distribution is not skewed (Figure 4–5 *A*). If $Q_3 - Q_2$ is greater than $Q_2 - Q_1$, then the distribution is positively skewed. (The relation *greater than* can also be expressed by the symbol $>$. Therefore, the preceding statement can be written $Q_3 - Q_2 > Q_2 - Q_1$.) (Figure 4–5 *B*.) Similarly, if $Q_3 - Q_2$ is less than $Q_2 - Q_1$, then the distribution is negatively skewed. (The relation

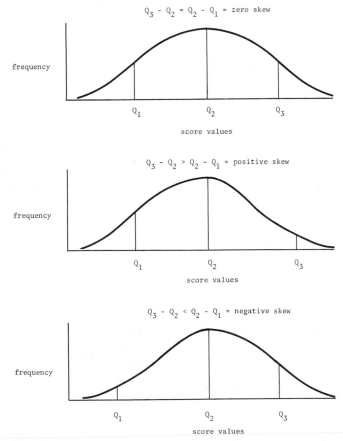

*Figure 4–5.*

*less than* can be expressed by the symbol $<$. Therefore, this statement can be written $Q_3 - Q_2 < Q_2 - Q_1$.) (Figure 4–5 C.)

**Range.**   One other measure of variability is the *range*. This is the difference between the highest and lowest values. While this measure is certainly easy to calculate (since it involves only the subtraction of the lowest from the highest observation), its disadvantages are numerous. The addition or subtraction of a single observation at either extreme can result in a substantial change in the value of the range and thereby can result in quite misleading estimates of variability. Since a change in only one observation can greatly change the range, it is not a stable statistic from a sampling viewpoint. Also, its interpretation depends on the size of the sample on which it is based. If we have only two observations in the distribution, the range would be determined by subtracting the lower value from the higher. If we now add a third observation we cannot decrease this range; the range will either stay the same or will increase. Since this will be true as we add observations, it is misleading to compare ranges if samples are of unequal size. As $N$ increases the range would be expected to increase, since the probability of sampling one of the infrequently occurring observations from either tail of the distribution is increased.

While statistics such as the range and interquartile range can be used as estimates of the standard deviation in large samples (cf. Chapter 15, Dixon and Massey*), their efficiency is still much less than if the estimates were based on sums of squares, and such estimates should be used only under specialized circumstances.

---

*Dixon, W. J., and Massey, F. J., Jr.: *Introduction to Statistical Analysis*, 2nd ed. New York, McGraw-Hill, 1957.

1. a. Calculate the sample variance for the following distribution of scores: 25, 37, 28, 33, 47, 21, 27, 32, 31, 29.
   b. Using distribution $C$ (Exercise 4), compute the sum of squares using the raw score formula. Compute the sample variance. Compute the sample standard deviation.
2. If you were told that two normal distributions had the same mean, would they be identical? Why?
3. A person's z-score on a test is $-1.5$. The mean on the test was 70, and the standard deviation was 6. What was the person's original score?
4. Find the semi-interquartile range for the following three distributions. Are any of the distributions skewed? In which directions?

| | A | | B | | C |
|---|---|---|---|---|---|
| Scores | f | Scores | f | Scores | |
| 52–53 | 1 | 95–99 | 6 | 12 | |
| 50–51 | 0 | 90–94 | 11 | 28 | |
| 48–49 | 5 | 85–89 | 16 | 19 | |
| 46–47 | 10 | 80–84 | 7 | 15 | |
| 44–45 | 9 | 75–79 | 9 | 15 | |
| 42–43 | 14 | 70–74 | 8 | 35 | |
| 40–41 | 7 | 65–69 | 2 | 14 | |
| 38–39 | 8 | 60–64 | 3 | 15 | |
| 36–37 | 6 | 55–59 | 2 | | |
| 34–35 | 5 | 50–54 | 1 | | |
| 32–33 | 3 | $N = 65$ | | | |
| $N = 68$ | | | | | |

5. Find the average deviation for distribution $C$.
6. What is the range in the following distribution: 7, 9, 13, 5, 12, 23, 54, 3, 5.
7. If you were told that the mean grade for a test in a class of 60

students was 74, the standard deviation was four and your grade is 2.3 standard deviations above the mean, what would your grade be?

8. If the mean for 60 students is 50, the median is 60, and $s$ is 5, and 5 points are added to each score the mean will become _____, the median will become _____, and the variance will be _____. If we multiply each score by 2 the mean will become _____, the median will become _____, and the variance will be _____.

9. Assume a normal distribution of scores with a mean of 60 and a standard deviation of 8. What raw score corresponds to the z-scores of $+1.28$ and $-1.28$?

## CHAPTER FIVE

# PROBABILITY AND THE NORMAL CURVE

Suppose, improbable though it may be, that you and a friend sitting next to you in class become bored by a lecture. To while away the time until the end of the hour, you try some inexpensive gambling. You cannot match pennies in the usual fashion, since this amount of activity would attract the attention of the instructor and few instructors would tolerate such activity during a lecture. However, your friend is sitting where he is not so easily seen when he flips a coin. You agree that he should flip a coin and if the coin comes up heads, he wins. If it comes up tails, you win.

Of course there are only two possible outcomes on each flip, and the odds are even; in the long run he should win half of the time and you should win half of the time. However, as gamblers, we know that sometimes we might get "lucky" and there will be a long run of, say, tails in our favor. If such a run is long enough, then one player might be bankrupt before the odds correct themselves, and in this case the lucky gambler wins from his bankrupt opponent.

Suppose you begin playing and the coin comes up heads (he wins) on the first five flips. This would not seem too unreasonable on an intuitive basis. What if he wins the first 10 flips; then the first 20; the first 50; the first 100? When would you decide that something was amiss and that it was unreasonable to continue on the assumption that the game was honest?

We know that, when gambling on outcomes of equally probable events, it is possible to have a "run of luck" for one of the events. On what basis, then, do we decide that this "lucky" run of events, say ten heads in a row, has exceeded what could reasonably be expected on the basis of luck alone? Essentially, we want to reason from a particular set of events (a sequence of coin tosses) to a general state of affairs (the "true" probability of each of the possible outcomes).

## PROBABILITY AND INFERENCE

Probability is central to statistical inference. For example, the experimenter who takes a group of rats, divides them randomly into two groups, administers a new drug to one group and an inert substance to the other, and then tests the ability of the rats to learn a maze, will end his experiment by analyzing his measure of learning in terms of probability statements. He will ask the question: What is the probability that a difference between the groups in the rate of maze learning is more than would be expected by chance alone?

Specifically, the experimenter is asking the question: Does the drug affect maze learning to the extent that I can conclude that there is a greater difference between the two groups of animals than would be expected by chance alone?

In this chapter we will expand on the concept of probability (symbolized as $p$) introduced in Chapter 2, and will present the basic rules for computing probabilities. The uses of normal curve models to determine probabilities will be presented, and the relationship of probability to the normal curve, and to statistical inference, will be developed.

In Chapter 2 the concept of probability was introduced and defined as the ratio of the ways something can happen to the ways it both can and cannot happen. If an event can happen in $X$ ways and not happen in $Y$ ways, the probability of $X$ occurring is equal to

**(5–1)**
$$X/(X + Y)$$

Let us now see how this formula can be applied to the example of coin tossing.

***Determining "Runs of Luck."***    It will help us to decide whether or not the coin game is honest if we have some idea about the probability of obtaining a "run of luck" against us, rather than having to relay on our intuitive judgment alone. In order to determine the probability of a given outcome we must know the probability of each of the possible single events. When we call a coin unbiased we mean that the likelihood that it will come up heads is the same as that it will come up tails on any single toss of the coin. Since these are the only two acceptable outcomes, we can say that the probability of heads on any toss of the coin is .50 (i.e., $p_H = .50$), and the probability of a tails on any toss of the coin is the same ($p_T = .50$). The probability of an event occurring (say heads) plus the probability of the event not occurring (tails) must equal 1.00.

The probability of obtaining either heads or tails on the first toss is, as we have seen, .50. What is the probability of obtaining heads on each of two independent tosses? There are four possible outcomes in this instance: the first toss can be heads and the second heads $(H, H)$; the first toss can be tails and the second heads $(T, H)$; the first heads and the second tails $(H, T)$; or both the first and the second can be tails $(T, T)$. Out of these four possible outcomes only one $(H, H)$ is favorable to getting two heads. Therefore, the probability of obtaining two heads on two independent coin tosses is one out of four, or $p = .25$. The probability of obtaining two tails is the same: 1/4 or $p = .25$. One head and one tail can be obtained in two ways $(T, H$ and $H, T)$. Therefore, the likelihood of obtaining this outcome is 2/4 or $p = .50$.

What is the probability of obtaining three heads in a row? The possible outcomes are shown below:

$$H, H, H; \quad H, T, H; \quad H, H, T; \quad T, H, H;$$
$$T, H, T; \quad T, T, H; \quad H, T, T; \quad T, T, T.$$

Of these eight possible outcomes only one is favorable to getting three heads $(H,H,H)$. Therefore, the likelihood of obtaining three heads in a row is one out of eight, or $p = .125$.

### Rules of Probability

We can state the general rule for determining the probability of obtaining *all* of an independent series of events as follows: If each of the specified events is independent of the outcome of the previous events, the probability that all of the set of independent events will occur is the product of the separate probabilities of each event.

Thus, the probability of obtaining two heads in a row is, as we have seen, $(1/2)(1/2) = (1/2)^2 = 1/4 = .25$. The probability of obtaining three heads in a row is $(1/2)(1/2)(1/2) = (1/2)^3 = 1/8 = .125$.

Now, we are able to answer our original question: What is the probability of flipping of a coin ten times and getting ten successive heads? $p = (1/2)(1/2)(1/2)(1/2)(1/2)(1/2)(1/2)(1/2)(1/2)(1/2) = (1/2)^{10} = 1/1024 = .00098$. A run like this, while possible, is very improbable, and perhaps you should suspect that the true probability of obtaining heads with this coin is *not* .50 and you might be well advised to discontinue the coin tossing game.

### PERMUTATIONS AND COMBINATIONS

Let us use a slightly different coin example. Assume that you toss six coins at a time and tally the frequency with which heads and tails appear; the chances are that you would have close to three heads and three tails. What is the probability that you would toss (given unbiased coins) four heads and two tails; five heads and one tails; six heads and no tails? To calculate the answers to such questions as these we need to make a distinction between *permutations* and *combinations.*

Permutations and combinations differ primarily in terms of the importance of order. Specifically, if the problem involves predicting the precise order of the outcome, we are interested in permutations. If there is no concern for the order of outcomes, we are interested in combinations. For example, given four objects labeled $A, B, C,$ and $D,$ what is the probability of picking object $A$ followed by object $B$? If we begin by randomly choosing one object, our chances of picking object $A$ are one in four. Assuming that we do obtain $A$ on the first choice, there are now three alternatives remaining (assuming that we cannot pick $A$ a second time). Thus we would have $4 \times 3$ or 12 permutations possible:

$$AB, AC, AD, BA, BC, BD, CA, CB, CD, DA, DB, DC.$$

Obviously only one of these permutations ($AB$) is the specified event; none of the others meets our specifications. Therefore the probability of selecting object $A$ followed by object $B$ on a purely random basis is one out of 12, and $1/12 = .083.$

Now let us assume that the order of selecting the two objects is unimportant. This is the same thing as saying that outcome $AB$ and outcome $BA$ are to be considered equivalent. Therefore the number of arrangements shrinks to the following six combinations:

$$AB, AC, AD, BC, BD, CD.$$

Two of the 12 permutations are the specified event ($AB$ and $BA$) and the probability, therefore, equals two out of 12, which equals one out of six. Therefore $p = .167.$

While it is possible to diagram all the permutations and combinations (as was done above) if the set of objects is fairly small, the process becomes extremely tedious when larger numbers become involved. Fortunately, there are formulas that will allow the calculation of permutations and combinations. However, to use the formulas it is necessary to become familiar with the concept of a *factorial.* The factorial of a number is obtained by multiplying the number times itself minus one, multiplying that product by the number minus two, and so forth, ending at one. (The factorial of zero is one.) The factorial of four (which is written as 4!) is calculated as follows:

$$4! = 4 \times 3 \times 2 \times 1.$$

Table 5–1 contains the factorial of the numbers from one to 15. To calculate the permutations of $N$ objects taken $K$ at a time, we substitute the necessary factorials into the following equation (the symbol "$P$" indicates permutations.):

$$P_K^N = \frac{N!}{(N-K)!} \cdot$$

After applying this formula to the earlier problem of the four objects $A$, $B$, $C$, and $D$ to be arranged in groups of two and then substituting the necessary values from Table 5–1 into the preceding formula, we have

$$P_2^4 = \frac{4!}{(4-2)!} = \frac{24}{2} = 12.$$

This is the number of possible permutations that was arrived at by actually counting the number of permutations. Similarly, the number of combinations of $N$ objects taken $K$ at a time can be calculated by the following equation (the symbol $C$ indicates combinations):

$$C_K^N = \frac{N!}{K!\,(N-K)!} \cdot \qquad (5\text{–}3)$$

By substituting values from Table 5–1 into the preceding formula we have

$$C_2^4 = \frac{4!}{2!\,(4-2)!} = \frac{4 \times 3 \times 2 \times 1}{(2 \times 1)(2 \times 1)} = \frac{24}{4} = 6,$$

which, again, is the value obtained earlier by actually counting the number of combinations.

We will apply these procedures to the questions raised earlier in the chapter concerning coin flipping. We want to know the probability that of six unbiased coins flipped in the air, four would come up heads and two would come up tails. Since we do not care which specific coins come up heads and which come up tails, we use our combinations formula. The first question concerns the number of possible combinations of six things taken four at a time. This is cal-

**Table 5-1.** FACTORIALS

| $n$ | $n!$ |
|---|---|
| 1 | 1 |
| 2 | 2 |
| 3 | 6 |
| 4 | 24 |
| 5 | 120 |
| 6 | 720 |
| 7 | 5,040 |
| 8 | 40,320 |
| 9 | 362,880 |
| 10 | 3,628,800 |
| 11 | 39,916,800 |
| 12 | 479,001,600 |
| 13 | 6,227,020,800 |
| 14 | 87,178,291,200 |
| 15 | 1,307,674,368,000 |

culated by substituting the appropriate values from Table 5-1 into the combinations formula:

$$C_4^6 = \frac{6!}{4! \ (6-4)!} = \frac{720}{24(2)} = \frac{720}{48} = 15.$$

Now from the result of this calculation we know that there are 15 ways that our six tossed coins can come up with four heads and two tails. We now know the number of ways the event can occur, but to calculate the probability we need to know all the other possibilities that can occur with six tossed coins. For example, what is the probability of one head and five tails? Six heads and no tails? If we are to calculate the probability of a certain event we must know all the other possibilities to determine the number of possible outcomes. We can calculate these in the same manner in which we determined the number of ways the event we are interested in (four heads and two tails) could occur.

To begin, let us specify all the other ways the event can occur:

6 heads and 0 tails,
5 heads and 1 tails,
4 heads and 2 tails (calculated above),
3 heads and 3 tails,
2 heads and 4 tails,
1 heads and 5 tails,
0 heads and 6 tails.

To calculate the probability of these outcomes, all that is necessary is to work the combinations formula for each of the above events. The calculations follow:

$$C_6^6 = \frac{6!}{6! \, (0)!*} = \frac{720}{720} = 1$$

$$C_5^6 = \frac{6!}{5! \, (1)!} = \frac{720}{120} = 6$$

$$C_4^6 = \frac{6!}{4! \, (2)!} = \frac{720}{48} = 15$$

$$C_3^6 = \frac{6!}{3! \, (3)!} = \frac{720}{36} = 20$$

$$C_2^6 = \frac{6!}{2! \, (4)!} = \frac{720}{48} = 15$$

$$C_1^6 = \frac{6!}{1! \, (5)!} = \frac{720}{120} = 6$$

$$C_0^6 = \frac{6!}{0! \, (6)!} = \frac{720}{720} = 1$$

$$\overline{64}$$

* $0! = 1$

When we finish this tedious series of computations, the sum of all these possible events will equal 64. Thus, there are 64 possible outcomes when tossing six coins. Now we apply the probability formula of $X/(X + Y)$ to determine the probability of obtaining four heads and two tails. $X = 15$ (the number of ways four heads can be obtained). $X + Y = 64$ (the total number of ways that the coins may distribute). When we divide 15 by 64 the answer is .234; therefore, the probability of obtaining four heads and two tails when six coins are tossed is .234.

**Table 5–2.** PASCAL'S TRIANGLE

| $N$ | Coefficients in Expansion of $(x + y)^n$ | | | | | | | | | | | Sum |
|---|---|---|---|---|---|---|---|---|---|---|---|---|
| 1 | | | | | | 1 | 1 | | | | | 2 |
| 2 | | | | | 1 | 2 | 1 | | | | | 4 |
| 3 | | | | 1 | 3 | 3 | 1 | | | | | 8 |
| 4 | | | 1 | 4 | 6 | 4 | 1 | | | | | 16 |
| 5 | | 1 | 5 | 10 | 10 | 5 | 1 | | | | | 32 |
| 6 | 1 | 6 | 15 | 20 | 15 | 6 | 1 | | | | | 64 |
| 7 | 1 | 7 | 21 | 35 | 35 | 21 | 7 | 1 | | | | 128 |
| 8 | 1 | 8 | 28 | 56 | 70 | 56 | 28 | 8 | 1 | | | 256 |
| 9 | 1 | 9 | 36 | 84 | 126 | 126 | 84 | 36 | 9 | 1 | | 512 |
| 10 | 1 | 10 | 45 | 120 | 210 | 252 | 210 | 120 | 45 | 10 | 1 | 1024 |

The computation of probabilities by the method illustrated above can be a tedious process. Fortunately, there is an easier method to achieve the same end. The actual probabilities may be obtained from a table known as Pascal's triangle for the special case when $p_x = p_y = .50$. This table, which is printed as Table 5–2, provides the exact probabilities and totals for all combinations of events up to ten. Examine the values for $n = 6$ and note that they are identical to the values calculated earlier for our six coin tosses. Also, note that the values total to 64, the sum of all the possible combinations for six separate events. The construction of Pascal's triangle is quite easy: the first and last values of the series for any number are always 1; all other terms are obtained by adding together the two values just above the one to be calculated. For example, the second term for $n = 6$ is obtained by summing the two values immediately above it; $1 + 5 = 6$; the next value is $5 + 10 = 15$; and so forth.

What do the combinatorial formula and Pascal's triangle have to do with the normal curve? As we stated in Chapter 2, the normal curve can be used to evaluate the probabilities of events occurring in much the same manner that the probability of tossing eight heads and two tails can be determined. To understand the relationship between the determination of probabilities as presented in the first part of this chapter and probabilities as determined from normal curve distributions, it must be understood that probability is a frequency ratio; it is the number of times an event happens divided by the number of times it can and cannot happen. *The probability distribution when $p = .50$ (as in coin tossing) and when n is infinitely large is a normal distribution.* When we consider the distribution of the outcomes that can occur when ten coins are tossed we find that there is only one way in which ten coins can be tossed and result in ten heads and no tails; there are nine ways in which there can be one head and nine tails; there are 45 ways in which there can be two heads and eight tails; and so on. These are exactly the values given in Pascal's triangle for $n = 10$. Using these values as frequencies and graphing them, we obtain a distribution similar in appearance to the normal curve. This figure is symmetrical about a central point, and the frequencies diminish as we move away from that central point. In fact, if we superimpose a normal curve on the graph the similarity between the results obtained on the basis of chance and the theoretical normal curve is quite striking.

Figure 5–1 shows distributions obtained by reading the values from Pascal's triangle for $N = 4, 6, 8,$ and 10 (taken from Table 5–1). The distributions begin to look more and more like the normal curve as $N$ gets larger and larger.

Frequency

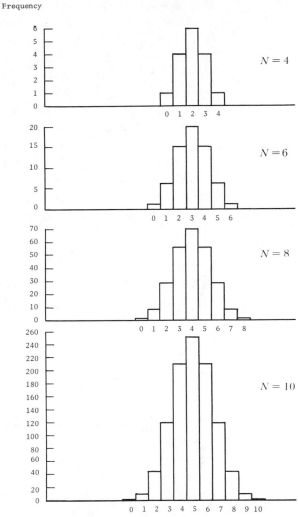

*Figure 5-1.* Values from Pascal's triangle for $N = 4$, 6, 8 and 10.

## NORMAL CURVE

The normal curve is a theoretical mathematical concept. The fact that it happens to describe the distribution of objects in the real world, such as the frequency with which things occur on the basis of chance alone, is one of those fortunate relationships between the world of mathematical equations and the world of observation. The normal curve can be used to determine the probability of specified events occurring.

This is done by representing the number of observations in the distribution in terms of the proportional area of the distribution. To do this we let the total number of observations, whether 30, 50, 1000, or 1,000,000 equal 1.00 of the total area under the curve defining the distribution. This procedure is similar to the method we use in plotting a bar diagram (also called a histogram). When plotting a bar diagram we represent each observation by a rectangle of a given size. If we knew the size of the rectangular unit we could determine the number of observations of any given value by measuring the height of a column of rectangles constructed for a given value. The theoretical distribution is a smooth curve. However, we are still representing the number of observations by proportional area. Therefore, if .20 of the total area under the curve falls between two values we know that .20 of the total number of observations lie between these two score values.

It is necessary that some common score unit be used in order to allow the normal distribution to be fitted to populations that are characterized by different numbers of observations, by different means, and by different variances. Just such a common score unit was presented in the last chapter–the standard score (z). A set of standard scores has a mean of zero and a standard deviation of one as a function of the way in which the scores are calculated. To transform the values from Table 2–1 into standard score form we use the equation $\dfrac{X - \bar{X}}{s}$. Figure 5–2 is the population of 1000 observations with both a scale of the original scores and of the standard scores corresponding to the original scores indicated along the horizontal axis.

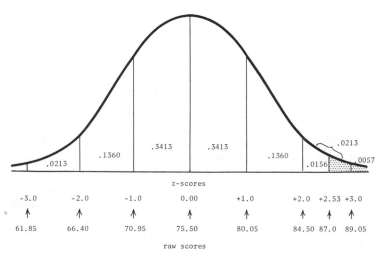

**Figure 5–2.** Area of the normal curve (shaded) falling beyond a z-score of +2.53.

(If you have forgotten the section on standard scores you should go back and review pages 56 and 57 before proceeding further.)

The normal distribution, then, is constructed using proportions of the total area to represent frequencies. The total area under the curve equals 1.00 and standard scores are used as the score units. Let us examine some of the properties of the normal curve in more detail. The normal curve is smooth, and it is symmetrical about its standard score mean of zero. Its range extends to plus and minus about four standard deviations (see Figure 4–4). Theoretically, the normal curve never quite reaches the baseline. For most practical purposes, however, ±4s is quite sufficient to enclose all of the frequencies in the distribution.

The area under the curve is equal to the total number of observations in the population (by definition). Since there is an invariant relationship between the standard deviation and the point at which it occurs in any normal distribution there is, then, a fixed relationship between the standard deviation and the proportion of the total area occurring between the mean and one standard deviation. Indeed, it can be seen that there is a fixed relationship between the proportional area of the curve and any given standard deviation distance. Since the normal curve is a graph that represents each case by an equal area, it follows that the proportion of the total area under the curve will equal the proportion of the total cases contained in any given region of the curve. Hence, proportional area is equal to the proportional frequency contained in any given region of the normal curve.

Table A–2 is used to find the area between the mean and any given standard score. The table is organized with the standard score values listed to the first decimal in the first column. The remaining columns list the values for the second decimal. In the body of the table is listed the proportion of the total area under the normal curve that falls between the mean and the particular standard score. A standard score value of 0.00 indicates that the score under consideration falls at the mean of the distribution. Since a standard score of 0.00 is at the mean, no area falls between that score and the mean; indeed, the entry in the table for 0.00 (the first score in the second column of the table) is .000. If the standard score is 0.01, then a small proportion of the total area falls between the mean and that standard score; the table indicates that .0040 of the total area falls between the mean and a z of .01. Inspection of the table reveals that between the mean and plus one standard deviation (+1$\sigma$) .3413 of the total area under the curve is found. Again, since proportional area equals proportional frequency, .3413 of the total number of the scores occur between the mean and plus one standard deviation (+1$\sigma$).

Thus, .6826 of the observations occur between plus and minus one standard deviation ($\pm 1\sigma$). Since .3413 of the observations occur between the mean ($\mu$) and one standard deviation ($+1\sigma$) and .4772 of the observations occur between $\mu$ and $+2\sigma$, then $.4772 - .3413 = .1359$ of the observations occur between $+1\sigma$ and $+2\sigma$. Thus, the probability of obtaining a score that is greater than $2\sigma$ away from $\mu$ is less (since there are fewer of them) than is the probability of obtaining a score greater than $1\sigma$ away from $\mu$.

Since the normal curve is symmetrical and .4772 of the observations occur between $\mu$ and either $+2\sigma$ or $-2\sigma$, $.4772 + .4772 = .9544$ of the observations occur between $\pm 2\sigma$. Since .4987 of the observations occur between $\mu$ and either $+3\sigma$ or $-3\sigma$, then $.4987 + .4987 = .9974$ of the observations occur between $\pm 3\sigma$.

If we have a table of the normal curve available, we can, by converting any observations to a standard score, determine the number of individuals who would be expected to obtain any given score value. To do this it is necessary to know $\mu$, $\sigma$, and $N$. The method for making such determinations is presented in the next section.

Normal curve methods can be used provided that the number of observations is at least 30. This is an arbitrary lower limit that is used because the bias in using samples varying in $N$ from size 30 to infinity ($\infty$) is negligible. If fewer than 30 observations are available, different methods of inference, referred to as small sample methods, are used. These small sample methods correct for the systematic bias introduced when small samples are used to infer normal curve parameters.

***Use of the Normal Curve Table.*** We can use normal curve methods to determine the probability that a subject chosen at random from the 1000 subjects represented in Table 2–1 will have a score higher than 87 on the scholarship examination. (See pages 12 to 15.)

If the normal curve is to be used to determine the probability of obtaining any given value, it is necessary to translate the value into standard scores. This sets the mean of the distribution at zero and the standard deviation at one. A value of 87, then, would be converted to standard score form as follows:

$$z_{87} = \frac{X - \overline{X}}{s}$$

$$= \frac{87 - 75.5}{4.55}$$

$$= \frac{11.50}{4.55}$$

$$= 2.53.$$

The population of 1000 scores is shown in Figure 5–2 with the horizontal axis labeled both in raw score units and in standard score units. It is helpful, when solving problems of this type, to visualize the region of the normal curve in which we are interested. In Figure 5–2 we have shaded the area of the curve about which we are concerned.

From Table A–2 we find that .4943 of the area above the mean falls between the $\bar{X}$ and a $z$ of $+2.53$. Therefore, only $.5000 - .4943 = .0057$ of the area remains above a $z$ of $+2.53$. Since relative area and relative frequency (and hence probability) are the same, we know the probability that an individual picked at random from the population will have a score higher than 87 is .0057. Since there are 1000 cases in the population we would expect to have $1000 \times .0057$, or about six scores higher than 87.

We can ask a series of questions concerning the probability of scores occurring at any point or within any region of the distribution provided that we know the $\bar{X}$ and $x$.

(a) What is the probability of obtaining a score lower than 87? In the previous example we found that a score of 87 is a standard score of $+2.53$. In this example, however, we are concerned with the shaded region of Figure 5–3. Since .0057 of the area falls above $z = 2.53$, then .4943 of the area falls between the mean and $z = 2.53$ and .5000 of the area falls below the mean: .5000 +

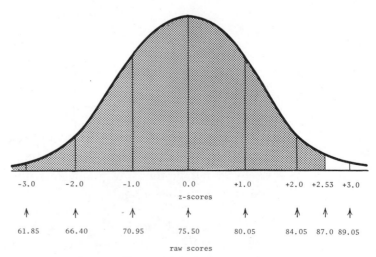

| -3.0 | -2.0 | -1.0 | 0.0 | +1.0 | +2.0 | +2.53 | +3.0 |

z-scores

| 61.85 | 66.40 | 70.95 | 75.50 | 80.05 | 84.05 | 87.0 | 89.05 |

raw scores

*Figure 5–3*

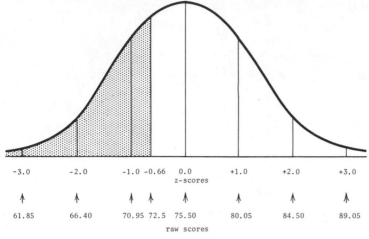

-3.0        -2.0        -1.0  -0.66    0.0         +1.0        +2.0        +3.0
                                   z-scores

61.85       66.40       70.95 72.5  75.50        80.05       84.50       89.05

raw scores

*Figure 5–4*

.4943 = .9943. Therefore, the probability of selecting a case at random that would be lower than 87 is .9943. Therefore, we could expect about 994 of our 1000 scores to be lower than 87.

(b) What is the probability of obtaining a score less than 72.5? Here, we are concerned with the shaded portion of Figure 5–4.

$$z_{72.5} = \frac{72.5 - 75.5}{4.55}$$

$$= \frac{-3}{4.55}$$

$$= -0.66.$$

Referring to the table, we find that .2454 of the area falls between the mean and a z of −.66 (since the normal curve is symmetrical, the proportional areas are the same for both plus and minus values). Since .5000 of the total area falls below the mean, and since .2454 of that .5000 falls between the mean and a z of −0.66, then .5000 − .2454 = .2546. The probability of obtaining a score lower than 72.5 when selecting at random from our population is .2546. Stated another way, about 255 subjects would be expected to score lower than 72.5.

(c) What is the probability of selecting someone with a score in the range 78 through 85?

In this problem we are concerned with the shaded area of Figure

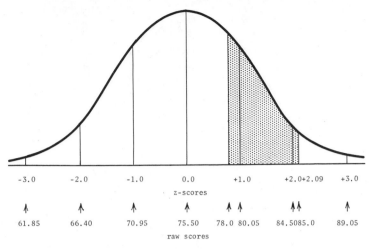

*Figure 5-5*

5-5. In order to answer this question we must find two different z scores as follows:

$$z_{78} = \frac{78 - 75.5}{4.55}$$

$$= \frac{2.5}{4.55}$$

$$= .55$$

$$z_{85} = \frac{85 - 75.5}{4.55}$$

$$= \frac{9.5}{4.55}$$

$$= 2.09.$$

Since we want to find the area between two z-scores above the mean, it is necessary to find the area from the mean to the lower score, then from the mean to the higher score, and to find the remainder by subtracting the smaller area from the larger. Between the mean and a z of +2.09 is .4817 of the total area under the curve; between the mean and a z of +.55 is .2088 of the total area. .4817 of the area occurs between the mean and a score of 85 while .2088 of the area occurs between the mean and a score of 78. Thus, .4817 − .2088 = .2729, which is the proportion of the area in the shaded range defined by the scores 78 through 85. Therefore, about 273 scores would be expected between 78 and 85.

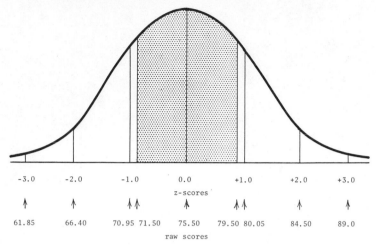

| -3.0 | -2.0 | -1.0 | 0.0 | +1.0 | +2.0 | +3.0 |

z-scores

| 61.85 | 66.40 | 70.95 71.50 | 75.50 | 79.50 80.05 | 84.50 | 89.0 |

raw scores

**Figure 5-6**

(d) What is the probability of selecting a score between the symmetrically placed scores of 71.50 and 79.50, as illustrated in
Figure 5–6? Since these are symmetrically placed scores it is
necessary to compute only one z-score:

$$z_{79.5} = \frac{79.50 - 75.50}{4.55}$$

$$= \frac{4.00}{4.55}$$

$$= .88.$$

Between the mean and a z of +.88 is .3106 of the total area. Since
the same area will fall between the mean and a z of −.88 we can
find the total area by adding .3106 and .3106 to obtain .6212.
Therefore, the probability of obtaining a score in the region
bounded by the scores 71.50 and 79.50 is .6212.

(e) What is the probability of selecting a score between the asym-
metrically placed scores of 72 and 76, as illustrated in Figure 5–7?

$$z_{76} = \frac{76 - 75.5}{4.55}$$

$$= \frac{.5}{4.55}$$

$$= .11.$$

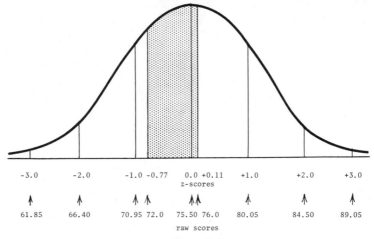

*Figure 5–7*

Between the mean and a $z$ of $+.11$ is .0438 of the total area.

$$z_{72} = \frac{72 - 75.5}{4.55}$$

$$= \frac{-3.5}{4.55}$$

$$= -.77.$$

Between the mean and a $z$ of $-.77$ is .2794 of the total area. Therefore, the probability of obtaining a score within the region bounded by scores of 72 and 76 is $.0438 + .2794 = .3232$.

It can be seen from the foregoing examples that the normal curve table can be used to solve a variety of problems if we can assume normality and if we know the mean and the standard deviation of the population. This fact provides us with some powerful inferential techniques, the development of which will be the subject of the next few chapters.

1. What is the probability of flipping a coin and getting four tails in a row followed by two heads in a row?
2. If there are ten cans and five of them are filled with water, in how many orders can the set of five water-filled cans be selected?
3. In how many ways can the five water-filled cans be selected from the ten cans when the order is ignored?
4. In a normal distribution the mean is 60 and the standard deviation is 4.3. If the acceptable scores are any scores within 1.56s of the mean, what is the range of acceptable scores?
5. In a normal distribution of 100 scores about how many scores would we expect to find between $z = 1.30$ and $z = 1.90$?
6. Explain the meaning of each of the entries in Pascal's triangle in the row to the right of $N = 5$.
7. In a normal distribution the mean is 50 and the standard deviation is 2.0.
   a. If an individual has a $z$-score of $-2.74$, what is his raw score?
   b. If his $z$-score is 1.34, what is his raw score?
8. In a normal distribution the mean is ten and the standard deviation is .5. What proportion of the scores would fall between a $z$-score of $+1.0$ and a $z$-score of $-1.0$?

## CHAPTER SIX

# NORMAL CURVE MODELS: PRECISION OF ESTIMATE

You now are acquainted with the process of drawing a random sample, calculating the mean, variance, and standard deviation, and determining the probability of obtaining a particular case from a normally distributed population.

The problem, at this point, is to determine the *precision* with which it is possible to estimate a population parameter from a sample value. In other words, we want to determine the probability that the parameters we have estimated fall within some prescribed range of values. As shown in Figure 3–1, our ability to estimate the mean on the basis of small samples is really quite good since most of the time we are quite close to the true population mean. However, some samples do vary more than others (see samples 2 and 4 in Figure 3–1). We would now like to say something more precise than merely stating that the accuracy of estimating the population mean from a sample mean is really quite good most of the time. The only way in which we could be absolutely sure of the accuracy of our estimates would be to calculate the population mean. But, if we could accomplish this, we would not need to collect samples in the first place.

A satisfactory approach to this problem would be to determine the probability that our estimate of the population mean did not exceed some stated range of values. It is possible to do this (1) by utilizing some properties of the normal curve, and (2) by taking advantage of the fact that many statistics calculated on random samples distribute normally.

Perhaps a brief review of some of the material in Chapter 5 will be helpful here. In Chapter 5, the characteristics of the normal curve were discussed and, from Figure 5–2, it can be seen that in a population distribution with the characteristics of the theoretical normal curve, .68 of the observations will fall between plus and minus one standard deviation and .95 of all the observations will fall between plus and minus 1.96 standard deviations from the mean.

Now, let us review briefly some aspects of sampling as presented in Chapter 2. In Chapter 2 there is a graph of 100 means calculated from samples of $N = 30$ from our "normal" population of 1000 observations (Figure 2–9 $A$). The mean of this normal population is 75.5 and the standard deviation is 4.55. Figure 2–9 $B$ is a graph of 100 means calculated from samples of $N = 30$ drawn randomly from an exponential population. The mean of this exponential population is 4.8 and the standard deviation is .803. The distributions of both of these calculated values form an approximately normal curve. If we were to calculate the percentage of observations falling within plus and minus one standard deviation and plus and minus 1.96 standard deviations, and then to compare these percentages to the values for the theoretical normal curve, we would find that the differences between the percentages for the two distributions are rather small. Figure 6–1 contains the results of these calculations.

With 100 normally distributed observations, we would expect five of them to lie outside the range of $\pm 1.96s$. For the 100 means calculated on samples drawn from a normal population (Figure 6–1 $A$), a total of six observations lie outside these ranges. For the means calculated on samples drawn from an exponential population (Figure 6–1 $B$), exactly five observations are outside this range. It is this remarkable correspondence of real events to mathematical expectations that makes the methods of statistical inference so valuable.

## SAMPLING DISTRIBUTIONS

In order to follow the discussion to be presented, it will be necessary both to make some assumptions and to take certain things on faith, since their proof is beyond the scope of this book. First of all, keep in mind that we want to estimate the population mean from only one sample. If we have drawn the observations in our sample under random conditions, this sample mean can itself be considered to be a random sample from a population of *means*. In fact, a set of 100 means calculated from our normal population of observations can be considered to be a population of means (although a very limited one); however, each "observation" is a sample *mean* instead of an individual *observation*. We can assume that our sample mean is one of an infinite number of sample means that could be calculated from the population of 1000 observations. Remember, if each observation is replaced in the population as soon as it is selected, the population of 1000 is theoretically infinitely large. Consequently, means calculated from

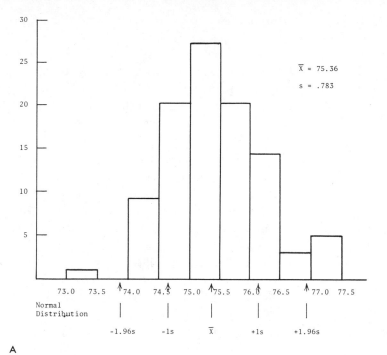

A

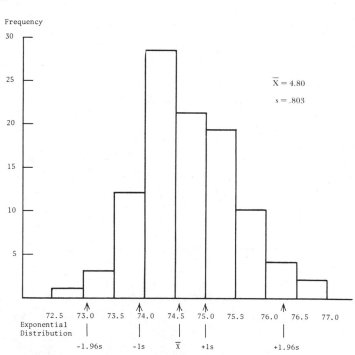

B

*Figure 6–1.* *A*, Distribution of 100 means calculated from samples of 30 observations each randomly selected from a normal population. *B*, Distribution of 100 means calculated from samples of 30 observations each randomly selected from an exponential population.

this population under these conditions represent samples from an infinitely large population of means. In statistics, populations such as these are called *sampling distributions.* The sampling distribution of means will have its own mean, which will be identical to the population mean.

The sample means will be located both above and below the true population mean (so that the average error will tend toward zero) and, provided that there is a large enough number of samples, will distribute themselves normally. As the number of observations contained in each sample increases, the amount of variability of the distribution of sample means will decrease. Consequently, there is a smaller probability that a large error will be made when a sample mean is used as an estimate of the population mean if the sample size is large.

Since we can assume that our sample mean is one of this population of means that are distributed in a normal curve fashion, we can rephrase our original question as follows: What is the probability that our obtained sample mean is between plus and minus one standard deviation of the mean of the distribution of means? To answer this, we need to know the standard deviation of the distribution of means. But all we have is a single sample! However, we can estimate the population mean on the basis of a single sample if we assume that this single sample is randomly selected from a distribution of means, which, as we know, will distribute as a normal curve. The statistic used to make this estimate is the *standard error of the mean* ($\sigma_{\bar{x}}$) and is calculated by the formula:

**(6–1)**
$$\sigma_{\bar{x}} = \frac{\sigma}{\sqrt{N}}.$$

(It should be noted that the formula for the standard error of the mean is stated in terms of population parameters. This has been indicated by the use of Greek symbols. Obviously, then, it would not be possible to use this formula to calculate the $\sigma_{\bar{x}}$ unless $\sigma$ is known.)

How does the preceding formula enable us to estimate where a given sample mean would be expected to fall in a distribution of sample means? The answer is twofold. First, it has been demonstrated previously that means computed from random samples distribute as a normal curve. Second, there is a demonstrable relationship between a population of observations and a distribution of means calculated from random samples drawn from this population of observations. The degree of variability that the sample means will display is a function of the degree of variability of the distribution of observations. Since this is a constant relationship, it is possible to estimate the standard deviation of a distribution of sample means *using only one single sample*. This statistic is called a *standard error*, and is an estimate of the standard deviation of the sampling distribution of a statistic, in this case the standard deviation of a distribution of sample means. Whenever the term standard error is used it means, then, that we are referring to the standard deviation of the sampling distribution of a statistic.

The relationship between a population of observations and a sampling distribution of means calculated on samples from this population is as follows: the means will distribute symmetrically and will approach the form of the normal curve. The sampling distribution of means will have the same mean as the population mean ($\mu$) and a standard deviation ($\sigma_{\bar{x}}$) equal to the population standard deviation ($\sigma$) divided by the square root of the sample size ($\sqrt{N}$).

### Calculation of the Standard Error

By way of illustration we will calculate the standard error of the mean, using the formula given earlier and the population parameters we have been using: $\mu = 75.5$; $\sigma = 4.55$. If we draw samples of $N = 30$ from this population the standard error of the mean is calculated as follows:

$$\sigma_{\bar{X}} = \frac{\sigma}{\sqrt{N}} = \frac{4.55}{\sqrt{30}} = \frac{4.55}{5.48} = .830.$$

This standard error value is interpreted in the same manner as the standard deviation values that we obtained earlier. Thus, between the mean and plus one $\sigma_{\bar{x}}$ we would expect to find .3413 of the total area of the curve occurring (and, of course, .3413 of the total number of means); between plus and minus one $\sigma_{\bar{x}}$ we would expect to find .6826 of the total area of the curve, and so forth. Put another way, between the $\mu$ of 75.5 (which we know in this example) and $75.5 + .83 = 76.33$ we would expect to find .3413 of the sample $\bar{X}$'s if we drew many samples from the population and calculated the mean for each sample. For the sample means, .6826 would be expected to be between 76.33 and 74.67 (which is $75.5 - .83$).

Usually, we do not have a population of sample means at our disposal and must rely on an estimate based on only one sample. In order to evaluate the adequacy of our estimate of the standard error of the mean using only one sample, let us draw some actual samples from a population whose parameters we know. We can then compare the estimate based on only one sample mean with the actual distribution of a large number of sample means drawn from the population. Figure 6–2 is the distribution of 100 sample means based on samples $N = 30$ drawn from the normally distributed population of scores that we have used throughout this book. The mean of these sample means is 75.45 (as compared to the population mean of 75.50). We found earlier that the standard error of the mean based on an $N$ of 30 and the $\sigma$ of 4.55 is equal to .83. The actual standard error of the mean for 100 means (found by calculating the standard deviation in the usual manner, using each mean as a score) is .80. This minor discrepancy from the estimated value of .83 is well within what would be expected on the basis of sampling variation alone.

Let us follow the procedure used to estimate the standard error of the mean as we would do it in actual practice. When we estimate $\sigma_{\bar{X}}$ using only a single sample we do not know the population standard deviation ($\sigma$). Therefore, we must use the best estimate of $\sigma$ that we have available. The best estimate of $\sigma$ is $s$, the standard deviation of our sample. The formula for the standard error of the mean thus becomes:

**(6–2)**
$$s_{\bar{X}} = \frac{s}{\sqrt{N}}.$$

The actual calculation of the standard error is done in Table 6–1.

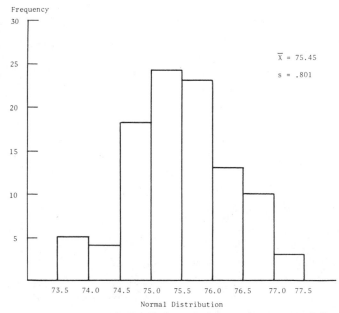

$\bar{X} = 75.45$

$s = .801$

Normal Distribution

*Figure 6–2.* The distribution of 100 sample means each based on random samples of 30 observations from a normal population with $\mu = 75.50$.

**Table 6–1.** CALCULATION OF THE STANDARD ERROR FOR A SAMPLE OF 30 OBSERVATIONS

*Observations*

| | | | | |
|---|---|---|---|---|
| 78 | 73 | 75 | 69 | 76 |
| 72 | 76 | 77 | 76 | 78 |
| 79 | 72 | 78 | 85 | 79 |
| 72 | 71 | 84 | 80 | 75 |
| 76 | 70 | 70 | 75 | 71 |
| 71 | 86 | 71 | 71 | 74 |

$$N = 30$$
$$\sum X = 2260$$
$$\overline{X} = 75.33$$
$$\sum X^2 = 170,842$$
$$(\sum X)^2 = 5,107,600$$
$$(\sum X)^2/N = 170,253.33$$
$$\sum x^2 = \sum X^2 - [(\sum X)^2/N] = 588.67$$
$$s^2 = \sum x^2/(N - 1) = 20.30$$
$$s = 4.51$$
$$s_{\overline{X}} = \frac{4.51}{\sqrt{30}}$$
$$= 4.50/5.48$$
$$= .82$$

Once the sample standard deviation has been calculated, the calculation of the standard error is quite straightforward. The standard error as estimated for this sample is .82, which compares quite well with the $\sigma_{\overline{X}}$ of .80 that we obtained when we actually drew 100 samples of $N = 30$ and calculated the $\sigma_{\overline{X}}$ directly.

## CONFIDENCE INTERVALS

We can now, with a few additional calculations, determine what are called *confidence intervals for the mean.* We know that a population of means calculated from random samples will distribute normally. The one available sample mean may be viewed as a single random mean drawn from an infinite population of sample means, each one based on the same number of observations. If the distribution is normal, .95

of the observations lie between plus and minus 1.96 standard deviations from the population mean. The mean of our single sample is the best estimate we have of the true population mean. We will use the standard error of the sample mean ($s_{\bar{X}}$) based on the data of Table 6–1 as an estimate of the standard deviation of the population of means ($\sigma_{\bar{X}}$). Consequently, we can determine the upper and lower limits within which the true population mean would be expected to fall by the following steps:

1. For the upper limit of the confidence interval, the equation is:

**(6–3)**
$$UL_{.95} = \bar{X} + 1.96s_{\bar{X}}.$$

2. For the lower limit:

**(6–4)**
$$LL_{.95} = \bar{X} - 1.96s_{\bar{X}}.$$

If we now apply these equations using the mean and the standard error of the mean taken from the earlier calculations we obtain the following values:

$$UL_{.95} = 75.33 + 1.96(.82) = 75.33 + 1.61 = 76.94$$
$$LL_{.95} = 75.33 - 1.61 = 73.72.$$

What does this mean? We have used the standard error of the mean calculated on the basis of one sample to estimate the standard deviation of a population of means. Then, using the normal curve model, we know that .95 of all the observations in a normal curve fall between plus and minus 1.96 standard deviations from the mean. We multiply the estimate ($s_{\bar{X}}$) of the standard deviation of the populations of means ($\sigma_{\bar{X}}$) by 1.96. This value, when added to the mean to determine the upper limit and subtracted to determine the lower limit, defines *the .95 confidence interval for the mean.* In other words, using the mean and the standard deviation of our sample, we expect the value of the population mean to fall between the upper and lower limits specified by $UL_{.95} = 76.94$ and $LL_{.95} = 73.72$. Any hypothesis concerning a value of the population mean that lies outside the limits specified by 76.94 and 73.72 we will reject at the .95 confidence level.

In the first chapter of this book, we remarked that the field of statistics is frequently characterized by a combination of strict rules and arbitrary assumptions. Estimating confidence limits is one example of this situation. We have a set of well-defined procedures for calculating the standard error and a set of requirements (such as minimum sample size) that must be met if the procedures are to be considered valid. However, the setting of confidence limits is a completely arbitrary matter. We could just as easily have determined the .45 confidence limits, or the .64 confidence limits, or any other set of confidence limits for that matter. All that is needed to set any given confidence limit is to determine from the normal curve table the standard scores that define the percentage of observations to be included within the confidence limits. For example, to set the .99 confidence limits, we find the percentage of observations included between the mean and the given standard score value from the table of the normal curve (Table A–2).

Assume that we want to set the limits for the .99 confidence interval. We know that half of the .99 will fall between the mean and the lower limit and half will fall between the mean and the upper limit. One-half of .99 is .495. From Table A–2 we find that .495 of the area under the curve falls between the mean and a z-score of 2.58 (the real value is 2.576, which becomes 2.58 when rounded off). To determine the .99 confidence limits, we substitute into the $UL$ and the $LL$ equations the value 2.58 (instead of 1.96, which we used for the .95 level) and multiply our standard error by this value. The results of this calculation are as follows:

$$UL_{.99} = \overline{X} + 2.58s_{\overline{X}} = 75.33 + 2.58(.82)$$
$$= 75.33 + 2.12 = 77.45$$
$$LL_{.99} = 75.33 - 2.12 = 73.21.$$

The interpretation of these values is as before; on the basis of our sample statistics we expect the value of the population mean to be located within the limits defined by the scores of 77.45 ($UL_{.99}$) and 73.21 ($LL_{.99}$). Any hypothesis concerning the value of the population mean outside these limits we reject at the .99 confidence level.

### Small Samples

The procedure just described is appropriate when the research worker has at least 30 observations in his sample. However, the research worker who has only small samples must employ a slightly different sampling distribution appropriate for small numbers of observations.

We have seen how a sampling distribution of means will assume a normal curve shape regardless of the shape of the population on which it is based, and we know that the approximation to the normal curve is usually closer and closer, the larger the sample size. By the same logic, we know that a sampling distribution of *differences between means* constructed by the equation:

**(6-5)**

$$\frac{\overline{X} - \mu}{\sigma_{\overline{X}}}$$

should also distribute normally.

This equation represents the sampling distribution of differences between means that we would obtain if we drew a sample, computed the mean ($\overline{X}$) subtracted from $\overline{X}$ the true population mean ($\mu$), and divided the difference by the standard deviation of the sampling distribution of means ($\sigma_{\overline{X}}$). Such a distribution would have a mean of zero and a standard deviation of one. As you may (or may not) have suspected, this becomes a sampling distribution of mean differences in standard score form. The equation $\frac{\overline{X} - \mu}{\sigma_{\overline{X}}}$ is basically a standard score equation.

For sample sizes greater than 30, this sampling distribution will distribute normally. However, for sample sizes smaller than 30, the curve changes shape.

In practice, if we were to develop such a sampling distribution, we would use $s_{\overline{X}}$ instead of $\sigma_{\overline{X}}$, since we would not know either the population mean ($\mu$) or the population standard deviation ($\sigma$) and thus could not calculate the $\sigma_{\overline{X}}$. Since the population standard deviation is systematically underestimated when using small samples, the normal curve model is inappropriate here. Therefore, an alternative procedure must be found. The sampling distribution for the equation $\frac{\overline{X} - \mu}{s_{\overline{X}}}$ can be developed with a correction included for the bias in the estimate of the standard error of the mean caused by small sample size. Suppose that we draw samples of ten observations each from our population of 1000 observations (for which we know the population mean), calculate the mean of each sample, subtract that mean from the population mean, and then divide by the standard error of the mean estimated on the basis of that sample. After doing this several thousand times we would have the sampling distribution labeled in Figure 6–3 as $df = 9$. (The meaning of the symbol $df$ will be explained in a moment. For our purposes here $df = N - 1$.)

## THE *t* DISTRIBUTION

The relationship of the new sampling distribution to the distribution of the normal curve is shown in Figure 6–3. This new distribution is referred to as the *t* distribution. The mathematical derivation

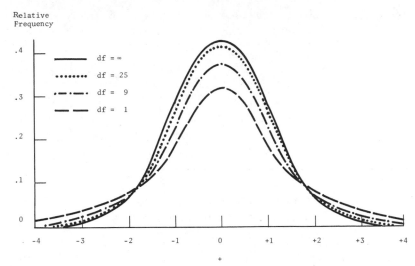

**Figure 6–3.** (From Ferguson, G. A., *Statistical Analysis in Psychology and Education*, 3rd edition. Copyright 1971 by McGraw-Hill Inc. and reproduced with their permission.)

of this distribution was first developed by W. S. Gossett, who published his findings under the pseudonym "Student" since the company that employed him had a rule that forbade the publication of the results of any research performed by its employees. Since the *t* distribution did not reveal any trade secrets dear to the industry concerned (Gossett was employed by the Guinness Brewing Corporation in Dublin), he was allowed to publish under this pseudonym. As a result this statistic is often referred to as Student's *t*.

Inspection of Figure 6–3 indicates: (1) that the *t* distribution for ten observations is symmetrical about zero; (2) that the observations are not as densely distributed in the center of the distribution of scores as is the case for the normal distribution; and (3) that there are more observations in the tails of the *t* distribution than in the normal distribution. There are slightly different distributions of *t* for every sample size until $N = 30$, at which point it becomes almost indistinguishable from the normal curve (which, you will remember, is based on a population of infinite size). Figure 6–3 illustrates the relationship of the *t* distributions for $df = 1$, 9, 25, and infinity ($\infty$). (The distribution for infinity is the normal curve.) Table 6–2 contains a comparison of the values of *t* and the normal curve values (*z*) for selected numbers of observations.

As is evident from examination of both Figure 6–3 and Table 6–2, the percentage of observations in the tails of the *t* distributions varies as a function of the number of observations. If the sampling distribution is calculated on the basis of samples with five *df*, the percentage of observations in the tails of the distribution is much higher

**Table 6–2.** COMPARISON OF AREAS BETWEEN LIMITS FOR THE NORMAL CURVE AND THE $t$ DISTRIBUTION FOR DIFFERING DEGREES OF FREEDOM

| Area between Confidence Limits | Normal Curve Value | $t$ Value for Varying Degrees of Freedom | | | | |
|---|---|---|---|---|---|---|
| | $z$ | 5 | 10 | 30 | 120 | $\infty$ |
| .90 | 1.64 | 2.01 | 1.81 | 1.70 | 1.66 | 1.64 |
| .95 | 1.96 | 2.57 | 2.23 | 2.04 | 1.98 | 1.96 |
| .99 | 2.58 | 4.03 | 3.17 | 2.75 | 2.62 | 2.58 |

than if the sampling distribution is calculated on the basis of samples with 20 $df$. When the number of $df$ reaches 30, the $t$ distribution is almost identical to the normal curve.

## Degrees of Freedom

The $t$ distribution can be used to set confidence intervals with small samples in the same manner that the normal curve is used with samples of more than thirty observations. To illustrate, we will determine the confidence limits of the mean for samples 1 and 2 from Table 2–1. However, before computing an estimate of the standard error of the mean and setting the confidence limits, we should explain the concept of degrees of freedom. The table of the $t$ distribution (Table A–3) is based on the number of degrees of freedom (abbreviated $df$). The number of degrees of freedom is always one less than the size of the sample on which the value of $t$ is based. For our example in which $N = 10$, the $df$ will be 9. The degrees of freedom for $t$ refer to the freedom of the observations to vary as a function of chance alone. Sample 1 has an $N$ of 10 and a mean of 75.2. When we calculate the mean of that sample we have thereby placed a restriction on the number of observations that are free to vary by chance alone. For example, we could add $+2$ to nine of the observations. However, if the mean is to remain at 75.2, then the tenth value would have to have 18 subtracted from it—there is no other way that the mean of the sample could remain at 75.2. This last value, then, is not free to vary randomly. It is restricted by the value of the mean and the sum of the other observations in the sample. The $t$ distribution is a distribution that we use to estimate the extent of variability to be expected on the basis of random sampling errors. Therefore, the equations for the $t$ distribution are based on the number of degrees of freedom rather than the number of observations in the sample. Since we are interested in estimating variability, and since we use the mean as the zero point around which we express variability, the mean must remain fixed. For our samples the proper $df$ would be 9, one less than the number of observations.

Making this allowance for the number of elements free to vary by chance is quite important when we have a small number of scores. The difference between basing our estimates of the variability of, say, four elements instead of five will make a considerable difference, although it may not make much difference when we have a sample size of 100 and use that value, rather than the appropriate value of 99.

Another way of understanding the importance of using the degrees of freedom rather than $N$ is to consider the fact that information on variation is contained in only $N-1$ elements in a distribution. If we have three scores, the number of possible differences can be found by the equation $1/2 \cdot N(N-1)$. Thus, we have $1/2 \cdot 3(3-1) = 1.5(2) = 3$. Of these three possible differences, only two ($N-1$) are independent differences. With three elements we have the differences $x_3 - x_1$; $x_2 - x_1$; $x_3 - x_2$. However, $x_3 - x_2$ is equal to $(x_3 - x_1) - (x_2 - x_1)$ and is not an independent difference as a consequence. For this reason we can see that the difference $x_3 - x_2$ is dependent on the other two differences in the sense that it gives no added information on variation.

There is no reason to select any one element as the zero point to express variability; the sample mean is used as a consequence. We have learned that the algebraic sum of the deviations from the mean must equal zero; that is a formal property of the mean. If $N = 4$ and you are told that the first three deviations are $x_1 = -4$, $x_2 = 7$, and $x_3 = 10$, then you know what the value of $x_4$ must be. Since the sum of the deviations equals $-4 + 7 + 10 = 13$, the value of $x_4$ must be fixed at $-13$ in order to obtain the required value of zero for the sum of the deviations. Hence, we have lost one degree of freedom when we express variation using the mean as a reference point.

The initial calculations to be carried out for confidence limits are the same as our earlier calculations.

|  |  |
|---|---|
| *Sample 1* | *Sample 2* |
| $\sum X_1 = 752$ | $\sum X_2 = 724$ |
| $N_1 = 10$ | $N_2 = 10$ |
| $\overline{X}_1 = 75.2$ | $\overline{X}_2 = 72.4$ |
| $s_1 = 4.89$ | $s_2 = 5.95$ |
| $s_{\overline{X}_1} = 1.55$ | $s_{\overline{X}_2} = 1.88$ |

### Establishing Confidence Intervals

However, when we estimate the confidence limits for the mean, we use the table of $t$ values in our $UL$ and $LL$ equations. These values are the small sample equivalent of the normal curve values. Using the normal curve table to determine the .95 confidence limits for our samples of $N = 30$, we multiply the standard error by 1.96, which is the standard score value that encloses .95 of the observations in the normal curve. For the $t$ distribution, we use Table A–3 and locate entry 9 in the column labeled "degrees of freedom." Having located 9 in that column, we read across that row and find the value of $t$ for the column headed 0.05. For our samples, this value is 2.26. This is the value of $t$ that encloses .95 of the cases in the $t$ distribution for nine degrees of freedom. It encloses exactly the same proportion of observations as does 1.96 for the normal curve, the larger value being due to the fact that the $t$ distribution has more observations in the tails of the distribution than does the normal curve. To calculate our upper and lower confidence limits, we simply substitute the value of $t$ for the normal curve value in the $UL$ and $LL$ equations.

| Sample 1 | Sample 2 |
|---|---|
| $UL_{.95} = \bar{X} + t_{.05}s_{\bar{X}} = 75.20 + 2.26(1.55)$ | $UL_{.95} = 72.40 + 2.26(1.88)$ |
| $= 75.20 + 3.50 = 78.70$ | $= 72.40 + 4.25 = 76.65$ |
| $LL_{.95} = 75.20 - 3.50 = 71.70$ | $LL_{.95} = 72.40 - 4.25 = 68.15$ |

Assuming, then, that we had only sample 1 available to us, we could, on the basis of our calculations, estimate that the true population mean is somewhere between 71.70 and 78.70. In addition, we could state these limits with confidence that we would be correct .95 of the time.

On the basis of sample 2 we could estimate that the true population mean is somewhere between 68.15 and 76.65, again with the expectation that we would be correct .95 of the time. Both of these estimates, we know, do include the true population mean of 75.5.

The procedure to determine the .99 confidence limits is the same. The value of $t$ in the 0.01 column for 9 $df$ is 3.25 (instead of the 2.58 for the normal distribution).

| Sample 1 | Sample 2 |
|---|---|
| $UL_{.99} = \bar{X} + t_{.01}s_{\bar{X}}$ | $UL_{.99} = 72.40 + 3.25(1.88)$ |
| $= 75.20 + 3.25(1.55)$ | $= 72.40 + 6.11 = 78.51$ |
| $= 75.20 + 5.04 = 80.24$ | |
| $LL_{.99} = 75.20 - 5.04 = 70.16$ | $LL_{.99} = 72.40 - 6.11 = 66.29$ |

It can be seen that the range of values we issue when estimating the .99 confidence limits is broader ($80.24 - 70.16 = 10.08$ for sample 1;

78.51 − 66.29 = 12.22 for sample 2) than those we issued for the .95 confidence limits (78.70 − 71.70 = 7.00 for sample 1; 76.65 − 68.15 = 8.50 for sample 2). The .99 range is broader than the .95 range; we are sacrificing precision of estimate in order to obtain greater confidence that the true population mean lies within the stated confidence limits.

Usually in research applications of statistical methods we are not interested in setting a range of values within which the true population mean would be expected to lie. The most common use of statistical procedures is to determine whether or not two samples could have been drawn from the same population, regardless of what the mean of that population might be. The next chapter develops the logic of statistical inference for this situation.

1. If you drew a sample of 30 scores from a population and found the mean of these scores to be 75 and the standard deviation to be 2, between what two symmetrically placed raw scores would you expect 97 per cent of the population scores to lie?

2. Given a sample of nine scores with a mean of 25 and a standard deviation of .73, what would be the upper and lower score limits within which 95 per cent of the raw scores would be expected to occur?

3. a. What would you estimate the standard error of the mean to be for the population given a standard deviation of 1.2 based on a sample of 36 cases?

   b. Given that the above population has a mean of 92, between what two symmetrically placed scores would you expect to find .6826 of the total area of the curve for the distribution of raw scores?

   c. Between what two symmetrically placed scores would you expect to find .6826 of the total area of the curve for the distribution of sample means?

4. If the following values are known, what is the standard error of the mean? $\bar{X} = 100$; $s = 15$; $N = 40$.

5. Given a sample $N$ of 81 with $\bar{X} = 21.1$ and $s = 3.62$, (a) calculate the standard error of the mean, and determine the confidence limits for the mean at (b) the .95 level of confidence and (c) the .99 level of confidence.

6. Determine the confidence limits for the mean at the .95 and .99 levels of confidence using the same statistics as in problem 5 except that the sample size is now 16 instead of 81.

7. Assume that the value of a population mean is 100 and the standard error of the mean for samples of size 120 is 3.5. What proportion of sample means based on a sample size of 120 would you expect to be between 96 and 103?

8. Find the .95 confidence limits for the mean given the following values: $\bar{X} = 97$; $s_{\bar{X}} = 10$; $N = 40$.

9. Find the .95 confidence limits for the mean, given the same values as in problem 8 except that the sample size is now ten instead of 40.

## CHAPTER SEVEN

# DIFFERENCES BETWEEN TWO GROUPS

You may have had some difficulty in relating what you have learned about statistics to what you have read in your other textbooks. For example, many textbooks in the field of psychology report experiments in which conclusions are drawn on the basis of "significant differences" between groups. These conclusions are based on statistical methods, but to date little that you have learned about statistical inference permits you to understand how these conclusions are reached. We will now examine the area of statistical inference that deals directly with problems of evaluating the results of experiments. Let us consider two types of situations.

(1) A psychologist interested in the physiological bases of learning suspects that a certain class of drugs, because of its mode of action on the central nervous system, may facilitate the rate at which animals learn. To evaluate the likelihood of this suspicion he takes a sample of 20 rats of approximately the same age and randomly assigns them to two groups: group A, which is injected with an inert substance, and Group B, which is injected with the drug. The animals then learn a multiple choice maze in order to find food. The investigator hypothesizes that the animals that are injected with the drug will learn the maze more quickly than will the animals that are injected with the inert substance. To test this hypothesis, he counts the number of trials each animal requires to reach an established criterion of learning; let us assume that the criterion is four errorless runs through the maze. After all the rats have been tested, the mean number of trials required to reach the criterion is calculated for Group A and for Group B. On what basis will the experimenter decide whether or not the drug facilitates learning?

(2) A social psychologist is interested in comparing different methods of influencing people's racial prejudices. He wishes to know whether direct contact with a member of a racial group about which prejudicial beliefs are held is more effective in changing attitudes than are methods that do not involve direct contact with a member of the group. To test this, he first administers a questionnaire to determine the degree of racial prejudice within the sample on which he proposes to test his methods. This sample is then divided into two groups that are matched so that the mean prejudice score is the same for both groups. One group is exposed to direct contact with members of the racial group against which prejudicial beliefs are held. The other group is given a series of lectures on the harmful effects of prejudice and is provided with information about the characteristics of the "prejudice group." At the end of the experimental period, a second measure of prejudice is administered. The average scores of the two groups are then compared to see if a positive change in attitudes toward the "prejudice group" has occurred. How big a difference in the amount of change between the two groups would there have to be for the difference to be considered statistically significant?

Although these two experiments, presented in capsule form, differ in many important respects, the fundamental statistical question remains basically the same: Are any differences found between the means of the two groups statistically significant? Can we conclude that one drug, or one method, is more effective than another in changing the behaviors in question? The basic paradigm for such experimentation is given in outline form in Figure 7–1. First, two random samples are drawn from the defined population. Each of these samples then receives the appropriate treatment and some relevant characteristic (called a *criterion measure*) is determined for each subject. Summary statistics are calculated for each group; these will be a measure of central tendency and a measure of variability. The bottom two boxes, which are connected by a two-headed arrow, represent the inference that is to be drawn from the experiment.

What is needed is an estimate of the probability that the observed difference between the location of the means for the two groups could have occurred as a result of random sampling deviations. On what basis do we determine the likelihood that a difference of a certain magnitude between two means is the result of chance factors rather than representing a real difference? Let us consider some data for the first experimental situation in order to clarify the steps of inference involved. In the first situation, you will remember, the effects of a drug on the rate at which rats learn a maze is being tested. The experimenter wishes to test the hypothesis that an injection of a

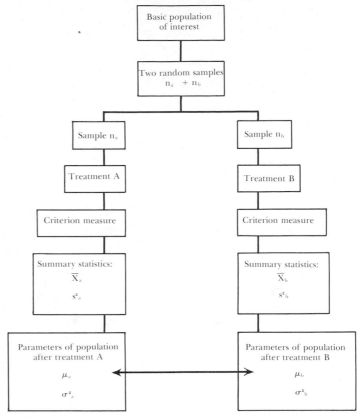

***Figure 7–1.*** Outline of steps in an experiment. (Adapted from Winer, B. J., *Statistical Principles in Experimental Design.* New York: McGraw-Hill, 1962.)

certain amount of a drug will affect the learning of the maze by hungry rats that are rewarded with food at the goal. A group of control rats is injected with the same amount of an inert substance known to have no effect on behavior. The measure of the rate of learning is the number of trials taken by the animals to run the maze without error four consecutive times. Table 7–1 lists the number of trials that each animal required to reach the criterion of four errorless runs. Table 7–2 contains the calculation of the mean, the variance, the standard deviation, and the standard error of the mean for both groups of animals.

These data indicate that the animals of Group B, which were injected with the drug, took fewer mean trials to reach the learning criterion than did the animals in Group A, which were injected with the control substance. Inspection of Figure 7–2 indicates that the distribution of the scores for the two groups is quite different.

**Table 7–1.** Number of Maze Trials Required to Reach Criterion of Four Errorless Trials

| Group A Scores (Inert Substance) | Group B Scores (Drug) |
| --- | --- |
| 10 | 5 |
| 13 | 8 |
| 13 | 8 |
| 14 | 9 |
| 14 | 9 |
| 14 | 10 |
| 16 | 10 |
| 17 | 11 |
| 17 | 12 |
| 19 | 12 |
| 19 | 12 |
| 19 | 14 |
| 20 | 14 |
| 20 | 15 |
| 22 | 15 |
| 22 | 17 |
| 22 | 17 |
| 24 | 17 |
| 25 | 23 |
| 26 | 24 |
| $N_A = 20$ | $N_B = 20$ |

How can we decide whether this difference between means could be expected to occur frequently on the basis of chance sampling differences or if it is too large to be considered a chance sampling deviation? After all, several of the animals in the two groups have the same scores. How much overlap can the groups have and still be statistically different?

## Sampling Distribution of Differences Between Means

To resolve this issue, it is necessary to consider yet another sampling distribution. In Chapter 6, the logic underlying the sampling

**Table 7–2.** Calculation of Mean, Variance, Standard Deviation and Standard Error of the Mean for Animals in Group A (Control) and Group B (Experimental)

| | |
|---|---|
| $N_A = 20$ | $N_B = 20$ |
| $\sum X_A = 366$ | $\sum X_B = 262$ |
| $\sum X_A^2 = 7072$ | $\sum X_B^2 = 3882$ |
| $\overline{X}_A = 18.30$ | $\overline{X}_B = 13.10$ |
| $(\sum X_A)^2 = 133{,}956$ | $(\sum X_B)^2 = 68{,}644$ |
| $(\sum X_A)^2/N_A = 6697.80$ | $(\sum X_B)^2/N_B = 3432.20$ |
| $\sum x_A^2 = \sum X_A^2 - (\sum X_A)^2/N_A$ | $\sum x_B^2 = \sum X_B^2 - (\sum X_B)^2/N_B$ |
| $\quad = 7072 - 6697.80$ | $\quad = 3882 - 3432.20$ |
| $\quad = 374.20$ | $\quad = 449.80$ |
| $s_A^2 = 19.69$ | $s_B^2 = 23.67$ |
| $s_A = 4.44$ | $s_B = 4.87$ |
| $s_{\overline{X}_A} = .99$ | $s_{\overline{X}_B} = 1.09$ |

distribution of means was developed and was discussed in terms of the precision of estimate possible using a single sample mean to estimate the population mean. To evaluate whether a difference in the means of two groups is larger than would be expected on the basis of chance, we must refer the obtained difference to a sampling distribution of differences between means.

In previous chapters, we have discussed random sampling and have presented the methods used to estimate population means and

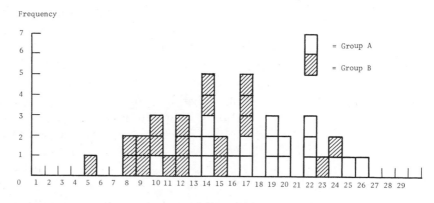

*Figure 7–2.* Graphic representation of maze learning scores for Group A (inert substance) and Group B (drug).

standard deviations using statistics calculated from random samples. A sampling distribution of the differences between means can be constructed in much the same manner as is the sampling distribution of differences $\dfrac{(\bar{X} - \mu)}{s_{\bar{X}}}$, which was developed in Chapter 6. If we draw pairs of samples by random methods, calculate the mean for each sample, and then subtract the mean of the second sample of the pair from the mean of the first sample, we could construct a sampling distribution of difference scores.

If we draw sample A and sample B from the same population on a random basis, calculate the mean for A and the mean for B, then subtract the mean for B from the mean for A, and do this several hundred times, we would have a distribution of differences. We can specify several properties of the resulting distribution without carrying out any calculations.

First of all, the mean of such a distribution of differences would be zero, because the population mean will be estimated quite accurately by the majority of the samples drawn. If the mean for sample A is an accurate estimate of the population mean and the mean for sample B is an accurate estimate of the population mean, the two estimates will be very similar, and the difference between them will be very small. A large number of such differences will center around zero. Figure 7–3 is a graphic representation of a distribution of 100 differences between means, obtained by drawing two random samples of 20 observations each 100 times from a normal population containing 6000 cases, calculating the mean for each sample and then subtracting the mean for the second sample (B) from the first sample (A).

Figure 7–3 indicates that the mean of the distribution does center on zero. Also, the distribution resembles the normal curve, although many more than 100 differences between means are needed to obtain a closer approximation to the normal curve. Thus, both the means calculated from random samples and the distribution of differences based on these means distribute normally.

The chances of obtaining a difference between means that is not zero diminish as the size of the differences increases, as is true of the other sampling distributions we have considered. In the distribution of differences shown in Figure 7–3, differences between means as large as $\pm 4.0$ occur only one time out of 100.

Could such a distribution be used to assess the probability of obtaining a difference between means of a certain size on the basis of chance alone? The answer is yes, if we take into account the amount of variability to be expected. Several sets of observations could have the same absolute difference between pairs of means but could differ

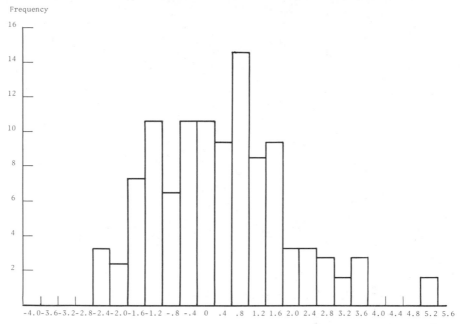

***Figure 7–3.*** One hundred differences between means based on samples of $N = 20$ from a normal population of 6000 cases.

drastically in the extent that the observations vary around their re-spective means. This point is illustrated in Figure 7–4. The pairs of samples shown all have the same difference between means but quite different variances. As a result there are different percentages of overlapping observations. Obviously, some way must be found to take this variability into account.

## STANDARD ERROR OF THE DIFFERENCE BETWEEN MEANS

The statistic used to characterize the degree of variability of a distribution of differences between means is called the standard error of the difference between means ($\sigma_{\bar{X}_1 - \bar{X}_2}$).

If pairs of samples are drawn randomly from one single popula-tion, a distribution of differences between means can be constructed, and this distribution will be normally distributed with $\mu = 0$. This is true only if the pairs of means are drawn from the same population. In the experiment presented earlier, we want to decide whether or not the mean learning scores of the drug and the control groups differ

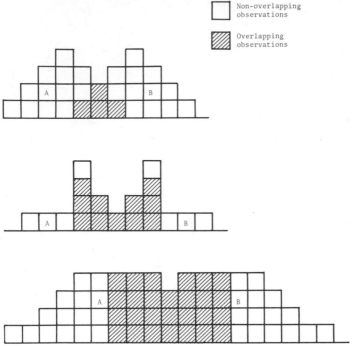

□ Non-overlapping observations

▨ Overlapping observations

*Figure 7–4.* Pairs of samples with identical mean differences and differing variances.

significantly following injection. If they do, then the two groups do not belong to the same population. However, we do not have any expectations on which to base a hypothesis concerning *how much* the population means would be expected to differ as a function of the experimental treatment. Therefore, we have no reasonable *a priori* basis on which we can assign expected values for either of the two population means. We do know, however, that if the treatment has no effect on the learning rate of the two groups, they can be considered to still belong to the same population. Therefore, the difference between means expected between the two groups would be zero. For this reason, whenever we test statistical hypotheses, we usually test the hypothesis that no difference exists between the two groups (in other words, that the two groups are randomly selected cases from the same population) and evaluate the probability that the difference between means that we have obtained could have occurred on the basis of random sampling deviation from the same population. This hypothesis—that there should be no difference between the two underlying population means in such a situation—is called the *null hypothesis.*

In order to decide whether any given difference between means could have occurred as a function of random sampling deviation, we must evaluate the probability of this difference occurring in relation to the amount of variability of the sample means. In order to do this, we must know the standard error of the distribution of differences between means.

The formula for the standard error of the difference between means is

$$\sigma_{\bar{X}_1 - \bar{X}_2} = \sqrt{\frac{\sigma_1^2}{N_1} + \frac{\sigma_2^2}{N_2}}, \tag{7-1}$$

where $\sigma_1^2$ and $\sigma_2^2$ are the variances of the respective populations from which the samples are drawn and $N_1$ and $N_2$ are the size of each of the samples. Since we do not know the parameters of $\sigma_1^2$ and $\sigma_2^2$ we must use our estimates of those in order to estimate the standard error of the difference as follows:

$$s_{\bar{X}_1 - \bar{X}_2} = \sqrt{\frac{s_1^2}{N_1} + \frac{s_2^2}{N_2}}, \tag{7-2}$$

where $s_1^2$ and $s_2^2$ are the variances calculated on the two samples we have taken. The quantity $s_{\bar{X}_1 - \bar{X}_2}$ is an estimate of the standard deviation of a sampling distribution of differences between sample means if the two samples are drawn from a single population of sample means.

## $t$-RATIO FOR INDEPENDENT GROUPS

In order to decide whether or not the obtained difference between means exceeds the difference that would be expected by chance, we will compute a $t$-ratio (see Chapter 6). The $t$ distribution, you will recall, is based on the ratio of a sample mean to its standard error. This distribution can be used to determine the probability of obtaining a difference of a given magnitude between two means as a result of sampling error. In order to do this, three assumptions are important.

1. The samples are assumed to represent a random selection from the population. For our example, the animals selected are random selections from a population of rats of a given age and species.

2. No differences are assumed to exist between the samples at the time they are selected. We must assume that the two groups of animals do not differ prior to the experimental treatment.

3. A null hypothesis is stated: that there is a zero difference between the means. This makes it possible for us to evaluate the probability of obtaining a difference between means as large as the one observed.

The $t$-ratio can be calculated using the following formula:

**(7-3)**

$$t = \frac{\text{Difference between means}}{\text{Standard error of difference between means}}$$

$$= \frac{\overline{X}_A - \overline{X}_B}{\sqrt{s^2 \dfrac{N_A + N_B}{N_A N_B}}}$$

Since both $s_A^2$ and $s_B^2$ are independent estimates of the same population variance we will combine them to obtain one pooled estimate of the population variance (the $s^2$ in formula [7–3] on which to base our standard error estimates). This quantity is calculated by formula (7–4).

**(7-4)**

$$s^2 = \frac{(N_A - 1)s_A^2 + (N_B - 1)s_B^2}{N_A + N_B - 2}$$

When formulas (7–3) and (7–4) are used it is assumed that $\sigma_A^2$ and $\sigma_B^2$ are equal (although, of course, they are unknown). This assumption is a reasonable one to make since we are testing the hypothesis that both samples are taken from the same population; hence, the statistical model we are applying assumes that they are equal. If the two samples are drawn from the two populations that have unequal variances, this will influence the inferential process little, if at all. Departures from the assumption of equal variances have been shown to have practically no effect on the operating characteristics of the $t$-ratio.*

---

*Boneau, C. A.: The effects of violations of assumptions underlying the $t$ test; *Psychological Bulletin,* 57:49–64, 1960; and Baker, B. O., Hardyck, C. D., and Petrinovich, L. F.: Weak measurements vs. strong statistics: An empirical critique of S. S. Stevens' proscriptions on statistics. *Educational and Psychological Measurement,* 26:291–309, 1966.

If we calculate the $t$-ratio on the data from the drug experiment, we obtain the following:

$$s^2 = \frac{(20-1)19.69 + (20-1)23.67}{20 + 20 - 2}$$

$$= \frac{19(19.69) + 19(23.67)}{38}$$

$$= \frac{374.11 + 449.73}{38}$$

$$= \frac{823.84}{38}$$

$$= 21.68$$

$$t = \frac{18.30 - 13.10}{\sqrt{21.68 \dfrac{20 + 20}{(20)(20)}}} = \frac{5.20}{\sqrt{21.68 \dfrac{40}{400}}} = \frac{5.20}{\sqrt{2.168}} = \frac{5.20}{1.47} = 3.54$$

How is this $t$-ratio of 3.54 to be interpreted? We have seen that the distribution of $t$ changes as a function of $N$. Again, the following rule applies: one degree of freedom is lost for each mean calculated. Since we calculate the means for two samples, two degrees of freedom are lost, and when $N = 40$ the total $df$ is equal to 38.

To interpret this obtained value, see Table A–3. You will recall that the first column lists the number of degrees of freedom and the successive columns list the values of $t$ beyond which a specified proportion of the area under the $t$-distribution occurs when the null hypothesis is true. Since we have 38 degrees of freedom and there is no exact value given for 38, we will be conservative and use the value entered for 35 degrees of freedom. For 35 $df$ we find the value of 2.72 listed in the column labeled .01. This value—2.72—is the value of $t$ that would be exceeded only one time out of 100 by chance sampling deviation alone. In other words, if we were to draw samples of $N = 20$ from a population and calculate the value of $t$, only one time out of 100 would we expect to obtain a value of $t$ as large as 2.72. Since our obtained value is 3.54, we conclude that the difference between the means of our two samples represents a real difference and did not occur as a consequence of a random sampling deviation within a single population. Since such a difference would have occurred less than one time in 100 by chance, and since the initial division of the sample into two groups was done randomly, we conclude that the drug administered to Group B does facilitate the rate at which rats learn the maze. In probability terms, the probability is less than .01

that this result is due to chance alone. Therefore, we reject the null hypothesis at greater than the .01 level of significance.

This is the basic sequence of steps used to decide whether a mean difference between two groups is due to random sampling differences or is due to the fact that the two groups are members of populations with different means. The $t$-test compares the ratio of the difference between two means to the combined standard error of the difference. On the basis of this ratio, the probability of obtaining a difference as large as that observed on a purely chance basis can be determined. While the mathematical basis for determining the critical values of the $t$ distribution is beyond the scope of this book, it can be easily demonstrated, using random sampling methods with a high-speed computer, that this mean-difference/standard error ratio will distribute exactly as do the values of $t$ calculated mathematically.

## Other Considerations

*Sample Size and the $t$ Distribution.* It can be seen from inspection of the table of the $t$ distribution that, as the number of $df$ increases, the size of the $t$-ratio required to reach a given level of significance becomes smaller. Therefore, if everything else remains constant, an increase in sample size permits us to detect differences between means more easily. This point will be discussed further when we discuss the concept of the power of a test.

*Significance Criteria.* In the example presented, the significance level used was .01. This level was chosen arbitrarily and is not related to the type of statistic used or to the number of subjects in the study. It is the arbitrary decision of the experimenter regarding the probability level that he will accept. The .05 level could have been chosen and would have been acceptable to most statisticians. There are circumstances in which a significance level of .10 might be appropriate, or in which we would demand the .001 level of significance before we would reject the null hypothesis. These are considerations that are determined by the nature of the problem and the relative cost of concluding that a chance difference is a real difference. This point will be discussed further when we consider the power of a test.

*Meaningfulness vs. Statistical Significance.* Because it is often forgotten, when we concentrate on the elegant and involved steps of logic involved in statistical inference we would like, at the outset, to emphasize the important distinction between statistical significance and meaningfulness. The end point of a set of statistical operations is one of two types. We make a judgment regarding whether or not some difference found between specified groups of individuals is large enough to represent a real difference—that they probably did not arise on the basis of chance alone. Or, we conclude that there is a real relationship between two or more sets of observations made on characteristics of the same individuals — again, that they probably did not arise on the basis of chance alone. This is an important point to determine; there is no use in speculating about the meaningfulness of differences or relationships unless they are likely to be real ones. However, merely establishing the existence of such statistically significant effects is only a preliminary step. The more important step is to decide whether or not these differences or relationships — granted that they are real — are *meaningful*.

We can approach this question in two ways. One is to ask the question of whether or not, for example, an observed difference in reading speed between children taught to read by two different methods, is worth the trouble of revising our methods of teaching reading. If the difference is small, even though it is real as judged by statistical standards, the effort involved in changing teaching methods, training teachers, and providing new reading materials might outweigh practically the small increase in speed obtained. Given a limited educational budget, we might decide that we could benefit our students more by expending money and effort in other ways. Practical considerations such as these will carry much more weight than will any statistical considerations.

Secondly, we have to keep in mind that when we observe that a significant difference or relationship exists we have yet to determine how important it is in the larger perspective. For example, assume that we want to understand some of the things that influence the happiness of individuals. We might devise a measure of people's expressed happiness and then choose to study some variables that would be expected to relate to happiness. Among these variables might be included intelligence, level of education, income, or type of employment. Assume that we study only level of education and find that people who have a high level of education score significantly higher on "happiness" than do people who have a lower level of education, and that this relationship is statistically significant. Is this sufficient evidence to conclude that educational level is an important determiner of happiness? The answer is no; it might be found, upon further examination, that, although level of education is a possible factor in the determination of happiness, it is one of the least important of the factors involved. In other words, finding that a variable is significantly related to some behavioral trait does not mean that it is very important in terms of its relative contribution as compared to other variables. In the present example, intelligence, income, and job type might all be of much more importance than educational level. All we know when we observe such a statistically significant difference or relationship is that it is *possible* for the variable to be an important determiner of a behavior. What we do not know — and what we really want to know — is how much influence the variable has on the behavior in question. In short, we want to know about those variables that exert the most influence and how much each variable does exert, not whether or not each variable has some influence of undetermined importance.

***Unequal Samples.*** In the example used both sets of observations were equal in number. There is no reason why two independent groups have to be equal in number of observations. However, if the two samples have drastically unequal variances (for example, if one group has twice the variance of the other), then an unfortunate interaction between the number of observations and the inequality of the variance is possible. It has been demonstrated that if two groups are unequal in size, and unequal in variance as well, the *t* distribution is not that which is tabulated in Table A–3. For example, if one sample has fewer observations and a larger variance than another, then the calculated *t*-ratio is likely to be larger than the tabled probability levels. Such a condition would result in an experimenter's deciding too often that there were real differences between his groups when no real differences existed.

The reverse is true if the sample with the smaller number of observations has the smaller variance. In this case the calculated *t*-ratio is likely to be smaller than the tabled probability levels. Here the researcher will fail to detect real differences and will conclude erroneously that his experimental treatment has no effect. This point is discussed further in Chapter 10, p. 179.

While these considerations may affect the inferences made, it has been demonstrated that small fluctuations in sample size and in variance will in general have little effect on the *t* distribution. The *t* statistic is considered by statisticians to be exceptionally "robust." This means that there are relatively few types of distributions of scores under which this statistic would result in misleading probability estimates. Another way of describing this is to say that if you conclude on the basis of the *t* statistic that there is a statistically meaningful difference between two groups you will seldom be wrong. The *t* statistic is remarkable in that it can be used with relatively little concern for the characteristics of the data.*

Let us now review the procedures involved in evaluating an experimental hypothesis:

1. The experimenter must state clearly the experimental hypothesis

---

*Baker, B. O., Hardyck, C. D., and Petrinovich, L. F.: Weak measurements vs. strong statistics: An empirical critique of S. S. Stevens' proscriptions on statistics. *Educational and Psychological Measurement, 26*:291–309, 1966.

that he wishes to test. In our example it is that Drug X will facilitate the learning of normal animals.

2. The experimenter must decide on the procedures, apparatus, subjects, etc., that he will use to test the experimental hypothesis. This step does not involve statistical procedures at all but depends on the wisdom of the researcher regarding the experimental procedures and theories of his particular field of specialization.

3. The experimenter, in the course of making the decisions involved in step 2, does become involved in one step requiring a decision on the basis of statistical considerations. If he decides to use the *t*-test for independent groups, which we have just outlined, then he must take steps to insure that the experimental group and the control group are randomly selected from the same population.

4. At this point the experimenter should formulate his *statistical* hypothesis. In the example we have used, the experimenter would have stated a null hypothesis to the effect that, with regard to their learning rate, the two groups of animals are two random samples from the same population. It is necessary to state an alternative hypothesis as well. In the example we have presented, the alternative hypothesis is that the two groups are not equal in terms of rate of learning and hence are not random samples from the same population. In statistical parlance this is called making a *two-tailed test* of the hypothesis, since we will consider a deviation in either direction from the hypothesized zero difference between means as a possible basis to reject the null hypothesis. In this case, if we reject the null hypothesis, we will accept the alternative hypothesis that the two groups are not equal, and it is possible that the experimental group could be judged to be significantly better or significantly worse than the control group, depending on the direction of the observed difference.

We could state a *one-tailed* alternative hypothesis as well. In this case the alternative to the null hypothesis is that the experimental group will be better than the control group. Here we are deciding (on non-statistical grounds) that the difference between the two groups can either be zero or that the mean differences will all fall in one tail of the distribution. This is tantamount to saying that we do not consider any mean differences in the opposite direction to be possible. The alternative hypothesis can be stated in the opposite direction also. In this case, if we reject the null hypothesis, we will conclude that the experimental group is worse than the control group. Again, this type of hypothesis would be justified on the grounds of non-statistical considerations. The use of one-tailed tests of statistical hypotheses merely involves reading a different column of the *t* table. The ordinary *t* distribution leaves, for the .05

level of confidence, .025 in each extreme tail of the distribution. If a one-tailed test is used, the extreme .05 is entirely within one tail of the distribution. Therefore, to obtain the one-tail entry for the .05 level it is necessary to read the table for the .10 level, since that level leaves .05 in each tail of the distribution. Similarly, if we desire to obtain the one-tail entry for the .01 level, the table must be entered for the .02 level of confidence.

Since the advisability of using one-tailed tests at all is still debated by statisticians, no more will be said on the matter. The student is advised, at his present level of preparation, to make two-tailed tests at all times since no question concerning the propriety of such tests will be raised.

5. At this point the experimenter is ready to perform the experiment, collect the data, and tabulate it in preparation for statistical analysis.

6. The final step is to calculate the appropriate statistics and either accept or reject the null hypothesis. If the null hypothesis is accepted, the experimenter concludes that the experimental manipulations do not affect the behavior under study. If the null hypothesis is rejected, the experimenter concludes that the experimental manipulations are effective influences on the behavior.

## *t*-TEST FOR NON-INDEPENDENT GROUPS

Testing the significance of differences between means based on independent groups of subjects has now been presented in some detail. There is, however, another type of research design in which the *t* statistic is frequently used. Situations arise in which only one group of subjects is used in an experiment. Here, the subjects are measured on some trait before the experiment, some experimental procedure is carried out, and the subjects are measured again on the same trait to see if there has been a change in the variable being measured.

Still another situation occurs when we have matched the subjects in two independent groups on a related variable. If we are interested in evaluating the efficiency of two different methods of teaching reading to first grade children it might be advantageous to match pairs of individuals in each of the groups in terms of intelligence. This matching would reduce the amount of variability present if intelligence is related to ability to read—a likely assumption.

Suppose that an experimenter is interested in a problem in which it is convenient to use the same subjects as both experimental

**Table 7–3.** SCORES

| S# | Pre-Experimental | Post-Experimental |
|----|------------------|-------------------|
| 1  | 13 | 17 |
| 2  | 12 | 15 |
| 3  | 11 | 15 |
| 4  | 13 | 16 |
| 5  | 9  | 10 |
| 6  | 11 | 16 |
| 7  | 8  | 7  |
| 8  | 12 | 15 |
| 9  | 13 | 18 |
| 10 | 11 | 15 |

and control subjects. In other words, the pre-experimental level of performance on the variable under study can be obtained as well as the level of performance following the introduction of the experimental manipulation. In this way, it is possible to determine how much subjects change from the initial pre-experimental level as a result of an experimental treatment. Table 7–3 lists pre-experimental and post-experimental scores for ten subjects.

It is possible to treat these two sets of scores as though they were based on independent groups and to carry out the computations shown earlier. However, such a procedure would nullify the precision that the repeated measures design allows. Since each subject provides his own control scores, the amount of variability present is greatly reduced over what would be present in two independent groups. In statistical terms, these scores are called *correlated* scores, meaning that there is a relationship between two sets of scores that are based on the same individual. Under such circumstances many of the factors that produce variability between individuals, such as level of motivation, intelligence level, and physical condition of the subject, would vary less between the pre- and post-experimental tests on the same individual than they would if the two measures were made on different subjects. Similarly, if such variables as intelligence are known to influence the behavior we are measuring, then matching individuals on such related variables will decrease the amount of variability in the scores due to uncontrolled factors.

Correlation methods will not be discussed until Chapters 11 and

12. However, $t$ can be calculated with scores that are not independent by a method that does not require the computation of correlation coefficients. This method allows us to take advantage of the reduction in uncontrolled variability produced when each subject is used as his own control, or when matched subjects are used.

The random sampling distribution of the statistic used to test for such changes would be a population of difference scores. The logic of this procedure is identical to that discussed earlier when the distributions of random sampling differences were discussed. Two samples drawn at random from the same population should be equally good estimates of the mean. In this chapter we discussed the fact that when we draw a random sample A from a population, calculate its mean, draw sample B from the same population, calculate its mean and then subtract the mean of sample B from sample A, this would most often produce a value of zero. This process, repeated thousands of times, produces a normal distribution of differences with the mean equal to zero. Exactly the same result occurs if sample A consists of 20 randomly drawn scores, and sample B of 20 randomly drawn scores; then we subtract the first score in sample B from the first score in sample A, and continue until we have 20 difference scores. If we add these difference scores and find the mean, we are likely to get a value of zero, just as we did when subtracting the mean of sample B from the mean of sample A.

If we repeated this process thousands of times, we would have a normal distribution of difference scores identical to the one discussed earlier on page 110.

The computation is quite simple and is illustrated with the data from Table 7–3. First, the post-experimental scores are subtracted from the pre-experimental scores, which results in a set of difference scores. The difference scores are then summed, keeping track of signs, and the mean difference $(\bar{D})$ is found. The standard error of these difference scores $(s_{\bar{D}})$ is then calculated, by the same formula used earlier to calculate the standard error of a single mean. The formula for the $t$-ratio is

(7–5)

$$t = \frac{\bar{D}}{s_{\bar{D}}},$$

where $s_{\bar{D}} = s_D / \sqrt{N}$, $s_D = \sqrt{\Sigma d^2 / N - 1}$ and $\Sigma d^2 = \Sigma D^2 - \dfrac{(\Sigma D)^2}{N}$. The term $s_D$ is the standard deviation of the difference scores, while the term $s_{\bar{D}}$ is the standard error of the mean difference scores. Thus, $s_D$ is analogous to the standard deviation of a distribution of raw scores while $s_{\bar{D}}$ is analogous to the standard error of the mean as discussed

**Table 7–4.** THE CALCULATION OF $t$ FOR CORRELATED SCORES

| Before | After | Difference (D) | $D^2$ |
|--------|-------|----------------|-------|
| 13 | 17 | −4 | 16 |
| 12 | 15 | −3 | 9 |
| 11 | 15 | −4 | 16 |
| 13 | 16 | −3 | 9 |
| 9 | 10 | −1 | 1 |
| 11 | 16 | −5 | 25 |
| 8 | 7 | +1 | 1 |
| 12 | 15 | −3 | 9 |
| 13 | 18 | −5 | 25 |
| 11 | 15 | −4 | 16 |

$$\sum D = -31 \qquad \sum D^2 = 127$$

$$\bar{D} = -3.10$$

$$\sum d^2 = \sum D^2 - \frac{(\sum D)^2}{N}$$

$$= 127 - \frac{(31)^2}{10}$$

$$= 127 - \frac{961}{10}$$

$$= 127 - 96.10$$

$$= 30.90$$

$$s_D^2 = \sum d^2/(N-1)$$

$$= 30.90/9$$

$$= 3.43$$

$$s_D = \sqrt{3.43}$$

$$= 1.85$$

$$s_{\bar{D}} = s_D/\sqrt{N}$$

$$= 1.85/\sqrt{10}$$

$$= 1.85/3.16$$

$$= .585$$

$$t = \bar{D}/s_{\bar{D}}$$
$$= -3.10/.585$$
$$= -5.30$$

$p < .01$ for 9 $df$

earlier. Since the scores themselves are expressed as difference scores, the $s_{\bar{D}}$ refers to a distribution of differences between means and the $s_{\bar{D}}$ is the appropriate term to use in the denominator of the test statistic.

We have ten difference scores and have calculated one mean difference. Therefore, we have nine degrees of freedom. Table 7–4 summarizes these calculations.

The $t$ value required for significance at the .01 level with 9 $df$ is 3.25. The calculated $t$ value of 5.30 exceeds this tabled value. Therefore, we reject the null hypothesis at better than the .01 level of significance. We conclude that the two samples are not drawn from the same population, which means that the post-experimental scores are different from the pre-experimental scores in terms of the location of the mean.

## Type I and Type II Errors

Obviously, the experimenter does not wish to make a faulty inference on the basis of the experimental data that he collects. The number of faulty inferences the experimenter will make of one type are dependent on the level of confidence chosen. You will recall that when we choose a level of confidence we risk making a certain percentage of mistaken inferences since we will reject the null hypothesis a certain percentage of the time even though the differences are, in truth, the result of random sampling deviations. Committing this error of concluding that there is a real difference between the groups when in fact there is none is known as making a Type I error. In other words, whenever we reject the null hypothesis when it is true, we are making a Type I error. The probability of making a Type I error (called $\alpha$) is determined in advance when we set our significance levels. Thus, if we set our significance levels at .05 then we expect to make five Type I errors out of every 100 inferences; if we set our limits at .01 we expect to make one Type I error out of every 100 inferences; if we set our limits at .001 we expect to make only one Type I error out of every 1000 inferences.

Why not always set our significance levels at .001, or even at .0001, in order that we make a minimal number of Type I errors? The reason is that there is another type of faulty inference, called a Type II error. We make this type of error any time we overlook a true difference by concluding that a true difference between means is due to random sampling deviation. A Type II error (called $\beta$) is committed whenever we accept the null hypothesis when in actuality it is false. Therefore, if we set our confidence limits so wide that we will practically never make a Type I error, we run the risk of overlooking many real differences and thereby making a large number of Type II errors.

In our example, a Type I error would be made when rats given the drug and rats not given the drug have the same mean learning rate but the mean difference was found to be at or beyond an acceptable significance level. Thus, it would be concluded (wrongly) that the two groups of animals are drawn from populations with different means. A Type II error would be made when the mean learning rates for the two populations of animals are different, but do not reach the predetermined level of significance. Thus, it would be concluded (again, wrongly) that the two groups of animals are drawn from populations with the same mean (this is the same as saying that they are drawn from the same population).

The probability of making a Type I error ($\alpha$) and the size of the samples ($N$) are set by the experimenter before collecting the data.

When $\alpha$ and $N$ are set, the probability of a Type II error ($\beta$) is determined. For a fixed $N$ there is an inverse relationship between $\alpha$ and $\beta$, such that an increase in $\alpha$ will decrease $\beta$. To reduce the possibility of Type II errors we must increase $N$.

## POWER OF A TEST

The probability of rejecting the null hypothesis when it is false is called the power of the test. This can also be expressed as $1 - \beta$, since $\beta$ is the probability of accepting the null hypothesis when it is false (overlooking real differences). The only other possible outcome when the null hypothesis is false is to reject it; therefore, $1 - \beta$ is the probability of rejecting the null hypothesis when it is, indeed, false. The next section presents a more technical discussion of the power of a test.

### POWER OF A TEST

Let us clarify these relationships with a numerical example utilizing the normal curve (Table A–2). Assume that we have a distribution of mean differences $(\bar{X}_1 - \bar{X}_2)$ with $\mu = 0.0$ and $\sigma_{\bar{X}_1 - \bar{X}_2} = 2.0$.

If we let $\alpha = .05$, what is the probability that we will make the correct inference—that $\mu = 0.0$? In this example our "null hypothesis" is that $\mu = 0.0$, and the alternative hypothesis is that $\mu$ is not equal to ($\neq$) 0.0.

We know from the table of the normal curve that .025 of the total area in a sampling distribution of differences between means will be located beyond $+1.96\sigma_{\bar{X}_1 - \bar{X}_2}$ and that .025 of the differences between means will be located beyond $-1.96\sigma_{\bar{X}_1 - \bar{X}_2}$. Our confidence limits for the mean will be $1.96\,(2.0) = 3.92$; $UL_{.95} = 0.00 + 3.92$; $LL_{.95} = 0.00 - 3.92 = -3.92$. Any time we obtain a difference between means that is greater than 3.92 or less than $-3.92$ we will reject the hypothesis that $\mu = 0.0$, and will do so at the .05 level of confidence.

Consider the operation of this test if we assume that $\mu = 0$ when actually $\mu = 0.5$. What is the power of our test to detect this true difference? In other words, we are interested in the power of our test to detect a difference between means of 0.5 when we assume a $\mu$ of 0.0 to be the true difference. We assume that reality is as illustrated in Figure 7–5 A and we will reject the hypothesis of $\mu = 0$ whenever a difference between means falls in the shaded region. If, however, the reality is as indicated in Figure 7–5 B, what is the probability that we will detect the difference? In other words, what is the probability that we will reject the hypothesis that $\mu = 0.0$ and will accept the alternative hypothesis that $\mu \neq 0.0$ when really $\mu = 0.5$? Again, we will reject the hypothesis that $\mu \neq 0.0$ whenever the sample mean falls in the shaded region of Figure 7–5 B.

Since the population distribution is centered around $\mu = 0.5$ rather than 0.0, we will have to recalculate our $z$-score values. We are going to reject any difference between means below $-3.92$ and above $+3.92$ and, therefore, must find the $z$-score values corresponding to those differences between means.

$$UL_z = \frac{3.92 - 0.50}{2.0} = \frac{3.42}{2.00} = 1.71$$

$$LL_z = \frac{-3.92 - 0.50}{2.0} = \frac{-4.42}{2.00} = -2.21.$$

Referring to the normal curve table, we find that .4564 of the total area falls between $\mu$ and a $z$ of 1.71 and that .4864 of the total area falls between $\mu$ and a $z$ of $-2.21$. It follows then that .0436 of the total area falls beyond a $z$ of 1.71 and .0135 falls beyond a $z$ of $-2.21$. Therefore, $1.0000 - .0436 - .0135 = .9429 = \beta$, which is the area contained in the unshaded portion of the curve shown in Figure 7–5 B.

The probability of *failing* to detect the difference between the "true" mean difference of 0.5 and the "assumed" mean difference of 0.0 equals $\beta = .9429$. The power of the test to detect a difference of this magnitude equals $1 - \beta = 1 - .9429 = .0571$.

Now, let us assume that the true mean difference is 1.0. The statistical model we are using assumes that the reality is the same as illustrated in Figure 7–5 A. However, the reality is illustrated in Figure 7–5 C.

We wish to determine the power of our test to detect a difference between means of 1.0 when we assumed a $\mu$ of 0.0 to be the true difference. We will reject the hypothesis of $\mu = 0$ whenever a difference between means falls in the shaded region of Figure 7–5 C.

$$UL_z = \frac{3.92 - 1.00}{2.00} = \frac{2.92}{2.00} = 1.46$$

$$LL_z = \frac{-3.92 - 1.00}{2.00} = \frac{-4.92}{2.00} = -2.46.$$

From the normal curve table we find that .4279 of the total area falls between $\mu$ and a $z$ of 1.46, and that .4931 of the total area falls between $\mu$ and a $z$ of $-2.46$. Therefore, $1.000 - .0721 - .0069 = .9210 = \beta$, which is the unshaded area of the curve shown in Figure 7–5 C. The probability of detecting the difference between the "true" mean difference of 1.0 and "assumed" mean difference of 0.0 equals $1 - \beta = 1 - .9210 = .0790$, which is the *power* of the test.

We could, by this procedure, determine the power function (with a fixed $\alpha$) to detect any presumed mean differences. Leaving $\alpha$ fixed we could calculate a family of curves with $N$ varying, such as is illustrated in Figure 7–6 for the $t$-test. A family of curves of this type could be generated for any given confidence level we wished and for any statistical test.

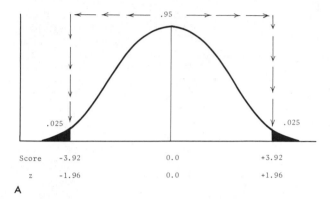

Score    -3.92           0.0           +3.92

z        -1.96           0.0           +1.96

A

*Figure 7–5*

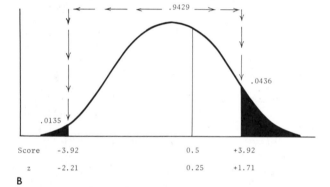

Score    -3.92           0.5    +3.92

z        -2.21           0.25    +1.71

B

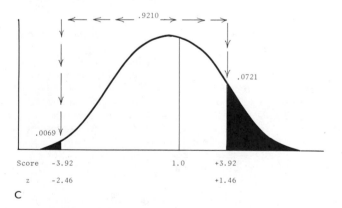

Score    -3.92           1.0    +3.92

z        -2.46                 +1.46

C

## Power Curves

To illustrate the concept of the power of a test in relation to differences between groups, assume that 10 subjects are selected from a population and assigned to two equal groups of five subjects each. One group is exposed to an experimental manipulation hypothesized to produce a change in the measured variable while the other group serves as the control and receives no special treatment. Upon completion of the experiment, the significance of the difference between the means for the groups is evaluated using the $t$-test. The null hypothesis is that the two groups are still from the same population following the differential treatment. Thus, any differences that occur are due to chance fluctuations around a population mean difference of zero.

$t$ is computed using formula (7–3) and a value of $t$ is obtained. Suppose that there is a real difference between the groups following the experimental treatment. What is the probability that the $t$-test will detect this difference? We can determine the power of the $t$-test to detect a difference from Figure 7–6. Along the horizontal axis the population difference is scaled in standard score units ranging from zero to $\pm 3$. Along the vertical axis the power of the test to detect a difference is scaled. The curves in the figure indicate the power of detecting a difference significant at the .05 level for different values of $N$. For our example, $N = 10$, and the power curve for $N = 10$ would be used. Suppose that there is a real difference between our two groups and, as a result of the experimental treatment, the two groups now belong to different populations. Suppose that our population difference is $\mu_0 = +.5\sigma$ in standard score values. We can determine from inspection of Figure 7–6 that there is about a 70 per cent chance of *failing* to detect this population difference. The power of the test to detect a difference of this size is .30. However, suppose that the population difference was $\mu_0 = -2.0\sigma$. Examination of the other side of the curve for $N = 10$ indicates that we would fail to detect this difference less than 1 per cent of the time. The power of the test to detect differences of this size is greater than .99.

Suppose that our population difference was $\mu_0 = +.5\sigma$ and our $N$ is 50. Examination of the curve for $N = 50$ indicates that we would fail to detect such a difference at the .05 level of significance only about 5 per cent of the time. The power of the test to detect a difference this large is, therefore, .95.

Inspection of these curves indicates the importance of sample size as a determinant of the power of a test to detect population differences. A comparison of the probability of detecting a real difference with $N = 10$ as compared to $N = 50$ should provide at least second thoughts for any experimenter who decides that an $N$ of 10 observations is enough to detect possible differences. If you suspect that a population difference is small, there is simply no substitute for large samples. On the other hand, the experimenter must decide whether a population difference that is so small that 100 observations are necessary to detect it is really of practical importance. The importance of a psychological, political, or any other kind of phenomenon is not a question to be decided statistically.

The choice of a significance level rests on a consideration of how costly, in practical terms, it is to the investigator to make a Type I as compared to a Type II error. If the decision to reject the null hypoth-

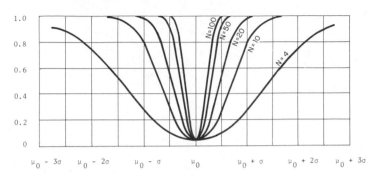

Population difference (in standard scores)

*Figure 7–6.* Power curves for the *t*-test; $\alpha = .05$; two-tailed test. (Reprinted from Dixon, W. J. and Massey, F. J. *Introduction to Statistics.* New York: McGraw-Hill, 1957.)

esis carries with it sweeping implications (e.g., in terms of financial expense or social consequences) the experimenter might well decide to demand a significance level of .0001, for example. We know that if he does demand such an extreme significance level he will probably overlook real differences. If he does reject the null hypothesis at this level of significance, however, he can be relatively certain that the observed difference is a real one. On the other hand, if he is performing a series of experiments to understand the effect of several environmental manipulations on behavior, it is extremely wasteful in terms of research energy as well as an accurate construction of reality to overlook real differences that do exist. The relative cost to the investigator of making a Type I or a Type II error, then, can only be decided on non-statistical grounds by the researcher. Once he has made this decision he can choose the proper significance level to minimize the expected number of Type I or Type II errors.

1. An experimenter wants to test the effect of a new drug on percep-
tion. He injects the experimental group with the drug and injects
the control group with saline. He records the number of seconds
between presentation of a light and the time when the presence of
the light was reported. Did his drug have any effect on perceptual
threshold? (Use .05 level of confidence.)

| Control | Experimental |
|---------|--------------|
| 13 | 9 |
| 12 | 8 |
| 11 | 9 |
| 9 | 12 |
| 12 | 10 |

2. In order to use a *t*-test, what three assumptions must be made?
3. Compute a *t* for the difference between means using the following
data: $N_1 = 11$; $N_2 = 26$; $\bar{X}_1 = 17.5$; $\bar{X}_2 = 14.8$; $\Sigma x_1^2 = 44$; $\Sigma x_2^2 = 68$.
4. A test of musical aptitude was given to a group of eighth grade and
a group of tenth grade students. Is the difference between the
means significant?

|  | 8 | 10 |
|--------|-------|-------|
| $\bar{X}$ | 90.76 | 99.32 |
| $s$ | 19.32 | 18.36 |
| $N$ | 200 | 200 |

5. The strength of the patellar reflex under two conditions, tensed
and relaxed, was measured for 10 minutes. Does tensing the patella
make any significant difference?

| Tensed | Relaxed |
|--------|---------|
| 31 | 35 |
| 19 | 14 |
| 22 | 19 |
| 26 | 29 |
| 36 | 34 |
| 30 | 26 |
| 29 | 19 |
| 36 | 37 |
| 33 | 27 |
| 34 | 24 |

6. Subjects were given an attitude test before and after viewing a motion picture designed to influence their attitudes favorably. A high score indicates a favorable attitude, and a low score an unfavorable attitude. Can we conclude that the motion picture resulted in a significant mean change?

| Subject | Pretest | Post test |
|---------|---------|-----------|
| 1 | 2.6 | 2.5 |
| 2 | 4.6 | 5.7 |
| 3 | 8.9 | 9.3 |
| 4 | 5.5 | 6.7 |
| 5 | 1.9 | 1.5 |
| 6 | 8.2 | 7.8 |
| 7 | 4.6 | 4.7 |
| 8 | 5.6 | 5.9 |
| 9 | 6.9 | 7.3 |
| 10 | 6.9 | 7.0 |

7. An experimenter found that the mean running speed of several groups of subjects with a specific magnitude of reinforcement was 50, $\sigma = 10$. He wishes to test the hypothesis that a change in magnitude of reinforcement will change the mean running speed. Accordingly, he employs a group of 100 subjects in a study and obtains a mean of 51.75. If $\alpha = .05$:

   a. Is he justified in concluding that running speed is a function of magnitude of reinforcement within the limit of the studies?
   b. What is the statistical hypothesis being tested?
   c. What is the probability of a Type I error in this experiment?
   d. What is the probability of a Type II error if the true mean ($\mu$) is 50.65 ($\alpha = .05$)?
   e. What is the power of the test?

# CHAPTER EIGHT

# ANALYSIS OF VARIANCE

The principles of statistical inference presented in Chapter 7 were developed to evaluate the significance of differences between the means of two groups. Other techniques exist that offer the research worker tremendous advantages in terms of flexibility in experimental design, and that enable the experimenter to extract the maximum amount of information from an experiment. These are called "analysis of variance" techniques, and are most often used when there are more than two groups in an experiment. They provide the research worker with some of the most powerful statistical tools available to analyze experimental data. For this reason analysis of variance is used more than any other statistical technique in contemporary social science research.* If you read journals publishing experimental research articles in the behavioral sciences, you will probably encounter more varieties of analysis of variance techniques than you will any other method. This statistic allows one to plan experiments of extreme complexity and to examine possibilities that could not be studied by any other method. It is also a statistic of considerable complexity, on which entire volumes have been written. In this presentation, we will of necessity be limited to a discussion of the basic logic underlying analysis of variance and of the simpler uses of the method.

By now, the logic underlying the comparison of two groups using a method such as the $t$ test should be clear. However, what do we do if we wish to make a comparison among more than two groups? Perhaps the first answer to come to mind would be to do all of the possible $t$-tests among the groups. Practical considerations alone suggest the limitations of this approach. For example, if we have three groups we wish to compare, we must make only three $t$-tests. If we have 10 groups to compare, however, we must make 45 $t$-tests! Apart

---

*Cf. *American Psychologist*, January, 1974.

from the incredible amount of computation required, the prospect of trying to make sense out of this number of comparisons would be sufficient to discourage even the most determined and obsessive investigator.

Entirely apart from both of these considerations is the simple fact that such comparisons violate the randomness requirement of the $t$-test. In comparing two groups by means of the $t$-test, we draw two samples randomly from the same population. Following experimental treatment the two samples are compared to determine whether the experimental treatment has had any significant effect upon the variable being measured. If the mean difference between the groups, relative to the estimate of variability, is more than we expect by chance, we conclude that our experimental treatment has had some effect; if the groups differ less than we would expect, we conclude that our experimental treatment has had little or no effect.

The critical assumption in the above formulation is that the two groups are random samples from the same population. If we have three groups and we compare groups one and two by means of the $t$-test, we are carrying out a perfectly legitimate comparison. However, if we now compare group 2 with group 3, the requirement of randomness has been violated, since after having performed a $t$-test to compare groups 1 and 2, the comparison of groups 2 and 3 is not independent of this first comparison. As the number of groups (and comparisons) increases, the seriousness of this problem becomes more extreme. The analysis of variance technique offers a way around this difficulty.

The concept of variance is scarcely new by now. It was first introduced in Chapter 4 and is defined as the average of the sum of the squared difference scores when each score is subtracted from the mean:

**(4–3)**
$$s^2 = \frac{\sum (X - \bar{X})^2}{N - 1}.$$

The computational formula we use to calculate the variance of a set of observations is the following:

**(8–1)**
$$s^2 = \frac{\sum X^2 - \frac{(\sum X)^2}{N}}{N - 1}.$$

The effectiveness of analysis of variance is due to the fact that the variability of several sets of observations can be divided into several parts with each part being associated with a given source of variability.

## SAMPLING DISTRIBUTION OF VARIANCES

Assume that we draw a random sample of five cases from a population, calculate its mean and variance, draw another sample of five cases and calculate its mean and variance. We then take the two variances and divide one by the other. If we do this the thousands of times necessary to construct a sampling distribution, we would have a distribution that looks rather different from anything we have seen so far. This sampling distribution of the ratio of two variances is called an *F* distribution and is shown in Figure 8–1.

This distribution will be positively skewed from a minimum value of zero and the mean will be slightly above 1.00 for the specific number of cases we have in this example. If the shape of this sampling distribution puzzles you, remember that there is no such thing as a negative variance. The variation of a set of scores around a mean may be zero—you may have a situation where all the scores are exactly the same—but you cannot have less than no variation.

Why is the mean just slightly above 1.00? Examine the process necessary to obtain this sampling distribution. You draw a random sample, calculate the mean and then calculate the variance of the scores around that mean. You do the same thing for a second sample. Just as two means are estimates of the population mean, the two variances are estimates of the population variance. Most of the time we would expect the two variances to be quite similar to each other, just as we expect the means to be quite similar. The result when you divide two identical quantities, one by the other, is 1.00, and this is approximately the value of the mean of this sampling distribution. The mean is slightly higher than 1.00 because the distribution is positively skewed.

A large value in this distribution of ratios would be obtained if

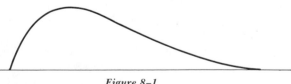

*Figure 8–1*

the first sample drawn happened to contain scores that came from the extremes of the population, resulting in a large variance, while the second sample happened to have all the scores drawn from one restricted section of the population, resulting in a very small variance. If the variance of the first sample is divided by the variance of the second sample, the resulting value will be considerably larger than 1.00. It is also the case that such values occur with steadily decreasing frequency as they become larger and larger.

How would we use this relationship between variances to test whether or not the differences between a set of sample means are larger than would be expected on the basis of chance sampling variation? Assume that an experimenter selects a sample of 30 subjects from a population suitable for his purposes. These subjects are randomly assigned to three groups. Since the assignment of a person to a given group is completely by chance it is quite safe to assume that the three groups do not differ on the characteristic being studied. Suppose that the experimenter is interested in whether people will improve more in a physical skill such as throwing a ball at a target if they are paid on the basis of how much their performance improves.

The three groups are defined as follows: Group A is the control group, the members of which engage in two minutes' practice throwing a ball at a target. Following this practice, they throw the ball at a target 20 times with the number of "hits" within a certain area of the target being counted. The control group receives no pay for doing this. The members of group B go through the identical procedure but are paid 25c for each "hit" during the testing period. The members of Group C also go through this procedure, but are paid 50c for each "hit" during the test period.

If payment to the subjects makes no difference in how accurate they are at their task, there should be no difference in the mean number of "hits" scored by the members of groups $A$, $B$, and $C$. Another way of saying this is that the mean scores are no different from what would be expected if all three groups went through the same procedure without payment. In Table 8–1, the calculation of the mean, the sum of squares, and the variance for each of the three groups is shown.

What can the experimenter conclude by looking at Table 8–1? The first thing to note is that group A has the lowest mean number of "hits," group B does better than A, and group C does best of all at hitting the target. From this information it appears that paying the subjects does seem to result in some improvement at the tasks. However, simple inspection of the data is not sufficient to conclude whether or not these differences are large enough to represent a real difference rather than being the result of chance variations. Perhaps if

Table 8–1. Scores Indicating the Number of Times a Target is Hit Accurately

| Group A | | | Group B | | | Group C | | |
|---|---|---|---|---|---|---|---|---|
| $X$ | $x$ | $x^2$ | $X$ | $x$ | $x^2$ | $X$ | $x$ | $x^2$ |
| 3 | −1 | 1 | 5 | −1 | 1 | 9 | −2 | 4 |
| 3 | −1 | 1 | 5 | −1 | 1 | 10 | −1 | 1 |
| 4 | 0 | 0 | 5 | −1 | 1 | 10 | −1 | 1 |
| 4 | 0 | 0 | 6 | 0 | 0 | 10 | −1 | 1 |
| 4 | 0 | 0 | 6 | 0 | 0 | 11 | 0 | 0 |
| 4 | 0 | 0 | 6 | 0 | 0 | 11 | 0 | 0 |
| 4 | 0 | 0 | 6 | 0 | 0 | 11 | 0 | 0 |
| 4 | 0 | 0 | 7 | +1 | 1 | 12 | +1 | 1 |
| 5 | +1 | 1 | 7 | +1 | 1 | 12 | +1 | 1 |
| 5 | +1 | 1 | 7 | +1 | 1 | 14 | +3 | 9 |
| $\Sigma X = 40$ | $\Sigma x = 0$ | $\Sigma x^2 = 4$ | $\Sigma X = 60$ | $\Sigma x = 0$ | $\Sigma x^2 = 6$ | $\Sigma X = 110$ | $\Sigma x = 0$ | $\Sigma x^2 = 18$ |
| $\bar X = 4.0$ | | | $\bar X = 6.0$ | | | $\bar X = 11.0$ | | |

all three groups had gone through the procedure without payment, mean differences as large as this still would have been obtained.

Keep in mind that what is being done here is not basically different from finding out whether or not the means of two groups are really different. The analysis of variance is a way to assess the meaningfulness of differences between means when more than two groups are involved. The arrangement of the arithmetic is somewhat different, but the purpose and the logic are quite similar.

To illustrate what is meant by "arranging the arithmetic," look at Table 8–2. This table contains the same 30 scores that are present in Table 8–1. However, here we have combined them and calculated the mean ($\bar X_T$) and sum of squares ($\Sigma x_T^2$) for all 30 subjects as one group. Now, look at what happens when we compare this result with the results of the calculations in Table 8–1.

The mean for all 30 subjects is close in value to the mean for group B, which is midway between the means of groups A and C. However, when the sums of squares of groups A, B, and C are added together ($4.0 + 6.0 + 18.00 = 28.00$) the resulting total is smaller than the sum obtained for all 30 scores treated as one group (288.0). How can this happen when exactly the same scores entered into both sets of calculations?

Understanding why this difference occurs is the basic key to understanding what happens in an analysis of variance. As mentioned earlier, this basic idea is that the variation present in a set of scores can be broken into two parts and that these parts can be compared with each other in the same way as when we take the variances of two samples drawn randomly and divide one into the other.

One of the sources of variation we have already discussed. It is the variation of a set of scores around their mean $\Sigma(X - \bar X)$,

**Table 8-2.** SCORES INDICATING THE NUMBER OF TIMES A TARGET IS HIT ACCURATELY. GROUPS A, B, AND C ARE COMBINED

| $X$ | $x$ | $x^2$ |
|---|---|---|
| 3 | −4 | 16 |
| 3 | −4 | 16 |
| 4 | −3 | 9 |
| 4 | −3 | 9 |
| 4 | −3 | 9 |
| 4 | −3 | 9 |
| 4 | −3 | 9 |
| 4 | −3 | 9 |
| 5 | −2 | 4 |
| 5 | −2 | 4 |
| 5 | −2 | 4 |
| 5 | −2 | 4 |
| 5 | −2 | 4 |
| 6 | −1 | 1 |
| 6 | −1 | 1 |
| 6 | −1 | 1 |
| 6 | −1 | 1 |
| 7 | 0 | 0 |
| 7 | 0 | 0 |
| 7 | 0 | 0 |
| 9 | +2 | 4 |
| 10 | +3 | 9 |
| 10 | +3 | 9 |
| 10 | +3 | 9 |
| 11 | +4 | 16 |
| 11 | +4 | 16 |
| 11 | +4 | 16 |
| 12 | +5 | 25 |
| 12 | +5 | 25 |
| 14 | +7 | 49 |
| $\Sigma X = 210$ | $\Sigma x = 0$ | $\Sigma x^2 = 288$ |
| $\bar{X} = 7.00$ | | |

which, as we know, equals zero. The differences squared are defined as $\Sigma (X - \bar{X})^2$. We have three such sums of squared differences, $\Sigma (X - \bar{X})^2$, for groups A, B, and C. These sums are 4.0 for group A, 6.0 for group B, and 18.0 for group C, the total for all three groups being 28.0. This can be represented as $\Sigma x_A^2 + \Sigma x_B^2 + \Sigma x_C^2 = \Sigma x_w^2$, where $\Sigma x_w^2$ refers to the sum of squares *within* groups.

The second source of variation is called the *between* variance and is obtained by adding the scores for all the groups together and calculating one mean, $\bar{X}_T$ (called the total mean) for all 30 subjects. Then we subtract each sample mean from the total mean, square this difference, and weight that value with the number of cases in the sample. The resulting value is called the *between* sum of squares $(\Sigma x_b^2)$. Thus, we go through the following steps.

1. Take the mean of group A and subtract it from the mean calculated on all 30 subjects. Square the resulting difference and multi-

ply that by the number of subjects in Group A. The numerical steps are shown next:

| $\bar{X}_T$ | $\bar{X}_A$ | $(\bar{X}_A - \bar{X}_T)$ | $(\bar{X}_A - \bar{X}_T)^2$ |
|---|---|---|---|
| 7.00 | 4.00 | 3.00 | 9.00 |

When $x^2$ is multiplied by the numbers of subjects in group A, we obtain $10(9.00) = 90.00$. $n_A(\bar{X}_A - \bar{X}_T)^2 = 10(4 - 7)^2 \doteq 10(3)^2 = 10(9) = 90.00$.

These steps are repeated for groups B and C and are shown below:

B:

| $\bar{X}_T$ | $\bar{X}_B$ | $(\bar{X}_B - \bar{X}_T)$ | $n_B(\bar{X}_B - \bar{X}_T)^2$ |
|---|---|---|---|
| 7.00 | 6.00 | 1.00 | $10(1.00) = 10.00$ |

C:

| $\bar{X}_T$ | $\bar{X}_C$ | $(\bar{X}_C - \bar{X}_T)$ | $n_C(\bar{X}_C - \bar{X}_T)^2$ |
|---|---|---|---|
| 7.00 | 11.00 | 4.00 | $10(16.00) = 160.00$ |

When the three numbers obtained by these processes are summed, $\Sigma x_b^2 = 90.00 + 10.00 + 160.00 = 260.00$. If this new total $(\Sigma x_b^2)$ is added to the sums of squared differences for groups A, B, and C, $(\Sigma x_w^2)$ we find that the new total is exactly the same as the sum of squared differences found when we treated all 30 subjects as one group $(\Sigma x_T^2)$.

The sum of squares $\Sigma x^2$ for 30 subjects as one group is:

| | |
|---|---|
| $\Sigma x_A^2$ | 4.00 |
| $\Sigma x_B^2$ | 6.00 |
| $\Sigma x_C^2$ | 18.00 |
| $\Sigma x_w^2$ | 28.00 |
| | |
| $\Sigma x_b^2$ | 260.00 |
| $\Sigma x_T^2$ | 288.00 |

The variation present in the 30 scores has been broken into two parts. The first part is the variation present within groups A, B, and C. It is just that—the variation of the scores in group A around the mean of group A, the variation of the scores in group B around the mean of group B, and the variation of the scores in group C around the mean of group C. When the sum of the variation for these groups is divided by the appropriate number of degrees of freedom it is called the *within groups variance*.

The other source of variation is the one obtained when we subtracted the mean of group A from the total mean, squared that difference, and multiplied it by the number of subjects in group A. This sum over groups A, B, and C divided by the appropriate number of degrees of freedom is known as the *between groups variance*. The ratio of these two variances is used to determine whether or not the differences between the group means are greater than would be expected by chance.

How does this work? Keep in mind that the between groups variance and the within groups variance are supposed to be estimates of the same thing—the variation present in a set of scores. The variation within groups is the variation we would expect to find in a set of scores because of individual differences. In the example of the target accuracy experiment, we would expect some people to be a little better at the task than others. However, we would not expect one group to do better than another if all groups received the same treatment. If all three groups were run on the experiment, with no group being paid, we would expect that the means of groups A, B, and C would differ only very slightly, if at all. Under these circumstances, if we subtracted the mean of group A from the total mean, that of group B from the total mean, and so forth, we would expect to end up with a rather small sum. If people actually do better on this task when paid, however, then the mean differences should be quite large. The larger the differences between the means of the groups, the larger the sum of squared differences for the between groups variance becomes. In other words, if the variance between groups is not much greater than the variance within groups, the groups are not very different from each other.

If you are still puzzled by this process, perhaps a graphic example will be of help. If we prepare a frequency distribution of the scores for groups A, B, and C, and connect each score to the mean by lines, we can represent how the scores vary around the mean for each group.

There are, of course, no lines connecting scores that have the value of the mean—that distance is zero. We can see by examining the dispersion of scores around the means of groups A, B, and C that the dispersion is limited. The same graphic representation for all scores treated as one group is shown below.

As can be seen from the illustrations, when all scores are combined into one group, the dispersion around the mean is much greater. It is this added dispersion that accounts for the additional variance, and it is this variance that forms the sum of the between groups sum of squares ($n(\bar{X}_C - \bar{X}_T)$).

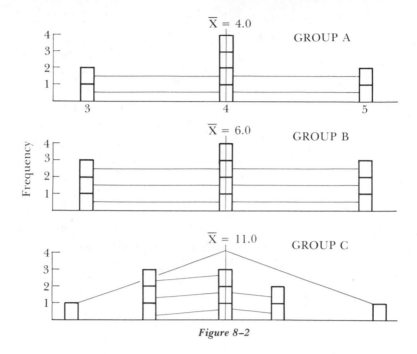

*Figure 8–2*

We are now ready to test for possible differences in our estimates of variance between and within groups. However, in order to calculate the statistic used here, some additional steps are necessary. The sums of squares within groups, $(\Sigma x_A^2 + \Sigma x_B^2 + \Sigma x_C^2)$, equals 28.00, and

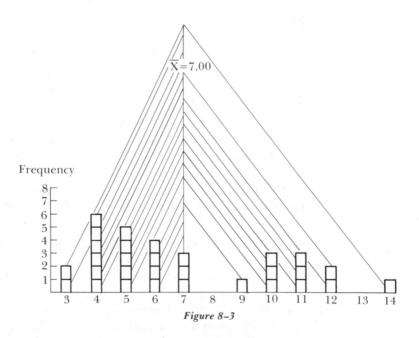

*Figure 8–3*

the sums of squares between groups, $[n_A(\bar{X}_A - \bar{X}_T) + n_B(\bar{X}_B - \bar{X}_T) + n_C(\bar{X}_C - \bar{X}_T)]$, equals 260.00. In calculating the test statistic we use the *mean squares*, which are an average of the sums of squares. Mean squares are calculated by dividing the separate sums of squares by the appropriate number of *degrees of freedom*. Degrees of freedom for analysis of variance are arrived at in much the same way as for the *t*-test — one degree of freedom is lost for each constant calculated from the data. The total number of degrees of freedom equals $N - 1$, since one degree of freedom is lost when we calculate the total mean. Since there are two separate variance estimates and two sums of squares, two calculations of degrees of freedom are required. The degrees of freedom for the between groups sums of squares is equal to the number of groups minus one. For our example the between groups $df = 3 - 1 = 2$. The degrees of freedom for within groups is equal to the number of subjects minus the number of groups. For our example with 30 subjects, $df = 30 - 3 = 27$. The $df$ for within groups and between groups sum to the total $df$ of $N - 1$; $27 + 2 = 29$. The final step in the calculations is to construct a summary table such as the following:

| Source of Variation | Sum of Squares | df | Mean Square | F | p |
|---|---|---|---|---|---|
| Between groups | 260.00 | 2 | 130.00 | 125.00 | .01 |
| Within groups | 28.00 | 27 | 1.04 | | |
| TOTAL | 288.00 | 29 | | | |

To calculate the test statistic — the value known as $F$ — the sums of squares are divided by their respective $df$'s and a mean square is calculated. In the above example, the sum of squares between groups is divided by the $df$ of 2 to produce a mean square of 130.00, and the within groups sum of squares is divided by its $df$ of 27 to produce a mean square of 1.04. The within mean square is then divided into the between mean square to produce the $F$ statistic of 125.00.

The calculation of the $F$-statistic is again a test of the *null hypothesis*: that there is zero difference between the two estimates of variation. In other words, we are testing the hypothesis that the different groups are all drawn from the same population. Since our value of $F$ is quite different from 1.00 — the value we would expect if there were no differences between groups — we can conclude that our experimental conditions have some effect. To complete the process, we turn to Table A–4 and determine the value of the $F$ statistic that would be expected to occur less than 5% (or 1%) of the time by chance when the degrees of freedom equal 2 and 27.

In Table A–4, the degrees of freedom for the between groups (the greater mean square) are located at the top of the column headed "2" on page 284. We then read down the column until we come to the row labeled "27." The point at which this row and column intersect contains the 5% and 1% values of the $F$ statistics.

Since a value of $F$ equal to 5.49 will occur only 1% of the time by chance, we can have considerable confidence in our obtained $F$ of 125.00 and can conclude that the experimental treatment is quite effective.

The processes used in our example to arrive at the necessary sums of squares are quite cumbersome. A more efficient calculation method will be shown with another three group problem.

## CALCULATION OF ANALYSIS OF VARIANCE

The use of the $F$-ratio in statistical inference will be illustrated using another three group problem. The data for this example represent the number of correct choices out of a total of 25 choices in a discrimination learning problem. The experiment was performed to determine the effects of a central nervous system stimulant on discrimination learning. Laboratory rats of the same age were randomly assigned to one of three groups. Group A is a control group that was injected with an inert substance known to have no effect on behavior. Group B was injected each day with 0.10 milligram of the drug per kilogram of body weight. Group C was injected each day with 0.05 milligram of the drug per kilogram of body weight. The scores indicate the number of times out of the 25 choices each rat chose the correct stimulus card to find food. The data are shown in Table 8–3.

**Table 8–3.** ACCURACY SCORES FOR DISCRIMINATION OF LEARNING IN THREE GROUPS OF LABORATORY RATS WITH DIFFERENT DRUG DOSAGES

| Group A (Control) | Group B (.10 mg/kg) | Group C (.05 mg/kg) |
|:---:|:---:|:---:|
| 7 | 21 | 18 |
| 10 | 17 | 19 |
| 10 | 12 | 23 |
| 14 | 18 | 13 |
| 13 | 13 | 15 |
| 13 | 12 | 12 |
| 10 | 16 | 16 |
| 16 | 20 | 16 |
| 12 | 10 | 20 |
|  | 16 |  |

**Table 8–4.** Summary Statistics for the Analysis of Variance

|  | A | B | C | Total |
|---|---|---|---|---|
| $n$ | 9 | 10 | 9 | $N = 28$ |
| $\bar{X}$ | 11.67 | 15.50 | 16.89 | $\bar{X}_T = 14.71$ |
| $\sum X$ | 105 | 155 | 152 | $\sum X_T = 412$ |
| $\sum X^2$ | 1283 | 2523 | 2664 | $\sum X_T^2 = 6470$ |
| $(\sum X)^2$ | 11,025 | 24,025 | 23,104 | $(\sum X_T)^2 = 169,744$ |
| $(\sum X)^2/n$ | 1225.00 | 2402.50 | 2567.11 | $\sum \dfrac{(\sum X)^2}{n} = 6194.61$ |
|  |  |  |  | $\dfrac{(\sum X_T)^2}{N} = 6062.29$ |

Note that groups A and C contain nine animals each while group B contains ten animals. At the start of the experiment all of the groups were equal, but shortly after the start, an animal in group A was found to have a severe infection and was removed from the study. An animal was lost from group C when a careless assistant injected the animal with the wrong solution. Problems such as these arise in experiments and it is well to be aware of the likelihood of such problems arising when an experiment is planned. As we will see, the small difference in the size of the groups will not affect the analysis.

Calculation of the sums of squares will be done by the usual computational formulas in this example. The summary statistics required to calculate the analysis of variance are contained in Table 8–4.

---

**COMMON CALCULATION ERRORS IN THE ANALYSIS OF VARIANCE**

The symbols used to indicate the quantities needed to calculate the analysis of variance are complex and, in a few instances, quite similar in appearance. It is important that you keep in mind the distinctions among these symbols. The following two comments may help:

1. Quantities such as $\Sigma X_T$ and $\Sigma X_T^2$ are obtained by summing the

values for the separate groups. In the computational example, $\Sigma X_T$ is obtained by adding $\Sigma X_A + \Sigma X_B + \Sigma X_C$ to obtain $\Sigma X_T$. $\Sigma X_T^2$ is obtained by adding $\Sigma X_A^2 + \Sigma X_B^2 + \Sigma X_C^2$.

Quantities such as $(\Sigma X_T)^2$ and $(\Sigma X_T)^2/N$ *cannot* be obtained by adding the quantities for the separate groups together. $(\Sigma X_T)^2$ is obtained by squaring $\Sigma X_T$. $(\Sigma X_A)^2$ is obtained by squaring $\Sigma X_A$. Similarly,

$(\Sigma X_T)^2/N$ is obtained by dividing $(\Sigma X_T)^2$ by the total number of observations in all of the groups combined and should not be confused with $\Sigma \dfrac{(\Sigma X)^2}{n}$, which is obtained by adding the values of $(\Sigma X)^2/N$ that have been calculated for each group.

1. Keep in mind the difference between $(\Sigma X)^2$ and $\Sigma X^2$. $(\Sigma X)^2$ instructs you to sum the scores in the column labeled $X$ and *then* to square that sum. $(\Sigma X)^2$ is read "the sum of $X$, quantity squared." $\Sigma X^2$ instructs you to square each of the scores and then to sum those squares. $\Sigma X^2$ is read "the sum of $X$-squared."

---

The number of quantities needed for even a simple analysis of variance may seem forbiddingly large, and the arithmetic may appear to be overwhelming. However, if a certain order of operations is followed, the computations are reasonably easy to follow. The number of observations in each of the samples is represented by the lower case letter $n$. The total number of cases in the analysis is represented by the upper case letter $N$. If necessary, subscripts can be used to identify particular samples, i.e., $n_A$, $n_B$, $n_C$ and $N_T$ (for total sample). The mean for each of the samples is symbolized as $\bar{X}_A$, $\bar{X}_B$, and $\bar{X}_C$, and the total (or overall) mean is identified by the symbol $\bar{X}_T$. The next quantities in the table should be quite familiar: $\Sigma X$ and $\Sigma X^2$ are the sum of the scores and the sum of the squared scores. The subscripts indicate which quantities are summed: $\Sigma X_T$ and $\Sigma X_T^2$ indicate that the sums are based on the total cases; $\Sigma X_A$ indicates that the sum is taken over sample $A$, and so forth. $\Sigma X_A = 105$; $\Sigma X_B = 155$; and $\Sigma X_C = 152$. The total of these is 412, which is the value of $\Sigma X_T$. $\Sigma X_T^2$ is obtained by adding the values $\Sigma X_A^2$, $\Sigma X_B^2$, and $\Sigma X_C^2$. $\Sigma X_A^2 = 1283$; $\Sigma X_B^2 = 2523$; and $\Sigma X_C^2 = 2664$. The sum of these quantities is 6470, which is the value of $\Sigma X_T^2$. The value $(\Sigma X_T)^2$ in the column headed "total" has a box around it. This is purely an attention getting device, since this quantity is *not* the sum of the quantities for groups A, B, and C. $(\Sigma X_T)^2$ is calculated by squaring $\Sigma X_T$, exactly as $(\Sigma X_A)^2$ is calculated by squaring $\Sigma X_A$.

The next item in the table $(\Sigma X)^2/n$, is obtained by dividing each $(\Sigma X)^2$ by its corresponding number of observations. The quantity $\Sigma \dfrac{(\Sigma X)^2}{n}$ is obtained by summing each of the separate quantities obtained in this way for samples A, B, and C.

The quantity $(\Sigma X_T)^2/N$ is calculated by dividing $(\Sigma X_T)^2$ (the first boxed item in the table) by $N$. For our example, 169,744 is divided by 28, which gives the value 6062.29 for $\dfrac{(\Sigma X_T)^2}{N}$.

The sums of squares needed for the analysis of variance can be obtained by the process of simple subtraction once the above sums have been calculated. The calculations are as follows:

For the total sum of squares:

**(8-2)**
$$\sum x_T^2 = \sum X_T^2 - (\sum X_T)^2/N.$$

For the sum of squares between groups:

**(8-3)**
$$\sum x_b^2 = \sum \frac{(\sum X)^2}{n} - \frac{(\sum X_T)^2}{N}.$$

For the sum of squares within groups:

**(8-4)**
$$\sum x_w^2 = \sum X_T^2 - \sum \frac{(\sum X)^2}{n}.$$

For our example, the total sum of squares $(\Sigma x_T^2) = 6470 - 6062.29 = 407.71$. The sum of squares between groups $(\Sigma x_b^2) = 6194.61 - 6062.29 = 132.32$. The sum of squares within groups $(\Sigma x_w^2) = 6470 - 6194.61 = 275.39$. If the calculations are correct, the sums of squares for $\Sigma x_b^2$ and $\Sigma x_w^2$ should equal $\Sigma x_T^2$.

To obtain our variance estimates the sums of squares are now divided by the appropriate number of degrees of freedom. For the within groups sum of squares, the $df$ is equal to the number of observations minus the number of groups. For our example, $N = 28$ and $k = 3$; therefore $df_w = 25$. For the between groups sum of squares, the $df_b$ is equal to the number of groups minus one. For our example, $k = 3$; $df_b = 3 - 1 = 2$. The value of the between groups and within groups variance estimates are usually arranged in an analysis of variance table such as Table 8-5.

In Table 8-5 the sums of squares are listed for the two independent estimates of variation. The degrees of freedom are listed and the mean square is calculated by dividing each of the sums of

Table 8-5.  SUMMARY TABLE FOR ANALYSIS OF VARIANCE

| Source of Variation | Sum of Squares | df | Mean Square | F |
|---|---|---|---|---|
| Between groups | 132.32 | 2 | 66.16 | 6.003 |
| Within groups | 275.39 | 25 | 11.02 | |
| Total | 407.71 | 27 | | |

squares by the *df* for that sum. For the between groups variance, the calculation of the mean square is 132.32/2, which equals 66.16. For the within groups variance the mean square is 275.39/25, which equals 11.02.

The only remaining step is the calculation of the *F*-ratio, which is done by dividing the mean square between groups by the mean square within groups. For our example, *F* is equal to 66.16/11.02, which equals 6.003.

### Interpretation of the *F*-Ratio

How is the value of *F* to be interpreted? The logic is basically the same as that used with the normal curve. If we were to randomly draw three samples from a normally distributed population, compute both the variance estimate between groups and the variance estimate within groups, and then compute the *F*-statistic, we would have one *F* value. This value of *F* is, you will recall, the ratio of the between variance estimate to the within variance estimate. The null hypothesis to be tested is that $\mu_1 = \mu_2 = \mu_3$. If this hypothesis is true, then $\bar{X}_1 = \bar{X}_2 = \bar{X}_3$ should be the case. As was indicated earlier, if the null hypothesis is true, all the variance will be due to the variance within groups, and any variance due to differences between groups is assumed to be the result of chance sampling deviation. Since we know that there will always be a certain amount of sampling variability of means, the values of *F* will, in the true null case, have a sampling distribution. Most of the values of *F* will be centered around one, and the frequency of an *F* value becomes smaller and smaller as the *F* value becomes larger.

The *F* distribution for two and 12 degrees of freedom is illustrated in Figure 8–4 A. The smooth line represents the theoretical distribution of *F* and the bar graph represents the obtained distribution of 19,486 actual *F* values obtained by drawing random samples and calculating the values of *F* with the aid of a high-speed computer.

In Figure 8–4 B the theoretical distribution of *F* for nine and 98 degrees of freedom is shown as a smooth line and the actual distribution of 1000 *F* values is plotted as a bar graph. There will be a different sampling distribution for *F*, depending on the number of degrees of freedom and on the manner in which they are apportioned to the within and the between variances. Each of these distributions of *F*, then, is what would be expected if the null hypothesis is true. Therefore, it is possible to state the probability of obtaining an

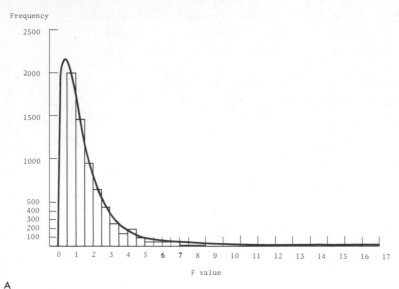

A

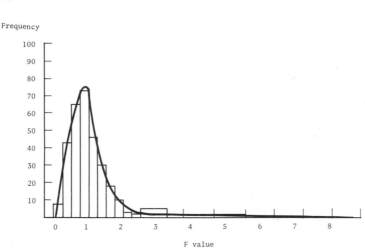

B

*Figure 8-4.* *A*, comparison of theoretical *F* distribution (smooth line) for 2 and 12 degrees of freedom with the distribution (bar graph) of 19,486 *F*-ratios for 2 and 12 degrees of freedom. *B*, comparison of theoretical *F* distribution (smooth line) for 9 and 98 degrees of freedom with the distribution (bar graph) of 1000 *F*-ratios for 9 and 98 degrees of freedom.

*F*-ratio of any given size by determining the proportion of the total area under the *F* distribution that falls beyond the given *F* value.

*Table of F.* The *F* distribution has been derived mathematically and complete tables of *F* can be constructed. However, such tables would fill several large volumes. Since investigators are usually interested in evaluating the null hypothesis only at certain stated probability levels, tables have been constructed which list the critical values for the 5 per cent and the 1 per cent points on the distribution of $F$. Table A–4 contains the 5 per cent and the 1 per cent points of the distribution of $F$ for degrees of freedom ranging from 1 and 1 to ∞ and ∞.

The sampling distribution of $F$ with which we are concerned in our computing example is for two and 25 degrees of freedom; two $df$ are associated with the between group effect (which is the greater mean square) and 25 $df$ are associated with the within group effect (which is the smaller mean square). We enter Table A–4 by locating the entry at the intersection of the column headed 2 and the row headed 25. The $F$ value for the 5 per cent level is 3.38 and that for the 1 per cent level is 5.57. The $F$-ratio in our example is 6.003. Since this $F$-ratio is larger than the tabled 1 per cent value we can reject the null hypothesis at the .01 level of significance since an $F$-ratio as large as the one obtained would occur less than 1 per cent of the time when the null hypothesis is true.

Upon rejecting the null hypothesis we will accept the alternative hypothesis that the three sample means are not drawn from the same population. The means of the three groups are $\bar{X}_1 = 10.89$; $\bar{X}_2 = 15.50$; and $\bar{X}_3 = 16.89$. The greatest difference among the groups is between the control group (A) and the smallest drug dosage group (C), while the difference between the largest drug dosage group (B) and group C is much smaller. We might suspect from this that the facilitating effect of the drug does not increase linearly with the dosage level. However, there is nothing in the present data to confirm this directly. To test this additional hypothesis, we would need several groups of animals given systematically increased amounts of the drug. We could then test for differences between the groups by more elaborate methods than are presented in this text. At present we can conclude that our first hypothesis—that the drug facilitates discrimination learning—is indeed supported by the data.

*Relationship of F and t.* The normal curve, the $t$ distribution, and the $F$ distribution are all related to one another. This can be illustrated by calculating $F$-ratios for two groups. The data and the calculation of both $t$ and $F$ are listed in Table 8–6.

The value of $t$ is 2.26 and the value of $F$ is 5.14. The square root of $F$ (5.14) equals 2.26. This value is the value of $t$. For all situations with two groups, $F = t^2$. The $t$-test is actually a special case of the more general $F$ distribution applicable only to two-group problems.

On the basis of both sets of calculations in Table 8–6, we reject the null hypothesis at the .05 level of significance. The $F$-test, it should be mentioned, is always a two-tailed test since the probability of obtaining a deviation as large as the one obtained, irrespective of the direction of the deviation, is being evaluated.

**Table 8–6.** CALCULATION OF $F$ WHEN THE NUMBER OF GROUPS $= 2$

| | A | | | B | | | | |
|---|---|---|---|---|---|---|---|---|
| | 17 | 21 | | 10 | 14 | | | |
| | 19 | 21 | | 12 | 17 | | | |
| | 11 | 16 | | 18 | 12 | | | |
| | 11 | 16 | | 8 | 10 | | | |
| | 11 | 16 | | 10 | 12 | | | |

$$\sum X_A = 159 \qquad \sum X_B = 123 \qquad \sum X_T = 282$$
$$n_A = 10 \qquad n_B = 10 \qquad N = 20$$
$$\sum X_A^2 = 2663 \qquad \sum X_B^2 = 1605 \qquad \sum X_T^2 = 4268$$
$$(\sum X_A)^2 = 25{,}281 \qquad (\sum X_B)^2 = 15{,}129 \qquad (\sum X_T)^2 = 79{,}524$$
$$(\sum X_A)^2/n_A = 2528.1 \qquad (\sum X_B)^2/n_B = 1512.9 \qquad \sum \frac{X^2}{n} = 4041.0$$
$$\bar{X}_A = 15.9 \qquad \bar{X}_B = 12.3 \qquad (\sum X_T)^2/N = 3976.2$$

*Calculation of t*

$$s^2 = \frac{\sum x_A^2 + \sum x_B^2}{n_A + n_B - 2}$$

$$\sum x_A^2 = 2663 - 2528.1$$
$$= 134.9$$

$$\sum x_B^2 = 1605 - 1512.9$$
$$= 92.1$$

$$= \frac{134.9 + 92.1}{18}$$

$$= 12.61$$

$$t = \frac{\bar{X}_A - \bar{X}_B}{\sqrt{\dfrac{s^2}{n_A} + \dfrac{s^2}{n_B}}} = \frac{15.9 - 12.3}{\sqrt{\dfrac{12.61}{10} + \dfrac{12.61}{10}}}$$

$$= \frac{3.6}{\sqrt{2.52}} = \frac{3.6}{1.59} = 2.26$$

$$t_{-.05} = 2.10$$

*Calculation of F*

$$\sum x_T^2 = \sum X_T^2 - (\sum X_T)^2/N = 4286 - 3976.2 = 291.8$$

$$\sum x_b^2 = \sum \frac{(\sum X)^2}{n} - \frac{(\sum X_T)^2}{N} = 4041.0 - 3976.2 = 64.8$$

$$\sum x_w^2 = \sum X_T^2 - \sum \frac{(\sum X)^2}{n} = 4268 - 4041 = 227$$

| Source of Variation | Sum of Squares | df | Mean Square | F |
|---|---|---|---|---|
| Total | 291.8 | 19 | 15.36 | |
| Between | 64.8 | 1 | 64.80 | 5.14 |
| Within | 227.0 | 18 | 12.61 | |

$$F_{.05} = 4.41$$

## Complex Analysis of Variance

The advantages of the analysis of variance techniques are difficult to appreciate until one attempts a more complex problem than has been presented in the examples shown so far. Suppose we are interested in knowing not only about differences among groups, but in the effects of combinations of variables. The analysis of variance allows us to examine the interrelationships of more than one variable under more than one condition. For example, suppose we wish to study experimentally a theoretical issue in the field of child development. One group of psychologists claims that the ability to solve certain kinds of logical problems is primarily a function of maturity and that early education will not improve the ability of children to solve problems. Another group, advocating early education, argues that training in certain kinds of problem solving will enable children to learn these ways of thinking at an earlier age than normally would be expected.

We decide to do a preliminary study with a very small number of children to see if further study is warranted. For our study we select 12 children at age 6 and 12 children at age 7, and assign each of them to one of two groups. One group will receive training in problem solving for a two-month period. The other group will be given an equivalent amount of training, but on subject matter that there is reason to believe will have no effect, positive or negative, on problem solving ability. At the end of the two-month period, the children are all given the same test of ability to solve problems requiring logical reasoning. Since the children are assigned at random to the training or no training groups, we are justified in assuming that there were no differences among the groups prior to the experiment.

The design of the study can be illustrated as follows:

| | Age 6 | Age 7 | |
|---|---|---|---|
| Trained in problem solving | $n = 6$ (6S) | $n = 6$ (7S) | Total trained group ($n = 12$) |
| Not trained in problem solving | $n = 6$ (6N) | $n = 6$ (7N) | Total group not trained ($n = 12$) |
| | Total 6 year old group ($n = 12$) | Total 7 year old group ($n = 12$) | Total number of subjects (T) ($N = 24$) |

The notation for each group is as follows: $6S$ = six year old children given training in problem solving; $7S$ = seven year old children given training in problem solving; $6N$ = six year old children given no training in problem solving; $7N =$ seven year old children given no training; $T =$ all subjects combined, the total group.

The scores and summary statistics for the four groups and for the total group are given in Table 8–7.

If we examine the means of the four groups we see that, as might be expected, the older children do much better on the problems. Also, the means of the groups receiving training in problem solving are higher than the means of the corresponding groups not receiving training. However, inspecting the mean differences does not allow us to decide whether or not any of these differences are significantly different from what would be expected by chance.

As a preliminary test, we can treat the data as a simple analysis of

Table 8–7

|  | AGE 6 | | | AGE 7 | |
|---|---|---|---|---|---|
|  | S# | Scores | | S# | Scores |
|  | 1 | 2.0 | | 7 | 4.0 |
|  | 2 | 2.0 | | 8 | 3.0 |
|  | 3 | 1.0 | | 9 | 4.0 |
|  | 4 | 2.0 | | 10 | 4.0 |
|  | 5 | 1.0 | | 11 | 4.0 |
| Given | 6 | 2.0 | | 12 | 4.0 |
| Training | | | 6S | | 7S |
|  | $\Sigma X = 10.00$ | | | $\Sigma X = 23.00$ | |
|  | $N = 6$ | | | $N = 6$ | |
|  | $\Sigma X^2 = 18.00$ | | | $\Sigma X^2 = 89.00$ | |
|  | $(\Sigma X)^2/n = 16.67$ | | | $(\Sigma X)^2/n = 88.17$ | |
|  | $\Sigma x^2 = 1.33$ | | | $\Sigma x^2 = .83$ | |
|  | $s^2 = .27$ | | | $s^2 = .17$ | |
|  | $s = .52$ | | | $s = .41$ | |
|  | $\bar{X} = 1.67$ | | | $\bar{X} = 3.83$ | |
|  | S# | Scores | | S# | Scores |
|  | 13 | 1.0 | | 19 | 2.0 |
|  | 14 | 2.0 | | 20 | 2.0 |
|  | 15 | 1.0 | | 21 | 1.0 |
|  | 16 | 1.0 | | 22 | 2.0 |
| Not | 17 | 2.0 | | 23 | 2.0 |
| Given | 18 | 1.0 | | 24 | 3.0 |
| Training | | | 6N | | 7N |
|  | $\Sigma X = 8.00$ | | | $\Sigma X = 12.00$ | |
|  | $N = 6$ | | | $N = 6$ | |
|  | $\Sigma X^2 = 12.00$ | | | $\Sigma X^2 = 26.00$ | |
|  | $(\Sigma X)^2/n = 10.67$ | | | $(\Sigma X)^2/n = 24.00$ | |
|  | $\Sigma x^2 = 1.33$ | | | $\Sigma x^2 = 2.00$ | |
|  | $s^2 = .27$ | | | $s^2 = .40$ | |
|  | $s = .52$ | | | $s = .63$ | |
|  | $\bar{X} = 1.33$ | | | $\bar{X} = 2.00$ | |
| TOTALS: | $\Sigma X = 53.00$ | | | $\Sigma x^2 = 27.95$ | |
|  | $N_T = 24$ | | | $s^2 = 1.39$ | |
|  | $\Sigma X^2 = 145.00$ | | | $s = 1.18$ | |
|  | $(\Sigma X)^2/N = 117.04$ | | | $\bar{X} = 2.46$ | |

four independent groups and do an analysis of variance identical to that shown on page 143. To do this we need to know (1) the total sum of squares, $\Sigma x_T^2$; (2) the sum of squares associated with variation within the groups (the variations of the group members around their own means), $\Sigma x_w^2$; and (3) the variation associated with difference between groups (the variation of group means around the total mean), $\Sigma x_b^2$.

Using the standard computational formula for the total sum of squares, $\Sigma X_T^2 - \dfrac{(\Sigma X_T)^2}{N_T}$, we obtain a total sum of squares

$145 - \dfrac{(53)^2}{24} = 145 - 2809/24 = 145 - 117.04 = 27.96$.

To calculate the sum of squares between groups, we substitute into formula (8.13) $\Sigma \dfrac{(\Sigma X)^2}{n} - \dfrac{(\Sigma X_T)^2}{N_T}$ and obtain a value of $16.67 + 88.17 + 10.67 + 24.00 = 139.51 - 117.04 = 22.47$. For the within groups sum of squares, substitution is made into formula (8–4), $\Sigma x_T^2 - \Sigma \dfrac{(\Sigma x)^2}{n} = 145 - 139.50$, and a value of 5.50 is obtained. Note that this is identical to the value obtained by adding together the $\Sigma x^2$ for each of the four cells of Table 8–7.

We can now prepare an analysis of variance summary table:

| Source of Variance | Sum of Squares | df | Mean Square | F | p |
|---|---|---|---|---|---|
| Between groups | 22.47 | 3 | 7.49 | 27.24 | .01 |
| Within groups | 5.50 | 20 | .275 | | |
| Total | 27.97 | 23 | | | |

Since the value of $F$ in Table A–4 for 3 and 20 degrees of freedom is 4.94 at the .01 level of significance, there is clearly a significant difference among groups. However, this does not really answer the questions that we asked. We are concerned about the effects of training on problem solving at different age levels and all we know from the above analysis is that there are statistically significant differences among the four groups. To find out how much variation is associated with the training and how much with age, a more detailed analysis is necessary.

In Table 8–8, the summary statistics from Table 8–7 have been reprinted and summed in two ways. By summing across the rows, we obtain a mean and a sum of squares for those children given preliminary training and for those not given training. The mean for children given training is 2.75 and for those children not receiving training it is 1.67.

Table 8–8

| | AGE 6 | AGE 7 | |
|---|---|---|---|
| Given Training | $\Sigma X = 10.00$<br>$\Sigma X^2 = 18.00$<br>$(\Sigma X)^2/n = 16.67$<br>$\Sigma x^2 = 1.33$<br>$s^2 = .27$<br>$s = .52$<br>$\bar{X} = 1.67$ | $\Sigma X = 23.00$<br>$\Sigma X^2 = 89.00$<br>$(\Sigma X)^2/n = 88.17$<br>$\Sigma x^2 = .83$<br>$s^2 = .17$<br>$s = .41$<br>$\bar{X} = 3.83$ | $\Sigma X_S = 33.00$<br>$\Sigma X_S^2 = 107.00$<br>$(\Sigma X)^2/n_S = 90.75$<br>$\Sigma x_S^2 = 16.25$<br>$s_S^2 = 1.48$<br>$s_S = 1.22$<br>$\bar{X}_S = 2.75$ |
| Not Given Training | $\Sigma X = 8.00$<br>$\Sigma X^2 = 12.00$<br>$(\Sigma X)^2/n = 10.67$<br>$\Sigma x^2 = 1.33$<br>$s^2 = .27$<br>$s = .52$<br>$\bar{X} = 1.33$ | $\Sigma X = 12.00$<br>$\Sigma X^2 = 26.00$<br>$(\Sigma X)^2/n = 24.00$<br>$\Sigma x^2 = 2.00$<br>$s^2 = .40$<br>$s = .63$<br>$\bar{X} = 2.00$ | $\Sigma X_N = 20.00$<br>$\Sigma X_N^2 = 38.00$<br>$(\Sigma X)^2/n_N = 33.33$<br>$\Sigma x_N^2 = 4.67$<br>$s_N^2 = .42$<br>$s_N = .65$<br>$\bar{X}_N = 1.67$ |
| | $\Sigma X_6 = 18.00$<br>$\Sigma X_6^2 = 30.00$<br>$(\Sigma X)^2/n_6 = 27.00$<br>$\Sigma x_6^2 = 3.00$<br>$s_6^2 = .27$<br>$s_6 = .52$<br>$\bar{X}_6 = 1.50$ | $\Sigma X_7 = 35.00$<br>$\Sigma X_7^2 = 115.00$<br>$(\Sigma X)^2/n_7 = 102.08$<br>$\Sigma x_7^2 = 12.92$<br>$s_7^2 = 1.17$<br>$s_7 = 1.08$<br>$\bar{X}_7 = 2.92$ | |

Similarly, we can sum down the columns to obtain means and sums of squares for the two age groups. For children age 6 the mean is 1.50 and for age 7, the mean is 2.92.

We can now take the between groups sum of squares $\Sigma x_b^2$ of 22.46 and divide it into specific sources of variance associated with our different conditions; variance associated with differences in age groups and variance associated with differences in training. The calculation of these sums of squares is a simple extension of the formulas used earlier. To find the sum of squares associated with age differences we substitute into the following equation:

$$\frac{(\Sigma X)^2}{n_6} + \frac{(\Sigma X)^2}{n_7} - \frac{(\Sigma X)^2}{N_T} = \frac{(18)^2}{12} + \frac{(35)^2}{12} - \frac{(53)^2}{24},$$

which produces the values of $27.00 + 102.08 - 117.04 = 12.04$, which is the variation associated with differences in age groups. To find the sum of squares for training effects, we carry out the equivalent calculation for the problem solving training vs. no training groups:

$$\frac{(\Sigma X)^2}{n_s} + \frac{(\Sigma X)^2}{n_n} - \frac{(\Sigma X)^2}{N_T} = \frac{(33)^2}{12} + \frac{(20)^2}{12} - \frac{(53)^2}{24}.$$

Solution of this equation gives the results $90.75 + 33.33 - 117.04 = 7.04$.

There is still some variance unaccounted for. The sum of squares associated with age (12.04) and the sum of squares associated with training (7.04) sum to only 19.08, while the total sum of squares for between groups variance is equal to 22.46. The difference is equal to 3.38.

This unaccounted for variance is variance that is not attributable to a specific source, such as age or training. This variance is due to the *interaction* of age and training and is a result of combinations of age with training. Interaction variance can be tested for its significance, just as the variance due to the main effects of age and training can be tested. To do so, we set up an analysis of variance table similar to the one used in the first analysis.

| Source of Variance | Sum of Squares | df | Mean Square | F | f |
|---|---|---|---|---|---|
| Training | 7.04 | 1 | 7.04 | 25.60 | < .01 |
| Age | 12.04 | 1 | 12.04 | 43.78 | < .01 |
| Interaction | 3.38 | 1 | 3.38 | 12.29 | < .01 |
| Within cells | 5.50 | 20 | .275 | | |

The procedure used to construct this analysis of variance table is identical to that used earlier. The only new steps are the calculation of the revised degrees of freedom. For training, the $df$ is equal to the number of training groups minus one, which equals $2 - 1 = 1$. For age, the $df$ is equal to the number of age groups minus one, also equal to $2 - 1 = 1$. Since the interaction is a joint function of age and training, the degrees of freedom are calculated by finding the product of age groups minus one and training groups minus one; $(2-1)(2-1) = 1$. The degrees of freedom for within groups are, as before, equal to $N - g$, where $g$ equals the number of groups, $(24 - 4) = 20$.

The main effects due to both age and training are significant beyond the .01 level. Also, the variation for interaction is significant. To understand the meaning of an interaction, a graphic representation will be helpful. In Figure 8–5, the mean values for the groups given training and not given training are plotted by age.

Figure 8–5 indicates that the rate of improvement of problem solving ability over age is much greater for the groups given training, but only for the older group. Thus, we conclude on the basis of this extremely small sample, that training in problem solving is beneficial, but only after the children have reached a certain age. If these results were to be substantiated in a larger, more comprehensive study, we would conclude that starting training at an early age—at least for

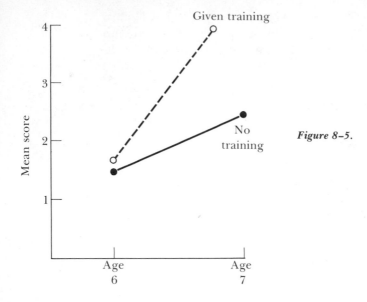

*Figure 8–5.*

the type of problem solving studied and within the age range studied — is not advantageous to the children.

Some appreciation for this approach to experimental design can be gained by considering how this result would be discovered by other approaches. Doing separate experiments in which age was compared and in which training versus no training was compared would not reveal the interaction between age and training that is present; there is simply no way in which that particular result would be found by conducting a series of experiments with pairs of groups. Analysis of variance is such a useful method because of this capability.

Designs of this type are called *factorial* designs and can be expanded to handle many more levels and variables than we have shown here. For example, we might wish to study the effect of three different methods of instruction on the level of scholastic achievement. In addition, we might want to know if there is any interaction between method of instruction and intelligence of the pupils. To study this we form three independent groups on the basis of IQ scores: high IQ, average IQ, and low IQ. One-third of each IQ group receives instruction under one of the instructional methods. The complete design is shown in Table 8–9.

It is possible by combining and recombining the variance due to the different treatments to determine whether or not there is a significant difference in achievement level between the methods of instruction independent of IQ effect (i.e., does $n_r = n_s = n_t$); whether there is an interaction between method of instruction and IQ level such that students of a certain IQ level score higher (or lower) using one particular method.

**Table 8–9.** INSTRUCTIONAL METHODS

|  |  | r | s | t |  |
|---|---|---|---|---|---|
|  | High | $n_a = 10$ | $n_b = 10$ | $n_c = 10$ | $n_h = 30$ |
| IQ | Medium | $n_d = 10$ | $n_e = 10$ | $n_f = 10$ | $n_m = 30$ |
|  | Low | $n_g = 10$ | $n_h = 10$ | $n_i = 10$ | $n_l = 30$ |
|  |  | $n_r = 30$ | $n_s = 30$ | $n_t = 30$ | $N = 90$ |

Although these methods may seem quite complex, it should be pointed out that we have barely scratched the surface of this topic in the present discussion. The analysis of variance is a complex topic and is the subject of many advanced texts in statistical methods and experimental design. To become an accomplished research worker in the behavioral sciences often requires considerable knowledge of these techniques and their applications.

# EXERCISES

Indicate, for each of the computational problems, the value of $F$, the values of each of the sums of squares, mean squares, and $df$'s. State whether the $F$ is significant and at what probability level.

1. An experimenter was interested in studying the effects of distribution of practice on the rate of learning. He performed an experiment in which three groups of subjects learned a list of ten nonsense syllables to a criterion of learning. The first groups had syllables presented to them every two seconds, the second group had a syllable presented every four seconds, and the third group had a syllable presented every six seconds. The number of trials required to reach criterion are listed for each subject below. Can you conclude that the rate at which the syllables are presented influences the rate of learning?

| 2 sec. | 4 sec. | 6 sec. |
|--------|--------|--------|
| 10     | 8      | 4      |
| 12     | 10     | 8      |
| 15     | 12     | 6      |
| 10     | 12     | 5      |
|        |        | 4      |

2. Three methods of instruction were used to train army recruits to shoot a rifle. Method 1 involved lectures only on the principles of marksmanship. Method 2 involved a combination of lectures and demonstrations. Method 3 involved practice only. The final marksmanship scores in terms of the number of "hits" in 15 shots are recorded below.

| Method 1 | Method 2 | Method 3 |
|----------|----------|----------|
| 3        | 4        | 6        |
| 5        | 4        | 7        |
| 2        | 3        | 8        |
| 4        | 8        | 6        |
| 8        | 7        | 7        |
| 4        | 4        | 9        |
| 3        | 2        | 10       |
| 9        | 5        | 9        |

**159**

What would you conclude regarding the relative merit of the three methods of instruction?

3. An experiment was performed to determine whether or not changes in the ratio of reinforced responses to total responses influenced the strength of a learned response. Five groups of rats were run 50 trials in a maze: the animals in group I were reinforced on every trial; group II animals were reinforced on 40 of the trials; group III animals were reinforced on 30 of the trials; group IV animals were reinforced on 20 of the trials; and group V animals were reinforced on ten of the trials. The measure of the strength of response was the number of trials required to reach an extinction criterion. What would you conclude concerning the effect of the partial reinforcement on the resistance to extinction based on the data presented below?

| I | II | III | IV | V |
|---|----|-----|----|----|
| 4 | 10 | 15 | 12 | 30 |
| 5 | 12 | 14 | 10 | 12 |
| 8 | 10 | 10 | 15 | 20 |
| 6 | 14 | 8  | 13 | 15 |
| 4 | 15 | 12 | 14 | 20 |
| 7 | 12 |    |    | 18 |
|   | 10 |    |    | 20 |
|   |    |    |    | 20 |

# CHI-SQUARE
# AND PROPORTIONS

The statistical techniques considered so far have all been based on observations scaled on some continuous scale of measurement. There are situations in which data are not based on measurements, but on categorization. Instead of continuous measurements, the data are based on frequencies of occurrence of various discrete events. If we want to decide whether or not there are any systematic deviations from some *a priori* pattern, we need a method by which we can compare frequencies of occurrence. The method that is most often used in this situation is called chi-square ($\chi^2$): if we can categorize individuals in some way we can use the $\chi^2$ test.

For example, assume that we are interested in learning whether or not the voters of a state are for or against capital punishment. We conduct a survey and determine the number opposed to capital punishment and the number in favor of capital punishment. Assume that, of a sample of 40 people questioned, 13 favor capital punishment and 27 oppose it. Does this represent a large enough deviation from a 20-20 split to conclude that more people oppose capital punishment than favor it in this state (assuming, of course, that our poll results are based on a representative sample of the voters)?

The $\chi^2$ technique is applicable in more complex situations, also. For example, suppose we want to know whether or not there is a relationship between preference for television programs and type of job. We might conduct a poll in which we categorize television preference into three types (e.g., current events, drama, and musicals) and categorize jobs into four types (e.g., laborers, blue collar workers, white collar workers, and professionals). Each individual is assigned to one of the job types and is asked to choose his preferred television fare. We could then determine whether or not the observed frequencies in each cell deviate from the frequencies that would be expected on the basis of chance distribution.

Table 9–1

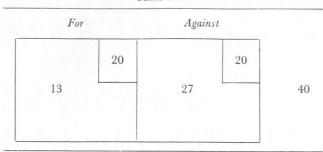

| For | | Against | |
|-----|-----|---------|-----|
| | 20 | | 20 |
| 13 | | 27 | 40 |

Usually, we want to know whether the frequencies observed in a sample deviate significantly from some theoretical or expected frequency. In both of the examples above we have assumed a chance distribution as our expected distribution. We could, however, assume any *a priori* distribution on use the $\chi^2$ technique. The $\chi^2$ test can be used to test any hypothesis regarding the expected frequency of events.

## ONE-WAY CLASSIFICATION PROBLEM

Let us use an example of opinions regarding capital punishment. Assume that we wish to test the hypothesis that there is an even split among the voters of the state. Since we have asked the opinion of 40 voters, we expect that 20 will oppose capital punishment and 20 will be in favor of capital punishment. These expected frequencies are contained in the small rectangle at the upper right-hand corner of the cells in Table 9–1.

We stated earlier that 13 people favored capital punishment and 27 opposed it. Now, we wish to determine whether the observed 13–27 split can be considered to be a significant deviation from our expected 20–20 split.

The formula for $\chi^2$ is:

(9–1)

$$\chi^2 = \Sigma \frac{(O - E)^2}{E},$$

where $O$ = observed frequency and $E$ = expected frequency. For our problem the calculation would be as follows:

$$\chi^2 = \frac{(27 - 20)^2}{20} + \frac{(13 - 20)^2}{20} = \frac{49}{20} + \frac{49}{20}$$

$$= 2.45 + 2.45 = 4.90.$$

To interpret this value we refer to Table A–5. The table is organized with $n$ standing for the number of degrees of freedom, and the probability of obtaining a $\chi^2$ equal to or larger than the tabled value listed in the body of the table.

***Degrees of Freedom in a One-way Classification.*** The number of degrees of freedom in this instance does not depend on the number of observations ($N$), as was the case with the $t$ and $F$ distributions. Rather, the number of $df$ depends on the number of deviations free to vary between the observed and the expected frequencies. In a one-way classification, such as the one we have here, only one deviation value is free to vary because the sum of the expected values must equal the sum of the observed values. The latter sum is fixed in our example at 40 (the number of individuals polled). Therefore, we have one $df$ in our $\chi^2$ problem.

In general, in a one-way classification, the number of $df$ equals the number of cells minus one. Therefore, if we had categorized our data into four degrees of opinion (strongly opposed; opposed; favor; strongly favor) we would have four cells on which the $\chi^2$ is based, and, hence, four deviation scores. This would give us 3 $df$. The method used to determine the number of $df$ in a two-way classification will be referred to in a later section.

## $\chi^2$ **Table**

The $\chi^2$ table (Table A–5) is interpreted in the same manner as is a $t$ table. If the value of the calculated $\chi^2$ exceeds the tabled value it is significant at or better than the probability level indicated at the head of the column. With 1 $df$ the value of $\chi^2$ required to reject the *a priori* hypothesis of a 20–20 split at the .05 level of significance is 3.84. Since our $\chi^2 = 4.90$, we will conclude that there is *not* an even balance

**Table 9–2**

| | *Candidate* | | | |
| --- | --- | --- | --- | --- |
| *A* | | *B* | *C* | |
| | 150 | 75 | 75 | |
| 237 | | 24 | 39 | 300 |

of opinion among the voters. On the basis of our results we will conclude that a majority of the voters in the state do not favor capital punishment.

We could, if we had some logical reason for doing so, assume any distribution of expected frequencies. For example, assume that on the basis of prior surveys we had reason to believe that twice as many people prefer candidate A over either candidate B or C, who are equally preferred. We ask 300 voters to choose their favorite candidate. Table 9–2 contains the data.

On the basis of our *a priori* hypothesis we would expect 150 voters to choose candidate A, 75 to choose candidate B, and 75 to choose candidate C. We observed that 237 chose A, 24 chose B, and 39 chose C. Can we consider the deviation from our expected frequencies to be within that expected by chance alone?

$$\chi^2 = \frac{(237 - 150)^2}{150} + \frac{(24 - 75)^2}{75} + \frac{(39 - 75)^2}{75}$$

$$= \frac{(87)^2}{150} + \frac{(-51)^2}{75} + \frac{(-36)^2}{75}$$

$$= \frac{7569}{150} + \frac{2601}{75} + \frac{1296}{75}$$

$$= 50.46 + 34.68 + 17.28$$

$$= 102.42.$$

Entering Table A–5 with 2 *df* (the number of cells minus one), we find a $\chi^2$ value of 5.99 listed for the .05 level of significance. Since our $\chi^2$ value exceeds the tabled value more than 18 times, we would conclude that our hypothesis concerning the respective popularities of the candidates is not supported by our results; candidate A is leading by a great deal more than we had believed on the basis of our prior surveys.

## TWO-WAY CLASSIFICATION PROBLEM

Now consider some data that have been categorized in two ways. Assume that we are interested in the problem-solving ability of college students as related to their academic major. We choose a difficult reasoning problem and decide to categorize individuals according to whether or not they are able to solve the problem. We categorize each individual according to academic major as well: Physical Science majors, Humanities majors, and Social Science majors. Sixty individuals are selected randomly from the college roster. They are then categorized according to academic major and are given the problem to solve. The data are in Table 9–3.

It was observed that 38 of the 60 students could solve the problem and 22 of them could not. Sixteen of the students were Physical Science majors (of whom ten solved the problem and six did not); 21 were Humanities majors (of whom 11 solved the problem and ten did not); and 23 of the students were Social Science majors (of whom 17 solved the problem and six did not). We have no reason to expect any differences in ability to solve the problem among the students in the three academic majors. Therefore, we expect an even distribution of cases in each cell. Determining the random distribution of frequencies is more complicated for this problem, since we do not have the same number of individuals in each category. To determine the expected frequency for each cell when the expected distribution is random, we multiply the number of frequencies contained in the entire row by the number of frequencies contained in the entire column in which the cell is located and divide that product by $N$. In order to determine

**Table 9–3**

| Problem Solving Ability | Academic Major | | |
| | Physical Science | Humanities | Social Science | |
|---|---|---|---|---|
| Solve problem | 10<br>10 | 13<br>11 | 15<br>17 | 38 |
| Do not solve problem | 6<br>6 | 8<br>10 | 8<br>6 | 22 |
| | 16 | 21 | 23 | 60 |

the expected frequency for those Physical Science majors who could solve the problem we multiply 38 (the total number who could solve the problem) by 16 (the total number of Physical Science majors), and divide that product by 60 (the total number of cases):

$$f_e = \frac{(38)(16)}{60} = \frac{608}{60} = 10.$$

The expected frequency of ten has been indicated in the small rectangle in the upper right-hand corner of the appropriate cell. If ten of the Physical Science majors are expected to solve the problem, and there are 16 Physical Science majors, then $16 - 10 = 6$ would be expected to be unable to solve the problem. That number is added to the table.

To determine the number of Humanities majors who would be expected to solve the problem, we perform the following calculation:

$$f_e = \frac{(38)(21)}{60} = \frac{798}{60} = 13.$$

The expected frequency is 13, and that number is added in the appropriate place in the table. Since there are 21 Humanities majors and 13 of them would be expected to solve the problem, $21 - 13 = 8$ of them would be expected to be unable to solve the problem. Since our marginal totals must be 38 and 22, the last two expected frequencies are fixed: $38 - 10 - 13 = 15$; $22 - 6 - 8 = 8$. The sum of the observed frequencies ($\Sigma O$) and the sum of the expected frequencies ($\Sigma E$), therefore, are the same, as they must be.

It was necessary to perform only two computations to determine the expected frequencies. The sum of the expected cell frequencies must equal the expected marginal frequencies and the expected marginal frequencies must equal the observed marginal frequencies. Once two cell frequencies are assigned, the others are all determined by the marginal frequencies. Thus, only two values are free to vary in this instance; there are 2 *df*.

The general formula used to determine the number of *df* is:

**(9–2)**
$$df = (r - 1)(c - 1),$$

where $r =$ number of rows and $c =$ number of columns.

We can now calculate our $\chi^2$ value:

$$\chi^2 = \Sigma \frac{(O - E)^2}{E}$$

$$= \frac{(10.0 - 10.0)^2}{10.0} + \frac{(11.0 - 13.0)^2}{13.0} + \frac{(17.0 - 15.0)^2}{15.0}$$

$$+ \frac{(6.0 - 6.0)^2}{6.0} + \frac{(10.0 - 8.0)^2}{8.0} + \frac{(6.0 - 8.0)^2}{8.0}$$

$$= \frac{(0.0)^2}{10.0} + \frac{(-2.0)^2}{13.0} + \frac{(2.0)^2}{15.0} + \frac{(0.0)^2}{6.0} + \frac{(2.0)^2}{8.0} + \frac{(-2.0)^2}{8.0}$$

$$= \frac{0.0}{10.0} + \frac{4.0}{13.0} + \frac{4.0}{15.0} + \frac{0.0}{6.0} + \frac{4.0}{8.0} + \frac{4.0}{8.0}$$

$$= .00 + .31 + .27 + .00 + .50 + .50$$

$$= 1.58.$$

The number of $df = (r - 1)(c - 1) = (2 - 1)(3 - 1) = 2$. From Table A–5 we find that, with 2 $df$, $\chi^2$ must be 5.99 to reach the .05 level of significance. Since our $\chi^2$ value falls far short of the critical value we will conclude that the observed distribution of frequencies is within the deviation expected on the basis of chance. We conclude that there is no reason to believe that the ability to solve the problem is different for the different academic majors.

## $\chi^2$ DISTRIBUTION

With one degree of freedom $\chi^2$ distributes as $F$ (and, of course, $t^2$). However, with more than one degree of freedom the sampling distribution of $\chi^2$ is not the same as $F$. There are a large number of $\chi^2$ distributions, depending on the number of degrees of freedom. The $\chi^2$ distributions for 1, 2, 4, 6, and 10 degrees of freedom are illustrated in Figure 9–1. With 30 $df$ the $\chi^2$ distribution is essentially normal. The $\chi^2$ test is a two-tailed test (see Chapter 7, pp. 119 and 120), as is $F$, since it does not take into account the direction of the deviation, but is based on the size of the deviation.

The $\chi^2$ table is used to determine the proportion of the total area that would be expected to be beyond the listed $\chi^2$ value if the *a priori* hypothesis is true, and the deviations from that hypothesis are due to chance deviations.

With over 30 $df$ the calculated $\chi^2$ value can be converted to a $z$ and the $z$ can be interpreted with a normal curve table. The formula for converting $\chi^2$ to $z$, with over 30 $df$, is as follows:

**(9–3)**
$$z = \sqrt{2\chi^2} - \sqrt{2n - 1},$$

where $n = df$.

## FOUR-FOLD CONTINGENCY TABLE

One of the most common uses of $\chi^2$ is in cases in which the data are arranged in a $2 \times 2$ table. In these instances individuals are categorized in two ways. For example, we could categorize individuals according to sex and according to blue vs. brown eye color. If the two ways of classifying the individuals are independent of one another, the $\chi^2$ will not be significant.

Since $\chi^2$ is used so often with the $2 \times 2$ table, a formula has been derived for this special case which eliminates the necessity of calculating the expected frequencies. When using this method, we assume that there is a random distribution of one trait on the other; that is, that they are independent traits. Assume for our sex-eye color example that when 40 individuals are categorized according to sex and eye color the data are as shown in Table 9–4.

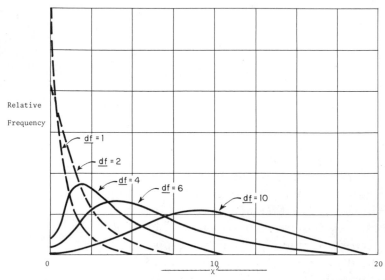

***Figure 9–1.*** Approximate forms of $\chi^2$ distribution for certain degrees of freedom. (From Lindquist, E. F., *Design and Analysis of Experiments in Psychology and Education.* Copyright © 1953 by Houghton Mifflin Company. Reprinted by permission of the publisher.)

**Table 9-4**

|  | Eye Color | | |
|---|---|---|---|
|  | Blue | Brown | |
| ♂ | 6 $\quad$ A | 9 $\quad$ B | 15 |
| Sex | | | |
| ♀ | 4 $\quad$ C | 21 $\quad$ D | 25 |
|  | 10 | 30 | 40 |

The formula for determining the value of $\chi^2$ in this example is:

$$\chi^2 = \frac{N(AD - BC)^2}{(A + B)(C + D)(A + C)(B + D)},$$

(9-4)

where $N =$ number of observations.

$$\chi^2 = \frac{40[(6)(21) - (9)(4)]^2}{(6 + 9)(4 + 21)(6 + 4)(9 + 21)}$$

$$= \frac{40[126 - 36]^2}{(15)(25)(10)(30)}$$

$$= \frac{40[90]^2}{112,500}$$

$$= \frac{324,000}{112,500}$$

$$= 2.88.$$

To determine the number of degrees of freedom for this example, we use formula (9-2); $df = (r - 1)(c - 1) = (2 - 1)(2 - 1) = 1$. Since our $\chi^2$ of 2.88 falls short of the value of 3.84 tabled at the .05

Table 9–5

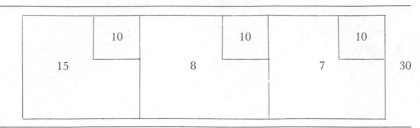

level, we accept the hypothesis that the two traits — eye color and sex —
are independent of one another.

## Yates' Correction for Continuity

If our $\chi^2$ had been significant, or if we want to estimate the true
probability level more accurately, we should apply Yates' correction
for continuity. This correction will lower the $\chi^2$ value slightly and
should be used if the $\chi^2$ is based on 1 $df$, or if any expected cell frequency is less than ten.

When we correct for continuity we allow for the fact that our
computed $\chi^2$ is based on observed frequencies that are whole numbers. Therefore, our observed frequencies vary in discrete steps. The
$\chi^2$ table, however, lists values that are based on a continuous scale.
To correct for this we reduce each observed difference by 0.5. This
reduces the $\chi^2$ value. It is important to make this correction whenever
$N$ is small and when the $\chi^2$ is on the border line of significance.

Let us calculate a $\chi^2$ with and without the correction for the data
of Table 9–5.

First, we will calculate $\chi^2$ without the correction:

$$\chi^2 = \sum \frac{(O - E)^2}{E} = \frac{(15 - 10)^2}{10} + \frac{(8 - 10)^2}{10} + \frac{(7 - 10)^2}{10}$$

$$= \frac{(5)^2}{10} + \frac{(-2)^2}{10} + \frac{(-3)^2}{10}$$

$$= \frac{25}{10} + \frac{4}{10} + \frac{9}{10}$$

$$= 2.5 + .4 + .9$$

$$= 3.80.$$

With Yates' correction the formula becomes:

(9–5)

$$\chi^2 = \sum \frac{(|O - E| - .5)^2}{E},$$

where $|O - E| - .5$ indicates that we should reduce the absolute size of the deviation by .5.

$$\chi^2 = \frac{(|15 - 10| - .5)^2}{10} + \frac{(|8 - 10| - .5)^2}{10} + \frac{(|7 - 10| - .5)^2}{10}$$

$$= \frac{(4.5)^2}{10} + \frac{(1.5)^2}{10} + \frac{(2.5)^2}{10}$$

$$= \frac{20.25}{10} + \frac{2.25}{10} + \frac{6.25}{10}$$

$$= 2.025 + .225 + .625$$

$$= 2.875.$$

In neither instance is the $\chi^2$ value significant at the .05 level of significance. However, it can be seen that the size of the $\chi^2$ has been reduced considerably.

To apply Yates' correction with the four-fold contingency table the formula becomes:

$$\chi^2 = \frac{N(|AD - BC| - N/2)^2}{(A + B)(C + D)(A + C)(B + D)} \tag{9-6}$$

Again, $|AD - BC| - N/2$ indicates that the size of the $AD - BC$ term is to be reduced toward zero by $N/2$, regardless of the sign of the deviation.

### Restrictions on the Use of $\chi^2$

$\chi^2$ is a useful and simple statistic to calculate as well as to interpret. However, it is also a frequently misused statistic. The requirement that all the individual events be independent is the most often violated in the use of $\chi^2$. To meet this requirement, no one individual can contribute more than one frequency to the $\chi^2$, since the frequencies would no longer be independent. Several measures based on the same individual are all dependent on that individual's abilities and background and cannot be used in a $\chi^2$ test.

Therefore, it is essential that no one individual contribute more than one observation to the frequency table. If this assumption is violated, then the nature of the population that is being sampled is confounded with the effects of the experimental treatment. For example, assume that we are studying the effect of crowding on the aggressive behavior of chimpanzees. We observe the animals in a large enclosure and then in a small one and note the number of minutes in a one-hour period that any animal was seen to hit another animal at least once. Assume that we observed 45 instances of hitting in the small enclosure and only 22 in the large one. It would not be appropriate to enter the 45 and the 22 in a one-way table, calculate a $\chi^2$ and conclude that chimpanzees are more aggressive in small enclosures than in large ones if the $\chi^2$ value was large enough to exceed the tabled value for one degree of freedom. The problem is that we wish to generalize our results to the population of all chimpanzees treated in the same manner as the ones we studied. Our results might not even be applied validly to characterize the behavior of the group we studied in large and small enclosures, since the entire increase in frequency of hitting could be due to an increase in the aggression of only one of the animals. If every instance of hitting by one animal is scored as an observed frequency this would violate the independence assumption, since each of an animal's repeated behaviors is not an event independent of the other behaviors. This, thereby, invalidates the use of $\chi^2$ since the increased aggressiveness observed might well be attributable to the behavior of one aberrant animal, and might not characterize the group that is being used as a sample from the population of chimpanzees. It is not possible to determine whether the observed effects are due to the effect of enclosure size or to the lack of independence of observations; the $\chi^2$ test will detect both and it is not possible to determine which of the two effects is producing the significant test statistic.

The proper way to analyze data of this type is to observe the identity of each animal observed to hit another in each of the enclosures and to tally whether or not each individual hit more often in the large or the small enclosure. Each chimp would contribute only one frequency to the contingency table, all of the observed frequencies in the table will be independent of the others, and a proper analysis can be done.

$\chi^2$ can be used only with frequency data. It cannot be used to test differences, for example, between an expected mean and an observed mean since the $\chi^2$ values would then vary with the size of the units of measurement and the $\chi^2$ table would not be appropriate.

There must be some rational basis for the manner in which the data are categorized. If the categorization is not meaningful, then there will be no way to draw a meaningful inference on the basis of the calculated $\chi^2$ value.

In order to obtain accurate estimates of probability there should not be too many small theoretical ($E$) frequencies. Some statisticians believe that the use of $\chi^2$ is inadvisable if there are any expected frequencies less than ten. This is perhaps an extreme position.

Walker and Lev (1953)* have outlined some "rules of thumb," which we believe are the most sensible positions on this issue:

1. If there is only one degree of freedom, follow the suggestion previously given for the use of Yates' correction.

2. If there are two or more degrees of freedom and the expectation in each cell is more than five, the chi-square table assures a good approximation of the exact probabilities.

3. If there are two or more degrees of freedom and roughly approximate probabilities are acceptable for the test of significance, an expectation of only two in a cell is sufficient.

4. If there are more than two degrees of freedom and the expectation in all the cells but one is five or more, then an expectation of only one in the remaining cell is sufficient to provide a fair approximation of the exact probabilities.

5. If the logic of the problem permits, combine some of the classes to increases the expectations in the cells when several cells have very small expectations.

## PROPORTIONS

There is another circumstance in which the data are not in the form of measurements, and in which we might want to evaluate the significance of a deviation from an *a priori* hypothesis. This circumstance is one in which the data are in the form of proportions. Assume that a cigarette company claims that 70 per cent of doctors smoke their brand (Brand A). We are suspicious of their advertising claims and conduct a survey on the smoking habits of doctors. The results of polling a random sample of 50 doctors indicate that 60 per cent of the 50 (30 of them) smoke Brand A.

The question now arises whether or not the proportion of doctors we found to smoke Brand A (.60) could have occurred as a result of sampling error when the true proportion is as the cigarette company claimed (.70). In other words, what is the probability that we would obtain a proportion of .60 when $N = 50$ if the true proportion is .70?

The solution to this problem is based on the fact that, if a large number of random samples are drawn from a population of proportions, the resulting distribution of proportions will distribute in a form similar enough to the normal curve to allow the use of the normal curve table. We have a statement concerning the true proportion in the population, which we assume is the $\mu$ of the distribution.

---

*Walker, H. M. and Lev, J.: *Statistical Inference.* New York, Holt, 1953.

We also know that the proportions around $\mu$ will be distributed almost normally. Therefore, if we can determine the standard error of this distribution of proportions, we can make the usual inferences based on the normal curve table. The formula for the standard error of a proportion is as follows:

**(9–7)**
$$\sigma_p = \sqrt{\frac{pq}{N}},$$

where $p$ = hypothetical true proportions,
$q = 1 - p$, and
$N$ = sample size.
The standard error of the proportion in our example, then, is

$$\sigma_p = \sqrt{\frac{(.7)(.3)}{50}} = \sqrt{\frac{.21}{50}} = \sqrt{.0042} = .065.$$

We can now determine the probability that we would obtain a proportion of .60 when the true proportion is .70. The problem is illustrated in Figure 9–2. We wish to find the proportion of the total area under the curve indicated by the shaded section. This proportion is the proportion of cases that would be expected to deviate as greatly as .10 from the true proportion on the basis of random sampling error, given the size of our sample.

To use the normal curve table we must calculate a $z$-score:

**(9–8)**
$$z = \frac{x}{\sigma_p} = \frac{.70 - .60}{.065} = 1.54.$$

From Table A–2 we find that .4382 of the area under the curve falls between the mean and a $z$ of 1.54: $.4382 + .4382 = .8764$ of the area under the curve would be expected to fall between a $z$ of $-1.54$ and a $z$ of $+1.54$. Therefore, .1236 of the area would remain in the tails of the distribution. Thus, the probability of observing a difference of .10 from the true proportion of .70 based on a sample of 50 cases is .1236. Since this probability is larger than the probability we usually require to reject a hypothesis (usually, we demand a significance level of .05), we conclude that the proportion we observed could reasonably have occurred due to chance sampling error from a population whose true proportion was .70. Hence, we accept the cigarette company's claim regarding the proportion of doctors who smoke Brand A.

***Corrections for Continuity.*** A problem arises when the value of $p$ becomes extreme. If, for example, $p = .10$ we will undoubtedly have a

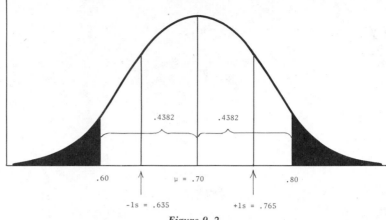

.4382 .4382

.60  μ = .70  .80

-1s = .635  +1s = .765

*Figure 9–2*

skewed distribution, since the smallest $p$ possible is .00, while the highest $p$ possible is 1.00. However, the degree of skewness is also dependent on the size of $N$. In order to compensate for the bias introduced in such instances we should correct for continuity when *either* $N_p$ or $N_q$ is between five and ten. If *both* $N_p$ and $N_q$ exceed ten we need not be concerned with correcting for continuity.

To correct for continuity we should reduce the value of the deviation of the observed proportion from the hypothetical proportion by $.5/N$. In our example the correction would be applied as follows:

$$z = \frac{|.7 - .6| - .5/50}{.065} = \frac{.1 - .01}{.065} = \frac{.09}{.065} = 1.38. \qquad (9\text{--}9)$$

Applying the correction reduces the size of $z$ from 1.54 to 1.38. The correction should always be applied when the size of $N_p$ or $N_q$ warrants it, and when the probability level is of a borderline value.

1. A die was tossed 60 times. The number of times each side was up is as follows: one, 8; two, 9; three, 9; four, 8; five, 10; six, 16. Would you conclude that the die is not evenly balanced?

2. It is claimed that 75 per cent of college students favor co-educational residential facilities. A sample of 100 students is polled and it is found that 65 of the students favor such housing arrangements. On the basis of these data, can you accept the claim?

3. It is further claimed that while 75 per cent of the total are in favor, 90 per cent of male students are in favor while only 60 per cent of female students are in favor of the proposed housing arrangements. The sample of 100 students is composed of 50 males and 50 females. Forty of the males and 35 of the females were found to be in favor. Can you accept this further claim that 90 per cent of males and 60 per cent of females are in favor on the basis of these data?

4. An experiment is performed in which subjects are categorized according to political affiliation and then are asked to state their preference for four political candidates. The data are tabled below:

|  |  | A | B | C | D |  |
|---|---|---|---|---|---|---|
|  | Liberal | 5 | 5 | 20 | 0 | 30 |
| Political Preference | Democrat | 10 | 20 | 30 | 20 | 80 |
|  | Republican | 21 | 19 | 20 | 20 | 80 |
|  | Conservative | 8 | 2 | 0 | 20 | 30 |
|  |  | 44 | 46 | 70 | 60 | 220 |

On the basis of these findings can you conclude that the obtained is other than that expected on the basis of a random distribution?

5. It is claimed that 85 per cent of college students favor fraternities on campus. A poll is conducted and it is found that of 60 students polled, 75 per cent favor fraternities. On the basis of these data, can you accept the claim? (Answer this using both the $\chi^2$ method and the standard error of a proportion.)

## CHAPTER TEN

# DISTRIBUTION-FREE METHODS

The chi-square method discussed in Chapter 9 is called a distribution-free, or non-parametric, method. This means that it is not necessary to make any assumptions about the shape of the underlying population distribution from which the samples are drawn. In contrast, to use statistical methods such as $t$ and $F$ you must assume that the statistics on which inferences are to be based distribute themseleves normally.

In practice, these assumptions can be largely ignored. Several studies* indicate that statistics such as $t$ and $F$, which are based on normal curve models, are not sensitive to violations of the normal distribution requirement. Therefore, the nature of the underlying distribution of scores can, in general, be disregarded since statistics computed from non-normal populations of scores distribute in a form sufficiently close to the normal curve to permit the use of methods based on the normal distribution.

While it is comforting to know that these assumptions are not essential, some misleading inferences can be made under certain circumstances. Perhaps the clearest demonstration of such circumstances was provided by Boneau, who used a computer to draw random samples and to calculate values of $t$ under conditions in which certain of the underlying assumptions for the use of $t$ were systematically violated. He found very few conditions that produced any systematic bias in the $t$-test. However, if samples are of unequal sizes and have unequal variances, some serious discrepancies do appear. The shape

---

*Boneau, C. A.: The effects of violations of assumptions underlying the $t$ test. *Psychological Bulletin*, 57:49–64, 1960. Baker, B. O., Hardyck, C. D., and Petrinovich, L. F.: Weak measurements vs. strong statistics: An empirical critique of S. S. Stevens' proscriptions on statistics. *Educational and Psychological Measurement*, 26:291–309, 1966.

of the $t$ distribution is shown in Figure 10–1 $A$ for the circumstances in which the smaller sample of the two has the larger variance. In Figure 10–1 $B$ we see the $t$ distribution for the circumstances in which the larger sample has the larger variance. Examination of these two figures indicates that, when the smaller sample has the larger variance, the $t$-ratio will fall beyond the .95 confidence limits many more times than the .05 expected on the basis of chance. When the larger sample has the larger variance, the reverse occurs—the $t$-ratio will fall beyond the .95 limits many *fewer* times than the .05 expected on the basis of chance.

For such occasions inferential methods have been developed that do not require any assumptions regarding the nature of the parent population. In this chapter a few additional techniques will be discussed that do not require normal curve assumptions.

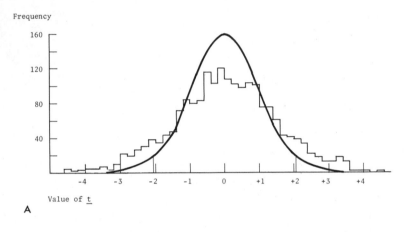

A

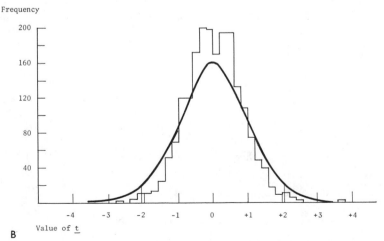

B

***Figure 10–1.*** $A$ and $B$. (From Boneau, C. A., The effects of violations of assumptions underlying the $t$ test. *Psychological Bulletin*, Vol. 57, No. 1, 1960. Copyright 1960 by the American Psychological Association. Reprinted by permission).

## SIGN TEST

The sign test takes its name from the fact that only the difference, + or −, around some reference point enters into the calculations; the actual score values themselves are not used in the computation. Suppose that an investigator is interested in the accuracy of visual recognition of objects under conditions of sunrise vs. sunset illumination. He obtains accuracy scores on a group of subjects, half of which are first tested at sunrise and half of which are first tested at sunset. The variances for the two conditions are so different that he decides not to use the *t*-test for correlated means. Rather, he decides to use a sign test to decide whether or not there is any significant difference in accuracy scores under the two conditions of illumination. Since his measures differ greatly in variability, he decides to subtract the sunset measurement from the sunrise measurement for each of the subjects. He then tallies the number of times the difference between the sunrise and the sunset score is + or −. Table 10–1 contains the data.

The number of times the sign with the smaller number of occurrences appears is counted (ignoring zero differences) and this number is called *r*. Then Table A–6 is entered. If the observed *r* is equal to or less than the value in the table, it can be concluded that *r* occurs less frequently than would be expected by chance. For the data of Table 10–1, the total *N* is equal to ten. This is reduced by two, because of zero differences, and the value of *r* is 2. Entering Table A–6 with an *N* of 8, we find that *r* can be no larger than zero to reach the 5 per cent level of confidence. Since the *r* in our example is 2, we will accept the

**Table 10–1.**  Calculation of the Sign Test

| A—Sunrise Accuracy Scores | B—Sunset Accuracy Scores | A-B Sign Difference |
|:---:|:---:|:---:|
| 12 | 18 | − |
| 19 | 20 | − |
| 11 | 17 | − |
| 8 | 24 | − |
| 12 | 18 | − |
| 17 | 17 | 0 |
| 22 | 19 | + |
| 14 | 14 | 0 |
| 18 | 15 | + |
| 13 | 21 | − |

Number of − signs = 6

Number of + signs = 2

hypothesis that there is no difference in the two sets of accuracy scores.

The sign test is subject to the same restrictions that apply when using $\chi^2$ regarding independence of events. Another example might help at this point. Assume that you wish to know whether or not a group of 10 coins are "honest"—that is, whether or not, when tossed into the air, they are as equally likely to come up heads as they are to come up tails. We could decide this by throwing the 10 coins a large number of times and counting how many heads and tails we observe each time they are tossed. We cannot evaluate the meaning of these results by use of a sign test if we want to make a generalization about the population of all coins of which this group of 10 is a sample. Since each coin is contributing more than one observation, an observed systematic bias could be the result of only one biased coin, with the other nine being "honest." All we can say, properly, is that this group of coins, considered as a group, is biased; that is, if we toss the 10 coins we would not expect half of them to come up heads and half of them to come up tails. Because we have violated the independence assumption, we can make no inference about the behavior of another group of 10 coins, about the characteristics of the individual coins in this sample, or about the characteristics of the population of coins of which this group of ten coins is a sample.

## Median Test

Given the situation in which we have two independent groups and do not wish to use the $t$-test, it is possible to test the hypothesis that the two groups come from populations having the same median. This test is a $\chi^2$ test; the only unique feature is that the groups are split at the median for all scores. To test this hypothesis, the two groups are combined and the overall median is determined (see Chapter 3, p. 35, for computing methods). Once the median has been located, a four-fold contingency table (cf. Chapter 9) is constructed. A tally is entered for each score of each group in the appropriate cell according to whether it is above or below the median for the combined groups. Once the tally has been completed, the hypothesis that the two groups are drawn from a population with the same median is tested using the chi-square statistic. Table 10–2 contains the calculation.

Since the critical $\chi^2$ value with one degree of freedom at the .05 level is 3.84, we accept the hypothesis that these two groups are drawn from populations with the same median. We conclude, therefore, that our experimental treatment has had no effect.

**Table 10–2.** Calculation of the Median Test

| | | |
|---|---|---|
| Step 1: Determine the median by finding the score above which 50 per cent of the cases lie. | *Sample A* | *Sample B* |
| | 16 | 15 |
| | 22 | 14 |
| | 20 | 12 |
| | 10 | 9 |
| | 23 | 8 |
| | 21 | 13 |
| | 10 | 19 |
| | $N = 7$ | $N = 7$ |

$$\begin{array}{ccccccccccc} & & 10 & & 13 \\ 8 & 9 & 10 & 12 & 13 & 14 & 16 & 19 & 20 & 21 & 22 & 23 \\ & & & & \uparrow \end{array}$$

Median $= 13.5$

(Scores in order of increasing magnitude)

Step 2: Prepare a contingency table

| | |
|---|---|
| *A* | *B* |
| *C* | *D* |

| | Sample A | Sample B | |
|---|---|---|---|
| Above median | 5 | 2 | 7 |
| Below median | 2 | 5 | 7 |
| | 7 | 7 | |

Step 3: Calculate $\chi^2$ for a four-fold table with correction for continuity (formula [9.6]) and $df = 1$.

$$\chi^2 = \frac{N(|BC - AD| - N/2)^2}{(A + B)(C + D)(A + C)(B + D)}$$

$$= \frac{14(|4 - 25| - 14/2)^2}{(7)(7)(7)(7)}$$

$$= \frac{14(|-21| - 7)^2}{2401} = \frac{14(14)^2}{2401}$$

$$= \frac{14(196)}{2401} = \frac{2744}{2401}$$

$$= 1.14$$

## Ranking Methods

Situations frequently arise in which data are collected in the form of ranks or in which scores are changed to ranks when they are unsuitable for analysis with parametric techniques. Two techniques for testing hypotheses using ranked data will be presented here.

*Mann-Whitney U Test.* The Mann-Whitney $U$ test is the equivalent of the $t$-test for independent groups for ranked measurements. If we wish to test the hypothesis that two sets of scores come from the same population, we first combine the sets of scores and rank them, giving the value of 1 to the lowest score, 2 to the next lowest, and so forth, until all scores have been ranked. Ties in rank are dealt with by assigning the average of the ranks that would have been assigned if they were not identical. Let us rank the following scores: 5, 7, 8, 10, 10, 10, 11, and 12. The first three scores that are identical in value are assigned the average of ranks 4, 5, and 6, which is 5. The rank order would read, then, 1, 2, 3, 5, 5, 5. Since rank positions 4, 5, and 6 have all been used by the scores of 10, we continue the ranking by assigning the rank of 7 to the score of 11. The completed ranking is 1, 2, 3, 5, 5, 5, 7, 8. The values of $U$ are found by the following calculation:

**(10–1a)**
$$U_1 = \left[ n_1 n_2 + \frac{n_1 (n_1 + 1)}{2} \right] - \Sigma R_1,$$

**(10–1b)**
$$U_2 = \left[ n_1 n_2 + \frac{n_2 (n_2 + 1)}{2} \right] - \Sigma R_2,$$

where $n_1$ and $n_2$ = the number of cases in samples 1 and 2, respectively, and $\Sigma R_1$ = the sum of ranks for group 1, where group 1 is the smaller sample. The smaller value of $U$, whether $U_1$ or $U_2$, is the one evaluated.

The critical values of $U$ for the .01 and .05 levels of confidence are listed in Table A–7 as a function of the size of the smaller sample ($n_1$) and the size of the larger sample ($n_2$). In order to be significant at the given level of confidence, the calculated value of $U$ must be as small as or smaller than the value listed in the table. Table 10–3 contains the computations.

To evaluate the $U$, we turn to Table A–7 and find that our $U$ is considerably larger than the tabled value of 23. Consequently, we conclude that our obtained difference is not significant and accept the hypothesis that the two samples have been drawn from the same population.

*Large Samples.* If either of the samples contains more than 20 cases, the normal curve table (Table A–2) can be used since the following formula gives a good approximation of $z$:

$$z = [U - (n_1 n_2/2)] / \sqrt{(n_1)(n_2)(n_1 + n_2 + 1)/12}, \qquad (10\text{-}2)$$

where $z$ is 1.96 for the .05 level and 2.58 for the .01 level.

*Kruskal-Wallis H Test.* The $U$ test just described is a ranked data analogue to the $t$-test for two independent groups. Similarly, the Kruskal-Wallis $H$ test is a ranked data analogue to the one-way analysis of variance. It is used to test the hypothesis that a number of groups have been drawn from the same population. The computational procedure is quite similar to the Mann-Whitney $U$. All groups are combined and ranked as in the Mann-Whitney. The statistic, $H$, is then calculated by the formula:

$$H = \frac{12}{N(N + 1)} \sum \frac{R^2}{n} - 3(N + 1), \qquad (10\text{-}3)$$

where $N$ = the total number of observations over all samples,

$n$ = the number of observations in any one sample, and

$R$ = the sum of ranks for any one sample.

The calculation of $H$ is illustrated with data based on three groups of subjects. The scores, their rank, and the sum of the ranks for each group are listed in Table 10–4.

The value of $H$ calculated using formula (10–3) is

$$H = \frac{12}{13(14)} \left[ \frac{20^2}{5} + \frac{25.5^2}{4} + \frac{45.5^2}{4} \right] - 3(14)$$

$$= \frac{12}{182} \left[ \frac{400.0}{5} + \frac{650.25}{4} + \frac{2070.25}{4} \right] - 42$$

$$= .066[80 + 162.6 + 517.6] - 42$$

$$= 50.17 - 42$$

$$= 8.17.$$

To evaluate the obtained $H$ of 8.2, we use Table A–8, which lists the values of $H$ for all combinations of three groups, where no $n$ is larger than five, at the .05 and .01 levels of confidence. For $n$'s of 5, 4, and 4 we find that the listed $H$ value is 7.74 at the .01 confidence level. Our value of 8.2 is larger than the tabled value and we reject the null hypothesis at the .01 level. We can conclude that the three samples are not drawn from the same population.

The size of $H$ is affected by the number of ties in rank. Therefore, a correction for ties should be made using the formula:

$$1 - \frac{\sum T}{N^3 - N}, \qquad (10\text{-}4)$$

**Table 10-3.** Calculation of the Mann-Whitney $U$ Test

Step 1: Rank the scores. Ties are settled by determining the average rank of the positions taken by the tied scores.

| Rank | 1 | 2 | 3.5 | 3.5 | 5.5 | 5.5 | 7 | 8 | 10 |
|------|-----|-----|-----|-----|-----|-----|-----|-----|-----|
| Score | 8 | 11 | 12 | 12 | 13 | 13 | 14 | 15 | 17 |
| Rank | 10 | 10 | 13 | 13 | 13 | 15.5 | 15.5 | 17 | 18 |
| Score | 17 | 17 | 18 | 18 | 18 | 19 | 19 | 20 | 21 |
| Rank | 19 | 20 | | | | | | | |
| Score | 22 | 24 | | | | | | | |

Step 2: Arrange the ranks by groups.

| | Group 1 | | Group 2 | |
|---|---|---|---|---|
| | Score | Rank | Score | Rank |
| | 8 | 1 | 13 | 5.5 |
| | 11 | 2 | 15 | 8 |
| | 12 | 3.5 | 17 | 10 |
| | 12 | 3.5 | 17 | 10 |
| | 13 | 5.5 | 18 | 13 |
| | 14 | 7 | 18 | 13 |
| | 17 | 10 | 19 | 15.5 |
| | 18 | 13 | 20 | 17 |
| | 19 | 15.5 | 21 | 18 |
| | 22 | 19 | 24 | 20 |
| Step 3: Sum the ranks for each of the groups. $\Sigma$ | | 80.0 | | 130.0 |

Step 4: Since Group 1 has the smaller sum, we will solve for $U$ using Group 1

$$U = n_1 n_2 + \frac{n_1(n_1 + 1)}{2} - \sum R_1$$

$$= (10)(10) + \frac{(10)(11)}{2} - 80.0$$

$$= 100 + 55 - 80$$

$$= 75.0$$

Step 5: The obtained value of $U$ is larger than the tabled value for .05, which is 23 (Table A-7).

Step 6: Accept the hypothesis that the two samples are drawn from the same population.

**Table 10–4**

| Group 1 | | Group 2 | | Group 3 | |
|---|---|---|---|---|---|
| *Score* | *Rank* | *Score* | *Rank* | *Score* | *Rank* |
| .50 | 1 | .73 | 3 | 2.00 | 9.5 |
| .63 | 2 | 1.27 | 6 | 2.60 | 11 |
| .84 | 4 | 1.55 | 7 | 3.00 | 12 |
| .87 | 5 | 2.00 | 9.5 | 3.40 | 13 |
| 1.66 | 8 | | | | |
| $\sum R_1 = 20$ | | $\sum R_2 = 25.5$ | | $\sum R_3 = 45.5$ | |

where $T = t^3 - t$, where $t$ is the number of tied observations in a set
  that is summed over all sets of ties, and
  $N =$ the total number of observations in the sample.
The correction is made by dividing the obtained value of $H$ by the
result of the preceding formula. In our example, one tie occurred.
Since two observations are involved in this tie, the number of tied
observations is two. Applying the formula, we find

$$T = t^3 - t = 8 - 2 = 6$$

$$N^3 - N = 2197 - 13 = 2184$$

$$1 - \frac{6}{2184} = 1 - .0027 = .9973.$$

The corrected value of $H$ is equal to:

$$H_c = 8.17/.9973$$

$$= 8.19$$

Since there was only one tie in this example, the difference between
the corrected $H$ (8.19) and the uncorrected $H$ (8.17) is quite small.
If the $H$ value is at the borderline of significance or if we want a
precise estimate of significance level, the $H$ value should be corrected
for ties.

*Larger Samples.*   When the number of observations exceeds the
values listed in Table A–8, $H$ can be evaluated by computing a chi-
square with the degrees of freedom equal to the number of groups
minus one. If we have more than three groups of subjects or have
more subjects than five in any one of three groups, our calculated $H$

can be treated as a $\chi^2$ value. If we do evaluate the $H$ statistic using the $\chi^2$ distribution, Table A–5 should be entered with

$$df = k - 1,$$

where $k$ = the number of groups.

If we have six groups of subjects the $df = 6 - 1 = 5$; the tabled value for $\chi^2$ at the .05 level of confidence with 5 $df$ (Table A–5) is 11.07. In order to reject the null hypothesis at the .05 level of confidence the value of $H$ must be at least as large as 11.07.

## Advantages and Disadvantages
## of Non-Parametric Methods

As a general rule, parametric methods are preferred because they have superior power and allow greater precision of estimation than do the corresponding non-parametric methods. Occasionally a non-parametric method is used because it is easier to compute. However, the efficiency of non-parametric methods is not as great as that of parametric methods. For example, a sign test done on 20 subjects is equivalent in power to a $t$-test done with 14 subjects at $\alpha = .04$. Use of the sign test in this case could be equivalent to throwing away six subjects! The $U$ and $H$ tests have somewhat better power, but still do not equal the power of the corresponding parametric measure. If a difference is significant with a non-parametric test it will usually be at least as significant with the corresponding parametric test, so it is usually not necessary to carry out the additional computation.

In general, non-parametric measures disregard information when compared to the corresponding parametric test. A sign test, for example, merely takes into account the sign of a difference; the magnitude of the differences is not taken into account.

Very few circumstances are encountered in which a parametric method is inappropriate. The only case in which one must use a non-parametric method are those instances in which the data are incomplete because some of the extreme measurements are not scaled. The empirical investigations cited earlier have established the fact that the parametric methods remain relatively unaffected by wide departures from the conventional normal curve models. In many situations it has been shown that parametric methods are *less* affected by unusual distributions than are the non-parametric methods.

1. Two experimenters are concerned about sampling biases in their selection of rats for their studies. In particular, they have been told that, when rats are housed two to a cage, the rat picked up first will be the larger and more aggressive rat of the two. Since they are conducting studies in emotionality in which any such biases would influence the outcome of their studies, they decide to test this claim. They cage ten pairs of rats together for one month; then an experimenter who is unaware of the purpose of the study picks one of the rats from each cage. They note which rat is chosen and they weigh all of the rats. The weights are listed below in grams:

| Cage # | 1 | 2 | 3 | 4 | 5 | 6 | 7 | 8 | 9 | 10 |
|---|---|---|---|---|---|---|---|---|---|---|
| Chosen rat | 250 | 241 | 232 | 215 | 283 | 200 | 234 | 189 | 250 | 226 |
| Cage mate | 225 | 236 | 234 | 180 | 198 | 200 | 220 | 210 | 231 | 207 |

One experimenter decides to run a sign test on these data. Can he conclude that there is a significant effect?

2. The second experimenter decided to do a median test on the data. Can he conclude that there is a significant effect?

3. The original informants explain to the two experimenters that the observed effect holds only for male rats. Since the experimenters used females in the first experiments they performed the study again with males. The weights are listed below in grams:

| Cage # | 1 | 2 | 3 | 4 | 5 | 6 | 7 | 8 | 9 | 10 |
|---|---|---|---|---|---|---|---|---|---|---|
| Chosen rat | 282 | 270 | 313 | 305 | 267 | 315 | 308 | 291 | 316 | 302 |
| Cage mate | 250 | 273 | 319 | 302 | 240 | 312 | 314 | 266 | 300 | 271 |

The second experimenter again decides to analyze the data using a median test. Can he conclude that there is a significant effect?

4. The first experimenter decides to do a sign test on the data. Can he conclude that there is a significant effect?

5. An experimenter is interested in studying the effect of motivation on the ability to make fine motor movements. He uses a task in which tweezers are used to insert tiny pegs into holes in a board. The score is expressed in terms of the number of pegs inserted in a five minute work period. One group of randomly selected subjects is paid 1¢ for each peg inserted (Group M). The other group of randomly selected subjects is not paid to do the task but is merely urged to do as well as they can (Group U). The data are listed below.

| Rank | 4 | 9 | 8 | 3 |
|---|---|---|---|---|
| Group $M$ | $X_1 = 254$ | $X_2 = 201$ | $X_3 = 210$ | $X_4 = 264$ |
| | 2 | 1 | 5 | |
| | $X_5 = 276$ | $X_6 = 281$ | $X_7 = 233$ | |

| Rank | 10 | 7 | 12 | 13 |
|---|---|---|---|---|
| Group $U$ | $X_1 = 195$ | $X_2 = 212$ | $X_3 = 173$ | $X_4 = 140$ |
| | 11 | 6 | | |
| | $X_5 = 183$ | $X_6 = 215$ | | |

The experimenter evaluates the significance of the difference between the two groups with the Mann-Whitney $U$ test. Can he conclude that there is a difference between the two groups?

6. (a) Another experimenter decides to test the difference between the two groups using the $t$-ratio. Can he conclude that there is a difference between the two groups?

(b) Which procedure to test the difference between the two groups is preferable? Why?

7. The following learning scores are based on three groups of subjects of different ages. The scores are expressed in terms of the number of items correctly recalled from a list of 20 nonsense syllables which the subjects had been instructed to learn.

| *15 year olds* | | *30 year olds* | | *45 year olds* | |
| Score | Rank | Score | Rank | Score | Rank |
| 10 | 5 | 13 | 2 | 9 | 7 |
| 9 | 7 | 8 | 9 | 7 | 10 |
| 12 | 3 | 6 | 11.5 | 4 | 13 |
| 11 | 4 | 7 | 7 | 2 | 14 |
| 15 | 1 | | 29.5 | 6 | 11.5 |
| | 20 | | | | 55.5 |

What is the value of the Kruskal-Wallis $H$ test calculated from these data? Can it be concluded that there is a significant difference among these groups?

## CHAPTER ELEVEN

# REGRESSION ANALYSIS

In Chapter 7, we presented the logic and techniques to determine whether or not an observed difference between the means of two groups of observations is statistically significant. In Chapter 8 we discussed the methods by which the variation present in a set of scores — the variance — can be divided into separate parts, each part associated with a different source. These methods provide us with some powerful tools for determining whether or not groups differ significantly from one another.

However, there are often circumstances in which classification of data into discrete groups or categories is inappropriate — situations in which we are interested in variations within sets of scores in the sense of knowing how scores change together. The approach to this type of analysis is fundamentally no different from the types of analysis covered in Chapters 7 and 8, but will require some new concepts.

The sum of squares, $\Sigma x^2 = \Sigma X^2 - \dfrac{(\Sigma X)^2}{N}$, and the variance, $s^2 = \dfrac{\Sigma x^2}{N-1}$, are by now quite familiar to you. If we have two sets of scores, $X$ and $Y$, we know how to calculate the sums of squares, variances, and, if we wish, to determine by use of the $t$ or $F$ statistic whether the means of the two sets of scores differ significantly. But what if we are interested in how change in one set of scores is related to change in another set? What are the possibilities of predicting a person's score on test $Y$ from knowing his score on test $X$?

For example, using the methods presented in Chapter 7, we can determine that a relationship exists between the ability of people to solve problems using principles of logic and their ability to learn to program a digital computer. To approach this question using the methods presented earlier, we could take two groups of subjects, one

group scoring high on a test of logical problem solving ability and the
other scoring low on the test, and calculate a $t$ statistic on the differences in the scores on the final examination in a course on computer
programming. The procedure is illustrated below:

| *Group A* | *Group B* |
|---|---|
| High scores on logical problem solving ability | Low scores on logical problem solving ability |
| $\bar{X}$ and $s$ on final examination in computer programming | $\bar{X}$ and $s$ on final examination in computer programming |

$t$ statistic to determine
significance of differ-
ence between groups on
the examination score

Such a design tells us that the groups differ significantly; that a
group selected because the members score high on one ability
measure (logical problem solving) differ significantly on another
measure (final examination in computer programming) as well.
However, this tells us little about how the two measures—problem
solving ability and computer programming ability—are related. To
approach the problem of evaluating how scores change in relation to
each other, a new concept is necessary. Just as the sum of squares for
a set of scores, $X$, is given by $\Sigma X^2 - \dfrac{(\Sigma X)^2}{N}$, and the sum of squares
for another set, $Y$, is given by $\Sigma Y^2 - \dfrac{(\Sigma Y)^2}{N}$, the variation associated
with change in one set as related to another is given by their cross-
products. If the sum of squares for $X$ is defined by $\Sigma(X - \bar{X})^2$ and
the sum of squares for $Y$ is defined by $\Sigma(Y - \bar{Y})^2$, then the sum of
squares for the new quantity, the *covariance*, is given by

**(11–1)**
$$\Sigma xy = \Sigma(X - \bar{X})(Y - \bar{Y}).$$

Just as the calculation formulas for the sums of squares are given by

$$\Sigma x^2 = \Sigma X^2 - \frac{(\Sigma X)^2}{N} \text{ and } \Sigma y^2 = \Sigma Y^2 - \frac{(\Sigma Y)^2}{N} \text{ for measures } X \text{ and } Y, \text{ the}$$

calculation formula for the covariance is given by

$$\Sigma xy = \Sigma XY - \frac{(\Sigma X)(\Sigma Y)}{N}$$

(11–2)

Basically, the only change that is made is the cross-multiplication of the pairs of scores to obtain the quantity $\Sigma XY$ instead of using the squares of the scores.

The concept of *covariance* is fundamental to *regression analysis* — an analysis by which we determine the amount of variation in one set of scores that can be accounted for by the variation in another set of scores. The ratio of the covariance of two measures to an average of the variances of the two separate measures provides us with the desired estimate of how much variation in one set of scores is determined by variation in another set of scores. This allows us to determine how accurately one set of scores can be predicted from another set.

This process and its relationship to the techniques discussed in Chapters 7 and 8 are best illustrated by reference to an example. By way of illustration, we will use data on husbands and wives — height measurements in centimeters. It seems reasonable that there should be more of a relationship between the heights of couples than there would be between pairs of persons selected at random. However, the degree to which the height of one member of a couple can be predicted from the height of the other remains to be seen.

The heights in centimeters of 14 couples are given in Table 11–1.

We want to examine the possibility that there is a systematic relationship between the pairs of scores — the possibility that, as one set of scores changes, the other measurements also change in a systematic and regular manner.

Earlier in this chapter, we introduced the concept of *covariance* and defined it as the sum of squares of the cross-products of two sets of measurements:

$$\Sigma xy = \Sigma (X - \bar{X})(Y - \bar{Y})$$

(11–1)

It is possible to use the covariance to determine the extent to which one score can be predicted from another and to estimate the accuracy with which this prediction can be made. This process — determining the accuracy with which one set of scores can be predicted from a related set — is known as *regression analysis*.

In the majority of circumstances in which we want to predict one set of measurements from another, we do not have anything ap-

**Table 11-1.** HEIGHTS (IN CENTIMETERS) OF 14 COUPLES

| Couple # | Husband | Wife | Difference | |
|---|---|---|---|---|
| 1 | 199 | 187 | 12.0 | |
| 2 | 179 | 170 | 9.0 | |
| 3 | 192 | 177 | 15.0 | $r = .88$ |
| 4 | 189 | 180 | 9.0 | $b = .875$ |
| 5 | 188 | 175 | 13.0 | $a = 10.50$ |
| 6 | 172 | 167 | 5.0 | |
| 7 | 192 | 177 | 15.0 | |
| 8 | 179 | 157 | 22.0 | |
| 9 | 178 | 162 | 16.0 | |
| 10 | 174 | 167 | 7.0 | |
| 11 | 174 | 162 | 12.0 | |
| 12 | 174 | 163 | 11.0 | |
| 13 | 177 | 164 | 13.0 | |
| 14 | 178 | 165 | 13.0 | *Totals* |
| | $n = 14$ | 14 | | 28 |
| | $\Sigma X = 2545$ | 2373 | 172 | 4918 |
| | $\Sigma X^2 = 463,585$ | 403,157 | 2342 | 866,742 |
| | $\Sigma x^2 = 940.36$ | 933.50 | 228.857 | 2930.43 |
| | $s^2 = 72.34$ | 71.81 | 176.044 | 108.53 |
| | $s = 8.50$ | 8.47 | 4.1957 | 10.42 |
| | $\bar{X} = 181.79$ | 169.5 | 12.2848 | 175.6 |
| | | | $\Sigma XY = 43220$ | |
| | | | $s_{\bar{D}} = 1.12$ | |
| | | | $t = 10.96$ | |

proaching an exact relationship. However, we would still like to utilize any relationship that exists between $X$ and $Y$ to improve our predictions.

## SCATTER DIAGRAMS

When we have reason to believe that there is a relationship between two variables, the first step is to prepare a *scatter diagram*. The scatter diagram is a special kind of graph based on two sets of measures — the values of $X$ and the matching values of $Y$ for the same individual. When constructing scatter diagrams, the variable that is to be used to predict (in our example, the heights of husbands) is called the $X$ variable and it is scaled along the horizontal axis of the graph. The variable to be predicted is referred to as the $Y$ variable and it is scaled along the vertical axis of the graph. Figure 11-1 is a scatter diagram of the data in Table 11-1.

The scatter diagram, Figure 11-1, is constructed by placing a tally mark in the box at the intersection of each pair of $X$ and $Y$ scores. For the first couple, the husband's height is 199 centimeters and the wife's is 187 centimeters. Therefore, a tally mark has been placed

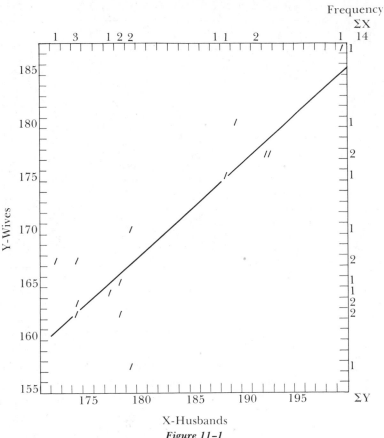

Figure 11–1

where these two scales intersect. As a check on accuracy, the frequency of each X measurement is noted at the top of each column and the frequency of each Y measurement is noted at the right margin of each row. The frequency of the X scores should equal 14, as should the frequency of the Y scores.

Table 11–2 contains the height measurements from Table 11–1 and illustrates the calculation process as well. The heights of husbands are labeled X and the heights of wives Y. The table also contains $X^2$, $Y^2$, and $XY$, as well as summary calculations that we will need later. The XY column is obtained by multiplying each Y by the corresponding X and summing over all pairs.

We can now carry out a calculation to permit us to draw a straight line that will do the best job possible of predicting Y from X. It must be emphasized that, if the relationship between the two variables is not a linear relationship, the best fit line will not be a straight line. We cannot use the method described here when a curved line would be the best fit line; the method works *only* when the best fit line is a straight line.

**Table 11–2.** Height Measurements and Calculation of Data from Table 11–1

| Couple # | Husband's Height, X | X² | Wife's Height, Y | Y² | XY |
|---|---|---|---|---|---|
| 1 | 199 | 39601 | 187 | 34969 | 37213 |
| 2 | 179 | 32041 | 170 | 28900 | 30430 |
| 3 | 192 | 36864 | 177 | 31329 | 33984 |
| 4 | 189 | 35721 | 180 | 32400 | 34020 |
| 5 | 188 | 35344 | 175 | 30625 | 32900 |
| 6 | 172 | 29584 | 167 | 27889 | 28724 |
| 7 | 192 | 36864 | 177 | 31329 | 33984 |
| 8 | 179 | 32041 | 157 | 24649 | 28103 |
| 9 | 178 | 31684 | 162 | 26244 | 28836 |
| 10 | 174 | 30276 | 167 | 27889 | 29058 |
| 11 | 174 | 30276 | 162 | 26244 | 28188 |
| 12 | 174 | 30276 | 163 | 26569 | 28362 |
| 13 | 177 | 31329 | 164 | 26896 | 29028 |
| 14 | 178 | 31684 | 165 | 27225 | 29370 |
| | Σ 2545 | 463585 | 2373 | 403157 | 432200 |

We could, of course, draw in the best fit line by visual inspection. The only drawback to this approach is that there might be disagreement among people as to which line is the best predictor. It is clearly not very sensible to base a prediction method on the subjective judgments of different individuals. By computing an equation to determine the line, we will obtain a line that allows us to make the best estimates possible of a $Y$ score from an $X$ score.

It is entirely reasonable to ask why a regression line is preferable to some other index, such as the average value of $Y$ for given values of $X$. Why not take the average of all the values of $Y$ present for a given $X$ and use the mean of the $Y$ values as the best prediction? The answer is that, from the standpoint of sampling stability, the line established by the regression equation is more stable than any other value indicating the relationship between $X$ and $Y$ since it is based on *all* of the measurements. Predictions based on the equation for the regression line will not be influenced by minor sampling fluctuations as much as would be the case if we used the values in the individual columns to make the predictions.

To find the line of "best fit" by more objective means than is possible with simple visual inspection, we will solve an equation that fits a straight line to the data of Table 11–1: the sum of the squares of the deviations from this line will be as small as possible. The equation we will use is the equation for a straight line.

**(11–3)**

$$Y' = a + bX$$

The formula for $b$ is the following:

$$b = \frac{\Sigma XY - \frac{(\Sigma X)(\Sigma Y)}{N}}{\Sigma X^2 - \frac{(\Sigma X)^2}{N}} \qquad \text{(11-4)}$$

where $b$ is the ratio of two sums of squares—the covariance of $X$ and $Y$ divided by the sum of squares for the $X$ measurements. Once the $b$ coefficient is known, the value of the $a$ constant can be obtained by subtraction as follows:

$$a = \bar{Y} - b\bar{X} \qquad \text{(11-5)}$$

To carry out a regression analysis, we have to calculate one new sum of squares—the covariance. To do this, we multiply each $Y$ by its corresponding $X$ value as follows:

$$X_1 \cdot Y_1 = XY_1$$
$$X_2 \cdot Y_2 = XY_2$$

All other sums of squares needed have been calculated earlier in Table 11-2 and can be used in our present calculations. To determine the $b$ coefficient for the data of Table 11-1, we calculate the ratio of the covariance sum of squares to the sum of squares for measure $X$, as shown in formula (11-4):

$$\frac{432200 - \frac{(2545)(2373)}{14}}{463585 - \frac{(2545)^2}{14}} = .875$$

Having obtained $b$, the value of $a$ can be found by subtraction:

$$169.50 - .875\,(181.79) = 10.4979$$

and the final equation to predict the heights of wives from their husbands' heights is

$$Y' = 10.50 + .875X$$

If we now solve the equation $Y' = a + bX$ for each value of $X$ in turn, we have the following results for the $X$ scores in Table 11–1:

$$X \quad b \quad + \quad a \quad = \quad Y'$$

$$199(.875) + 10.50 = 184.5567$$
$$179(.875) + 10.50 = 167.0634$$
$$192(.875) + 10.50 = 178.4341$$
$$189(.875) + 10.50 = 175.8101$$
$$188(.875) + 10.50 = 174.9354$$
$$172(.875) + 10.50 = 160.9407$$
$$192(.875) + 10.50 = 178.4341$$
$$179(.875) + 10.50 = 167.0634$$
$$178(.875) + 10.50 = 166.1887$$
$$174(.875) + 10.50 = 162.6900$$
$$174(.875) + 10.50 = 162.6900$$
$$174(.875) + 10.50 = 162.6900$$
$$177(.875) + 10.50 = 165.3140$$
$$178(.875) + 10.50 = 166.1887$$

If we examine this set of values and compare it to the actual scores on $Y$, we can see how well we do at predicting the $Y$ scores. If we take the difference between the actual $Y$ score and the predicted $Y'$ score, we have the following table of differences between $Y$ and $Y'$.*

It can be seen that our predictions compare quite favorably with the obtained $Y$'s. The discrepancy between $Y$ and $Y'$ is called the error of estimate, the error of prediction, or the residual error. The sum of squares of the residual error, $(Y'-Y)^2$, is 214.0850. We could have used the single most representative value of $Y$, the mean of $Y$, as our predicted value if we had disregarded any relationship that might exist between $X$ and $Y$. If we do this we find the sum of the squared deviations from the mean value of $\bar{Y}$, $\Sigma(Y-\bar{Y})^2$ is 933.503, a value considerably larger than the value of 214.0850 we obtained when we used the information regarding the relationship of the two variables. Thus, it would pay us to take advantage of this information regarding the relationship of the two variables when attempting to predict the value of any score.

---

*Normally, we do not carry as many as four decimal places, as we have done in this example. Here we have done so because we wish to demonstrate certain relationships between different components of regression and correlation analysis and to avoid any confusion that might result from the presence of rounding errors.

Table 11–3

| $Y'$ | $Y$ | $Y'-Y$ | $(Y'-Y)^2$ |
|---|---|---|---|
| 184.5567 | 187 | −2.4432 | 5.9693 |
| 167.0634 | 170 | −2.9365 | 8.6234 |
| 178.4341 | 177 | 1.4341 | 2.0566 |
| 175.8101 | 180 | −4.1898 | 17.5552 |
| 174.9354 | 175 | −.0645 | .0041 |
| 160.9407 | 167 | −6.0592 | 36.7145 |
| 178.4341 | 177 | 1.4341 | 2.0566 |
| 167.0634 | 157 | 10.0634 | 101.2725 |
| 166.1887 | 162 | 4.1887 | 17.5456 |
| 162.6900 | 167 | −4.3099 | 18.5753 |
| 162.6900 | 162 | .6900 | .4762 |
| 162.6900 | 163 | −.3099 | .0960 |
| 165.3140 | 164 | 1.3140 | 1.7268 |
| 166.1887 | 165 | 1.1887 | 1.4131 |

$\Sigma y' = 402942.6801$
$\Sigma y'^2 = 402223.2627$

$\Sigma = 0.0$      214.0852

$\Sigma y^2 = 933.502599$
$\Sigma y'^2 = 719.417399$
$\Sigma y_{res}^2 = 214.0852$

## LINEAR REGRESSION

Perhaps a simple example of a *perfect* linear regression of variable $Y$ on $X$ will be instructive. Assume that such a perfect relationship exists between monthly income from contracts and interest income and the amount of yearly income of a small business. The monthly income throughout the year is the same since all income comes from fixed amount contracts for a 12-month period. In addition to this income, the company receives $1000 interest on investments over the year. If we know this information, we can calculate the yearly income. The equation we use is the equation for a straight line:

$$Y' = a + bX, \qquad\qquad (11\text{–}3)$$

where $Y'$ = the to-be-predicted yearly income,
    $X$ = the monthly income from contracts,
    $a$ = the interest income, and
    $b$ = the number of months over the year the income is collected.
In this equation $a$ and $b$ are constants, the function of which we will discuss below. We will assume the following values: $X = \$1000$, $a = \$1000$, $b = 12$ months. Therefore: $Y' = 1000 + 12(1000) = 13,000$.

Keeping everything else constant, let us assume that $X$ takes the value $1500. Therefore: $Y' = 1000 + 12(1500) = 19,000$. Again keeping everything else constant, let us assume that $X$ takes the value $2000. Therefore: $Y' = 1000 + 12(2000) = 25,000$. Let $X$ take the value $2500. Therefore: $Y' = 1000 + 12(2500) = 31,000$.

Figure 11–2 is a graph of these four points, which are plotted as crosses and connected by a solid straight line. If both constant $a$ and constant $b$ stay the same, we can predict the yearly income from the monthly income with complete accuracy. In fact, we could do so after calculating only two points, connecting them, and using the regression line to predict $Y$ contingent on a given value of $X$.

Suppose that everything stays the same except the number of months over which the income is collected. The decision of the company president is to close the business for two months during the summer for a vacation. Thus, $b$ will take the value of 10, rather than 12. Our four equations will now give the following values:

$$Y' = 1000 + 10(1000) = 11,000$$

$$Y' = 1000 + 10(1500) = 16,000$$

$$Y' = 1000 + 10(2000) = 21,000$$

$$Y' = 1000 + 10(2500) = 26,000$$

These four points are plotted as crosses in Figure 11–2 and connected by a dashed line. The effect of changing the constant $b$ is to change the slope of the straight line.

If we change the value of the constant $a$ we will not affect the slope but will change the position of the line on $Y$. For example, assume that the investment income ($a$) becomes \$2000 per year and everything else is as depicted in the solid line. Now, our four equations become:

$$Y' = 2000 + 12(1000) = 14,000$$

$$Y' = 2000 + 12(1500) = 20,000$$

$$Y' = 2000 + 12(2000) = 26,000$$

$$Y' = 2000 + 12(2500) = 32,000$$

These four points are represented in Figure 11–2 as open circles connected with a solid line. It can be seen that changing the constant $a$ does not affect the slope of the line at all but merely the position of the line on $Y$.

On the basis of this example it is evident that if a perfect linear relationship exists all of the points in the distribution fall on the regression line; thus, if we know the parameters $a$ and $b$, and are given a value of $X$, we can predict $Y$ with complete accuracy.

## ACCURACY OF PREDICTION

Earlier, the analogy was drawn between the present situation in which we predict one set of measurements from another and the earlier situation in which we estimate a population parameter from a sample statistic. When we estimate a population parameter, we want

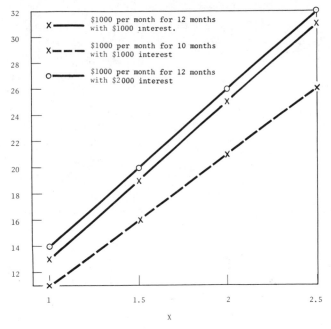

Monthly income (in thousands)

***Figure 11–2***

to know how accurately we have estimated the population value. In regression analysis, we want to know how accurate our predictions are. To do this, we need some estimate of the standard deviation of the predicted $Y$ minus the $Y'$. This is called the *standard error of estimate*, or the standard error of prediction, and is defined by the following formula:

$$s_{y \cdot x} = \sqrt{\frac{\Sigma(Y - Y')^2}{N - 2}}$$

(11–6)

where $s_{y \cdot x}$ is the symbol for the standard error of the regression of $Y$ on $X$, and $N$ refers to the number of pairs of scores. The rest of the terms have been defined many times before. The formula is quite similar to the definitional formula for the standard deviation of any set of scores $(s_x = \sqrt{\Sigma x^2/N - 1})$, which can be written as:

$$s_x = \sqrt{\frac{\Sigma(X - \bar{X})^2}{N - 1}}$$

The only difference between the standard error of estimate and the ordinary standard deviation formula is that two constants $a$ and $b$

(see page 198) have been calculated from the data, and thus two degrees of freedom are lost.

For the example, the value of $\Sigma(Y-Y')^2$ is available and can be substituted into formula (11–5):

$$s_{y \cdot x} = \sqrt{\frac{214.0852}{12}} = \sqrt{17.8404} = 4.2238$$

Solving for the value of the standard error of estimate results in a value of 4.22. If this value is interpreted as an ordinary standard deviation and confidence limits are set (see Chapter 6), we can establish the limits within which any predicted value of $Y$ is expected to fall a given proportion of the time. For example, if we calculate the $Y'$ for an $X$ of 199, we obtain a value of 184.5567. If we then calculate the confidence limits of $y' = 184.5567 + 1.96 s_{y \cdot x}$, we obtain the following value: $184.5567 + 1.96(4.2238) = 184.5567 + 8.2786$, which is equal to 192.8353 for the upper confidence interval. When we do the same calculation to find the lower confidence interval we obtain the following value: $184.5567 - 1.96(4.2238) = 184.5567 - 8.2786 = 176.2781$. These two values define the 5 per cent confidence limits for the predicted value of $Y$. We can now state that our predicted value of $Y$ should be within these two limits 95 per cent of the time.

Since calculating the standard error of estimate using deviation

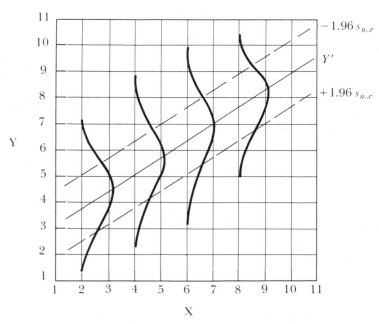

***Figure 11–3.*** Tabulation of bivariate data from Table 11–1.

scores involves too many tedious steps in calculation, a more efficient calculation method for $s_{y \cdot x}$ will be shown after we have discussed some other aspects of regression analysis. (See Chapter 12, p. 218.)

For a graphic representation of the process described above, see Figure 11–3. The center diagonal line is the regression line and the dotted lines above and below the regression line are set equal to $1.96 s_{y \cdot x}$.

Given any $X$ value we can predict the value of $Y$ by the equation $Y' = a + bX$, which for our example is equal to $Y' = 10.50 + .875X$. The only assumption necessary here is that the values of $Y$ are distributed normally about $Y'$ in the population from which our sample is drawn. The standard deviation of that distribution is given by $s_{y \cdot x}$. The estimates of $Y'$ can then be made in terms of $Y'$ plus and minus $1.96s_{y \cdot x}$. In this manner we can say that the actual value of $Y$ should lie between the values of $Y'$ plus and minus $1.96s_{y \cdot x}$ 95 per cent of the time. Only in 5 per cent of the predictions should the actual value of $Y$ be found outside of the above limits.

1. Given the following data for test $X$ and test $Y$

$$\sum X = 183 \qquad \sum Y = 144$$
$$\sum X^2 = 1119 \qquad \sum Y^2 = 962$$
$$(\sum X)^2 = 33489 \qquad (\sum Y)^2 = 20736$$
$$N = 35 \qquad \sum XY = 846.97$$

   compute the regression equation for $Y$.
2. Predict $Y$, given $X = 25$.
3. Predict $Y$, given $X = -1.877$.
4. Given the following data on two forms of the same test

$$\sum X = 87 \qquad \sum Y = 97$$
$$\sum X^2 = 1732 \qquad \sum Y^2 = 1203$$
$$(\sum X)^2 = 7569 \qquad (\sum Y)^2 = 9409$$
$$N = 25 \qquad \sum XY = 1356.87$$

   calculate the regression equation for $Y$.
5. Predict $Y$, with $X = 3.48$.
6. Predict $Y$, with $X = 4.85$.

# CHAPTER TWELVE

# CORRELATION

In the last chapter we concentrated on the process by which variation in a variable $Y$ associated with variation in a variable $X$ can be identified, and can be used to predict values of one variable from knowledge of values of the other one. In the example we presented it was found that there was a significant amount of variation in the heights of wives that was associated with variation in the heights of their husbands, and that this covariation was sufficiently high to allow us to predict values in one group from values of the other. (In our example we predicted the heights of wives from those of their husbands. It would have been just as easy to predict the heights of husbands from those of wives.) Clearly, there is a high degree of association between the two sets of scores.* What we would like at this point is a single value that would allow us to make some statement regarding the degree of association between two variables. Such a value is known as the *coefficient of correlation.*

## THE COEFFICIENT OF CORRELATION (PEARSON $r$)

The coefficient of correlation (or the Pearson $r$, after the statistician Karl Pearson who developed it) is a measure of the *linear* (straight line) relationship between two variables, and is an expression of the degree to which two measures $X$ and $Y$ are related. It is valid only for circumstances in which the relationship between the two variables is linear. The simplest way to assess linearity is to construct a scatter diagram, as in Figure 11–1.

Figure 12–1 contains four such scatter diagrams, illustrating a linear positive relationship ($A$), a linear negative relationship ($B$), no

---

*Later in this chapter, where the relationship of regression analysis and analysis of variance is illustrated, the method of calculating the significance of the regression is developed.

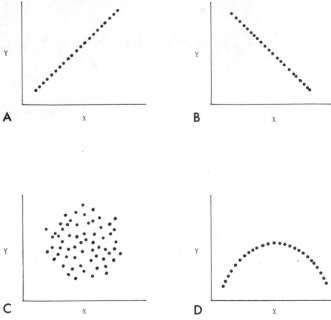

**Figure 12-1.** *A*, positive relationship. *B*, negative relationship. *C*, no relationship. *D*, curvilinear relationship.

relationship between $X$ and $Y$ ($C$), and what is known as a *curvilinear* relationship ($D$).

Calculation of the coefficient of correlation is appropriate only for scatter diagrams $A$, $B$, and $C$; $A$ and $B$ are perfect linear relationships and $C$ represents no relationship whatever. Since the scatter of points in $C$ is circular, any arbitrarily chosen straight line passed through the center of the points will fit as well as any other. It is inappropriate to calculate the Pearson $r$ for ($D$), since the relationship between $X$ and $Y$, although obviously very high, is not linear—scores on $Y$ at first increase as $X$ increases, then do not change, and finally decrease as the values of $X$ increase. In this instance no straight line will fit the points adequately and we would seriously underestimate the relationship through use of the linear regression method. In cases such as this we must use special correlational methods designed for curvilinear relationships. These methods are more complicated since it takes more constants to fit the "best" curved line through a set of points.

One further requirement must be mentioned for the calculation of the coefficient of correlation. It is necessary to assume that scores are dispersed approximately equally throughout the total range of scores. The technical term for this is *homoscedasticity*. In Figure 12–2, three illustrations of homoscedasticity are shown. In Figure 12–2 *A*, the change is linear and the dispersion is even throughout the range of scores. In Figure 12–2 *B*, the change is linear, but the dispersion is not even. In Figure 12–2 *C*, the relationship is not linear and the dispersion is not even. Only in the case of Figure 12–2 *A* should we calculate a Pearson *r*.

The Pearson *r* is basically a ratio of the covariance sum of squares to a mean of the sums of squares of the two variables. One definition formula for the Pearson *r* is

$$r = \frac{\sum (X - \bar{X})(Y - \bar{Y})}{\sqrt{\sum (X - \bar{X})^2 \sum (Y - \bar{Y})^2}} \, .$$

(12–1)

This formula can also be written as

$$r = \frac{\sum xy}{\sqrt{\sum x^2 \sum y^2}} \, .$$

(12–2)

The Pearson correlation coefficient is best considered as a ratio that indicates the degree to which variation in one variable is associated with variation in another variable. The denominator in formula (12–3) you will recognize as the square root of the sum of squares for variable *X* times the sum of squares for variable *Y*. This term is actually a type of arithmetic mean. We did not discuss this among the measures of central tendency referred to in Chapter 3 simply because this type of average has only limited use. The value $\sqrt{\Sigma x^2 \Sigma y^2}$ is called the *geometric mean* of the sums of squares for *X* and *Y*. A geometric mean is defined as the *n*th root of the product of *N* values. For example, the geometric mean of 3, 5, and 6 is equal to $\sqrt[3]{90}$, since three values enter into the total. If four values were involved, the fourth root would be taken. For correlation where only two values are involved in determining the geometric mean, the square root is taken.

The numerator represents the sum of squares for the cross products of *X* and *Y*. In Chapter 2 the relationship between the calculation formulas for the sum of squares and for the covariance were shown to be

$$\sum x^2 = \sum X^2 - \frac{(\sum X)^2}{N} \, , \, \sum xy = \sum XY - \frac{(\sum X)(\sum Y)}{N} \, .$$

Put in this fashion, the formula for $r$ can be written as follows:

**(12–3)**

$$r = \frac{\sum XY - \frac{(\sum X)(\sum Y)}{N}}{\sqrt{\left[\sum X^2 - \frac{(\sum X)^2}{N}\right]\left[\sum Y^2 - \frac{(\sum Y)^2}{N}\right]}},$$

where $\left[\sum X^2 - \frac{(\sum X)^2}{N}\right]$ and $\left(\sum Y^2 - \frac{(\sum Y)^2}{N}\right)$ are the familiar formulas for determining the sum of squares as shown in Chapter 4.

You have already encountered the concept of *covariance* in the discussion of regression. If we were to take the scores on measure $X$ and measure $Y$ and transform them to standard scores with a mean of 0 and a standard deviation of 1 (see Chapter 4, pp. 56 to 57) by the equations

$$z_x = \frac{(X - \bar{X})}{s_x} \quad \text{and} \quad z_y = \frac{(Y - \bar{Y})}{s_y}$$

the formula for the correlation coefficient becomes

**(12–4)**

$$r = \frac{\sum z_x z_y}{N}$$

from which we see that if the variances of $X$ and $Y$ are made equal by the standard score transformation, $r$ is simply the average covariance of the two measures. The larger the value of the covariance, the larger the value of $r$. To visualize this, see Table 12–1, which contains three sets of standard score pairs—one for a high positive correlation, one for a high negative correlation, and one for a zero correlation.

In part (*a*) of the table the standard scores for the individuals on $X$ and $Y$ match perfectly and the algebraic sum of the covariance is equal to $N$, resulting in an $r$ of $+1.00$ (remember that a negative number times a negative number results in a positive number). In part (*b*) the algebraic sum of the $z_x z_y$ multiplications is $-11.00$ (again equal to $N$), and the $r$ is $-1.00$. In part (*c*) the algebraic sum of the covariances is zero and the $r$ is also zero. The use of formulas (12–1), (12–2), (12–3), and (12–4) all result in the same answers.

### Calculation of the Correlation Coefficient

The formulas shown thus far for $r$ are not convenient computational formulas. To calculate $r$, the most efficient formula is a slight rearrangement of formula (12–3), as follows:

$$r = \frac{N \sum XY - (\sum X)(\sum Y)}{\sqrt{\{N \sum X^2 - (\sum X)^2\}\{N \sum Y^2 - (\sum Y)^2\}}}$$ (12–5)

If we use the data on the heights of husbands and wives and substitute the proper values into this formula, we obtain the following value for the correlation coefficient:

$$r = \frac{14(432200) - (2545)(2373)}{\sqrt{[14(463585) - (2545)^2][14(403157) - (2373)^2]}}$$

$$= \frac{6050800 - 6039285}{\sqrt{(6490190 - 6477025)(5644198 - 5631129)}}$$

$$= \frac{11515.00}{\sqrt{(13165)(13069)}}$$

$$= \frac{11515.00}{\sqrt{(114.7388)(114.3197)}}$$

$$= \frac{11515.00}{13116.9052}$$

$$r = .8779$$

**Table 12–1.** ILLUSTRATION OF CORRELATION AS THE MEAN OF CROSS-PRODUCTS WHEN VARIANCES ARE IDENTICAL

| | a | | | b | | | c | | |
|---|---|---|---|---|---|---|---|---|---|
| | Std. Score | Std. Score | | Std. Score | Std. Score | | Std. Score | Std. Score | |
| Subject | $z_x$ | $z_y$ | $z_x z_y$ | $z_x$ | $z_y$ | $z_x z_y$ | $z_x$ | $z_y$ | $z_x z_y$ |
| 1 | −1.58 | −1.58 | +2.50 | −1.58 | +1.58 | −2.50 | +1.58 | +1.58 | +2.50 |
| 2 | −1.26 | −1.26 | +1.59 | −1.26 | +1.26 | −1.59 | −1.26 | +1.26 | −1.59 |
| 3 | −.95 | −.95 | +.90 | −.95 | +.95 | −.90 | +.95 | +.95 | +.90 |
| 4 | −.63 | −.63 | +.40 | −.63 | +.63 | −.40 | −.63 | +.63 | −.40 |
| 5 | −.32 | −.32 | +.11 | −.32 | +.32 | −.11 | +.32 | +.32 | +.11 |
| 6 | .00 | .00 | .00 | .00 | .00 | .00 | .00 | .00 | .00 |
| 7 | +.32 | +.32 | +.11 | +.32 | −.32 | −.11 | −.32 | +.32 | −.11 |
| 8 | +.63 | +.63 | +.40 | +.63 | −.63 | −.40 | +.63 | +.63 | +.40 |
| 9 | +.95 | +.95 | +.90 | +.95 | −.95 | −.90 | +.95 | −.95 | −.90 |
| 10 | +1.26 | +1.26 | +1.59 | +1.26 | −1.26 | −1.59 | +1.26 | +1.26 | +1.59 |
| 11 | +1.58 | +1.58 | +2.50 | +1.58 | −1.58 | −2.50 | −1.58 | +1.58 | −2.50 |

$$\sum z_x z_y = 11.00 \qquad \sum z_x z_y = -11.00 \qquad \sum z_x z_y = .00$$

$$r = \frac{\sum z_x z_y}{N} \qquad r = \frac{-11.00}{11.00} \qquad r = \frac{.00}{11.00}$$

$$= \frac{11.00}{11.00} \qquad = -1.00 \qquad = .00$$

$$= +1.00$$

## Inferences Regarding r

Usually we test the hypothesis that the population correlation ($\rho$, following the convention of using Greek letters to represent population parameters) is zero, and test our obtained $r$ against this hypothesis. In a sense, we are testing a null hypothesis—that there is no relationship between the two variables in the population. If we reject this hypothesis, we will accept the alternative hypothesis: that there is a statistically significant relationship between the two variables. We could test two obtained correlation coefficients against one another to determine whether or not they are drawn from the same population. However, the occasions on which this is done are so rare that the procedures for doing so will not be presented here. We could also test for population values other than zero. To do this we must transform $r$ to normalize the distribution since the sampling distribution of $r$ depends on the size of $\rho$. As $\rho$ approaches $+1.00$ or $-1.00$, a skewed sampling distribution of $r$'s results because $r$ cannot exceed these values. For example, if $\rho = .80$, the distribution of $\rho$ will be negatively skewed, since the highest value $r$ can be is $+1.00$ (.20 points away from $\rho$) while the lowest value $r$ can take is $-1.00$ (1.80 points from $\rho$). Figure 12–2 contains the sampling distributions for $\rho = .80$ and $\rho = .00$. It can be seen that the distribution around $\rho = .00$ is symmetrical, while that around $\rho = .80$ is highly negatively skewed.

The transformation used to test for population values other than zero is called the $r$ to $z$ transformation and the methods used to make this transformation can be found in Walker and Lev and in McNemar.*

The only case we will consider here is testing the hypothesis that no relationship exists between the two variables; that is, that the population correlation is zero. Again, if we reject this hypothesis we will conclude that *some* relationship exists.

The coefficient of correlation, as with every statistic we have considered, is subject to errors of sampling. If $\rho = 0$ and we take successive samples of ten pairs of observations each, the sample $r$'s will fluctuate around the population value. Some of the sample $r$'s will be above the mean, some will be below, and the distribution will be normal around $\rho$. (Remember, this is true only if $\rho = 0$.) Therefore, if we could determine the standard error of $r$ we could apply normal curve methods to evaluate our statistical hypothesis concerning the value of $\rho$.

---

*Walker, H., and Lev, J.: *Statistical Inference*. New York, Holt, 1953; and McNemar, Q.: *Psychological Statistics*. 4th Edition. New York, Wiley, 1969.

The formula for the standard error of $r$ ($\sigma_r$) when $N > 30$ is as follows:

$$\sigma_r = \frac{1 - \rho^2}{\sqrt{N - 1}}. \tag{12-6}$$

If $\rho = 0$, as it does in the case we are considering, this formula reduces to:

$$\sigma_r = \frac{1}{\sqrt{N - 1}}. \tag{12-7}$$

Assume that we have gathered data on 87 subjects and found an $r$ of .30. We now want to determine the likelihood that an $r$ this large could have arisen in the course of sampling from a population in which $\rho = 0$. We decide that we will use the .05 level of significance. We know that a $z$ of $\pm 1.96$ defines this significance level.

$$\sigma_r = \frac{1}{\sqrt{37 - 1}} = \frac{1}{\sqrt{36}} = \frac{1}{6} = .167.$$

To determine the $z$-ratio we use the formula:

$$z = \frac{r - \rho}{\sigma_r} = \frac{.30 - 0}{.167} = 1.80. \tag{12-8}$$

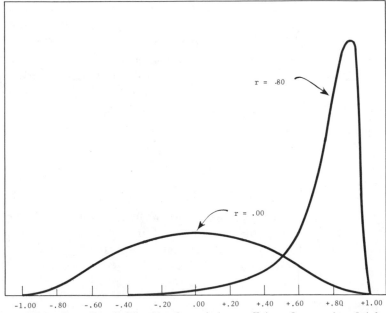

*Figure 12-2.* Sampling distribution of correlation coefficients for samples of eight pairs drawn from two populations having the indicated values of $r$. (From Edwards, A. L.: *Statistical Method,* 3rd ed. New York: Holt, Rinehart and Winston, 1973, and reprinted with their permission.)

From the table of the normal curve, Table A–2, we find that .4641 of the total area falls between the mean ($\rho$) and a $z$ of 1.80. Thus, .9282 of the total area will fall between $z$'s of ±1.80, and $1 - .9282 = .0718$. Since this proportion of the total area is greater than .05, we conclude that an $r$ of .30 could have occurred by chance when $\rho = 0$. Therefore, we conclude that there is no relationship between the two variables.

Let us now test the hypothesis that the $r$ calculated from the data in Table 11–1 could have arisen by chance when $\rho = 0$. Since $N$ is only 14 we must use small sample statistics. Therefore, we will calculate a $t$ value by the following formula:

**(12–9)**

$$t = \frac{r\sqrt{N - 2}}{\sqrt{1 - r^2}}$$

$$= \frac{.8779\sqrt{14 - 2}}{\sqrt{1 - (.8779)^2}}$$

$$= \frac{.8779(3.464)}{\sqrt{1 - .7707}}$$

$$= \frac{3.041}{\sqrt{.2293}} = \frac{3.041}{.4789} = 6.350.$$

With 12 $df$ we find, from Table A–3, that a $t$ value of this size would occur fewer than .01 times by chance, and reject the hypothesis that $\rho = 0$. We accept the alternative hypothesis that $\rho \neq 0$ and we conclude that there is a relationship between the two variables.

*Table of Significant Values of* $r$. We do not have to calculate $\sigma_r$ and then find a $z$ or a $t$ value, however, since the size of $\sigma_r$ varies as a function of $N$ alone when $\rho = 0$. Consequently, it is a simple task to table the values of $r$ that would occur at the 5 per cent and 1 per cent levels of significance as a function of the number of degrees of freedom. Table A–9 lists these values. The number of degrees of freedom is listed in the left column and the values of $r$ for the .10, .05, .02, and .01 levels are listed in the columns headed "Level of Significance for Two-Tailed Tests." Once $r$ is calculated no further calculation is necessary, since its significance can be evaluated using the table.

In the example for which we computed the $t$-ratio we have 12 $df$. The values of $r$ that reach the .05 and the .01 levels of confidence for 12 $df$ are .532 and .661, respectively. Since our $r$ of .8779 exceeds these values, we again reject the hypothesis that $\rho = 0$.

## Interpretation of r

The value of $r$ may range from $+1.00$, which indicates a perfect positive correlation, through $-1.00$, which indicates a perfect negative correlation. This means that 100 per cent of the variance of $Y$ could be predicted by knowledge regarding variation in $X$; there is no residual variance. Note that an association can be systematically negative as well as positive; scores in $Y$ can decrease as scores in $X$ increase. The closer $r$ is to zero, the less variation in $Y$ is associated with variation in $X$. The closer $R$ is to 1.00, whether positive or negative, the more variation in $Y$ can be predicted from variation in $X$.

The relationship of $r$ to the regression equation can best be understood by looking at it in terms of the ratio of two sums of squared deviations—the sum of the squared deviations of the actual values $(Y)$ to the predicted values $(Y')$, $[\Sigma (Y - Y')^2]$ to the sum of the squared deviations of the actual $Y$ score from the mean of $Y$ $[\Sigma (Y - \bar{Y})^2]$. If the prediction of $Y$ is exact, then every $Y'$ will equal $Y$ and the ratio $\Sigma (Y - Y')^2/\Sigma (Y - \bar{Y})^2$ will be zero since every $(Y - Y')^2$ is zero. If the association between $X$ and $Y$ is zero, the ratio becomes 1, since the best possible prediction of any $Y$ value from any $X$ value is the mean of $Y$, which is the single most representative value of the distribution of $Y$ scores.

This ratio provides us with a useful way to interpret the meaning of $r$. Since the ratio is 0 when prediction is exact and is 1 when there is no predictability possible, we can express the degree of association by subtracting the ratio from 1. In the former case, in which the relationship is exact, $1 - 0 = 1$. In the latter case, in which there is no relationship, $1 - 1 = 0$. Thus, the degree of relationship can be represented by a value ranging from 0 to $+1$.

We are in this way determining the amount of the total variance in $Y$ that is accounted for by knowledge of $X$. This term is called the *coefficient of determination*, and can be obtained by squaring $r$. Therefore,

$$r^2 \times 100 = \text{the percentage of the variance in } X \qquad \textbf{(12–10)}$$
$$\text{associated with variance in } Y.$$

Since a correlation coefficient is not expressed in the units of measurement from which it is obtained, as are the mean and standard deviation, we must exercise some caution in deciding on the meaning of a correlation coefficient. A coefficient of .60 does not indicate twice as great a relationship as does one of .30. However, if $r = .60$, $r^2 = .36$; this indicates that 36 per cent of the variance in $X$ and $Y$ are associated. If $r = .30$, $r^2 = .09$; only nine per cent of the variance in $X$ and $Y$ are associated. If we wished to predict values of $Y$ from knowledge of $X$, an $R$ of .60 is four times as useful as is a value of .30.

## Calculation of the
## Standard Error of Estimate

In Chapter 11, page 202, in our discussion of accuracy of prediction, we introduced the *standard error of estimate* of $Y$ from $X$ (also known as the standard error of prediction of $Y$ from $X$), which was defined as

(11–6)
$$s_{y \cdot x} = \sqrt{\frac{\Sigma Y - Y'}{N - 2}}$$

The calculation of $s_{y \cdot x}$ was not given in Chapter 11, since the computation from raw scores is laborious. Now that $r$ has been calculated, computing the standard error of estimate of $Y$ from $X$ can be done by formula 12–11

(12–11)
$$s_{y \cdot x} = s_y \sqrt{1 - r^2}$$

and the estimate of $X$ from $Y$ by formula 12–12

(12–12)
$$s_{x \cdot y} = s_x \sqrt{1 - r^2}$$

For example, if we compute the standard error of estimate of $Y$ from $X$ for the data on heights of husbands and wives, we have

$$s_{y \cdot x} = 8.474 \sqrt{1 - .8779^2}$$
$$= 8.474 \sqrt{.2293}$$
$$= 8.474(.4788)$$
$$= 4.06$$

which is a sufficient approximation to the value of 4.22 obtained in Chapter 11 through use of formula 11–6.

## REGRESSION ANALYSIS AND THE
## ANALYSIS OF VARIANCE

We have presented our discussion of regression and correlation with no more than passing reference to the discussion of analysis of variance in Chapter 8. However, there are some direct relationships between the analysis of variance and regression analysis that, if mastered, we believe will make the process of understanding much simpler. (This section should be skipped if Chapter 8 was not covered.)

In a simple analysis of variance we partition the total sum of squares into two parts: variation associated with differences between groups, and variation associated with differences within groups. The two sources of variance add up to the total sum of squares, $\Sigma x_b^2 + \Sigma x_w^2 = \Sigma_T^2$. In much the same manner we can break the sum of squares of the $Y$ variable, $\Sigma y^2$, into two parts: one part associated with the variation predicted by the $X$ variable, and the other part associated with variation not predicted by the $X$ variable. We can determine whether a significant amount of variation in $Y$ can in fact be predicted by $X$ by comparing these two sources of variance.

The comparison of the variance predicted by $X$ to that not predicted is similar to what is done when groups are compared on the variance between groups relative to the variance within groups. If all groups were randomly drawn from the same population, we would expect the variance between groups to be identical to the variance within groups and the result of our variance ratio should be close to 1.00. If there are real differences between our groups, the variance between groups will be quite large relative to the variance within groups. Exactly the same logic holds for our comparison of variance that can be predicted with the variance that cannot be predicted. If $Y$ cannot be predicted from $X$ at better than chance levels, the variance associated with changes in $X$ should be no different from variance not associated with $X$ and the ratio of these two variances should be close to 1.00. If it is possible to predict $Y$ from $X$, with considerable accuracy, there should be a significant component of variance associated with the prediction, or *regression*, of $Y$ on $X$ as compared to the variance not associated. To test this we calculate the total sum of squares for $Y$,

$$\Sigma y^2 = 933.50$$

(given on page 201 as part of the calculation for the regression analysis), calculate the sum of squares for the predicted $Y'$ as given above,

$$\Sigma Y'^2 - \frac{(\Sigma Y')^2}{N} = 402942.68 - 402223.26 = 719.42$$

and calculate the sum of squares for the variance not predicted by $X$, which is given by the differences between $Y$ and $Y'$.

$$\Sigma (Y - Y')^2 = 214.08$$

These two sources of variance sum to the total sum of squares for $Y$,

$$\Sigma y'^2 + \Sigma y_{res}^2 = \Sigma y^2$$
$$719.417 + 214.085 = 933.50$$

Just as in the analysis of variance, we can calculate a mean square by dividing the sums of squares by the appropriate degrees of freedom. The degrees of freedom for regression are equal to the number of variables $(v)$ minus one; in this example, $v - 1 = 1$. The degrees of freedom for the variance not associated with the predictor variable is equal to $N - (v)$, which is equal to $14 - 2 = 12$. It is now possible to compute the mean squares for the regression and for the *residual*, the variance not associated with the predictor variable.

$$MS_{Y'} = 719.42/1 = 719.42$$

$$MS_{(Y-Y')^2} = 214.08/12 = 17.84$$

The $F$ statistic can be calculated by dividing the residual mean square into the regression mean square. The resulting $F$ statistic can be evaluated from Table A–4 with 1 and 12 degrees of freedom,

$$719.42/17.84 = 40.326.$$

The value of the $F$ statistic at the .01 level for 1 and 12 degrees of freedom is 9.33, which indicates that there is clearly a significant component of variance in variable $Y$ associated with variance in variable $X$.

## THE $F$ STATISTIC IN MAKING INFERENCES ABOUT CORRELATION COEFFICIENTS

When we test the statistical significance of a correlation coefficient we are asking whether or not a significant amount of variation in the $Y$ variable can be accounted for by variation in the $X$ variable. If the amount of variation accounted for is not significantly different from zero, the correlation coefficient is judged to be zero. The logic is identical to that in our discussion of analysis of variance. We have a total sum of squares around a grand mean which can be divided into two sources of variance. The sum of squares for prediction is the sum of $Y$ that can be predicted by variance in $X$ and the residual is the sum that cannot be predicted.

The correlation coefficient enters into this prediction rather directly. We know already that the value of $r$ is the average covariance of how $X$ and $Y$ scores covary together. If the value of $r$ is squared, it can be interpreted directly as a proportion of variance in $Y$ associated with variance in $X$. In the example at the beginning of the chapter, $r$ is equal to .8779 and $r^2$ is equal to .7707, which indicates that .77 of the variance in $Y$ is associated with variance in $X$. Since $r^2$ is a direct indication of associated variance between the two measures, it can be used to evaluate the significance of the regression as follows:

$$F = \frac{r^2}{(1 - r^2)/(N - 2)} \qquad \text{(12-13)}$$

with degrees of freedom equal to 1 and $N - 2$.

If we solve (12–13) for the data of our first problem, the resulting $F$ is equal to

$$\frac{.7707}{.2293/12} = \frac{.7707}{.019} = 40.5632$$

The obtained $F$ is identical (within rounding error) to the value of $F$ obtained by our other calculations.

**Using the Value of $r$ to Calculate $b$.**   If we have calculated the correlation coefficient we can eliminate some of the computation involved in calculating regression coefficients. Since we know that $r$ increases as the accuracy of prediction increases, we can use $r$ to calculate the coefficient $b$. Remember that the formula for determining the ratio of change of $X$ to $Y$ in regression is given by

$$b = \frac{\Sigma XY - \dfrac{(\Sigma X)(\Sigma Y)}{N}}{\Sigma X^2 - \dfrac{(\Sigma X)^2}{N}} \qquad \text{(11-4)}$$

and is the ratio of the covariance to the sum of squares of $X$. Since $r$ is the average covariance (see formula 12–4, p. 212), its use in calculating the $b$ coefficient really simplifies matters. All that is needed to calculate the $b$ coefficient if we have $r$ are the standard deviations of $X$ and $Y$, as shown below.

(12–14)
$$b = r \left( \frac{s_y}{s_x} \right)$$

If we apply this formula to our example we have $.878 \left( \frac{8.474}{8.505} \right) = .875$, which is identical to the value obtained earlier.

## CORRELATION AND CAUSATION

It is necessary to emphasize that the existence of a correlation between two variables does not tell us anything about causation. The example we have used in this chapter — heights of couples — illustrates this point quite well; it would be difficult to claim that the husband's height is caused by the wife's height (or vice versa). Although there is clearly a high degree of association, this would not result in someone's concluding that "Sam is so short because his wife is only 157.5 centimeters in height;* if she had been 183 centimeters in height, he would really have been tall."

Another factor that makes it difficult to imply causation from the existence of a correlation is the fact that both of the variables might really be caused by changes in a third variable.

An educator has discovered that there is a correlation between the size of school children's feet and the quality of their handwriting. Are we to assume that the size of feet is a factor determining the quality of handwriting? Perhaps the increase in quality of handwriting causes the feet to grow longer. If this is true, to obtain children with larger feet we should give them practice aimed at improving the quality of their handwriting. Obviously, neither of these alternatives is the correct one. Both size of feet and quality of handwriting are related to a third variable, age of the child; older children have larger feet and a higher quality of handwriting than do younger children.

Similarly, it has been pointed out that there is a relationship between teachers' salaries and the amount of beer consumed in the United States. Can we conclude from this that teachers are, therefore, consuming more beer as their incomes increase? Or perhaps we should conclude that as beer consumption increases those controlling teachers' salaries relax their control and raise salaries in their beery

---

*5 feet, 2 inches. One inch = 2.54 centimeters.

condition? It seems that the most likely possibility is that the change in both variables is related to the economic condition of the country. As the economic conditions improve, both teachers' salaries and beer consumption increase.

## Factors Affecting the Size of Correlation Coefficients

There are several factors that affect the size of correlation coefficients. One is linearity of regression. If the regression is not linear, the Pearson $r$ will underestimate the degree of relationship.

Another factor that will lead to an underestimation of the degree of relationship is the presence of variable errors of measurement. This reduction in $r$ as a result of variable errors of measurement is called *attenuation*. We can correct for attenuation to estimate the true degree of the relationship between two variables. However, $r$'s corrected for attenuation cannot be used in prediction equations, because prediction is based on fallible rather than on true scores.

The magnitude of a correlation coefficient also varies as a function of the degree of heterogeneity of the sample with respect to the variables being correlated. Assume that we are correlating IQ and grades. If all of the students have an IQ of 100, then the range of IQ scores is zero. Since $r$ is an estimate of the proportional change in one variable in relation to the proportional change in another variable, $r$ under these conditions will be an indeterminate value near zero. As the range of scores becomes greater, the obtained correlation will become higher, other things being equal. There are methods used to correct for spread of talent and for attenuation. The student is referred to a more advanced text* for presentation of these methods.

A highly spurious correlation coefficient might be obtained as a function of the manner in which cases are selected. If, for some reason, we eliminate cases near the mean, $r$ will increase since we have eliminated cases from the middle of the distribution where the dispersion is likely to be the greatest. If any relationship exists between the two variables it should be most apparent at the extremes.

Figure 12–3 illustrates why the correlation of a composite group made up of subgroups with unequal means is misleading. In Figure 12–3 $A$ groups with unequal means on both $X$ and $Y$ are combined.

---

*McNemar, Q.: *Psychological Statistics*, 4th edition. New York, Wiley, 1969; Winer, B. J.: *Statistical Principles in Experimental Design*, 2nd edition. New York, McGraw-Hill, 1971; Lindquist, E. F.: *Design and Analysis of Experiments in Psychology and Education*. Boston, Houghton Mifflin, 1963; Walker, H. M., and Lev, J.: *Statistical Inference*. New York, Holt, 1953.

Within each group there is no relationship between $X$ and $Y$ ($r = 0$). However, the composite correlation is positive and fairly high. In Figure 12–3 *B* we see the effect of combining three groups whose means differ on $X$ and $Y$. Within each group the $r$ is highly negative while in the composite it is zero. In Figure 12–3 *C* the $r$ within each group is positive while in the composite it is negative. Therefore, extreme caution must be exercised when combining groups for the purpose of determining the degree of relationship if the means of the individual samples tend to be quite different.

**Statistical vs. Practical Significance.** We can, of course, interpret the meaning of $r$ solely in terms of statistical significance. But we must remember not to confuse statistical significance with practical significance. For example, we see from examination of Table A–9 that with 1000 degrees of freedom an $r$ of .062 is significant at the 5 per cent level of confidence. However, $r^2 = .0036$, which means that we are accounting for only 0.36 per cent of the variance in $Y$ from knowledge of $X$. Predictions of $Y$ from $X$ will be very poor. These

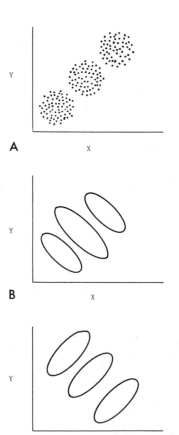

A

B

C

*Figure 12–3.* *A, B*, and *C*. See text for explanation.

predictions of $Y$ will, of course, be better than would be expected without using $X$, but the gain will be very small.

The same point is true when we test the significance of differences between means. A difference between means might be highly significant statistically if the $N$ is large enough, but might not mean anything *practically*. Only the researcher's judgment can be used to decide whether statistically significant results have any practical meaning.

One other way to interpret an $r$ is in terms of the use for which it is intended. Often, correlation coefficients are calculated to determine either the reliability or the validity of a measuring instrument, such as a test. The next two sections will discuss the use of $r$ to estimate reliability and validity.

*Reliability of Measurement.* The problem of reliability of measurement is one of the most important that a scientist must face. A measurement is said to be reliable if it is dependable, in the sense that you obtain the same reading each time you measure the same thing on different occasions. For example, a reliable ruler would be one that does not change from reading to reading, while an unreliable ruler would be one made of rubber, which must be stretched to make the reading. If you do not stretch it the same amount on repeated measurements of the same thing, you will not obtain the same reading.

What sort of factors lower the reliability of a measuring instrument? One factor would be presence of errors in the instrument or test itself, such as intermittent mechanical defects in a piece of apparatus or mistakes in printing on some copies of a printed test. Another factor would be any physiological variations in the individual that occur from testing to testing; for example, on one testing the individual may be rested and not hungry while on the second testing he may be tired and very hungry. Another factor lowering reliability would be the presence of errors caused by extraneous physical disturbances present during the testing; perhaps on one testing the room is quiet and of normal temperature while on the second testing there is a great deal of noise and it is quite warm. Yet another factor lowering reliability would be errors in reading the instrument or in scoring the test. Each of these factors would make it difficult to obtain the same reading on successive measurements of the same thing, and would be said to lower the reliability of the measurement. If we want to use a measuring instrument for some purpose, it at least must be reliable.

The correlation coefficient between any two measurements of the same thing is called a reliability coefficient. It is easy to determine the reliability of such things as measurements of length and time:

measure the same objects twice and calculate the correlation coefficient between the two sets of readings. Many times, however, repetition of the measurement is not feasible, since the measurement cannot be made without changing the object of the measurement. An example of this is a learning task in which the second reading would not be the same as the first because the individual remembers some of the items from the first reading. In such cases we could construct comparable alternate forms of the test, and then correlate the performance on these two forms. This involves a considerable amount of effort and would probably underestimate the true reliability, since the two separate testings would still be influenced by the factors that produce day to day variation, such as physiological variations in the subjects and extraneous physical distractions.

*Split-Half Reliability.* The other solution to this problem is to estimate what is called the split-half reliability. This method requires us to compare the results of one half of the test with the results of the second half of the test. If the test does not vary systematically in difficulty we can compare the first half of the test directly with the second half. If the test is one that gets progressively more difficult we can compare alternate items, thereby obtaining a score for even numbered items and another score for the odd-numbered items. The estimate of reliability based on two halves of the same test is found using what is known as the Spearman-Brown prophecy formula:

**(12–15)**
$$R = \frac{2r}{1 + r},$$

where $R$ = the correlation between two comparable test forms, and
$r$ = the correlation between two half-tests.

This formula compensates for the fact that the correlation between two half-tests will be lower than the correlation between two complete tests. The use of this formula will probably lead to an overestimation of the reliability because chance day-to-day errors will be correlated. However, this method will provide a closer estimation of the true reliability than will the use of the uncorrected $r$ based on two half-tests.

A detailed discussion of reliability theory will be found in Ghiselli's book.*

*Validity.* A valid measurement is one that measures whatever it is supposed to measure. If we are using a ruler to measure length in centimeters it is important that the centimeter scale be accurate. If the basic scale units are inaccurate, we can obtain highly reliable

---

*Ghiselli, E.: *Theory of Psychological Measurement.* New York, McGraw-Hill, 1964.

measurements, but they will not be valid since the centimeters as indicated on the scale do not correspond to the agreed upon length for a centimeter.

When we report a correlation coefficient between some predictor and the measure that is to be predicted, we call that correlation a validity coefficient. Assume that we wish to know whether or not the IQ of mothers is a valid predictor of the IQ of their first born children. To decide this we might measure the IQ of the mother using a standard test and also measure the IQ of the first born children using another standard test. We could then correlate the IQ score of each mother with the IQ score of the first born child. This validity coefficient would then be used to decide whether or not a mother's IQ is a valid predictor of a first born child's IQ.

If we are in a situation in which we wish to use, for example, a measure of a person's aptitude (say, clerical aptitude) to predict his success on a job, two problems arise. The first problem involves the selection of a measure of performance that relates to the ultimate job performance. The second problem involves the selection of a criterion that is an indicator of on-the-job performance. Since the solution to these problems depends on the specific situation and on the ingenuity of the investigator, there is little more that can be said here.

Validity depends directly on reliability. If a test is not reliable, it *cannot* be valid. We must have stable indicators of the values under consideration in order to make measurements that have meaning as predictors. However, a test can be highly reliable and still not be valid. An example of this would be a clock that runs at the wrong speed. It might be highly reliable since the same results would be obtained on successive readings, but the readings would not be valid, since they would not conform to the standards agreed upon for seconds, minutes, and hours.

### Spearman's Rank Order Correlation

One special correlational method will be presented because of its usefulness in a wide variety of situations. This method, Spearman's rank order (or rank difference) correlation (rho), is used with data that are in the form of ranks. If all we have is the rank order of data and do not know the value of the actual measurements, we can use this technique. With a small number of cases rho can be determined quickly and provides a fast and accurate estimate of $r$.

To use this method the data must be in the form of ranks. The formula is as follows:

$$\text{rho} = 1 - \frac{6 \sum d^2}{N(N^2 - 1)},$$

(12–16)

where $N$ = number of paired ranks, and

$d$ = difference between pairs of ranks.

Let us compute rho for a sample of ten pairs of observations. Table 12–2 lists the scores and their corresponding ranks as well as the difference scores and their squares. The lowest score has been assigned the rank of one. Again, it is important to square each difference score and then sum the squared difference scores. The rho, which is calculated in Table 12–2, is +.77.

The rank difference correlation has a larger standard error than does $r$. Therefore, it is not as powerful a test as is $r$. To determine whether or not a rho of .77 based on an $N$ of ten could have arisen by chance when the true population correlation is zero, we will use Table A–10. This table is entered using $N$ and *not* the degrees of freedom. We see that with an $N$ of ten a rho of .65 is significant at the .05 level of significance. Since our rho of .77 exceeds the tabled value, we assume that a correlation this large did not occur by chance from a population whose true correlation is zero. Therefore, we will conclude that there is a relationship between the two variables. Since

**Table 12–2.**

| Subject | $X$ | $Y$ | $X$ Rank | $Y$ Rank | $d$ | $d^2$ |
|---------|-----|-----|----------|----------|------|-------|
| A | 12 | 11 | 1 | 1 | .0 | .00 |
| B | 13 | 13 | 2 | 2.5 | −.5 | .25 |
| C | 14 | 13 | 4 | 2.5 | 1.5 | 2.25 |
| D | 14 | 16 | 4 | 9 | −5.0 | 25.00 |
| E | 14 | 14 | 4 | 4.5 | −.5 | .25 |
| F | 15 | 15 | 7 | 7 | .0 | .00 |
| G | 15 | 14 | 7 | 4.5 | 2.5 | 6.25 |
| H | 15 | 15 | 7 | 7 | .0 | .00 |
| I | 16 | 15 | 9 | 7 | 2.0 | 4.00 |
| J | 17 | 18 | 10 | 10 | .0 | .00 |
| | | | | | $\Sigma$ | 38.00 |

$$\text{rho} = 1 - \frac{6 \sum d^2}{N(N^2 - 1)}$$

$$= 1 - \frac{6(38)}{10(99)}$$

$$= 1 - \frac{228}{990}$$

$$= 1 - .23$$

$$\text{rho} = .77$$

the table is a two-tailed table, we accept the hypothesis that the population correlation is not zero.

It is important to remember that the rank difference correlation can *only* be calculated after the scores have been transformed to ranks. It cannot be used with the raw scores themselves.

In the last two chapters the basic methods used to express the degree of relationship have been presented. Many other coefficients of correlation have been developed for use with special kinds of measurement scales. For example, it is possible to estimate the correlation between two variables when one is a continuous variate and the other can take only two values. It is also possible to estimate the correlation between two variables when both variables can take only two values. Earlier it was indicated that the degree of correlation can be determined between two variables that are related curvilinearly. In addition, methods exist that allow us to hold constant a third variable that might affect the size of the correlation between two variables. It is possible to determine the correlation of several variables with one variable. The basic logic underlying this variety of techniques all stems from that of the Pearson $r$. These techniques, which are among the most elegant and sophisticated in statistics, are the topics of advanced courses in statistics. A brief account of some of these methods will be presented in Chapter 13.

1. Calculate a Pearson $r$ from the following data:

$$N = 54,$$
$$\sum z_X z_Y = 19.71.$$

2. Is the obtained correlation significant at the .05 level of significance?

3a. Calculate the Pearson $r$ for the following two measures of social adjustment:

$$\sum X = 183 \qquad \sum Y = 144$$
$$\sum X^2 = 1119 \qquad \sum Y^2 = 962$$
$$(\sum X)^2 = 33489 \qquad (\sum Y)^2 = 2073$$
$$\sum XY = 864.97 \qquad N = 35$$

3b. Calculate the standard error of estimate of $Y$ from $X$.

4. Is the obtained $r$ significant at the .01 level? What would you conclude about the relationship between these two measures?

5. Transform the following set of data to ranks and calculate a Spearman rank-difference correlation:

| Case | $X$ Score | $Y$ Score |
|------|---------|---------|
| 1 | 16 | 14 |
| 2 | 14 | 17 |
| 3 | 13 | 11 |
| 4 | 10 | 5 |
| 5 | 8 | 8 |
| 6 | 7 | 15 |
| 7 | 5 | 6 |
| 8 | 4 | 9 |
| 9 | 2 | 2 |
| 10 | 1 | 3 |

6. Determine the significance of the obtained Spearman rank-difference correlation.

7. Calculate the Pearson $r$ on the following data:

$$\sum X = 60 \qquad \sum Y = 40$$
$$\sum X^2 = 494 \qquad \sum Y^2 = 212$$
$$(\sum X)^2 = 3600 \qquad (\sum Y)^2 = 1600$$
$$\sum XY = 288 \qquad N = 10$$

8. Determine the significance of the correlation for the data of problem 7.

9. A psychologist, dissatisfied with all existing measures of work aptitude, decided to develop another test which would measure work aptitude for precision tasks more effectively than any existing measures. In order for him to evaluate his new test it was necessary (1) to give the test twice over a two-month interval to determine reliability, (2) to compare his test scores with actual ratings of job performance on precision tasks. On a small sample, he obtained the following data:

| Individual | Score on First Administration | Score on Second Administration | Score on Work Sample |
|---|---|---|---|
| A | 104 | 104 | 104 |
| B | 98 | 100 | 98 |
| C | 130 | 127 | 133 |
| D | 76 | 85 | 85 |
| E | 109 | 119 | 111 |
| F | 110 | 111 | 111 |
| G | 68 | 63 | 64 |
| H | 149 | 145 | 143 |
| I | 100 | 105 | 100 |
| J | 103 | 100 | 102 |
| K | 96 | 96 | 93 |
| L | 85 | 86 | 87 |
| M | 121 | 118 | 118 |
| N | 118 | 115 | 118 |
| O | 86 | 85 | 80 |

Calculate the reliability coefficient for these data and determine the significance.

10. Determine the validity coefficient between the scores on the first administration and the scores on the work sample and determine its significance.

11. On the basis of these data he concluded that his test was both reliable and valid and decided to publish his test. Do you think that his decision was justified? Why?

## CHAPTER THIRTEEN

# MULTIVARIATE STATISTICAL ANALYSIS

What is a chapter on multivariate statistical analysis doing in an elementary statistics book? Since multivariate analysis, as a topic of study, would normally follow after an *intermediate* level statistics course, what possible purpose can there be in even mentioning such things? After all, a lot of people are sufficiently traumatized by their first statistics course to avoid the topic forever after, unless required to encounter it once again while pursuing a particular field of study. Why present a preview of one of the more difficult statistical methods to understand?

We include this chapter because we firmly believe that multivariate methods will dominate statistical analysis in the behavioral sciences in years to come. The methods and techniques that were developed to study one variable at a time almost always introduce artificiality into the study of human behavior. The research worker who uses single variable methods either assumes that the ignoring of other variables has no effect on the results of his experiment or is aware that the phenomenon is being studied under artificial conditions—a situation that he must tolerate since he knows of no other way to attack the problem.

Multivariate methods allow the researcher not only to consider multiple measures when studying a particular problem, but to study how these variables change in relation to each other as well. This provides a more complete and realistic picture of the phenomenon under study. The additional information gained represents an immense increase in the power of the methods used to understand a problem. Since we are seldom interested in just one aspect of a problem, multivariate methods allow us to study phenomena under conditions more nearly approaching their natural complexity.

Multivariate analysis, as we define it here, refers to any situation in which more than one variable at a time is studied under controlled conditions. We have already examined one multivariate method in our discussion of the analysis of variance with more than one variable (see Chapter 8, pp. 151–157).

Such praise for multivariate methods in relation to single variable methods may produce considerable irritation on the part of someone who has just completed the material in this book. All this effort to learn an outmoded set of procedures? Perhaps, yet it would have been pointless to instruct anyone about the techniques used to study multiple variables before the procedures of dealing with one variable at a time were understood. The material covered in this text is useful, but it does have its limitations. Furthermore, it provides the fundamental background essential for an understanding of multivariate analysis, since multivariate techniques are logical extensions of the techniques used to study single variables.

This chapter, then, is a preview of approaches that you may learn in the future. At least, you should know about the existence of multivariate methods.

This chapter differs considerably from the other chapters in this book. There are no examples to work out, no calculations to do, and no exercises to complete. This is an attempt to show you how a research worker using multivariate analysis approaches certain types of problems.

The lack of examples and problem calculations is a necessity, given the nature of multivariate analysis. Just as certain types of single variable problems are laborious to calculate without the assistance of a desk calculator, multivariate problems are difficult, if not impossible, without a large digital computer. Multivariate techniques do not exist, in a practical sense, unless a large digital computer is available. The time needed to carry out calculations is prohibitive under any other circumstances.

We must emphasize the fact that you will find these methods to be more difficult than much of the preceding material. However, any understanding that is gained will be repaid with a heightened appreciation of the conceptual complexity that we can attain using these statistical procedures. Use of these methods makes it unnecessary to distort reality and artificially to isolate variables from meaningful contexts in order to study them scientifically.

A total of four multivariate methods will be discussed: two-group discriminant function analysis; multiple group discriminant function analysis; stepwise multiple regression analysis; and multivariate analysis of variance.

These methods will be presented through the discussion of

examples we have encountered in research settings. Since a computer is necessary to carry out these methods, we will, in the course of our discussion, present some printed results generated by a computer, discuss the elements, and interpret some of the material shown. Hopefully, this will facilitate your acquaintance with the accomplishments of these methods.

## Preparing Data for a Digital Computer

Before we proceed with the statistical example, a few words about how such analyses are prepared may be helpful. The observations are punched on cards such as the one below, usually referred to as IBM cards. Almost all computing machinery uses this type of card, which was developed by International Business Machines, and used by all the different types of computers.

For the computing system used by the authors (a Control Data Corporation CDC 6400 computer at the University of California, Berkeley) a computer run would be prepared as follows:

This set of numbers is interpreted below:

J6782,—the account number to which the cost of the computing will be charged;

, ,—if a magnetic tape were to be used in the computations to follow, the number "1" would have been punched between the commas. Since no tape is needed, this space is left blank;

100,—this is an estimate of the time needed to do the calculations.

The units of time are specialized for the computer and will not be dealt with here, other than to comment that 100 is equal to about one

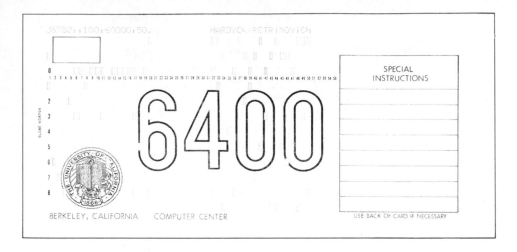

minute. In other words, you are estimating that your computing will take less than one minute of computer time (the actual time needed to do the calculations was 3.74 seconds);

60000,—this is an estimate of the amount of memory needed in the computer to carry out the computing;

50,—this is an estimate of the number of pages to be printed. Note that a period follows this number, which indicates that no more information is contained on this card other than the name of the person requesting the computing.

## Two-Group Discriminant Function Analysis

To illustrate how multivariate techniques work, we will examine a problem, first as it would be studied by univariate methods, and then by the more appropriate multivariate technique. Suppose that a manufacturing firm has been accused of discriminatory practices in the hiring of women. The claim is made that women are paid less than men for the same work, even when women employees are better educated and have worked more years for the company.

The firm denies this and agrees that an analysis should be made of one of their departments as a test case. The variables that are to be examined are:

1. Number of years employed by the company.
2. Number of years of education.
3. Months of appropriate professional experience prior to being employed by the current company.
4. Job classification.
5. Pay.

6. Percentage of midpoint pay (This refers to the salary ranges for a given job classification. For example, a job classified at level 5 might have a salary range from $1000 to $2500 per month. The midpoint of this range is $1750. The percent of midpoint pay is an individual's salary in relation to this midpoint. An individual earning $1000 would be earning 57 per cent of the midpoint pay. An individual at the same job level earning $2000 per month is earning 114 per cent of midpoint pay.)

In our problem, the department of the manufacturing firm has 73 employees, 24 women and 49 men. Six of the women employees (25 per cent) have college degrees and 41 of the men (84 per cent) have college degrees. There are 18 women (75 per cent) with no college degree and 8 men (16 per cent) with no college degree. The ratios of men and women with degrees are clearly quite different, but such a difference between ratios is not sufficient to argue that the firm discriminates against women.

A univariate analysis of this problem could be done by dividing employees into men and women and calculating a $t$-statistic (Chapter 7) for each of the above variables to see if the groups differ. This would be a total of six $t$-tests, which must then be interpreted to provide an overall answer. Rather than take this approach, a computer is used to perform a two-group discriminant function analysis. In this analysis, the two groups, men and women, are identified, and a procedure is carried out that produces the optimal linear combination of measures that will predict group membership.

The process of predicting group membership is conceptually similar to the procedure carried out in the ordinary prediction equations discussed in Chapter 11, pp. 198 to 201. In the prediction example discussed in Chapter 11, the problem is solved for one variable with a straight line equation of the form $Y' = a + bX$ (see pp. 198 to 201 for examples). This allows us to predict an individual's $Y$ score from his score on the $X$ variable. In a discriminant function analysis, the task is to predict into which of two groups an individual should be classified. A discriminant function analysis can be done with as few as two variables or with an extremely large number—the computing routine determines the maximum amount of variation that can be associated with differences between the defined groups and develops the prediction equations that will predict this difference.

In our example—the problem of sex discrimination in employment—we assume the statistical hypothesis that it is impossible to predict sex on the basis of such measures as professional experience, years employed, or pay. In other words, if there are no systematic differences on the measure, classification into groups by means of the discriminant function technique should be no better than we would obtain by tossing a coin and deciding on the basis of heads or tails whether a person is female or male.

The computer routine used to carry out these particular calculations (such routines are called computer programs) was developed by the Health Sciences Computing Facility at the University of California, Los Angeles and is one of a series known collectively as BMD, standing for Biological-Medical computing routines. The program that will be used for the discriminant function is known as BMD 04M — Discriminant Function analysis.

The instruction card for the discriminant function routine (usually known as the control card or cards) is reproduced on p. 239. In this analysis, we will compare the men and women who do not have college degrees on the six measures listed earlier.

The results of the calculations produced by the computer are reproduced on the following pages. Initially, the program computes the arithmetic means for the defined groups on each variable and lists the difference between means. The numbers listed under "Mean 1, Women:" are the means for women on the six variables listed earlier (see page 236). The six letter code preceding each variable is an identifying code:

1. YRSEMP = number of years employed by the company
2. YRSED = number of years of education
3. MOPROX = months of professional experience prior to current employment
4. JOBCL = job classification
5. PAY = pay
6. PMDPAY = percentage of midpoint pay

The next items of interest are the "discriminant function coefficients," which are listed in order for each of the six variables. These coefficients are the values used in predicting group membership and are an extension of the type of linear prediction discussed in Chapter 11. When only one variable is used to predict $Y$ from $X$, we use the equation $Y' = a + bX$. Similarly, the discriminant function coefficients predict group membership from multiple measures. For any given individual, the prediction is made by multiplying the coefficients times the score on each of the six variables. The actual equation would be of the following form:

$$.01595YRSEMP + .13681YRSED + .00040MOPROX$$

$$+ .03771JOBCL + -.0061PAY$$

$$+ -.01408PMDPAY = \text{prediction of group membership.}$$

```
PROBLM22 6 18  8      DISCRIMINANT FUNCTION INSTRUCTIONS                    1
```

After solving this equation, the computing routine then makes a probability judgment of group membership based on the relationship of the predicted score to the means of the two groups and assigns membership accordingly.*

The statistic computed for this type of analysis is known as the Mahalanobis $D^2$ and is a measure of the distance between the two groups over all variables when the measurement units are equalized. The Mahalanobis $D^2$ is evaluated by means of an $F$ statistic (see Chapter 8). The $F$ statistic is used to evaluate the significance of the amount of variance associated with differences between groups. For this example, the tabled value of the $F$ statistic at the .001 level is 6.18. Since our calculated value is 6.58, we conclude that there is a significant amount of variance in the measures used and that this variance can predict group membership—in this example, sex.

An even more striking indication of the differences is shown in the columns headed "Rank of Women" and "Rank of Men." In our example, the first 18 ranks are composed entirely of the women employees. In other words, the ability to predict sex from the measures used is perfect—no member of any group is misclassified.

To appreciate this, consider what would happen if the groups were classified on the basis of chance. Since there are eight men and 18 women in this sample, the probability of selecting a woman for group 1 by chance is equal to 18 divided by 26, which equals .6923077. The probability that all 18 women would be placed in group 1 by chance is equal to .6923077[18] or .00133.

---

*This may provide some illumination as to why multivariate analysis is done only with computers. Apart from the matrix calculations (several thousand multiplications) necessary to obtain the coefficients, calculating the final prediction equations as given above requires six multiplications and additions for each individual—all done to 12 decimal place accuracy (even though only five places are printed out).

```
BMDO4M - DISCRIMINANT ANALYSIS-TWO GROUPS - VERSION OF MAY  26, 1964
HEALTH SCIENCES COMPUTING FACILITY, UCLA

PROBLEM NO.  03
NUMBER OF VARIABLES   6

VARIABLE MEANS BY GROUP AND DIFFERENCE IN MEANS
      VARIABLE      MEAN 1            MEAN 2          DIFFERENCE
YRSCOMP   1          5.61111          5.87500          -.26389
YRSED     2         13.05556         12.25000           .80556
MOPROX    3         93.16667        167.25000         -74.08333
JOBCL     4          6.27778          7.37500          -1.09722
PAY       5       1036.38889       1310.00000        -273.61111
%MDPAY    6         81.12778         93.50000         -12.37222

SUM OF PRODUCTS OF DEV. FROM MEANS
      655.15278        -20.36111       1739.41667        137.31944      17072.72222        243.39444
      -20.36111         12.44444        508.33333         -2.02778        434.61111         30.97222
     1739.41667        508.33333     264364.00000       3648.41667     505859.83333       7658.31667
      137.31944         -2.02778       3648.41667        187.48611      18201.05556         34.26111
    17072.72222        434.61111     505859.83333      18201.05556    2057628.27778      17352.30556
      243.39444         30.97222       7658.31667        -34.26111      17352.30556       1016.75611

INVERSE OF SUM OF PRODUCTS OF DEV. FROM MEANS
       .00258           .00526           .00005           .00307          -.00006          -.00025
       .00526           .10480          -.00007           .01955          -.00021          -.00094
       .00005          -.00007           .00001           .00035          -.00001           .00000
       .00307           .01955           .00035           .11514          -.00125           .01344
      -.00006          -.00021          -.00001          -.00125           .00001          -.00014
      -.00025          -.00094           .00000           .01344          -.00014           .00303

DISCRIMINANT FUNCTION COEFFICIENTS
       .01595           .13691           .00040           .03771          -.00061          -.01408

MAHALANOBIS DSQUARE=          9.00911

F( 6,  19)=          5.58358

POP. NO.     SAMPLE SIZE       MEAN Z            VARIANCE Z        STD. DEV. Z
    1             18            .37729             .01797            .13404
    2              8            .00191             .00999            .09995

            FIRST GROUP      SECOND GROUP     FIRST GROUP    SECOND GROUP
RANK          VALUES           VALUES          ITEM NO.       ITEM NO.
   1           .74807                              14
   2           .54311                               3
   3           .54246                               2
   4           .45936                               4
   5           .42982                              18
   6           .41915                              16
   7           .40070                              11
   8           .39358                              13
   9           .33604                              10
  10           .32707                              17
  11           .32578                               1
  12           .31428                               7
```

```
  13           .29077                              12
  14           .28157                               9
  15           .27868                              15
  16           .24921                               6
  17           .23152                               8
  18           .20281                               5
  19                            .13846                               3
  20                            .06530                               2
  21                            .04555                               7
  22                            .04317                               5
  23                            .02291                               4
  24                           -.03157                               8
  25                           -.08438                               6
  26                           -.15423                               1
```

*Figure 13-1.* Computer output for two-group discriminant function analysis.

What can we conclude from this analysis? We have shown that it is possible to predict perfectly group membership on the basis of the measures used. In relation to this, examination of the means for each of the measures shows that the women have worked longer for the company, have slightly more education, have much less professional experience, are paid less, have lower job classifications, and earn a lower percentage of midpoint pay. Unless a substantial argument can be made that the months of professional experience (the only variable on which men have the higher value) justify the other differences, we would conclude that there is a good deal of evidence for discriminatory hiring practices against women.

If we now wish to check our results on a second sample of employees, we could select another department within the company, take the same six measures that were used in the first study, and apply the equations to all individuals under conditions in which we do not know which are men and which are women. If we are still able to separate the sexes on a second sample, we would conclude that the hiring practices of the entire company are characterized by sexual discrimination.

## Discriminant Function Analysis of Multiple Groups

The two-group discriminant function analysis just discussed can be generalized to allow classification of multiple groups. As an example, let us use some data from a study of problem solving ability in children growing up in three different environmental settings and attempt to predict the environmental settings in which the children live. In our example, a total of nine measures of problem solving ability were taken on 271 children: 91 children living in an isolated farm area where they do not see other children (other than siblings) until they begin school; 91 living in a small village; and 89 children living in a medium sized city.

An analysis of variance of the three groups indicates that there is a significant amount of variance associated with differences in environmental setting as compared to differences present within the various groups. However, we would like to know more than the fact that significant differences are present for all the tests given (note that this requires nine separate univariate analyses of variance, one for each measure). We would like to know if there is some combination of measures that will allow us to predict membership in the three groups.

To calculate this, we again use a BMD computing routine—for this problem the routine known as BMD 05M—Discriminant Analysis for Multiple Groups.

The computing instructions will not be shown here, since the process is quite similar to that shown for the two-group example. The groups are identified and the computing routine again calculates the optimal combination of measures to identify group membership. The first part of the computer print (known as computer output) again lists the means for each group on each measure. The statistic is again a version of Mahalanobis $D^2$, which is referred to in the output as the "generalized Mahalanobis $D^2$." The value of $D^2 = 105.80835$, and can be interpreted with reference to a table of chi-square. For 18 degrees of freedom, the tabled value of chi-square at the .001 level is equal to 42.31. There is clearly a significant amount of variance in the measures and it is associated with differences between environmental groups, since our obtained value of 105.80835 far exceeds the tabled value of 42.31.

The coefficients for the nine measures for each group are then printed. The process of solving the equation is similar to that described for the two-group example and will not be repeated. The next section, entitled "Evaluation of Classification Function for Each Case," indicates how each person is classified. The prediction equations are solved for each person and the probability of that person being a member of group 1, 2, or 3 is calculated. The person is then assigned to the group on the basis of this probability. For the first subject (case #1), the largest probability is .55848 for group 1 and he

```
BMD05M - DISCRIMINANT ANALYSIS-SEVERAL GROUPS - VERSION OF MAY 27, 1964
HEALTH SCIENCES COMPUTING FACILITY, UCLA

PROBLEM NO.    AG
NUMBER OF VARIABLES    9
```

| GROUP | 1 | 2 | 3 | TOTAL |
|---|---|---|---|---|
| SAMPLE | 91 | 91 | 89 | 271 |
| MEAN SCORES | | | | |
| 1  CLSINC | 2.51848 | 2.82413 | 3.40449 | |
| 2  YULCLS | 2.48352 | 2.73626 | 2.94342 | |
| 3  YULREL | 2.19780 | 2.28571 | 2.73034 | |
| 4  CONVOL | 2.28571 | 2.81319 | 3.08989 | |
| 5  CINTVL | 2.42857 | 2.74725 | 2.86517 | |
| 6  COCCVL | 2.39560 | 2.57143 | 2.59551 | |
| 7  PERSPC | 3.38462 | 3.47253 | 3.24719 | |
| 8  VEREGO | 2.47253 | 2.84615 | 3.14607 | |
| 9  ROLTAK | 2.73626 | 2.86813 | 3.28090 | |

```
THE VALUE  105.80835 CAN BE USED AS CHI-SQUARE WITH 18
DEGREES OF FREEDOM TO TEST THE HYPOTHESIS THAT THE MEAN
VALUES ARE THE SAME IN ALL THE   3 GROUPS FOR THESE  9
VARIABLES.
```

| FUNCTION | 1 | 2 | 3 |
|---|---|---|---|

**Figure 13–2.**  Computer output for discriminant function analysis of multiple groups.

*Figure 13–2 continued on opposite page.*

is accordingly classified as a member of group 1—children from the isolated farm area. The classifications and probabilities are shown only for the first 20 subjects, since there is little purpose here in printing out the full table for all 271 children. The "classification matrix" at the end provides us with a summary of the overall accuracy of group membership classification. For this example, the number of subjects in each group is sufficiently close to make unnecessary the computing of probabilities of assignment by chance. A chance level of classification would be 33 per cent. Examining the frequencies for group 1, we find that 49 out of 91 persons were accurately classified, a gain of 21 per cent over chance. For group 2, the accuracy is poor; only 35 out of 91, or 6 per cent over chance. For group 3, the accuracy is best of all; 60 out of 89, or 35 per cent improvement over chance. We can conclude that while our ability to predict membership is far from the phenomenal result found for our first example, in which

COEFFICIENT

| | 1 | 2 | 3 |
|---|---|---|---|
| 1 | 2.61755 | 2.86509 | 3.50126 |
| 2 | 2.03249 | 2.26058 | 2.20874 |
| 3 | 1.30570 | 1.07587 | 1.60553 |
| 4 | -1.77915 | -1.96419 | -1.57442 |
| 5 | 1.80202 | 1.97195 | 2.32432 |
| 6 | 4.35221 | 4.38790 | 4.21359 |
| 7 | 5.83221 | 5.91744 | 5.83331 |
| 8 | 1.15194 | 1.48195 | 1.72069 |
| 9 | 3.47033 | 3.55463 | 4.09992 |

| CONSTANT | -28.55371 | -31.99963 | -35.59365 |
|---|---|---|---|

EVALUATION OF CLASSIFICATION FUNCTIONS FOR EACH CASE

| FUNCTION | 1 | 2 | 3 | LARGEST PROBABILITY | FN.NO.FOR LARGEST PROBABILITY |
|---|---|---|---|---|---|
| GROUP 1 | | | | | |
| CASE | | | | | |
| 1 | .55848 | .37706 | .06446 | .55848 | 1 |
| 2 | .10677 | .17686 | .71436 | .71436 | 3 |
| 3 | .44463 | .50060 | .05536 | .50060 | 2 |
| 4 | .45611 | .40104 | .14286 | .45611 | 1 |
| 5 | .43759 | .23447 | .32794 | .43759 | 1 |
| 6 | .29950 | .45745 | .24305 | .45745 | 2 |
| 7 | .52400 | .36725 | .10875 | .52400 | 1 |
| 8 | .73625 | .21085 | .05290 | .73625 | 1 |
| 9 | .24733 | .38772 | .36245 | .38772 | 2 |
| 10 | .28943 | .46954 | .24604 | .46954 | 2 |
| 11 | .23242 | .46551 | .30107 | .46551 | 2 |
| 12 | .73459 | .22572 | .03965 | .73459 | 1 |
| 13 | .82846 | .16484 | .00670 | .82846 | 1 |
| 14 | .21623 | .21926 | .56450 | .56450 | 3 |
| 15 | .57447 | .35163 | .07390 | .57447 | 1 |
| 16 | .34570 | .34605 | .30816 | .34605 | 2 |
| 17 | .27975 | .31702 | .40323 | .40323 | 3 |
| 18 | .59493 | .35347 | .05161 | .59493 | 1 |
| 19 | .43410 | .31140 | .25450 | .43410 | 1 |
| 20 | .33381 | .35939 | .30680 | .35939 | 2 |

CLASSIFICATION MATRIX

| FUNCTION | 1 | 2 | 3 | TOTAL |
|---|---|---|---|---|
| GROUP | | | | |
| 1 | 49 | 23 | 19 | 91 |
| 2 | 26 | 35 | 30 | 91 |
| 3 | 13 | 16 | 60 | 89 |

*Figure 13-2 continued.*

prediction was perfect, our ability to identify environment groups on the basis of the tests used is a great improvement over chance alone.

The accuracy of the predictions obtained here is not as phenomenal as the predictions in the two-group problem. However, the analysis serves to sharpen our focus in continuing research on problems such as this. From this analysis, we have learned that there are characteristics of the measures used that help to identify differences between groups. We can now continue research and attempt to determine what specific characteristics of the measures used are most effective in detecting differences between the groups. In doing this, we hope to understand the characteristics that differentiate the groups and to determine the implications of these findings for theories of children's learning, problem solving ability, and thinking. The multiple discriminant function analysis was useful in that it enabled us to determine those variables that were most important in discriminating between the groups. Clearly there would be no point in simply identifying the groups, since we already knew which children belonged in which group. However, use of the discriminant function techniques allowed us to find exactly which measures are most effective in determining differences between the groups, thus providing direction for future studies.

## Stepwise Multiple Regression

In Chapters 11 and 12, the concepts of regression and correlation were discussed at some length, and the relationship of regression to the analysis of variance was presented in the final section of Chapter 12.

To appreciate the relationship of correlation and analysis of variance, it is useful to think of a correlation as an index of the amount of variance in one variable associated with variance in another variable. To the extent that two sets of variance are associated, one set can then be predicted from the other. In the analysis of variance, the total variance present in a set of measurements is separated into two components, variance within groups and variance between groups (review Chapter 8, if necessary). In multiple correlation and regression—the use of several measures to predict another measure—the variance present in a set of scores (which we will call variable $Y$) can be broken into several components: variance that can be predicted from several other measures such as $A$, $B$, $C$, and $X$; and variance that cannot be predicted from any combination of these other measures. The ratio of variance that can be predicted to variance that cannot be predicted is analogous to the ratio of variance between groups to the variance within groups in the analysis of variance. Since the variance that can be predicted relative to the variance that cannot be predicted is analogous to the situation found in analysis of variance, this ratio can be tested with the $F$ statistic just as the ratio of variance between groups to within groups is tested in the analysis of variance for independent groups.

To illustrate, we will begin with a univariate example. In the prediction example in Chapter 11, we predicted the height of wives from the height of their husbands by means of the equation $Y' = a + bX$, where $X$ is the height of the husband, $Y'$ is the predicted height of the wife, and $a$ and $b$ are constants that determine a reference point and the rate at which $X$ changes relative to $Y$, respectively. We also commented that the correlation coefficient $r$ was best interpreted by squaring it to obtain $r^2$, which can be interpreted as the proportion of variance in $Y$ associated with variance in $X$. It is also possible to calculate an $F$ statistic to determine whether or not the amount of variance in $Y$ predicted by variance in $X$ is statistically significant. If the correlation between $X$ and $Y$ is known, the calculation of the $F$ statistic is quite simple, being given by

$$\frac{r^2}{(1 - r^2)/(N - 2)},$$

as was shown at the end of Chapter 12.

If we substitute the values from the example in Chapter 12, where the correlation between the heights of couples is equal to .8779 for 14 couples, we obtain the following:

$$F = \frac{.8779^2}{(1 - .8779^2)/(14 - 2)} = \frac{.7707}{.2293/12} = \frac{.7707}{.019} = 40.5632.$$

The tabled value of the $F$ statistic for 1 and 11 $df$ at the .01 level is 9.65. Therefore, we can conclude that a significant amount of variance in $Y$ is predicted by corresponding variance in $X$.

When we use stepwise regression analysis, we are doing exactly the same thing, except that we now use several variables to predict a single $Y$ variable. Just as we use the $F$ statistic to evaluate whether or not a single variable produces a significant effect, we use the $F$ statistic to evaluate the degree of improvement in prediction as we add each of several variables to the prediction equation.

The logic of the method with a single variable and that with multiple variables is exactly the same. However, the computational complexity changes drastically. Computing a prediction equation for one predictor variable is a moderately easy task; computing the prediction equations with multiple predictor variables (as we have seen in the equation shown for the discriminant function analysis) is practically impossible without a computer.

To illustrate the use of stepwise multiple regression methods, we will use the data of the last example, in which there were nine measures of problem solving ability. In addition to these nine measures, we developed a new measure of verbal problem solving ability and administered it to the 134 children on whom we obtained the other nine measures. In developing a new test, there is always the possibility that you have found only another way to measure something already measured completely by your existing tests. Therefore, we would like to know to what extent the new verbal skills measure overlaps with the other tests of problem solving ability. One way to do this is to attempt to predict the scores on the new measure by combinations of the other tests. If we can perfectly predict the scores on the new test from some combination of the previous tests, then we would conclude that the new test does not measure anything not already measured by the existing tests. We again use one of the BMD computing routines, BMD 02R.

The means and standard deviations for all variables are printed at the beginning of the computer output. The six letter codes preceding each variable are, as before, identifying descriptions. The variable to be predicted is the last one, PRNOUN. The next step is the calculation of the correlation coefficients among all the variables.

*Text continued on page 253.*

```
BMD02R - STEPWISE REGRESSION
HEALTH SCIENCES COMP. FAC., UCLA VERSION 4/13/65
FSU - CAL VERSION 8/18/71
(IF ALTERNATE INPUT TAPE IS USED, SPECIFY TAPE3 ON
BOTH THE COC REQUEST CARD AND THE BMD PROBLM CARD.)

PROBLEM CODE                        HUNPRN
NUMBER OF CASES                        134
NUMBER OF ORIGINAL VARIABLES            10
NUMBER OF VARIABLES ADDED               -0
TOTAL NUMBER OF VARIABLES               10
NUMBER OF SUB-PROBLEMS                    1
```

| VARIABLE | | MEAN | STANDARD DEVIATION |
|---|---|---|---|
| CLSINC | 1 | 3.00000 | .91766 |
| MULCLS | 2 | 2.81343 | .79631 |
| MULREL | 3 | 2.39552 | 1.02612 |
| CONVOL | 4 | 2.78358 | 1.11963 |
| CINTVL | 5 | 2.82090 | 1.06093 |
| CECCVL | 6 | 2.58209 | .64071 |
| PERSPC | 7 | 3.41791 | .76874 |
| VEREGO | 8 | 2.85821 | .89403 |
| ROLTAK | 9 | 2.82836 | .81827 |
| PRNOUN | 10 | 2.54478 | .92269 |

*Figure 13–3.* Computer output for stepwise multiple regression.

CORRELATION MATRIX

| VARIABLE NUMBER | 1 | 2 | 3 | 4 | 5 | 6 | 7 | 8 | 9 | 10 |
|---|---|---|---|---|---|---|---|---|---|---|
| 1 | 1.000 | | | | | | | | | |
| 2 | .247 | 1.000 | | | | | | | | |
| 3 | .256 | .404 | 1.000 | | | | | | | |
| 4 | .351 | .384 | .350 | 1.000 | | | | | | |
| 5 | .154 | .227 | .342 | .568 | 1.000 | | | | | |
| 6 | .205 | .259 | .253 | .347 | .398 | 1.000 | | | | |
| 7 | -.021 | -.019 | -.011 | -.027 | -.073 | .052 | 1.000 | | | |
| 8 | .119 | .026 | .012 | .172 | .044 | .132 | .262 | 1.000 | | |
| 9 | .110 | .089 | .010 | .156 | -.062 | -.023 | .079 | .265 | 1.000 | |
| 10 | .249 | .017 | -.007 | -.173 | -.030 | .045 | .122 | .477 | .155 | 1.000 |

SUB-PROBLEM 1

| | |
|---|---|
| DEPENDENT VARIABLE | 10 |
| MAXIMUM NUMBER OF STEPS | 20 |
| F-LEVEL FOR INCLUSION | .010000 |
| F-LEVEL FOR DELETION | .005000 |
| TOLERANCE LEVEL | .001000 |

STEP NUMBER 1
VARIABLE ENTERED 8

MULTIPLE R .4772
STD. ERROR OF EST. .8139

ANALYSIS OF VARIANCE

| | DF | SUM OF SQUARES | MEAN SQUARE | F RATIO |
|---|---|---|---|---|
| REGRESSION | 1 | 25.780 | 25.780 | 38.913 |
| RESIDUAL | 132 | 87.451 | .663 | |

VARIABLES IN EQUATION

| VARIABLE | | COEFFICIENT | STD. ERROR | F TO REMOVE |
|---|---|---|---|---|
| (CONSTANT | ) | 1.13724 | | |
| VEREGO | 8 | .49245 | .07894 | 38.9132 |

VARIABLES NOT IN EQUATION

| VARIABLE | | PARTIAL CORR. | TOLERANCE | F TO ENTER |
|---|---|---|---|---|
| CLSINC | 1 | .21980 | .9858 | 6.6502 |
| MULCLS | 2 | .00478 | .9993 | .0030 |
| MULREL | 3 | -.01463 | .9998 | .0281 |
| CONVOL | 4 | .10531 | .9704 | 1.4692 |
| CINTVL | 5 | -.05845 | .9940 | .4491 |
| COCCVL | 6 | -.02112 | .9826 | .0585 |
| PERSPC | 7 | -.00371 | .9314 | .0018 |
| ROLTAK | 9 | .03354 | .9300 | .1476 |

*Figure 13–3 continued on following page.*

STEP NUMBER 2
VARIABLE ENTERED 1

MULTIPLE R .5143
STD. ERROR OF EST. .7971

ANALYSIS OF VARIANCE

| | DF | SUM OF SQUARES | MEAN SQUARE | F RATIO |
|---|---|---|---|---|
| REGRESSION | 2 | 30.005 | 15.003 | 23.615 |
| RESIDUAL | 131 | 83.226 | .635 | |

VARIABLES IN EQUATION

| VARIABLE | COEFFICIENT | STD. ERROR | F TO REMOVE |
|---|---|---|---|
| (CONSTANT | .61876 ) | | |
| CLSINC 1 | .19562 | .07586 | 6.6502 |
| VEREGO 8 | .46853 | .07784 | 36.2109 |

VARIABLES NOT IN EQUATION

| VARIABLE | | PARTIAL CORR. | TOLERANCE* | F TO ENTER |
|---|---|---|---|---|
| MULCLS | 2 | -.05205 | .9390 | .3532 |
| MULREL | 3 | -.07515 | .9344 | .7384 |
| CONVOL | 4 | -.03375 | .8595 | .1482 |
| CINTVL | 5 | -.09488 | .9755 | 1.1810 |
| COCCVL | 6 | -.06612 | .9464 | .5708 |
| PERSPC | 7 | .00856 | .9286 | .0095 |
| ROLTAK | 9 | .01594 | .9237 | .0330 |

STEP NUMBER 3
VARIABLE ENTERED 5

MULTIPLE R .5212
STD. ERROR OF EST. .7965

ANALYSIS OF VARIANCE

| | DF | SUM OF SQUARES | MEAN SQUARE | F RATIO |
|---|---|---|---|---|
| REGRESSION | 3 | 30.755 | 10.252 | 16.158 |
| RESIDUAL | 130 | 82.477 | .634 | |

*Figure 13–3 continued on opposite page.*

| VARIABLES IN EQUATION | | | | | VARIABLES NOT IN EQUATION | | | |
| VARIABLE | COEFFICIENT | STD. ERROR | F TO REMOVE | | VARIABLE | PARTIAL CORR. | TOLERANCE | F TO ENTER |
|---|---|---|---|---|---|---|---|---|
| (CONSTANT) | .77683 | | | | MULCLS 2 | -.03413 | .9024 | .1504 |
| CLSINC 1 | .20815 | .07668 | 7.3694 | | MUREL 3 | -.04773 | .8404 | .2945 |
| CINTVL 5 | -.07163 | .06591 | 1.1810 | | CONVOL 4 | .10491 | .5920 | 1.4355 |
| VEREGO 8 | .47077 | .07783 | 36.5826 | | COCCVL 6 | -.03280 | .8110 | .1389 |
| | | | | | PERSPC 7 | -.00087 | .9225 | .0001 |
| | | | | | ROLTAK 9 | .00747 | .9163 | .0072 |

STEP NUMBER 4
VARIABLE ENTERED 4

MULTIPLE R .5289
STD. ERROR OF EST. .7952

ANALYSIS OF VARIANCE

| | DF | SUM OF SQUARES | MEAN SQUARE | F RATIO |
|---|---|---|---|---|
| REGRESSION | 4 | 31.662 | 7.916 | 12.518 |
| RESIDUAL | 129 | 81.569 | .632 | |

| VARIABLES IN EQUATION | | | | | VARIABLES NOT IN EQUATION | | | |
| VARIABLE | COEFFICIENT | STD. ERROR | F TO REMOVE | | VARIABLE | PARTIAL CORR. | TOLERANCE | F TO ENTER |
|---|---|---|---|---|---|---|---|---|
| (CONSTANT) | .78990 | | | | MULCLS 2 | -.06555 | .8353 | .5523 |
| CLSINC 1 | .17816 | .08054 | 4.8937 | | MUREL 3 | -.06425 | .8221 | .5305 |
| CONVOL 4 | .09590 | .08004 | 1.4355 | | COCCVL 6 | -.05040 | .7905 | .3259 |
| CINTVL 5 | -.12462 | .07929 | 2.4706 | | PERSPC 7 | -.00487 | .9198 | .0030 |
| VEREGO 8 | .45653 | .07860 | 33.7420 | | ROLTAK 9 | -.01112 | .8882 | .0158 |

*Figure 13-3 continued on following page.*

STEP NUMBER 5
VARIABLE ENTERED 2

MULTIPLE R             .5317
STD. ERROR OF EST.     .7966

ANALYSIS OF VARIANCE

|  | DF | SUM OF SQUARES | MEAN SQUARE | F RATIO |
|---|---|---|---|---|
| REGRESSION | 5 | 32.013 | 6.403 | 10.090 |
| RESIDUAL | 128 | 81.219 | .635 | |

VARIABLES IN EQUATION

| VARIABLE | COEFFICIENT | STD. ERROR | F TO REMOVE |
|---|---|---|---|
| (CONSTANT | .92321 ) | | |
| CISTHC 1 | -.18623 | .08160 | 5.2336 |
| MULCLS 2 | -.07053 | .09490 | .5523 |
| CONVOL 4 | .11277 | .08333 | 1.8314 |
| CINTVL 5 | -.12369 | .07943 | 2.4245 |
| VEPEGO 8 | .45354 | .07894 | 33.0892 |

VARIABLES NOT IN EQUATION

| VARIABLE | PARTIAL CORR. | TOLERANCE | F TO ENTER |
|---|---|---|---|
| MULREL 3 | -.04694 | .7491 | .2804 |
| COCCVL 6 | -.04267 | .7783 | .2317 |
| PERSEC 7 | -.00574 | .9196 | .0042 |
| ROLTAK 9 | -.00842 | .8867 | .0090 |

STEP NUMBER 6
VARIABLE ENTERED 3

MULTIPLE R             .5332
STD. ERROR OF EST.     .7988

ANALYSIS OF VARIANCE

|  | DF | SUM OF SQUARES | MEAN SQUARE | F RATIO |
|---|---|---|---|---|
| REGRESSION | 6 | 32.192 | 5.365 | 8.408 |
| RESIDUAL | 127 | 81.040 | .638 | |

VARIABLES IN EQUATION

| VARIABLE | COEFFICIENT | STD. ERROR | F TO REMOVE |
|---|---|---|---|

VARIABLES NOT IN EQUATION

| VARIABLE | PARTIAL CORR. | TOLERANCE | F TO ENTER |
|---|---|---|---|

*Figure 13–3 continued on opposite page.*

```
(CONSTANT)           .92272
CLSINC 1      .19208    .08238    5.4367         COCCVL 6    -.04026    .7760    .2045
MULCLS 2     -.05479    .09970     .3020         PERSPC 7    -.00464    .9191    .0027
MULREL 3     -.04130    .07799     .2804         ROLTAK 9    -.00961    .8851    .0116
CONVOL 4      .11566    .08375    1.9073
CINTVL 5     -.11517    .08127    2.0084
VEREGO 8      .45198    .07912   32.6320


STEP NUMBER       7
VARIABLE ENTERED  6

MULTIPLE R          .5343
STD. ERROR OF EST.  .8013

ANALYSIS OF VARIANCE
                 DF    SUM OF SQUARES   MEAN SQUARE   F RATIO
REGRESSION        7        32.323          4.618       7.191
RESIDUAL        126        80.903           .642

            VARIABLES IN EQUATION                              VARIABLES NOT IN EQUATION

VARIABLE  COEFFICIENT  STD. ERROR  F TO REMOVE      VARIABLE  PARTIAL CORR.  TOLERANCE  F TO ENTER
(CONSTANT)  1.00417                                 PERSPC 7    -.00231      .9160       .0007
CLSINC 1     .19459     .08282      5.5200          ROLTAK 9    -.01300      .8801       .0211
MULCLS 2    -.05010     .10055       .2482
MULREL 3    -.02946     .07855       .2529
CONVOL 4     .12016     .08460      2.0175
CINTVL 5    -.10638     .08381      1.6113
COCCVL 6    -.05568     .12311       .2045
VEREGO 8     .45537     .07973     32.6247
```

*Figure 13–3 continued on following page.*

```
STEP NUMBER    8
VARIABLE ENTERED    9

MULTIPLE R            .5344
STD. ERROR OF EST.   .8045

ANALYSIS OF VARIANCE
                DF      SUM OF SQUARES    MEAN SQUARE    F RATIO
REGRESSION       8         32.337           4.042        6.246
RESIDUAL       125         80.895            .647
```

| VARIABLES IN EQUATION | | | | VARIABLES NOT IN EQUATION | | | |
|---|---|---|---|---|---|---|---|
| VARIABLE | COEFFICIENT | STD. ERROR | F TO REMOVE | VARIABLE | PARTIAL CORR. | TOLERANCE | F TO ENTER |
| (CONSTANT | 1.03302 ) | | | | | | |
| CLSINC 1 | .19507 | .08321 | 5.4955 | PERSPEC 7 | -.00226 | .9160 | .0006 |
| MULCLS 2 | -.04929 | .10110 | .2576 | | | | |
| MULREL 3 | -.03964 | .07868 | .2538 | | | | |
| CRMVL 4 | .12226 | .08615 | 2.0140 | | | | |
| CINTVL 5 | -.10815 | .08501 | 1.6186 | | | | |
| CHOCVL 6 | -.05717 | .12402 | .2125 | | | | |
| VERPGO 8 | .45823 | .08249 | 30.8612 | | | | |
| RDLTAK 9 | -.01320 | .09087 | .0211 | | | | |

F-LEVEL INSUFFICIENT FOR FURTHER COMPUTATION

FINISH CARD ENCOUNTERED
PROGRAM TERMINATED

*Figure 13-3* continued.

Once these are calculated, the solution of the prediction equation can begin.

In examining the correlation matrix, we can see that the highest correlation with variable 10 is variable 8. The computing routine selects this as the first predictor variable. The "multiple R" is actually only the correlation between variables 8 and 10 at this first step and the value of .262 is identical to the univariate $r$ between variables 8 and 10.

The significance of this relationship can be tested by the $F$ statistic as shown in the next two lines of print. The $F$ statistic of 38.913 is clearly significant since it exceeds the tabled $F$ value of 6.81 for 1 and 132 degrees of freedom by a considerable margin. This means that a significant amount of variance in variable 10 can be predicted from variance in variable 8.

The columns on the right list the variables not included in the equation. The column headed "Partial Correlations" is of particular interest here. If you examine the original intercorrelation matrix, you can see that the variable having the next to the highest correlation with variable 10 (after variable 8) is variable 1, with an $r$ of .249. If we now look at the column for variable 8, which is already in the prediction equation, we see that variables 1 and 8 intercorrelate only .119, which is less than they correlate with variable 10. However, variables 1 and 8 do have some variance in common, as indicated by the $r$ of .119. The value of .21980 in the "Partial Correlations" column is the correlation of variable 1 with variable 10, minus the effects of the correlation between variables 1 and 8. The net effect is to reduce the correlation of 1 with 10 from .249 to .21980. The other partial correlations in the column are interpreted in the same manner. The general rule is that the more the two measures have the same variance in common, the more they will be reduced in size by the subtraction process. For example, variable 9 (which correlated .265 with variable 8 and .155 with variable 10) has been reduced to .03354 by the subtraction of the variance that variable 8 and 9 have in common.

In step two of the analysis, the computing routine selects variable 1, since it has the next highest correlation (.2198) with number 10 after the subtraction of common variance is completed. The effect on the multiple $R$ is to raise it from .4772 to .5148 and the amount of variance predicted (given by $R^2$) from .23 to .26. The $F$ statistic is again calculated and found to be 23.615, which is significant. This means that a statistically significant amount of variance over that already accounted for has been predicted by the addition of variable 1 to the prediction equation.

The computing routine continues in this manner, entering new variables and testing to determine whether or not a significant amount of variance is accounted for by the addition of each new variable in turn.

Note, however, that the multiple $R$ increases very slowly after the first few variables have been entered. The correlation between the first variable (8) and variable 10 was .4772; with the next variable entered (1) it rose to .5148; and with the third variable, .5212. By the time the last of 8 variables was entered into the equation, the multiple $R$ was only .5344. There is relatively little gain, then, with the addition of each variable after the first one. If economy were a factor here it would probably not pay to continue using any variable other than the first one to predict the value of variable 10.

The process of entering new variables is continued until the results of the $F$ statistic computation indicate that no significant contribution is made by the addition of more variables. The final multiple $R$ of .5344 and $R^2$ of .2856 indicate that only .286 of the variance in variable 10 can be predicted from the combination of the 8 variables entered into the equation. If we are satisfied that our tests are reliable, then we are safe in concluding that variable 10 is a measure of abilities not predicted by our other nine tests.

## Multivariate Analysis of Variance

Analysis of variance has already been dealt with at some length in Chapter 8 and, as we mentioned at the beginning of this chapter, the examples illustrate one way to deal with relationships among more than one variable. In the multivariate analysis of variance, it is possible to study multiple measures as well as to consider the extent to which the various measures are interrelated.

To illustrate a multivariate analysis of variance, we will examine two comparisons using the same set of data used earlier to demonstrate discriminant function analysis of multiple groups. The variables are measures of problem solving ability and of social cognitive skills. The tests were given to children aged 7, 8, and 9 in three different environmental settings: isolated farms, a small village, and a medium-sized town. The design can be graphically represented as follows:

|  | AGE | | |
|---|---|---|---|
|  | 7 | 8 | 9 |
| *Isolated farm* |  |  |  |
| LOCATION   *Small village* |  |  |  |
| *Medium-sized town* |  |  |  |

We are interested in knowing whether there are significant differences associated with environmental settings and with age. In the univariate model, we could carry out ten separate analyses of variance (one for each measure) and assess the significance of each measure separately—a cumbersome procedure, both in terms of the labor required and in the process of trying to interpret all the separate analyses.

The computer program used to carry out these computations is known as MULTIVARIANCE.* For illustrative purposes, we will consider two of the possible comparisons for the location and age problem. The first hypothesis tested is that there are statistically significant differences associated with different environmental settings on the 10 measures administered.

The computer output for MULTIVARIANCE indicates that the multivariate $F$ is equal to 5.6885 for environmental setting, a value that is significant at lesss than the .0001 level. We conclude that there is a significant difference among the groups. Basically the multivariate $F$ statistic is obtained from a set of linear prediction equations, similar to those encountered in discriminant function analysis and stepwise multiple regressions. These equations maximize the amount of variance associated with differences in location.

The columns below the multivariate $F$ value list, from left to right, the names of the variables and the calculations for each measure independently. The column headed "HYPOTHESIS MEAN SQUARE:" contains the estimates of the variance associated with between group differences on a particular measure. The first value in the "UNIVARIATE F" column is the $F$ statistic we would obtain if we carried out a univariate analysis of variance on variable 1, CLSINC. The next column indicates the probability, or statistical significance, of the univariate $F$.

The next column, "STEP DOWN F" is a more complex measure. This is a measure of the significance of the $F$ statistic when all variance from the preceding measure has been removed. As an illustration, suppose that two measures that had a correlation of .90 were given to groups of subjects. If a statistically significant difference were found between groups for the first measure, there would probably also be a statistically significant difference on the second measure since the two are so highly related. For the "STEP DOWN F" the first value in the column is identical to the value in the "UNIVARIATE F" column. However, the next value down in the column decreases in size from the univariate value of 7.5977 to a step down value of

---

*Additional information about MULTIVARIANCE can be obtained from National Educational Resources, Inc., 215 Kenwood Avenue, Ann Arbor, Michigan, 48103. However, their manual assumes a knowledge of multivariate analysis.

1,0,  LOCATION ONE, ALL AGES VS LO 2 AND 3 ALL AGES      LO1AAG
2,0,  LOCATION TWO ALL AGES VS LOCATION 1 AND 3 ALL AGES   LO2AAG

F-RATIO FOR MULTIVARIATE TEST OF EQUALITY OF MEAN VECTORS= 5.6885

D.F.= 20. AND 232.0000   P LESS THAN .0001

| VARIABLE | HYPOTHESIS MEAN SQ | UNIVARIATE F | P LESS THAN | STEP DOWN F | P LESS THAN |
|---|---|---|---|---|---|
| 1 CLSINC | 2.0631 | 2.8332 | .0627 | 2.8332 | .0627 |
| 2 MULCLS | 4.2346 | 7.5977 | .0008 | 6.0892 | .0031 |
| 3 NULREL | 9.6143 | 11.7194 | .0001 | 6.1415 | .0029 |
| 4 CONVOL | 5.4502 | 5.5900 | .0044 | 1.2301 | .2959 |
| 5 CINTVL | 14.7957 | 16.7042 | .0001 | 10.1666 | .0001 |
| 6 COCCVL | 2.1073 | 5.4822 | .0053 | .3429 | .7247 |
| 7 PERSPC | 1.9682 | 3.5114 | .0329 | 3.3343 | .0390 |
| 8 VEREGO | 4.6463 | 7.2815 | .0011 | 5.3415 | .0061 |
| 9 ROLTAK | 5.8714 | 10.8250 | .0001 | 8.2089 | .0005 |
| 10 PRNOUN | 6.6479 | 11.0490 | .0001 | 6.8547 | .0016 |

DEGREES OF FREEDOM FOR HYPOTHESIS= 2
DEGREES OF FREEDOM FOR ERROR= 125.

*Figure 13-4.* Computer output for multivariate analysis of variance.

*Figure 13-4 continued on opposite page.*

```
0,1,   AGE 1 VS AGES 2 AND 3 ALL LCCATIONS      AG1-23
0,2,   AGES 2 VS AGES 1 AND 3 ALL LCCATIONS     AG2-13

      F-RATIO FOR MULTIVARIATE TEST OF EQUALITY OF MEAN VECTORS=  4.6628

             D.F.=  20.  AND   232.0000    P LESS THAN  .0001
```

| VARIABLE | HYPOTHESIS MEAN SQ | UNIVARIATE F | P LESS THAN | STEP DOWN F | P LESS THAN |
|----------|--------------------|--------------|-------------|-------------|-------------|
| 1 CLSINC | 7.5083 | 10.3109 | .0001 | 10.3109 | .0001 |
| 2 MULCLS | 2.6988 | 4.9421 | .0095 | 3.3322 | .0390 |
| 3 MULREL | 6.6913 | 6.1564 | .0005 | 4.3022 | .0157 |
| 4 CONVOL | 14.7673 | 15.4169 | .0001 | 7.7794 | .0007 |
| 5 CINTVL | 4.2154 | 4.7591 | .0102 | .4371 | .6473 |
| 6 COCCVL | .4423 | 1.1506 | .3198 | 1.0244 | .3604 |
| 7 PERSPC | .3779 | .6741 | .5115 | .5070 | .6037 |
| 8 VEREGO | 5.3472 | 8.8501 | .0003 | 4.8580 | .0094 |
| 9 ROLTAK | 4.0944 | 7.5488 | .0009 | 2.5128 | .0855 |
| 10 PRNOUN | 10.0507 | 16.7047 | .0001 | 7.8352 | .0007 |

```
DEGREES OF FREEDOM FOR HYPOTHESIS= 2
DEGREES OF FREEDOM FOR ERROR=  125
ERROR TERM IS ON PAGE
```

*Figure 13–4*  continued.

6.0892. This decrease is due to the removal of variation that measure 1 and measure 2 have in common. Thus, we learn not only that measure 2 is statistically significant, but that what it measures is essentially independent of measure 1. The results for measure 4 are quite different. Here, the univariate $F$ of 5.6900 is significant at the .004 level. The stepwise $F$ value shrinks to 1.2301 and the probability of .2959 fails to reach acceptable significance levels. The reason for this shrinkage is that the variance accounted for by measure 4 is largely accounted for by the first three measures. Thus, we learn not only which of our separate measures are making significant contributions to the measured differences between groups, but we also learn the extent of the independence of the contributions they make to those measurements.

If we now look at a second part of the analysis, we can examine the extent of the differences associated with ages 7, 8, and 9. For this comparison, the multivariate $F$ is 4.6428, again significant at the .0001 level. The univariate $F$ values for each measure indicate that all but measures 6 and 7 are also significant. However, when we examine the step down $F$ values, we find that measures 5, 6, and 7 do not reach an acceptable level of significance under the step down tests. We can conclude that, although the differences attributable to differences in age are significant, they are not very powerful, nor are they as effective over as many measures as are the differences attributable to differences in environmental setting.

In our opinion the multivariate analysis of variance is an extraordinarily powerful tool, since multiple conditions can be studied using multiple measurements in a way in which the individual effects and interactions of conditions and measurements can be assessed directly. We know of no other measures that give the research worker in the behavioral sciences such a wide variety of flexible procedures to apply to the complex situations with which such scientists must contend.

## EPILOGUE

The material presented in this chapter on multivariate analysis has been more difficult reading than the rest of this book. Although this is unfortunate, it is unavoidable since multivariate techniques represent a step forward in the techniques available to study natural phenomena. In our opinion, multivariate analysis methods will predominate in the future and will result in drastic changes in the manner in which research workers think about problems and how they design their research. These methods make it possible to ask specific and precise questions of considerable complexity in natural settings. This makes it possible to conduct theoretically significant research and to evaluate the effects of naturally occurring parametric variations in the context in which they normally occur. In this way, the natural correlations among the manifold influences on behavior can be preserved and the separate effects of these influences can be studied statistically without causing atypical isolation of either individuals or variables.

Note that we mentioned *theoretically* significant research. Statistical techniques are useful only for answering questions that the research worker wants to ask; if he is confused, no statistical technique will help. One danger of multivariate techniques is the tendency of the research worker to hope that they will provide answers when he has no clear idea of the question he wishes to ask. There is all too often a tendency to hope, in vain, that the computer will solve the confusions and ambiguities that are present and somehow make sense out of the relationship of many variables. Multivariate analysis will not help clear up confusion about multiple variables any more than single variable statistics will clear up confusion about a single variable. When dealing with more powerful statistical methods, it is important that the reasoning behind the calculations be just as powerful as the statistical method. Statistical calculations are no substitute for sound thinking.

# CHAPTER FOURTEEN

# SOME APPLICATIONS TO EXPERIMENTAL PSYCHOLOGY

This chapter contains a series of experiments similar to those that most students will encounter in an experimental psychology laboratory course. Usually, the beginning experimental psychology course is the first stage at which the psychology student must apply statistical methods to experimental data. Frequently, the transition from the study of statistics to the application of statistical methods to an experimental problem is a difficult one for the student to accomplish. The material in this chapter is intended to provide the student with "real data" on which he may practice and to illustrate the types of problems to which the various statistical procedures can be applied.

We will illustrate six statistical techniques used to test for the significance of differences between two or more groups and two methods to determine correlation. These techniques are presented in the following order:

1. The $t$-test for independent groups (Chapter 7).
2. The $t$-test for correlated groups (repeated measures) (Chapter 7).
3. The one-way Analysis of Variance (Chapter 8).
4. The Chi-square ($\chi^2$) test (Chapter 9).
5. The Mann-Whitney $U$ test (Chapter 10).
6. The Kruskal-Wallis analysis of variance of ranks (Chapter 10).
7. The Pearson coefficient of correlation (Chapter 12).
8. The Spearman rank difference correlation (Chapter 12).

Each method is complete within its section; thus, the order in which the methods are considered is completely arbitrary.

*1. A Reaction-Time Experiment: The $t$-Test for Independent Groups (Chapter 7).* An experimenter wished to test what is called a "response compatibility hypothesis" using reaction time as his outcome measure.

He used a two choice reaction time apparatus with two stimulus lights 12 inches apart. A response key was located beneath each stimulus light. Figure 14–1 is an illustration of the type of apparatus used.

The experimenter's hypothesis is that reaction time will be longer if the response is not compatible with the stimulus. A compatible response is defined as one in which the response key to be pressed is located beneath the stimulus light that is illuminated. An incompatible response is defined as one in which the key to be pressed is located beneath the stimulus light that is not illuminated. Each subject was seated at the apparatus and neither light was illuminated. Each subject was instructed to keep his left forefinger on the left key and his right forefinger on the right key. Those subjects assigned to the compatible condition were instructed to press the left key as quickly as possible when the left stimulus was illuminated and to press the right key as quickly as possible when the right stimulus was illuminated.

A total of 25 subjects were available for this experiment and were randomly assigned to either the compatible or incompatible response groups. Thirteen subjects were assigned to the compatible group and 12 were assigned to the incompatible group. Each subject was given 20 trials. The stimulus light was presented on the left for one-half of the trials and on the right for the other half in a random order. When the stimulus light was illuminated, a timer registering thousandths of a second was started. When the subject pressed the key this stopped the timer. Each subject's score for each trial was recorded in thousandths of a second and the average for each subject over his 20 trials was taken as that subject's "score."

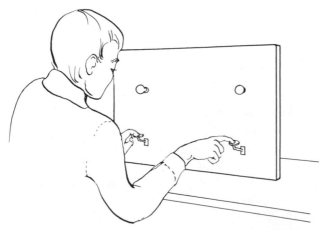

*Figure 14–1.* Two choice reaction-time apparatus.

The statistical hypothesis to be tested is that the compatible and incompatible response groups are drawn from a population with common mean reaction time. In terms of the experimental treatment, the statistical hypothesis would be that "compatibility" or "incompatibility" of a response as defined in the experiment has no effect on the subjects' reaction time. The alternative statistical hypothesis is that they are drawn from different populations in terms of mean reaction time. The statistic used to test these hypotheses is the $t$-test for independent groups.

The subject's scores and the computations for the $t$-test are given in Table 14–1.

The value of the $t$ statistic, as shown in Table 14–1, is 9.30. Examination of Table A–3 reveals that, for 23 degrees of freedom, a $t$ value of 2.069 is required to reach the .05 level of significance and a $t$ value of 2.807 is required to reach the .01 level of significance. The obtained $t$ of 9.30 exceeds both of the tabled values. Therefore, the experimenter rejects at the .01 level of significance the hypothesis of "no difference." He accepts the alternative hypothesis that the two means are drawn from different populations. Also, since the mean response time of the "incompatible" group is much higher, he considers his "response compatibility hypothesis" to be supported by the data.

**2. The Muller-Lyer Illusion: The $t$-Test for Correlated Means (Chapter 7).** One of the standard illusions used in the study of perceptual processes is the Muller-Lyer illusion illustrated in Figure 14–2.

Line segment $A$ is equal to line segment $B$. Perceptually, however, $A$ appears to be shorter than $B$. It is possible to study the effects of many variables on the magnitude of this illusion. One variable that has been studied is the magnitude of the illusion when a variable arrow "$Y$" is adjusted beginning on some trials from the segment "$B$" as compared to beginning on other trials from the segment "$A$." The following experiment was performed to determine whether the direction from which the variable is adjusted has any effect on the magnitude of the illusion when the subject is instructed to adjust $Y$ until the two line segments look equal. Fifteen subjects performed the equality adjustment 16 times; on eight of the trials the variable was moved from the $A$ region and on eight of the trials the variable was moved from the $B$ region.

Each subject sat five feet from the apparatus and was instructed to adjust the arrow until Segment $A$ was equal to Segment $B$. Figure 14–3 illustrates the nature of the experimental situation. By pulling one of the strings on either side, the arrow can be moved in either direction. $Y$ was started in segment $A$ half of the time and in segment

**Table 14–1.** REACTION TIMES IN THOUSANDTHS OF A SECOND FOR SUBJECTS MAKING COMPATIBLE AND INCOMPATIBLE RESPONSES (EACH SCORE IS THE AVERAGE OF 20 RESPONSES)

| A | | | | B | | | |
|---|---|---|---|---|---|---|---|
| Subject # | | Compatible Response Group | | Subject # | | Incompatible Response Group | |
| 2 | 4 | 230 | 207 | 1 | 3 | 320 | 315 |
| 6 | 9 | 196 | 217 | 5 | 7 | 289 | 335 |
| 11 | 12 | 235 | 265 | 8 | 10 | 317 | 309 |
| 13 | 14 | 209 | 195 | 16 | 18 | 365 | 297 |
| 15 | 17 | 240 | 222 | 20 | 21 | 305 | 319 |
| 19 | 23 | 211 | 201 | 22 | 24 | 291 | 281 |
| 25 | | 250 | | | | | |

$$\Sigma X_A = 2878 \qquad\qquad \Sigma X_B = 3743$$
$$\Sigma X_A^2 = 642{,}716 \qquad\qquad \Sigma X_B^2 = 1{,}173{,}203$$
$$(\Sigma X_A)^2 = 8{,}282{,}884 \qquad\qquad (\Sigma X_B)^2 = 14{,}010{,}049$$

$$\Sigma x_A^2 = \Sigma X_A^2 - \frac{(\Sigma X_A)^2}{N_A} \qquad\qquad \Sigma x_B^2 = \Sigma X_B^2 - \frac{(\Sigma X_B)^2}{N_B}$$

$$= 642{,}716 - \frac{8{,}282{,}884}{13} \qquad\qquad = 1{,}173{,}203 - \frac{14{,}010{,}049}{12}$$

$$\Sigma x_A^2 = 5571 \qquad\qquad \Sigma x_B^2 = 5699$$

$$\bar{X}_A = \frac{\Sigma X_A}{N_A} \qquad\qquad \bar{X}_B = \frac{\Sigma X_B}{N_B}$$

$$= \frac{2878}{13} \qquad\qquad = \frac{3843}{12}$$

$$= 221.38 \qquad\qquad = 311.92$$

$$s_A^2 = \frac{\Sigma x_A^2}{N_A - 1} = \frac{5571}{12} \qquad\qquad s_B^2 = \frac{\Sigma x_B^2}{N_B - 1} = \frac{5699}{11}$$

$$= 464.25 \qquad\qquad = 518.08$$

$s^2$ (For combined groups)

$$s^2 = \frac{\Sigma x_A^2 + \Sigma x_B^2}{N_A + N_B - 2} \qquad\qquad t = \frac{\bar{X}_A - \bar{X}_B}{\sqrt{s^2 \dfrac{N_A + N_B}{N_A N_B}}}$$

$$= \frac{5571.00 + 5699.00}{13 + 12 - 2} \qquad\qquad = \frac{221.38 - 311.92}{\sqrt{(490)\dfrac{13 + 12}{156}}}$$

$$= \frac{11{,}270.00}{23} \qquad\qquad = \frac{-90.54}{\sqrt{490(.1602)}}$$

$$s^2 = 490.00 \qquad\qquad = \frac{-90.54}{\sqrt{78.50}}$$

$$= \frac{-90.54}{8.86}$$

$$t = -10.22$$

A           B

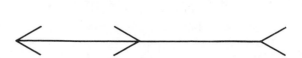

*Figure 14–2.* Muller-Lyer illusion.

*B* half of the time according to a random sequence. For each subject a mean score was obtained for the eight trials starting in *A* and for the eight starting in *B*. This score was expressed in terms of the number of millimeters the *Y* arrow was located from objective zero; positive numbers indicate that *Y* was located in segment *B*, and negative numbers indicate that *Y* was located in segment *A*.

The hypothesis to be tested is that the magnitude of the illusion is the same when *Y* is moved starting from segment *B* as when it is started from segment *A*. The statistic chosen to test this hypothesis is the *t*-test for correlated means since we have measurements made on each subject in each of the two conditions. The data for each subject in terms of mean number of millimeters from zero in each of the conditions are listed in Table 14–2. Also, the difference score (found by subtracting each subject's mean when starting from *A* from his mean when starting from *B*) is listed, as well as the computations necessary to make the *t*-test.

Remember that in a *t*-test for correlated means, the degrees of freedom are equal to the number of pairs minus one. Since we have 15 subjects, the number of degrees of freedom for the differences between *A* and *B* is equal to the number of subjects minus one degree of freedom, or 14.

In Table A–3 the *t* value for 14 degrees of freedom is 2.145 at

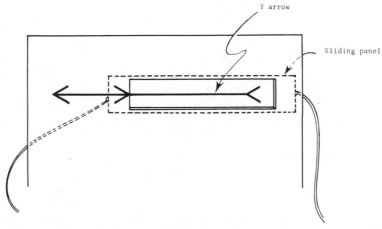

*Figure 14–3.* Adjustable Muller-Lyer illusion.

the .05 level of significance and 2.977 at the .01 level of significance. Since our obtained $t$ in Table 14–2 is 4.06, we may safely conclude that the two means are drawn from different underlying populations. Our experimental evidence clearly indicates that the magnitude of the illusion is greater when the adjustable arrow is moved from the $B$ line segment than when it is moved from the $A$ line segment.

*3. The Effect of Associate Strength on Recall: The One-Way Analysis of Variance (Chapter 8).* An experimenter wished to study

**Table 14–2.** Error Scores in Millimeters for the Muller-Lyer Illusion When Judgment of Equality is Made from Left (Segment A) and Right (Segment B)

| Subject # | Adjusted from Segment B | Adjusted from Segment A | Difference B minus A |
|-----------|-------------------------|-------------------------|----------------------|
| 1 | 10.9 | 2.8 | 8.1 |
| 2 | 1.9 | 5.1 | −3.2 |
| 3 | 8.6 | 2.7 | 5.9 |
| 4 | 7.4 | 2.2 | 5.2 |
| 5 | 11.9 | 2.1 | 9.8 |
| 6 | 7.1 | 2.9 | 4.2 |
| 7 | 6.2 | 2.1 | 4.1 |
| 8 | 6.0 | 3.1 | 2.9 |
| 9 | 8.9 | 3.8 | 5.1 |
| 10 | 10.5 | 2.7 | 7.8 |
| 11 | 5.4 | 3.3 | 2.1 |
| 12 | 1.8 | 3.6 | −1.8 |
| 13 | 10.2 | 4.0 | 6.2 |
| 14 | 8.8 | 2.9 | 5.9 |
| 15 | 1.9 | 3.9 | −2.0 |

$$\sum {+}\text{'s} \quad 67.3$$

$$\sum {-}\text{'s} = 7.0$$

$$\sum D = 60.3$$

$$\bar{D} = 4.02$$

$$\sum D^2 = 448.35$$

$$(\sum D)^2 = 3636.09$$

$$\sum d^2 = \sum D^2 - \frac{(\sum D)^2}{N}$$

$$= 448.35 - \frac{3636.09}{15}$$

$$= 448.35 = 242.41$$

$$\sum d^2 = 205.94$$

$$s_D^2 = \frac{\sum d^2}{N-1}$$

$$= \frac{205.94}{14}$$

$$= 14.71$$

$$s_D = \sqrt{14.71}$$

$$= 3.84$$

$$s_{\bar{D}} = \frac{3.84}{3.87}$$

$$= .99$$

$$t = \frac{\bar{D}}{s_{\bar{D}}}$$

$$t = \frac{4.02}{.99}$$

$$= 4.06$$

the effect of varying the association value of a list of nonsense syllables on the number of syllables correctly recalled. The association value of a nonsense syllable can be defined in terms of the number of meaningful verbal responses that subjects can give to it. In other words, the more things a nonsense syllable reminds people of, the higher is its association value. For example, a syllable with an association value of 21–40 per cent is one to which 21 to 40 per cent of a sample of subjects is reminded of at least one thing. A standard list of association values was used to construct five lists of 20 syllables each. Each list of syllables is presented to each subject in the experiment four times, each time in a different order. After the four presentations of each list, the subject is asked to recall all the syllables he can remember. The syllables presented to the different groups have different association values as follows: Group I, 1–20 per cent; Group II, 21–40 per cent; Group III, 51–70 per cent; Group IV, 81–100 per cent. Forty subjects were assigned randomly to each of four groups. Three subjects had to be discarded for failure to follow instructions, which resulted in an unequal number of subjects in the different groups: Group I, $n = 9$; Group II, $n = 10$; Group III, $n = 8$; Group IV, $n = 10$.

Table 14–3 lists the number of syllables correctly recalled for each group. The computations necessary to construct the analysis of variance table are also included.

Table 14–4 is the summary analysis of variance table constructed from the computations shown in Table 14–3.

From Table A–4 we find that with three degrees of freedom for the numerator and 33 degrees of freedom for the denominator (use 32 $df$) an $F$ value of 2.90 is required at the .05 level of significance and an $F$ value of 4.46 is required at the .01 level of significance. Since our obtained $F$ value of 10.72 exceeds these tabled values, it is concluded that the means for the four samples were not drawn from the same underlying population. Therefore, the number of syllables correctly recalled does differ as a function of the association value of the nonsense syllables. Since the overall test of significance reaches an acceptable level it would be permissible to perform individual tests of significance between the individual groups using a multiple comparison procedure. These procedures are not described in this textbook, but appropriate references are listed in Chapter 12 (see p. 223).

**4. Position Preferences in Rats: The Chi-Square Test (Chapter 9).** An experimenter is interested in studying the ability of rats to detect differences among four stimuli. He constructs an apparatus that has a start box and a Y-shaped choice compartment with four doors at the end, on each of which stimulus cards can be mounted. Each door is four inches from the adjacent door and the two end doors are four inches from the side walls. Before starting the experiment it is

**Table 14-3.** NUMBER OF NONSENSE SYLLABLES CORRECTLY RECALLED BY EACH EXPERIMENTAL GROUP

| Group I Association Value 1-20% | | Group II Association Value 21-40% | | Group III Association Value 51-70% | | Group IV Association Value 81-100% | |
|---|---|---|---|---|---|---|---|
| Subject # | Score | Subject # | Score | Subject # | Score | Subject # | Score |
| 1 | 11 | 9 | 13 | 5 | 10 | 2 | 16 |
| 4 | 6 | 11 | 9 | 7 | 11 | 3 | 19 |
| 6 | 10 | 13 | 11 | 18 | 14 | 15 | 17 |
| 8 | 12 | 14 | 14 | 19 | 20 | 16 | 16 |
| 10 | 15 | 21 | 14 | 24 | 17 | 17 | 20 |
| 12 | 13 | 23 | 17 | 27 | 19 | 20 | 19 |
| 25 | 13 | 30 | 12 | 29 | 17 | 26 | 15 |
| 28 | 10 | 32 | 11 | 36 | 16 | 33 | 19 |
| 31 | 13 | 35 | 13 | | | 37 | 19 |
| | | 38 | 16 | | | 40 | 17 |
| | — | | — | | — | | — |

$$n = 9 \qquad\qquad 10 \qquad\qquad 8 \qquad\qquad 10$$
$$\sum X = 103 \qquad 130 \qquad 124 \qquad 177$$
$$\overline{X} = 11.44 \qquad 13.0 \qquad 15.5 \qquad 17.7$$
$$\sum X^2 = 1233 \qquad 1742 \qquad 2012 \qquad 3159$$
$$(\sum X)^2 = 10{,}609 \qquad 16{,}900 \qquad 15{,}376 \qquad 31{,}329$$
$$\frac{(\sum X)^2}{N} = 1178.7 \qquad 1690 \qquad 1922 \qquad 3132.9$$

Total: $N_T = 37$ $\qquad \overline{X}_T = 14.41 \qquad (\sum X_T)^2 = 285{,}156 \qquad \dfrac{(\sum X_T)^2}{N} = 7706.9$

$$\sum X_T = 534 \qquad \sum X_T^2 = 8146 \qquad \sum \frac{(\sum X)^2}{n} = 7923.6$$

$$\sum x_T^2 = \sum X_T^2 - \frac{(\sum X_T)^2}{N} = 8146.0 - 7706.9 = 439.1$$

$$\sum x_b^2 = \sum \frac{(\sum X)^2}{n} - \frac{(\sum X_T)^2}{N} = 7923.6 - 7706.9 = 216.7$$

$$\sum x_w^2 = \sum X_T^2 - \sum \frac{(\sum X)^2}{n} = 8146.0 - 7923.6 = 222.4$$

**Table 14-4.** ANALYSIS OF VARIANCE SUMMARY TABLE

| Source | Sum of Squares | df | Mean Square | F |
|---|---|---|---|---|
| Between groups | 216.7 | 3 | 72.23 | 10.72 |
| Within groups | 222.4 | 33 | 6.74 | |
| Total | 439.1 | 36 | | |

pointed out to the experimenter that rats might have position preferences since rats tend to run along walls when they can. Therefore, the rats might show a strong preference for the two outside doors, a factor that would have to be taken into account in designing the experiment and interpreting the data. If the rats have no preference in this apparatus they should distribute their choices evenly among the four doors if the doors are all left open. However, if they do have a position preference the distribution of choices would be uneven, probably tending to favor the outside two doors.

To determine whether or not there is any pattern of preference in the apparatus, each of the 40 rats to be used in the discrimination experiment is run once through the apparatus.

If there is no position preference, then about 25 per cent (10 rats) would be expected to choose each door. If any door is chosen significantly more often than the expected 25 per cent, then the experimenter will have to take this factor into account; either he must allow for this in the experimental design or he must redesign the apparatus.

Remember that in a $\chi^2$ test each observation must be independent and the marginal totals for the observed and expected frequencies must be equal. Since our expected frequencies are distributed on the basis of what would be expected by chance, an expected frequency of ten will be entered in each cell. The observed frequencies and the calculations are given in Table 14–5.

From Table A–5 we find that with three degrees of freedom a

**Table 14–5.** Observed and Expected Frequencies and Chi-Square Calculations for Position Preferences of 40 Rats

|  | A | B | C | D |  |
|---|---|---|---|---|---|
| Observed | 18 | 5 | 6 | 11 | $\sum O = 40$ |
| Expected | 10 | 10 | 10 | 10 | $\sum E = 40$ |

$$\chi^2 = \sum \frac{(O - E)^2}{E}$$

$$= \frac{(18 - 10)^2}{10} + \frac{(5 - 10)^2}{10} + \frac{(6 - 10)^2}{10} + \frac{(11 - 10)^2}{10}$$

$$= \frac{64}{10} + \frac{25}{10} + \frac{16}{10} + \frac{1}{10}$$

$$= 6.4 + 2.5 + 1.6 + .1$$

$$= 10.6$$

$\chi^2$ value of 7.82 is required at the .05 level of significance and a $\chi^2$ value of 11.34 is required at the .01 level of significance. Since our obtained $\chi^2$ value exceeds the tabled values for the .05 level of significance, it is concluded that the choices are not distributed evenly. Therefore, the experimenter must consider the problem of position preferences.

*5. A Retroactive Inhibition Experiment: The Mann-Whitney U Test (Chapter 10).* The phenomenon of "retroactive inhibition" is said to occur when material just learned interferes with the memory of material learned at an earlier date. This can be demonstrated by interpolating verbal material between the learning and the recall of a list of nonsense syllables. Each subject in Group A first learns a list of 20 nonsense syllables to a criterion of 18 syllables correct. Ten minutes later each subject learns a second list of 20 nonsense syllables to the same criterion. Ten minutes after learning the second list, the subject is asked to recall the original list. Each subject in Group B also learns the list of 20 nonsense syllables to the criterion of 18 correct syllables. The subjects in this group name colors for the same approximate time period the subjects in Group A take to learn the second, interpolated list. Each subject then recalls the original list. If the subjects in Group A show the effects of retroactive inhibition, their recall level will be lower as a function of having learned the interpolated list as compared to the recall level of Group B, which performed an irrelevant task during the interpolation interval.

Twenty subjects were assigned randomly to the groups. Two subjects from Group B had to be discarded because of an error on the part of the experimenter. Thus, there are ten subjects in Group A and eight subjects in Group B. The experimenter decides to test the significance of the difference using the Mann-Whitney $U$ statistic.

Table 14–6 contains the original scores in terms of the number of nonsense syllables recalled correctly, the rank order of each, and the computation required to make the test of significance.

From Table A–7 we find that the tabled value of $U$ when $n_1 = 8$ and $n_2 = 10$ is 17 at the .05 level of significance and is 12 at the .01 level of significance. Since our obtained value of $U$ is smaller than the tabled value for the .01 level of significance, it is concluded that the two groups are not drawn from the same population of scores; Group B recalls significantly more syllables than does Group A. This result supports the conclusion that for Group A the original list did suffer from the effects of retroactive inhibition.

*6. The Effect of Water Deprivation on Bar Pressing: The Kruskal-Wallis Ranked One-Way Analysis of Variance (Chapter 10).* One of the commonly used methods of studying motivation in animals is to determine how frequently an animal will perform a given response in

**Table 14–6.** ORIGINAL SCORES FOR NUMBER OF NONSENSE SYLLABLES RECALLED
CORRECTLY FOR EACH SUBJECT AND EQUIVALENT RANKS FOR THE
MANN-WHITNEY $U$ TEST

| Group A | | | Group B | | |
|---|---|---|---|---|---|
| Subject # | Score | Rank | Subject # | Score | Rank |
| 2 | 11 | 4 | 1 | 15 | 9.5 |
| 3 | 15 | 9.5 | 4 | 19 | 17 |
| 5 | 10 | 1.5 | 7 | 15 | 9.5 |
| 6 | 11 | 4 | 10 | 12 | 6.5 |
| 8 | 11 | 4 | 11 | 18 | 15.5 |
| 9 | 16 | 12.5 | 12 | 17 | 14 |
| 13 | 12 | 6.5 | 14 | 20 | 18 |
| 16 | 10 | 1.5 | 15 | 18 | 15.5 |
| 17 | 15 | 9.5 | | | |
| 18 | 16 | 12.5· | | | |
| | $R_1 = \overline{65.5}$ | | | $R_2 = \overline{105.5}$ | |

Since Group $B$ has the smaller number of subjects it is $n_1$, since $n_1$ is the notation for the smaller sample.

$$U = \left[ n_1 n_2 + \frac{n_1(n_1 + 1)}{2} \right] - \sum R_1$$

$$= \left[ (8)(10) + \frac{8(9)}{2} \right] - 105.5$$

$$= (80 + 36) - 105.5$$

$$= 116 - 105.5$$

$$= 10.5$$

order to receive a given reward. If an animal that has learned to press a lever to obtain water is deprived of water for a number of hours and is then allowed to obtain water by pressing the lever, the frequency of lever pressing can be used to indicate the strength of the motivation to obtain water. With this method a number of factors can be varied, such as the amount of effort required to press the bar and the number of times the bar must be pressed to obtain a reward. We know from earlier work that animals (including humans!) will continue to perform a response for a longer period of time when reward is discontinued altogether if they have not been rewarded for every response.

An experimenter wished to study the effect of the number of hours of water deprivation on the number of times a rat would press a heavily weighted lever during a 15 minute period when the response was rewarded an average of one out of every five times the lever pressing response occurred. Each reward consisted of a few drops of

**Table 14-7.** AVERAGE NUMBER OF BAR PRESSES PER MINUTE OVER A 15 MINUTE PERIOD AND EQUIVALENT RANKS FOR FOUR GROUPS OF RATS UNDER DIFFERING AMOUNTS OF WATER DEPRIVATION

| A | | | B | | | C | | | D | | |
|---|---|---|---|---|---|---|---|---|---|---|---|
| *1 Hour Deprivation* | | | *12 Hours Deprivation* | | | *24 Hours Deprivation* | | | *36 Hours Deprivation* | | |
| *Sub. #* | *Score* | *Rank* | *Sub. #* | *Score* | *Rank* | *Sub. #* | *Score* | *Rank* | *Sub. #* | *Score* | *Rank* |
| 3 | 7 | 1.0 | 4 | 14 | 9.5 | 1 | 16 | 13.0 | 2 | 11 | 4.5 |
| 5 | 12 | 6.0 | 7 | 19 | 16.5 | 12 | 23 | 20.0 | 6 | 18 | 14.5 |
| 9 | 11 | 4.5 | 11 | 14 | 9.5 | 14 | 21 | 18.5 | 8 | 18 | 14.5 |
| 13 | 10 | 2.5 | 16 | 14 | 9.5 | 15 | 21 | 18.5 | 10 | 15 | 12.0 |
| 19 | 10 | 2.5 | 20 | 14 | 9.5 | 18 | 19 | 16.5 | 17 | 13 | 7.0 |

$$\sum R_1 = 16.5 \qquad \sum R_2 = 54.5 \qquad \sum R_3 = 86.5 \qquad \sum R_4 = 52.5$$

$$R_1^2 = 272.25 \qquad R_2^2 = 2970.25 \qquad R_3^2 = 7482.25 \qquad R_4^2 = 2756.25$$

$$\frac{R_1^2}{n_1} = 54.45 \qquad \frac{R_2^2}{n_2} = 594.05 \qquad \frac{R_3^2}{n_3} = 1496.45 \qquad \frac{R_4^2}{n_4} = 551.25$$

$$H = \left[ \frac{12}{N(N+1)} \left( \sum \frac{R^2}{n} \right) \right] - 3(N+1)$$

$$= \left[ \frac{12}{20(21)} (54.45 + 594.05 + 1496.45 + 551.25) \right] - 3(21)$$

$$= \left[ \frac{12}{420} (2696.2) \right] - 63$$

$$= [.029(2696.2)] - 63$$

$$= 78.19 - 63$$

$$= 15.19$$

Applying the correction for ties: $\dfrac{H}{1 - \dfrac{\sum T}{N^3 - N}}$, $t = 2; 2; 2; 2; 2; 4.$

This indicates that there were five instances where two cases were tied and one instance where four cases were tied.

$$\sum T = (t^3 - t)$$

$$= (2^3 - 2) + (2^3 - 2) + (2^3 - 2) + (2^3 - 2) + (2^3 - 2) + (4^3 - 4)$$

$$= 6 + 6 + 6 + 6 + 6 + 60 = 90$$

$$\frac{H}{1 - \dfrac{\sum T}{N^3 - N}} = \frac{15.19}{1 - \dfrac{90}{7980}} = \frac{15.19}{1 - .011} = \frac{15.19}{.989} = 15.36$$

water. Four levels of water deprivation were used: 1 hour; 12 hours; 24 hours; and 36 hours. Five animals were assigned randomly to each group. The experimenter decided to rank the data and to test for significance using the Kruskal-Wallis one-way ranked analysis of variance method.

The data in terms of the average number of bar presses per minute are listed for each rat in Table 14–7.

Since we have four groups of five subjects each, we can treat our obtained $H$ value as a $\chi^2$ with three degrees of freedom. (See Chapter 10, p. 187, if this part of the procedure is not clear to you.) From Table A–5 we find a $\chi^2$ value of 7.82 listed at the .05 level of significance and a value of 11.34 listed at the .01 level of significance. Since our obtained $H$ of 15.36 exceeds both of these values, we can reject the hypothesis that these four samples were drawn from the same underlying population. Inspection of the data indicates that the animals in the one hour deprived group perform at a much lower level than do the animals in the other group. It also appears that the animals in the 24 hour deprived group perform at a higher level than do the other groups. In order to evaluate the likelihood of these possibilities it is necessary to make individual comparisons among the groups.

**7. A Relationship Between Height and Weight: The Pearson Product-Moment Correlation (Chapter 12).** To demonstrate correlation methods, a statistics teacher obtains the height in inches and the weight in pounds of each of his students. He is interested in demonstrating that height and weight co-vary. Table 14–8 contains each student's height $(X)$ and weight $(Y)$ and the computations leading to the groups.

When Table A–9 is entered with nine degrees of freedom we find that $r$ must equal .602 to be considered significantly different from zero at the .05 level of significance and that it must reach .735 to reach significance at the .01 level of significance. The $r$ of .84 calculated between height and weight is larger than either of these values. Therefore, it can be concluded on the basis of this sample that height and weight do co-vary in the population represented by these 11 students.

**8. A Relationship Between Brightness and Pattern Discrimination: The Spearman Rank Difference Correlation (Chapter 12).** An experimenter is studying various aspects of discrimination learning in cats. He has reason to believe that a cat's ability to discriminate patterns is related to its ability to discriminate brightness. To evaluate this proposition he trains eight cats to discriminate black from white in a two-choice discrimination apparatus. He then trains the same eight cats to discriminate between two patterns in the same apparatus.

A problem develops, however. Cat $C$ shows no evidence of learn-

**Table 14–8.** HEIGHT IN INCHES ($X$) AND WEIGHT IN POUNDS ($Y$) FOR ELEVEN SUBJECTS.

| Subject # | Inches<br>X | Pounds<br>Y |
|:---:|:---:|:---:|
| 1 | 63 | 158 |
| 2 | 68 | 171 |
| 3 | 65 | 159 |
| 4 | 73 | 197 |
| 5 | 59 | 165 |
| 6 | 69 | 175 |
| 7 | 74 | 203 |
| 8 | 70 | 173 |
| 9 | 61 | 155 |
| 10 | 58 | 151 |
| 11 | 65 | 148 |

$$\sum X = 725$$
$$\sum X^2 = 48,075$$
$$(\sum X)^2 = 525,625$$

$$\sum Y = 1855$$
$$\sum Y^2 = 366,013$$
$$(\sum Y)^2 = 3,441,025$$

$$\sum XY = 123,073$$

$$r = \frac{N \sum XY - (\sum X)(\sum Y)}{\sqrt{[N \sum X^2 - (\sum X)^2][N \sum Y^2 - (\sum Y)^2]}}$$

$$= \frac{(11)(123,073) - (725)(1855)}{\sqrt{[(11)(48,075) - 525,625][(11)(316,013) - 3,441,025]}}$$

$$= \frac{8928}{\sqrt{(3,200)(35,118)}}$$

$$= \frac{8928}{\sqrt{112,366,600}}$$

$$= \frac{8928}{10,601}$$

$$= .84$$

ing the pattern discrimination in 80 trials. Since the experimenter is running only one trial a day he does not wish to prolong the experiment, especially in the face of results that suggest that the cat will not learn the problem for some time to come. The experimenter also does not wish to discard the data for Cat $C$ if he can avoid it. Therefore, he decides to stop the experiment and to assign Cat $C$ a score of 80+. He then ranks the data (Cat $C$ will, then, have the highest rank) and calculates a Spearman rank difference correlation. The data, in trials to criterion for each cat on each of the discrimination tasks, are presented in Table 14–9.

**Table 14–9.** NUMBER OF CORRECT RESPONSES FOR EIGHT CATS ON BRIGHTNESS AND DISCRIMINATION TRIALS AND EQUIVALENT RANKS FOR CALCULATION OF THE SPEARMAN RANK-DIFFERENCE CORRELATION

| Cat | Score | | Rank | | d | d² |
|-----|-------|---------|-------|---------|---|-----|
| | Brightness | Pattern | Brightness | Pattern | | |
| A | 27 | 30 | 1 | 1 | 0 | 0 |
| B | 49 | 57 | 6 | 7 | −1 | 1 |
| C | 65 | 80+ | 8 | 8 | 0 | 0 |
| D | 37 | 41 | 4 | 4 | 0 | 0 |
| E | 29 | 31 | 2 | 2 | 0 | 0 |
| F | 39 | 42 | 5 | 5 | 0 | 0 |
| G | 57 | 55 | 7 | 6 | +1 | 1 |
| H | 31 | 32 | 3 | 3 | 0 | 0 |

$$\text{rho} = 1 - \frac{6(\Sigma d^2)}{N(N^2 - 1)}$$

$$= 1 - \frac{6(2)}{8(63)}$$

$$= 1 - \frac{12}{504}$$

$$= 1 - .024$$

$$= .976$$

$$\Sigma d^2 = 2$$

From Table A–10 we find that with an $N$ of eight the rank difference correlation coefficient must be .74 to be considered significantly different from zero at the .05 level of significance. The obtained coefficient of .976 is larger than this value. Therefore, it can be concluded that there is a significant relationship between the ability of cats to discriminate brightness and pattern, given the conditions of this experiment.

## EPILOGUE

Hopefully, these eight experiments with their attendant calculations have served to provide a transition from statistics in an abstract sense to statistical method as an integral part of experimental design. All too frequently a research worker becomes concerned with statistical treatment of data to such an extent that he loses sight of the purpose of his experiments.

In any scientific investigation, the experiment must take precedence. Excellent statistical treatment will not save or salvage a poorly designed and executed experiment. Similarly, misapplication of statistics can result in inappropriate or incorrect conclusions from a well designed experiment. Statistics is one of the tools of experimentation and as such should be used with care and precision.

# APPENDICES

# CODING SCORES FOR HAND CALCULATION

Anyone who is planning to do any significant amount of statistical work will almost certainly have access to an electric calculator. For large scale statistical calculations an electronic digital computer that can be programmed to carry out hundreds of calculations in a few seconds is often used.

There are still situations in which it is necessary to carry out calculations by hand. Use of raw score formulas in hand calculations often requires the manipulation of rather large numbers. Consequently, it is useful to know ways of simplifying the computations so as to keep the size of the numbers to a minimum. However, a few preliminary steps are necessary in order to use these techniques.

## Grouping of Scores

If a statistic is to be calculated directly from the raw scores, there is little advantage to be gained by arranging the scores in order or grouping them in any fashion. If they can be coded in any manner, the work will be greatly simplified if the scores are arranged into a set of *class intervals*. This procedure shortens the number of values it is necessary to work with. Table I–1 contains 30 raw scores and a set of class intervals constructed from these scores.

Table I–1 is constructed from scores taken from our original set of scores which range from 30 to 77. They are grouped in class intervals of 5, giving us a total of 10 class intervals.

What determines the number of class intervals we will choose to use? This is largely arbitrary, since the nature of the scores to be

**Table I–1.** SETTING CLASS INTERVALS FOR RAW SCORES

*Scores:*

| 34 | 35 | 61 | 39 | 57 | 41 |
|----|----|----|----|----|----|
| 51 | 71 | 39 | 76 | 57 | 67 |
| 31 | 65 | 60 | 33 | 46 | 59 |
| 70 | 73 | 73 | 77 | 41 | 48 |
| 66 | 36 | 46 | 69 | 38 | 30 |

| Class Intervals | Frequency | |
|:---:|:---:|:---:|
| 75–79 | II | (2) |
| 70–74 | IIII | (4) |
| 65–69 | IIII | (4) |
| 60–64 | II | (2) |
| 55–59 | IIII | (4) |
| 50–54 | I | (1) |
| 45–49 | III | (3) |
| 40–44 | II | (2) |
| 35–39 | IIII | (4) |
| 30–34 | IIII | (4) |

$$N = 30$$

grouped must be taken into consideration. Too fine a grouping defeats the purpose for grouping scores and too coarse a grouping tends to lose information. Usually, 10 to 15 intervals are satisfactory. The usual rule to use to start the class limits is that the lower limit of each class interval must be divisible by the class interval, $i$. For the example in Table I–1, the class interval, $i$, is 5. The lowest score, 30, is evenly divisible by five, so our lowest class interval can start with 30. If we have had a score of 29, our lowest interval would start with 25 and encompass the range 25–29.

In statistical terminology, the class intervals we have used are in terms of *working limits*. The *theoretical limits* for the lowest interval are 29.5–34.5. This means that the interval *theoretically* encompasses all values within the range 29.5 to 34.5. Keep in mind that these are the limits in the mathematical sense.

How does the grouping change the scores? When using class intervals the midpoint of the class interval represents all the scores in that interval. Thus the class interval 75–79, which contains two scores of 76 and 77 in raw score form, now in effect has two scores of 77 – the midpoint of the class interval.

## The Coding of Scores

The coding or transformation of scores is basically a very simple process, and will be illustrated by calculating the arithmetic mean. Table I–2 illustrates the sequence of steps.

The column headed $x'$ contains the values 0 through 9, beginning with 0 in the first class interval and progressing by steps of 1 up to the highest class interval. The column headed $fx'$ is the result of multiplying the $x'$ values by the values in the frequency $(f_x)$ column. The sum of this column is then taken and substituted into the formula for obtaining the mean from coded scores.

It is important to keep in mind that the formulas for obtaining the mean from raw scores and from coded scores are the same formula. The only difference in the coded score version lies in the necessity to specify the point of origin for the coding and in correcting for the class interval size. Note that scores can be coded using a class interval of 1, just as if they were raw scores under which circumstances the multiplication by $i$ has no effect on the value of the mean.

The point of origin for coding does not need to be placed at the

**Table I–2.** Calculation of the Mean by Coded Scores (Data from Table I–1)

| | Scores | Frequency | $x'$ | $fx'$ |
|---|---|---|---|---|
| Step I: Set up a column labeled $x'$ next to the column containing the frequencies of the scores. Enter the value of zero in the lowest class interval, the value of 1 in the next interval, and continue, increasing the value of $x'$ by 1 for each interval. | 75–79 | 2 | 9 | 18 |
| | 70–74 | 4 | 8 | 32 |
| | 65–69 | 4 | 7 | 28 |
| | 60–64 | 2 | 6 | 12 |
| Step 2: Multiply the values in the $x'$ column by the corresponding row values in the frequency $(f_x)$ column. For interval 75–79, $2 \times 9 = 18$. The value of 18 is entered in the $fx'$ column. | 55–59 | 4 | 5 | 20 |
| | 50–54 | 1 | 4 | 4 |
| | 45–49 | 3 | 3 | 9 |
| | 40–44 | 2 | 2 | 4 |
| Step 3: The formula for determining the mean from coded scores is: | 35–39 | 4 | 1 | 4 |
| | 30–34 | 4 | 0 | 0 |

$$\bar{X} = M + [\sum fx'/N]i,$$

where $M$ = the midpoint of the interval containing the 0 value,

$\sum fx'$ = the sum of the $fx'$ column,

$i$ = the size of the class interval,

$N$ = the number of observations.

| $\sum$ | 30 | — | 131 |
|---|---|---|---|

$\bar{X} = M + [\sum fx'/N]i$   $M = 32$

$= 32 + [131/30]5$   $i = 5$

$= 32 + [4.37]5$

$= 32 + 21.85$

$= 53.85$

lowest score interval—it can be placed in the center of the class intervals, for example. This method is advantageous in that numbers are kept even smaller than in the calculations of Table I-2. However, one disadvantage lies in the fact that the signs of numbers must be noted.

To illustrate this, Table I-3 repeats the calculation of the mean placing the point of origin at interval 50–54. The calculation is identical with the calculation of Table I-2, with the difference that the algebraic sum of $fx'$ must be obtained.

## Calculation of the Variance

To calculate the variance in terms of coded scores an additional column is necessary. Table I-4 repeats the calculations of Table I-2, with the additional calculations required to obtain the variance.

Note that the formula for the sum of squares from coded scores

**Table I-3.** CALCULATION OF THE MEAN FROM A POINT OF ORIGIN IN THE CENTER OF THE DISTRIBUTION

| Scores | $f_x$ Frequency | $x'$ | $fx'$ |
|---|---|---|---|
| 75–79 | 2 | 5 | 10 |
| 70–74 | 4 | 4 | 16 |
| 65–69 | 4 | 3 | 12 |
| 60–64 | 2 | 2 | 4 |
| 55–59 | 4 | 1 | 4 |
| 50–54 | 1 | 0 | 0 |
| 45–49 | 3 | −1 | −3 |
| 40–44 | 2 | −2 | −4 |
| 35–39 | 4 | −3 | −12 |
| 30–34 | 4 | −4 | −16 |
| $\Sigma$ | 30 | | 11 |

$$\overline{X} = M + [\Sigma\, fx'/N]i$$
$$= 52 + [11/30]5$$
$$= 52 + [.37]5$$
$$= 52 + 1.85$$
$$= 53.85$$

**Table I-4.** CALCULATION OF THE VARIANCE

| Scores | $f_x$ | $x'$ | $fx'$ | $fx'^2$ |
|--------|-------|------|-------|---------|
| 75–79 | 2 | 9 | 18 | 162 |
| 70–74 | 4 | 8 | 32 | 256 |
| 65–69 | 4 | 7 | 28 | 196 |
| 60–64 | 2 | 6 | 12 | 72 |
| 55–59 | 4 | 5 | 20 | 100 |
| 50–54 | 1 | 4 | 4 | 16 |
| 45–49 | 3 | 3 | 9 | 27 |
| 40–44 | 2 | 2 | 4 | 8 |
| 35–39 | 4 | 1 | 4 | 4 |
| 30–34 | 4 | 0 | 0 | 0 |
| $\Sigma$ | 30 | — | 131 | 841 |

The only change from the calculations of Table I–2 is in the calculation of the values in the column labeled $fx'^2$. These values are obtained by multiplying each value in the $fx'$ column by its corresponding $x'$ value. For interval 60–64 $x' = 6$ and $fx' = 12$, resulting in an $fx'^2$ value of 72.

$$\Sigma x^2 = [\Sigma fx'^2 - \{(\Sigma fx')^2/N\}]i^2 \qquad s^2 = \Sigma x^2/(N - 1)$$

$$= [841 - \{(131^2)/30\}]5^2 \qquad\qquad = 6724.25/29$$

$$= [841 - \{(17161)/30\}]25 \qquad\qquad = 231.87$$

$$= [841 - 572.03]25$$

$$= [268.97]25$$

$$= 6724.25$$

$$s = \sqrt{s^2} \qquad\qquad\qquad\qquad s = \sqrt{s^2}$$

$$= \sqrt{185.7} \qquad\qquad\qquad s = \sqrt{231.87}$$

$$= 13.7 \qquad\qquad\qquad\qquad s = 15.22$$

is identical to the raw score form, the only difference being the difference in symbols.

## Hand Calculation of the Correlation Coefficient

The example given in Chapter 11 will be used to illustrate the procedures used in the hand calculation of the Pearson correlation coefficient. Table I–5 illustrates the computation.

The scores are coded in exactly the same manner as for a single array of scores (cf. Table I–1). However, for the correlation, the coding is done on two sides of the bivariate frequency distribution to allow for the simultaneous coding of $X$ and $Y$. The coding is arranged so that the values of the coded scores increase with increases in the value of the observations. The first row at the bottom of the bivariate frequency distribution labeled $f_x$ contains the frequencies for the values of the variable X. The first column to the right of the frequency distribution labeled $f_y$ lists the frequencies for variable Y. The second row is labeled $x'$ and contains the coding values for X. The corresponding column for Y contains the coding for Y and is labeled $y'$. The remaining columns and rows, $fx'$, $fy'$, $fx'^2$, and $fy'^2$, are all calculated in the same manner as for the mean and standard deviation.

The first new calculation is in the row labeled $fy' \cdot x'$, which can be translated as "the sum of the $fy'$ coding on the corresponding $fx'$ coding."

To illustrate what is meant by this rather cumbersome definition, look at the first entry in the $x'$ row. There is one score tallied for that entry and the $x'$ code is 0. Now we look over to the $y'$ column and see that the $y'$ code is also 0. Since there is only one score, the value of 0 is entered at the beginning of the $fy' \cdot x'$ row. For the next entry, where the $x'$ code is 1, there is also only one score, and its $y'$ code is 2, so the value of 2 is entered in the next position in the $fy' \cdot x'$ row. For the third position, there are 3 scores which have $y'$ scores of 2, 3, and 5, respectively, and the entry in the $fy' \cdot x'$ column will be the sum of these, which is 10. The sum of this row, when completed, should be identical to the sum of the $fy'$ column. If it does not agree exactly, an error has been made. When this process is completed, the final row, labeled $fx'y'$, can be calculated. This is done by multiplying the $fy' \cdot x'$ values by the $x'$ values in the same column. For the first entry $0 \times 0$, for the second entry $1 \times 2 = 2$, for the third entry $2 \times 10 = 20$, and so forth.

We are now ready to calculate $r$. We will need the sums of the $fx'$, $fy'$, $fx'^2$, $fy'^2$, $fy' \cdot x'$, and $fx'y'$. The remaining calculations are shown on table on opposite page. To find the covariance, we substitute into the formula:

$$\sum xy = \left[ \sum fx'y' - \frac{(\sum fx')(\sum fy')}{N} \right] i_x i_y,$$

and for the sums of squares for X and Y:

$$\sum x^2 = \left[ \sum fx' - \frac{(\sum fx')^2}{N} \right] i_x^2, \quad \sum y^2 = \left[ \sum fy' - \frac{(\sum fy')^2}{N} \right] i_y^2.$$

When these calculations are completed, $r$ may be found by substituting into

$$r = \frac{\sum xy}{\sqrt{\sum x^2 y^2}}.$$

**Table I-5.** Hand Calculation of the Correlation Coefficient.

|  | Score on X | | | | | | | | | | |
|---|---|---|---|---|---|---|---|---|---|---|---|
|  | 1 | 2 | 3 | 4 | 5 | 6 | 7 | $f_y$ | $y'$ | $fy'$ | $fy'^2$ |
| 8 |  |  |  |  |  |  | 1 | 1 | 7 | 7 | 49 |
| 7 |  |  |  |  |  |  |  | 0 | 6 | 0 | 0 |
| 6 |  |  | 1 |  |  |  |  | 1 | 5 | 5 | 25 |
| 5 |  |  |  | 11 |  | 1 |  | 3 | 4 | 12 | 48 |
| 4 |  |  | 1 | 1 |  |  |  | 2 | 3 | 6 | 18 |
| 3 |  | 1 | 1 | 1 |  |  |  | 2 | 2 | 4 | 8 |
| 2 |  |  |  |  |  |  |  | 0 | 1 | 0 | 0 |
| 1 | 1 |  |  |  |  |  |  | 1 | 0 | 0 | 0 |
| $f_x$ | 1 | 1 | 3 | 3 | 0 | 1 | 1 | 10 |  | 34 | 148 |
| $x'$ | 0 | 1 | 2 | 3 | 4 | 5 | 6 |  |  |  |  |
| $fx'$ | 0 | 1 | 6 | 9 | 0 | 5 | 6 | 27 |  |  |  |
| $fx'^2$ | 0 | 1 | 12 | 27 | 0 | 25 | 36 | 101 |  |  |  |
| $fy' \cdot x'$ | 0 | 2 | 10 | 11 | 0 | 4 | 7 | 34 |  | ← CHECK |  |
| $fx'y'$ | 0 | 2 | 20 | 33 | 0 | 20 | 42 | 117 |  |  |  |

(Score on Y is shown along the left; Score on X across the top.)

$$\sum xy = \left[\sum fx'y' - \frac{(\sum fx')(\sum fy')}{N}\right] i_x i_y \qquad\qquad \sum y^2 = \left[\sum fy'^2 - \frac{(\sum fy')^2}{N}\right] i_y^2$$

$$= \left[117 - \frac{(27)(34)}{10}\right] 1 \cdot 1 \qquad\qquad = \left[148 - \frac{(34)^2}{10}\right] 1$$

$$= \left[117 - \frac{918}{10}\right] 1 \cdot 1 \qquad\qquad = \left[148 - \frac{1156}{10}\right] 1$$

$$= [117 - 91.8]1 \cdot 1 \qquad\qquad = [148 - 115.6]1$$

$$= 25.2 \qquad\qquad = 32.4$$

$$\sum x^2 = \left[\sum fx'^2 - \frac{(\sum fx')^2}{N}\right] i_x^2$$

$$= \left[101 - \frac{(27)^2}{10}\right] 1$$

$$= [101 - 72.9]$$

$$= 28.1$$

$$r = \frac{\sum xy}{\sqrt{\sum x^2 \sum y^2}} = \frac{25.2}{\sqrt{(28.1)(32.4)}} = \frac{25.2}{\sqrt{910.44}} = \frac{25.2}{30.17} = .83$$

# APPENDIX II

# STATISTICAL TABLES

**Table A–1.** Random Numbers

This table may be entered at any point and read in any direction. For example, to randomly select a sample of ten observations from a total of 100, begin in the upper left hand corner and read two-digit groups until the sample is selected. In this example, observation No. 10 would be the first to be selected, followed by No. 9, then No. 73 and so forth until the entire sample has been selected. The point of origin is unimportant—you may begin anywhere and read in any direction.

**Table A-1.** RANDOM NUMBERS*

| | | | | | | | | | |
|---|---|---|---|---|---|---|---|---|---|
| 10097 | 32533 | 76520 | 13586 | 34673 | 54876 | 80959 | 09117 | 39292 | 74945 |
| 37542 | 04805 | 64894 | 74296 | 24805 | 24037 | 20636 | 10402 | 00822 | 91665 |
| 08422 | 68953 | 19645 | 09303 | 23209 | 02560 | 15953 | 34764 | 35080 | 33606 |
| 99019 | 02529 | 09376 | 70715 | 38311 | 31165 | 88676 | 74397 | 04436 | 27659 |
| 12807 | 99970 | 80157 | 36147 | 64032 | 36653 | 98951 | 16877 | 12171 | 76833 |
| | | | | | | | | | |
| 66065 | 74717 | 34072 | 76850 | 36697 | 36170 | 65813 | 39885 | 11199 | 29170 |
| 31060 | 10805 | 45571 | 82406 | 35303 | 42614 | 86799 | 07439 | 23403 | 09732 |
| 85269 | 77602 | 02051 | 65692 | 68665 | 74818 | 73053 | 85247 | 18623 | 88579 |
| 63573 | 32135 | 05325 | 47048 | 90553 | 57548 | 28468 | 28709 | 83491 | 25624 |
| 73796 | 45753 | 03529 | 64778 | 35808 | 34282 | 60935 | 20344 | 35273 | 88435 |
| | | | | | | | | | |
| 98520 | 17767 | 14905 | 68607 | 22109 | 40558 | 60970 | 93433 | 50500 | 73998 |
| 11805 | 05431 | 39808 | 27732 | 50725 | 68248 | 29405 | 24201 | 52775 | 67851 |
| 83452 | 99634 | 06288 | 98083 | 13746 | 70078 | 18475 | 40610 | 68711 | 77817 |
| 88685 | 40200 | 86507 | 58401 | 36766 | 67951 | 90364 | 76493 | 29609 | 11062 |
| 99594 | 67348 | 87517 | 64969 | 91826 | 08928 | 93785 | 61368 | 23478 | 34113 |
| | | | | | | | | | |
| 65481 | 17674 | 17468 | 50950 | 58047 | 76974 | 73039 | 57186 | 40218 | 16544 |
| 80124 | 35635 | 17727 | 08015 | 45318 | 22374 | 21115 | 78253 | 14385 | 53763 |
| 74350 | 99817 | 77402 | 77214 | 43236 | 00210 | 45521 | 64237 | 96286 | 02655 |
| 69916 | 26803 | 66252 | 29148 | 36936 | 87203 | 76621 | 13990 | 94400 | 56418 |
| 09893 | 20505 | 14225 | 68514 | 46427 | 56788 | 96297 | 78822 | 54382 | 14598 |
| | | | | | | | | | |
| 91499 | 14523 | 68479 | 27686 | 46162 | 83554 | 94750 | 89923 | 37089 | 20048 |
| 80336 | 94598 | 26940 | 36858 | 70297 | 34135 | 53140 | 33340 | 42050 | 82341 |
| 44104 | 81949 | 85157 | 47954 | 32979 | 26575 | 57600 | 40881 | 22222 | 06413 |
| 12550 | 73742 | 11100 | 02040 | 12860 | 74697 | 96644 | 89439 | 28707 | 25815 |
| 63606 | 49329 | 16505 | 34484 | 40219 | 52563 | 43651 | 77082 | 07207 | 31790 |
| | | | | | | | | | |
| 61196 | 90446 | 26457 | 47774 | 51924 | 33729 | 65394 | 59593 | 42582 | 60527 |
| 15474 | 45266 | 95270 | 79953 | 59367 | 83848 | 82396 | 10118 | 33211 | 59466 |
| 94557 | 28573 | 67897 | 54387 | 54622 | 44431 | 91190 | 42592 | 92927 | 45973 |
| 42481 | 16213 | 97344 | 08721 | 16868 | 48767 | 03071 | 12059 | 25701 | 46670 |
| 23523 | 78317 | 73208 | 89837 | 68935 | 91416 | 26252 | 29663 | 05522 | 82562 |
| | | | | | | | | | |
| 04493 | 52494 | 75246 | 33824 | 45862 | 51025 | 61962 | 79335 | 65337 | 12472 |
| 00549 | 97654 | 64051 | 88159 | 96119 | 63896 | 54692 | 82391 | 23287 | 29529 |
| 35963 | 15307 | 26898 | 09354 | 33351 | 35462 | 77974 | 50024 | 90103 | 39333 |
| 59808 | 08391 | 45427 | 26842 | 83609 | 49700 | 13021 | 24892 | 78565 | 20106 |
| 46058 | 85236 | 01390 | 92286 | 77281 | 44077 | 93910 | 83647 | 70617 | 42941 |
| | | | | | | | | | |
| 32179 | 00597 | 87379 | 25241 | 05567 | 07007 | 86743 | 17157 | 85394 | 11838 |
| 69234 | 61406 | 20117 | 45204 | 15956 | 60000 | 18743 | 92423 | 97118 | 96338 |
| 19565 | 41430 | 01758 | 75379 | 40419 | 21585 | 66674 | 36806 | 84962 | 85207 |
| 45155 | 14938 | 19476 | 07246 | 43667 | 94543 | 59047 | 90033 | 20826 | 69541 |
| 94864 | 31994 | 36168 | 10851 | 34888 | 81553 | 01540 | 35456 | 05014 | 51176 |
| | | | | | | | | | |
| 98086 | 24826 | 45240 | 28404 | 44999 | 08896 | 39094 | 73407 | 35441 | 31880 |
| 33185 | 16232 | 41941 | 50949 | 89435 | 48581 | 88695 | 41994 | 37548 | 73043 |
| 80951 | 00406 | 96382 | 70774 | 20151 | 23387 | 25016 | 25298 | 94624 | 61171 |
| 79752 | 49140 | 71961 | 28296 | 69861 | 02591 | 74852 | 20539 | 00387 | 59579 |
| 18633 | 32537 | 98145 | 06571 | 31010 | 24674 | 05455 | 61427 | 77938 | 91936 |
| | | | | | | | | | |
| 74029 | 43902 | 77557 | 32270 | 97790 | 17119 | 52527 | 58021 | 80814 | 51748 |
| 54178 | 45611 | 80993 | 37143 | 05335 | 12969 | 56127 | 19255 | 36040 | 90324 |
| 11664 | 49883 | 52079 | 84827 | 59381 | 71539 | 09973 | 33440 | 88461 | 23356 |
| 48324 | 77928 | 31249 | 64710 | 02295 | 36870 | 32307 | 57546 | 15020 | 09994 |
| 69074 | 94138 | 87637 | 91976 | 35584 | 04401 | 10518 | 21615 | 01848 | 76938 |

*This table is reproduced with permission from the RAND Corporation: *A Million Random Digits*, 1955.

*Table continued on the following page*

Table A-1. *Continued*

| | | | | | | | | |
|---|---|---|---|---|---|---|---|---|
| 03991 | 10461 | 93716 | 16894 | 66083 | 24653 | 84609 | 58232 | 88618 | 19161 |
| 38555 | 95554 | 32886 | 59780 | 08355 | 60860 | 29735 | 47762 | 71299 | 23853 |
| 17546 | 73704 | 92052 | 46215 | 55121 | 29281 | 59076 | 07936 | 27954 | 58909 |
| 32643 | 52861 | 95819 | 06831 | 00911 | 98936 | 76355 | 93779 | 80863 | 00514 |
| 69572 | 68777 | 39510 | 35905 | 14060 | 40619 | 29549 | 69616 | 33564 | 60780 |
| | | | | | | | | |
| 24122 | 66591 | 27699 | 06494 | 14845 | 46672 | 61958 | 77100 | 90899 | 75754 |
| 61196 | 30231 | 92962 | 61773 | 41839 | 55382 | 17267 | 70943 | 78038 | 70267 |
| 30532 | 21704 | 10274 | 12202 | 39685 | 23309 | 10061 | 68829 | 55986 | 66485 |
| 03788 | 97599 | 75867 | 20717 | 74416 | 53166 | 35208 | 33374 | 87539 | 08823 |
| 48228 | 63379 | 85783 | 47619 | 53152 | 67433 | 35663 | 52972 | 16818 | 60311 |
| | | | | | | | | |
| 60365 | 94653 | 35075 | 33949 | 42614 | 29297 | 01918 | 28316 | 98953 | 73231 |
| 83799 | 42402 | 56623 | 34442 | 34994 | 41374 | 70071 | 14736 | 09958 | 18065 |
| 32960 | 07405 | 36409 | 83232 | 99385 | 41600 | 11133 | 07586 | 15917 | 06253 |
| 19322 | 53845 | 57620 | 52606 | 66497 | 68646 | 78138 | 66559 | 19640 | 99413 |
| 11220 | 94747 | 07399 | 37408 | 48509 | 23929 | 27482 | 45476 | 85244 | 35159 |
| | | | | | | | | |
| 31751 | 57260 | 68980 | 05339 | 15470 | 48355 | 88651 | 22596 | 03152 | 19121 |
| 88492 | 99382 | 14454 | 04504 | 20094 | 98977 | 74843 | 93413 | 22109 | 78508 |
| 30934 | 47744 | 07481 | 83828 | 73788 | 06533 | 28597 | 20405 | 94205 | 20380 |
| 22888 | 48893 | 27499 | 98748 | 60530 | 45128 | 74022 | 84617 | 82037 | 10268 |
| 78212 | 16993 | 35902 | 91386 | 44372 | 15486 | 65741 | 14014 | 87481 | 37220 |
| | | | | | | | | |
| 41849 | 84547 | 46850 | 52326 | 34677 | 58300 | 74910 | 64345 | 19325 | 81549 |
| 46352 | 33049 | 69248 | 93460 | 45305 | 07521 | 61318 | 31855 | 14413 | 70951 |
| 11087 | 96294 | 14013 | 31792 | 59747 | 67277 | 76503 | 34513 | 39663 | 77544 |
| 52701 | 08337 | 56303 | 87315 | 16520 | 69676 | 11654 | 99893 | 02181 | 68161 |
| 57275 | 36898 | 81304 | 48585 | 68652 | 27376 | 92852 | 55866 | 88448 | 03584 |
| | | | | | | | | |
| 20857 | 73156 | 70284 | 24326 | 79375 | 95220 | 01159 | 63267 | 10622 | 48391 |
| 15633 | 84924 | 90415 | 93614 | 33521 | 26665 | 55823 | 47641 | 86225 | 31704 |
| 92694 | 48297 | 39904 | 02115 | 59589 | 49067 | 66821 | 41575 | 49767 | 04037 |
| 77613 | 19019 | 88152 | 00080 | 20554 | 91409 | 96277 | 48257 | 50816 | 97616 |
| 38688 | 32486 | 45134 | 63545 | 59404 | 72059 | 43947 | 51680 | 43852 | 59693 |
| | | | | | | | | |
| 25163 | 01889 | 70014 | 15021 | 41290 | 67312 | 71857 | 15957 | 68971 | 11403 |
| 65251 | 07629 | 37239 | 33295 | 05870 | 01119 | 92784 | 26340 | 18477 | 65622 |
| 36815 | 43625 | 18637 | 37509 | 82444 | 99005 | 04921 | 73701 | 14707 | 93997 |
| 64397 | 11692 | 05327 | 82162 | 20247 | 81759 | 45197 | 25332 | 83745 | 22567 |
| 04515 | 25624 | 95096 | 67946 | 48460 | 85558 | 15191 | 18782 | 16930 | 33361 |
| | | | | | | | | |
| 83761 | 60873 | 43253 | 84145 | 60833 | 25983 | 01291 | 41349 | 20368 | 07126 |
| 14387 | 06345 | 80854 | 09279 | 43529 | 06318 | 38384 | 74761 | 41196 | 37480 |
| 51321 | 92246 | 80088 | 77074 | 88722 | 56736 | 66164 | 49431 | 66919 | 31678 |
| 72472 | 00008 | 80890 | 18002 | 94813 | 31900 | 54155 | 83436 | 35352 | 54131 |
| 05466 | 55306 | 93128 | 18464 | 74457 | 90561 | 72848 | 11834 | 79982 | 68416 |
| | | | | | | | | |
| 39528 | 72484 | 82474 | 25593 | 48545 | 35247 | 18619 | 13674 | 18611 | 19241 |
| 81616 | 18711 | 53342 | 44276 | 75122 | 11724 | 74627 | 73707 | 58319 | 15997 |
| 07586 | 16120 | 82641 | 22820 | 92904 | 13141 | 32392 | 19763 | 61199 | 67940 |
| 90767 | 04235 | 13574 | 17200 | 69902 | 63742 | 78464 | 22501 | 18627 | 90872 |
| 40188 | 28193 | 29593 | 88627 | 94972 | 11598 | 62095 | 36787 | 00441 | 58997 |
| | | | | | | | | |
| 34414 | 82157 | 86887 | 55087 | 19152 | 00023 | 12302 | 80783 | 32624 | 68691 |
| 63439 | 75363 | 44989 | 16822 | 36024 | 00867 | 76378 | 41605 | 65961 | 73488 |
| 67049 | 09070 | 93399 | 45547 | 94458 | 74284 | 05041 | 49807 | 20288 | 34060 |
| 79495 | 04146 | 52162 | 90286 | 54158 | 34243 | 46978 | 35482 | 59362 | 95938 |
| 91704 | 30552 | 04737 | 21031 | 75051 | 93029 | 47665 | 64382 | 99782 | 93478 |

**Table A-1.**  *Continued*

| | | | | | | | |
|---|---|---|---|---|---|---|---|
| 19612 | 78430 | 11661 | 94770 | 77603 | 65669 | 86868 12665 | 30012 75989 |
| 39141 | 77400 | 28000 | 64238 | 73258 | 71794 | 31340 26256 | 66453 37016 |
| 64756 | 80457 | 08747 | 12836 | 03469 | 50678 | 03274 43423 | 66677 82556 |
| 92901 | 51878 | 56441 | 22998 | 29718 | 38447 | 06453 25311 | 07565 53771 |
| 03551 | 90070 | 09483 | 94050 | 45938 | 18135 | 36908 43321 | 11073 51803 |
| | | | | | | | |
| 98884 | 66209 | 06830 | 53656 | 14663 | 56346 | 71430 04909 | 19818 05707 |
| 27369 | 86882 | 53473 | 07541 | 53633 | 70863 | 03748 12822 | 19360 49088 |
| 59066 | 75974 | 63335 | 20483 | 43514 | 37481 | 58278 26967 | 49325 43951 |
| 91647 | 93783 | 64169 | 49022 | 98588 | 09495 | 49829 59068 | 38831 04838 |
| 83605 | 92419 | 39542 | 07772 | 71568 | 75673 | 35185 89759 | 44901 74291 |
| | | | | | | | |
| 24895 | 88530 | 70774 | 35439 | 46758 | 70472 | 70207 92675 | 91623 61275 |
| 35720 | 26556 | 95596 | 20094 | 73750 | 85788 | 34264 01703 | 46833 65248 |
| 14141 | 53410 | 38649 | 06343 | 57256 | 61342 | 72709 75318 | 90379 37562 |
| 27416 | 75670 | 92176 | 72535 | 93119 | 56077 | 06886 18244 | 92344 31374 |
| 82071 | 07429 | 81007 | 47749 | 40744 | 56974 | 23336 88821 | 53841 10536 |
| | | | | | | | |
| 21445 | 82793 | 24831 | 93241 | 14199 | 76268 | 70883 68002 | 03829 17443 |
| 72513 | 76400 | 52225 | 92348 | 62308 | 98481 | 29744 33165 | 33141 61020 |
| 71479 | 45027 | 76160 | 57411 | 13780 | 13632 | 52308 77762 | 88874 33697 |
| 83210 | 51466 | 09088 | 50395 | 26743 | 05306 | 21706 70001 | 99439 80767 |
| 68749 | 95148 | 94897 | 78636 | 96750 | 09024 | 94538 91143 | 96693 61886 |
| | | | | | | | |
| 05184 | 75763 | 47075 | 88158 | 05313 | 53439 | 14908 08830 | 60096 21551 |
| 13651 | 62546 | 96892 | 25240 | 47511 | 58483 | 87342 78818 | 07855 39269 |
| 00566 | 21220 | 00292 | 24069 | 25072 | 29519 | 52548 54091 | 21282 21296 |
| 50958 | 17695 | 58072 | 68990 | 60329 | 95955 | 71586 63417 | 35947 67807 |
| 57621 | 64547 | 46850 | 37981 | 38527 | 09037 | 64756 03324 | 04986 83666 |
| | | | | | | | |
| 09282 | 25844 | 79139 | 78435 | 35428 | 43561 | 69799 63314 | 12991 93516 |
| 23394 | 94206 | 93432 | 37836 | 94919 | 26846 | 02555 74410 | 94915 48199 |
| 05280 | 37470 | 93622 | 04345 | 15092 | 19510 | 18094 16613 | 78234 50001 |
| 95491 | 97976 | 38306 | 32192 | 82639 | 54624 | 72434 92606 | 23191 74693 |
| 78521 | 00104 | 18248 | 75583 | 90326 | 50785 | 54034 66251 | 35774 14692 |
| | | | | | | | |
| 96345 | 44579 | 85932 | 44053 | 75704 | 20840 | 86583 83944 | 52456 73766 |
| 77963 | 31151 | 32364 | 91691 | 47357 | 40338 | 23435 24065 | 08458 95366 |
| 07520 | 11294 | 23238 | 01748 | 41690 | 67328 | 54814 37777 | 10057 42332 |
| 38423 | 02309 | 70703 | 85736 | 46148 | 14258 | 29236 12152 | 05088 65825 |
| 02463 | 65533 | 21199 | 60555 | 33928 | 01817 | 07396 89215 | 30722 22102 |
| | | | | | | | |
| 15880 | 92261 | 17292 | 88190 | 61781 | 48898 | 92525 21283 | 88581 60098 |
| 71926 | 00819 | 59144 | 00224 | 30570 | 90194 | 18329 06999 | 26857 19238 |
| 64425 | 28108 | 16554 | 16016 | 00042 | 83229 | 10333 36168 | 65617 94834 |
| 79782 | 23924 | 49440 | 30432 | 81077 | 31543 | 95216 64865 | 13658 51081 |
| 35337 | 74538 | 44553 | 64672 | 90960 | 41849 | 93865 44608 | 93176 34851 |
| | | | | | | | |
| 05249 | 29329 | 19715 | 94082 | 14738 | 86667 | 43708 66354 | 93692 25527 |
| 56463 | 99380 | 38793 | 85774 | 19056 | 13939 | 46062 27647 | 66146 63210 |
| 96296 | 33121 | 54196 | 34108 | 75814 | 85986 | 71171 15102 | 28992 63165 |
| 98380 | 36269 | 60014 | 07201 | 62448 | 46385 | 42175 88350 | 46182 49126 |
| 52567 | 64350 | 16315 | 53969 | 80395 | 81114 | 54358 64578 | 47269 15747 |
| | | | | | | | |
| 78498 | 90830 | 25955 | 99236 | 43286 | 91064 | 99969 95144 | 64424 77377 |
| 49553 | 24241 | 08150 | 89535 | 08703 | 91041 | 77323 81079 | 45127 93686 |
| 32151 | 07075 | 83155 | 10252 | 73100 | 88618 | 23891 87418 | 45417 20268 |
| 11314 | 50363 | 26860 | 27799 | 49416 | 83534 | 19187 08059 | 76677 02110 |
| 12364 | 71210 | 87052 | 50241 | 90785 | 97889 | 81399 58130 | 64439 05614 |

*Table continued on the following page*

Table A–1. *Continued*

| | | | | | | | | |
|---|---|---|---|---|---|---|---|---|
| 94015 | 46874 | 32444 | 48277 | 59820 | 96163 | 64654 | 25843 | 41145 | 42820 |
| 74108 | 88222 | 88570 | 74015 | 25704 | 91035 | 01755 | 14750 | 48968 | 38603 |
| 62880 | 87873 | 95160 | 59221 | 22304 | 90314 | 72877 | 17334 | 39283 | 04149 |
| 11748 | 12102 | 80580 | 41867 | 17710 | 59621 | 06554 | 07850 | 73950 | 79552 |
| 17944 | 05600 | 60478 | 03343 | 25852 | 58905 | 57216 | 39618 | 49856 | 99326 |
| | | | | | | | | |
| 66067 | 42792 | 95043 | 52680 | 46780 | 56487 | 09971 | 59481 | 37006 | 22186 |
| 54244 | 91030 | 45547 | 70818 | 59849 | 96169 | 61459 | 21647 | 87417 | 17198 |
| 30945 | 57589 | 31732 | 57260 | 47670 | 07654 | 46376 | 25366 | 94746 | 49580 |
| 69170 | 37403 | 86995 | 90307 | 94304 | 71803 | 26825 | 05511 | 12459 | 91314 |
| 08345 | 88975 | 35841 | 85771 | 08105 | 59987 | 87112 | 21476 | 14713 | 71181 |
| | | | | | | | | |
| 27767 | 43584 | 85301 | 88977 | 29490 | 69714 | 73035 | 41207 | 74699 | 09310 |
| 13025 | 14338 | 54066 | 15243 | 47724 | 66733 | 47431 | 43905 | 31048 | 56699 |
| 80217 | 36292 | 98525 | 24335 | 24432 | 24896 | 43277 | 58874 | 11466 | 16082 |
| 10875 | 62004 | 90391 | 61105 | 57411 | 06368 | 53856 | 30743 | 08670 | 84741 |
| 54127 | 57326 | 26629 | 19087 | 24472 | 88779 | 30540 | 27886 | 61732 | 75454 |
| | | | | | | | | |
| 60311 | 42824 | 37301 | 42678 | 45990 | 43242 | 17374 | 52003 | 70707 | 70214 |
| 49739 | 71484 | 92003 | 98086 | 76668 | 73209 | 59202 | 11973 | 02902 | 33250 |
| 78626 | 51594 | 16453 | 94614 | 39014 | 97066 | 83012 | 09832 | 25571 | 77628 |
| 66692 | 13986 | 99837 | 00582 | 81232 | 44987 | 09504 | 96412 | 90193 | 79568 |
| 44071 | 28091 | 07362 | 97703 | 76447 | 42537 | 98524 | 97831 | 65704 | 09514 |
| | | | | | | | | |
| 41468 | 85149 | 49554 | 17994 | 14924 | 39650 | 95294 | 00556 | 70481 | 06905 |
| 94559 | 37559 | 49678 | 53119 | 70312 | 05682 | 66986 | 34099 | 74474 | 20740 |
| 41615 | 70360 | 64114 | 58660 | 90850 | 64618 | 80620 | 51790 | 11436 | 38072 |
| 50273 | 93113 | 41794 | 86861 | 24781 | 89683 | 55411 | 85667 | 77535 | 99892 |
| 41396 | 80504 | 90670 | 08289 | 40902 | 05069 | 95083 | 06783 | 28102 | 57816 |
| | | | | | | | | |
| 25807 | 24260 | 71529 | 78920 | 72682 | 07385 | 90726 | 57166 | 98884 | 08583 |
| 06170 | 97965 | 88302 | 98041 | 21443 | 41808 | 68984 | 83620 | 89747 | 98882 |
| 60808 | 54444 | 74412 | 81105 | 01176 | 28838 | 36421 | 16489 | 18059 | 51061 |
| 80940 | 44893 | 10408 | 36222 | 80582 | 71944 | 92638 | 40333 | 67054 | 16067 |
| 19516 | 90120 | 46759 | 71643 | 13177 | 55292 | 21036 | 82808 | 77501 | 97427 |
| | | | | | | | | |
| 49386 | 54480 | 23604 | 23554 | 21785 | 41101 | 91178 | 10174 | 29420 | 90438 |
| 06312 | 88940 | 15995 | 69321 | 47458 | 64809 | 98189 | 81851 | 29651 | 84215 |
| 60942 | 00307 | 11897 | 92674 | 40405 | 68032 | 96717 | 54244 | 10701 | 41393 |
| 92329 | 98932 | 78284 | 46347 | 71209 | 92061 | 39448 | 93136 | 25722 | 08564 |
| 77936 | 63574 | 31384 | 51924 | 85561 | 29671 | 58137 | 17820 | 22751 | 36518 |
| | | | | | | | | |
| 38101 | 77756 | 11657 | 13897 | 95889 | 57067 | 47648 | 13885 | 70669 | 93406 |
| 39641 | 69457 | 91339 | 22502 | 92613 | 89719 | 11947 | 56203 | 19324 | 20504 |
| 84054 | 40455 | 99396 | 63680 | 67667 | 60631 | 69181 | 96845 | 38525 | 11600 |
| 47468 | 03577 | 57649 | 63266 | 24700 | 71594 | 14004 | 23153 | 69249 | 05747 |
| 43321 | 31370 | 28977 | 23896 | 76479 | 68562 | 62342 | 07589 | 08899 | 05985 |
| | | | | | | | | |
| 64281 | 61826 | 18555 | 64937 | 13173 | 33365 | 78851 | 16499 | 87064 | 13075 |
| 66847 | 70495 | 32350 | 02985 | 86716 | 38746 | 26313 | 77463 | 55387 | 72681 |
| 72461 | 33230 | 21529 | 53424 | 92581 | 02262 | 78438 | 66276 | 18396 | 73538 |
| 21032 | 91050 | 13058 | 16218 | 12470 | 56500 | 15292 | 76139 | 59526 | 52113 |
| 95362 | 67011 | 06651 | 16136 | 01016 | 00857 | 55018 | 56374 | 35824 | 71708 |
| | | | | | | | | |
| 49712 | 97380 | 10404 | 55452 | 34030 | 60726 | 75211 | 10271 | 36633 | 68424 |
| 58275 | 61764 | 97586 | 54716 | 50259 | 46345 | 87195 | 46092 | 26787 | 60939 |
| 89514 | 11788 | 68224 | 23417 | 73959 | 76145 | 30342 | 40277 | 11049 | 72049 |
| 15472 | 50669 | 48139 | 36732 | 46874 | 37088 | 73465 | 09819 | 58869 | 35220 |
| 12120 | 86124 | 51247 | 44302 | 60883 | 52109 | 21437 | 36786 | 49226 | 77837 |

**Table A-1.** *Continued*

| | | | | | | |
|---|---|---|---|---|---|---|
| 09188 20097 | 32825 39527 | 04220 86304 | 83389 87374 | 64278 58044 |
| 90045 85497 | 51981 50654 | 94938 81997 | 91870 76150 | 68476 64659 |
| 73189 50207 | 47677 26269 | 62290 64464 | 27124 67018 | 41361 82760 |
| 75768 76490 | 20971 87749 | 90429 12272 | 95375 05871 | 93823 43178 |
| 54016 44056 | 66281 31003 | 00682 27398 | 20714 53295 | 07706 17813 |
| | | | | |
| 08358 69910 | 78542 42785 | 13661 58873 | 04618 97553 | 31223 08420 |
| 28306 03264 | 81333 10591 | 40510 07893 | 32604 60475 | 94119 01840 |
| 53840 86233 | 81594 13628 | 51215 90290 | 28466 68795 | 77762 20791 |
| 91757 53741 | 61613 62269 | 50263 90212 | 55781 76514 | 83483 47055 |
| 89415 92694 | 00397 58391 | 12607 17646 | 48949 72306 | 94541 37408 |
| | | | | |
| 77513 03820 | 86864 29901 | 68414 82774 | 51908 13980 | 72893 55507 |
| 19502 37174 | 69979 20288 | 55210 29773 | 74287 75251 | 65344 67415 |
| 21818 59313 | 93278 81757 | 05686 73156 | 07082 85046 | 31853 38452 |
| 51474 66499 | 68107 23621 | 94049 91345 | 42836 09191 | 08007 45449 |
| 99559 68331 | 62535 24170 | 69777 12830 | 74819 78142 | 43860 72834 |
| | | | | |
| 33713 48007 | 93584 72869 | 51926 64721 | 58303 29822 | 93174 93972 |
| 85274 86893 | 11303 22970 | 28834 34137 | 73515 90400 | 71148 43643 |
| 84133 89640 | 44035 52166 | 73852 70091 | 61222 60561 | 62327 18423 |
| 56732 16234 | 17395 96131 | 10123 91622 | 85496 57560 | 81604 18880 |
| 65138 56806 | 87648 85261 | 34313 65861 | 45875 21069 | 85644 47277 |
| | | | | |
| 38001 02176 | 81719 11711 | 71602 92937 | 74219 64049 | 65584 49698 |
| 37402 96397 | 01304 77586 | 56271 10086 | 47324 62605 | 40030 37438 |
| 97125 40348 | 87083 31417 | 21815 39250 | 75237 62047 | 15501 29578 |
| 21826 41134 | 47143 34072 | 64638 85902 | 49139 06441 | 03856 54552 |
| 73135 42742 | 95719 09035 | 85794 74296 | 08789 88156 | 64691 19202 |
| | | | | |
| 07638 77929 | 03061 18072 | 96207 44156 | 23821 99538 | 04713 66994 |
| 60528 83441 | 07954 19814 | 59175 20695 | 05533 52139 | 61212 06455 |
| 83596 35655 | 06958 92983 | 05128 09719 | 77433 53783 | 92301 50498 |
| 10850 62746 | 99599 10507 | 13499 06319 | 53075 71839 | 06410 19362 |
| 39820 98952 | 43622 63147 | 64421 80814 | 43800 09351 | 31024 73167 |
| | | | | |
| 59580 06478 | 75569 78800 | 88835 54486 | 23768 06156 | 04111 08408 |
| 38508 07341 | 23793 48763 | 90822 97022 | 17719 04207 | 95954 49953 |
| 30692 70668 | 94688 16127 | 56196 80091 | 82067 63400 | 05462 69200 |
| 65443 95659 | 18288 27437 | 49632 24041 | 08337 65676 | 96299 90836 |
| 27267 50264 | 13192 72294 | 07477 44606 | 17985 48911 | 97341 30358 |
| | | | | |
| 91307 06991 | 19072 24210 | 36699 53728 | 28825 35793 | 28976 66252 |
| 68434 94688 | 84473 13622 | 62126 98408 | 12843 82590 | 09815 93146 |
| 48908 15877 | 54745 24591 | 35700 04754 | 83824 52692 | 54130 55160 |
| 06913 45197 | 42672 78601 | 11883 09528 | 63011 98901 | 14974 40344 |
| 10455 16019 | 14210 33712 | 91342 37821 | 88325 80851 | 43667 70883 |
| | | | | |
| 12883 97343 | 65027 61184 | 04285 01392 | 17974 15077 | 90712 26769 |
| 21778 30976 | 38807 36961 | 31649 42096 | 63281 02023 | 08816 47449 |
| 19523 59515 | 65122 59659 | 86283 68258 | 69572 13798 | 16435 91529 |
| 67245 52670 | 35583 16563 | 79246 86686 | 76463 34222 | 26655 90802 |
| 60584 47377 | 07500 37992 | 45134 26529 | 26760 83637 | 41326 44344 |
| | | | | |
| 53853 41377 | 36066 94850 | 58838 73859 | 49364 73331 | 96240 43642 |
| 24637 38736 | 74384 89342 | 52623 07992 | 12369 18601 | 03742 83873 |
| 83080 12451 | 38992 22815 | 07759 51777 | 97377 27585 | 51972 37867 |
| 16444 24334 | 36151 99073 | 27493 70939 | 85130 32552 | 54846 54759 |
| 60790 18157 | 57178 65762 | 11161 78576 | 45819 52979 | 65130 04860 |

**Table A–2.** AREAS OF A STANDARD NORMAL DISTRIBUTION*

Standard score values are listed in the column headed "$z$." To find the proportion of the total area occurring between the mean and any given $z$-score, locate the entry indicated by the $z$-score. For example, a $z$-score of $+1.96$ is located by reading across to column 6 from the value of 1.9 in the "$z$" column. The value in the body of the table is .4750. Since the total area above the mean is equal to .5000, this means that only .0250 of the area is beyond the $z$-score of $+1.96$. Similarly, a $z$-score of $-2.58$ has a value of .4951, indicating that only .0049 of the area lies beyond the $z$-score of $-2.58$.·

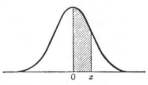

| $z$ | .00 | .01 | .02 | .03 | .04 | .05 | .06 | .07 | .08 | .09 |
|-----|-----|-----|-----|-----|-----|-----|-----|-----|-----|-----|
| 0.0 | .0000 | .0040 | .0080 | .0120 | .0160 | .0199 | .0239 | .0279 | .0319 | .0359 |
| 0.1 | .0398 | .0438 | .0478 | .0517 | .0557 | .0596 | .0636 | .0675 | .0714 | .0753 |
| 0.2 | .0793 | .0832 | .0871 | .0910 | .0948 | .0987 | .1026 | .1064 | .1103 | .1141 |
| 0.3 | .1179 | .1217 | .1255 | .1293 | .1331 | .1368 | .1406 | .1443 | .1480 | .1517 |
| 0.4 | .1554 | .1591 | .1628 | .1664 | .1700 | .1736 | .1772 | .1808 | .1844 | .1879 |
| 0.5 | .1915 | .1950 | .1985 | .2019 | .2054 | .2088 | .2123 | .2157 | .2190 | .2224 |
| 0.6 | .2257 | .2291 | .2324 | .2357 | .2389 | .2422 | .2454 | .2486 | .2517 | .2549 |
| 0.7 | .2580 | .2611 | .2642 | .2673 | .2703 | .2734 | .2764 | .2794 | .2823 | .2852 |
| 0.8 | .2881 | .2910 | .2939 | .2967 | .2995 | .3023 | .3051 | .3078 | .3106 | .3133 |
| 0.9 | .3159 | .3186 | .3212 | .3238 | .3264 | .3289 | .3315 | .3340 | .3365 | .3389 |
| 1.0 | .3413 | .3438 | .3461 | .3485 | .3508 | .3531 | .3554 | .3577 | .3599 | .3621 |
| 1.1 | .3643 | .3665 | .3686 | .3708 | .3729 | .3749 | .3770 | .3790 | .3810 | .3830 |
| 1.2 | .3849 | .3869 | .3888 | .3907 | .3925 | .3944 | .3962 | .3980 | .3997 | .4015 |
| 1.3 | .4032 | .4049 | .4066 | .4082 | .4099 | .4115 | .4131 | .4147 | .4162 | .4177 |
| 1.4 | .4192 | .4207 | .4222 | .4236 | .4251 | .4265 | .4279 | .4292 | .4306 | .4319 |
| 1.5 | .4332 | .4345 | .4357 | .4370 | .4382 | .4394 | .4406 | .4418 | .4429 | .4441 |
| 1.6 | .4452 | .4463 | .4474 | .4484 | .4495 | .4505 | .4515 | .4525 | .4535 | .4545 |
| 1.7 | .4554 | .4564 | .4573 | .4582 | .4591 | .4599 | .4608 | .4616 | .4625 | .4633 |
| 1.8 | .4641 | .4649 | .4656 | .4664 | .4671 | .4678 | .4686 | .4693 | .4699 | .4706 |
| 1.9 | .4713 | .4719 | .4726 | .4732 | .4738 | .4744 | .4750 | .4756 | .4761 | .4767 |
| 2.0 | .4772 | .4778 | .4783 | .4788 | .4793 | .4798 | .4803 | .4808 | .4812 | .4817 |
| 2.1 | .4821 | .4826 | .4830 | .4834 | .4838 | .4842 | .4846 | 4850 | .4854 | .4857 |
| 2.2 | .4861 | .4864 | .4868 | .4871 | .4875 | .4878 | .4881 | .4884 | .4887 | .4890 |
| 2.3 | .4893 | .4896 | .4898 | .4901 | .4904 | .4906 | .4909 | .4911 | .4913 | .4916 |
| 2.4 | .4918 | .4920 | .4922 | .4925 | .4927 | .4929 | .4931 | .4932 | .4934 | .4936 |
| 2.5 | .4938 | .4940 | .4941 | .4943 | .4945 | .4946 | .4948 | .4949 | .4951 | .4952 |
| 2.6 | .4953 | .4955 | .4956 | .4957 | .4959 | .4960 | .4961 | .4962 | .4963 | .4964 |
| 2.7 | .4965 | .4966 | .4967 | .4968 | .4969 | .4970 | .4971 | .4972 | .4973 | .4974 |
| 2.8 | .4974 | .4975 | .4976 | .4977 | .4977 | .4978 | .4979 | .4979 | .4980 | .4981 |
| 2.9 | .4981 | .4982 | .4982 | .4983 | .4984 | .4984 | .4985 | .4985 | .4986 | .4986 |
| 3.0 | .4987 | .4987 | .4987 | .4988 | .4988 | .4989 | .4989 | .4989 | .4990 | .4990 |

*Reproduced with permission from Hoel, P. G.: *Elementary Statistics*, 2nd Ed. New York: John Wiley and Sons, Inc., 1966.

**Table A–3.** STUDENT'S *t* DISTRIBUTION

The first column contains the number of degrees of freedom (*df*). The values in the body of the table are the values of *t* that must be exceeded to attain a certain probability value. For example, a *t* value of 3.63 with 9 degrees of freedom will occur less than 0 .01 of the time since it exceeds the tabled value of 3.2498 shown for the probability of .01 and 9 *df*.

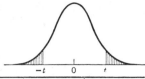

| P \\ df | 0.50 | 0.25 | 0.10 | 0.05 | 0.025 | 0.01 | 0.005 |
|---|---|---|---|---|---|---|---|
| 1 | 1.00000 | 2.4142 | 6.3138 | 12.706 | 25.452 | 63.657 | 127.32 |
| 2 | 0.81650 | 1.6036 | 2.9200 | 4.3027 | 6.2053 | 9.9248 | 14.089 |
| 3 | 0.76489 | 1.4226 | 2.3534 | 3.1825 | 4.1765 | 5.8409 | 7.4533 |
| 4 | 0.74070 | 1.3444 | 2.1318 | 2.7764 | 3.4954 | 4.6041 | 5.5976 |
| 5 | 0.72669 | 1.3009 | 2.0150 | 2.5706 | 3.1634 | 4.0321 | 4.7733 |
| 6 | 0.71756 | 1.2733 | 1.9432 | 2.4469 | 2.9687 | 3.7074 | 4.3168 |
| 7 | 0.71114 | 1.2543 | 1.8946 | 2.3646 | 2.8412 | 3.4995 | 4.0293 |
| 8 | 0.70639 | 1.2403 | 1.8595 | 2.3060 | 2.7515 | 3.3554 | 3.8325 |
| 9 | 0.70272 | 1.2297 | 1.8331 | 2.2622 | 2.6850 | 3.2498 | 3.6897 |
| 10 | 0.69981 | 1.2213 | 1.8125 | 2.2281 | 2.6338 | 3.1693 | 3.5814 |
| 11 | 0.69745 | 1.2145 | 1.7959 | 2.2010 | 2.5931 | 3.1058 | 3.4966 |
| 12 | 0.69548 | 1.2089 | 1.7823 | 2.1788 | 2.5600 | 3.0545 | 3.4284 |
| 13 | 0.69384 | 1.2041 | 1.7709 | 2.1604 | 2.5326 | 3.0123 | 3.3725 |
| 14 | 0.69242 | 1.2001 | 1.7613 | 2.1448 | 2.5096 | 2.9768 | 3.3257 |
| 15 | 0.69120 | 1.1967 | 1.7530 | 2.1315 | 2.4899 | 2.9467 | 3.2860 |
| 16 | 0.69013 | 1.1937 | 1.7459 | 2.1199 | 2.4729 | 2.9208 | 3.2520 |
| 17 | 0.68919 | 1.1910 | 1.7396 | 2.1098 | 2.4581 | 2.8982 | 3.2225 |
| 18 | 0.68837 | 1.1887 | 1.7341 | 2.1009 | 2.4450 | 2.8784 | 3.1966 |
| 19 | 0.68763 | 1.1866 | 1.7291 | 2.0930 | 2.4334 | 2.8609 | 3.1737 |
| 20 | 0.68696 | 1.1848 | 1.7247 | 2.0860 | 2.4231 | 2.8453 | 3.1534 |
| 21 | 0.68635 | 1.1831 | 1.7207 | 2.0796 | 2.4138 | 2.8314 | 3.1352 |
| 22 | 0.68580 | 1.1816 | 1.7171 | 2.0739 | 2.4055 | 2.8188 | 3.1188 |
| 23 | 0.68531 | 1.1802 | 1.7139 | 2.0687 | 2.3979 | 2.8073 | 3.1040 |
| 24 | 0.68485 | 1.1789 | 1.7109 | 2.0639 | 2.3910 | 2.7969 | 3.0905 |
| 25 | 0.68443 | 1.1777 | 1.7081 | 2.0595 | 2.3846 | 2.7874 | 3.0782 |
| 26 | 0.68405 | 1.1766 | 1.7056 | 2.0555 | 2.3788 | 2.7787 | 3.0669 |
| 27 | 0.68370 | 1.1757 | 1.7033 | 2.0518 | 2.3734 | 2.7707 | 3.0565 |
| 28 | 0.68335 | 1.1748 | 1.7011 | 2.0484 | 2.3685 | 2.7633 | 3.0469 |
| 29 | 0.68304 | 1.1739 | 1.6991 | 2.0452 | 2.3638 | 2.7564 | 3.0380 |
| 30 | 0.68276 | 1.1731 | 1.6973 | 2.0423 | 2.3596 | 2.7500 | 3.0298 |
| 40 | 0.68066 | 1.1673 | 1.6839 | 2.0211 | 2.3289 | 2.7045 | 2.9712 |
| 60 | 0.67862 | 1.1616 | 1.6707 | 2.0003 | 2.2991 | 2.6603 | 2.9146 |
| 120 | 0.67656 | 1.1559 | 1.6577 | 1.9799 | 2.2699 | 2.6174 | 2.8599 |
| ∞ | 0.67449 | 1.1503 | 1.6449 | 1.9600 | 2.2414 | 2.5758 | 2.8070 |

*Reproduced with permission from Hoel, P. G.: *Elementary Statistics*, 2nd Ed. New York: John Wiley and Sons, Inc., 1966.

## Table A–4. F Distribution*

Find the column containing the number of degrees of freedom for the numerator ($f_1$) and the row containing the number of degrees of freedom for the denominator ($f_2$). If the value in the body of the table is exceeded by the obtained $F$ value, the 5 per cent significance level has been reached. For example, an $F$ of 5.02 with $df$ for the numerator equal to 1 and $df$ for the denominator equal to 10 exceeds the table value of 4.96 at the 5 per cent level and would be judged significant at that level.

Each cell gives the 5 per cent value (upper) and the **1 per cent value (lower, bold)**.

$f_1$, Degrees of Freedom (for greater mean square)

| $f_2$ | 1 | 2 | 3 | 4 | 5 | 6 | 7 | 8 | 9 | 10 | 11 | 12 | 14 | 16 | 20 | 24 | 30 | 40 | 50 | 75 | 100 | 200 | 500 | ∞ |
|---|---|---|---|---|---|---|---|---|---|---|---|---|---|---|---|---|---|---|---|---|---|---|---|---|
| **1** | 161 / **4,052** | 200 / **4,999** | 216 / **5,403** | 225 / **5,625** | 230 / **5,764** | 234 / **5,859** | 237 / **5,928** | 239 / **5,981** | 241 / **6,022** | 242 / **6,056** | 243 / **6,082** | 244 / **6,106** | 245 / **6,142** | 246 / **6,169** | 248 / **6,208** | 249 / **6,234** | 250 / **6,261** | 251 / **6,286** | 252 / **6,302** | 253 / **6,323** | 253 / **6,334** | 254 / **6,352** | 254 / **6,361** | 254 / **6,366** |
| **2** | 18.51 / **98.49** | 19.00 / **99.00** | 19.16 / **99.17** | 19.25 / **99.25** | 19.30 / **99.30** | 19.33 / **99.33** | 19.36 / **99.36** | 19.37 / **99.37** | 19.38 / **99.39** | 19.39 / **99.40** | 19.40 / **99.41** | 19.41 / **99.42** | 19.42 / **99.43** | 19.43 / **99.44** | 19.44 / **99.45** | 19.45 / **99.46** | 19.46 / **99.47** | 19.47 / **99.48** | 19.47 / **99.48** | 19.48 / **99.49** | 19.49 / **99.49** | 19.49 / **99.49** | 19.50 / **99.50** | 19.50 / **99.50** |
| **3** | 10.13 / **34.12** | 9.55 / **30.82** | 9.28 / **29.46** | 9.12 / **28.71** | 9.01 / **28.24** | 8.94 / **27.91** | 8.88 / **27.67** | 8.84 / **27.49** | 8.81 / **27.34** | 8.78 / **27.23** | 8.76 / **27.13** | 8.74 / **27.05** | 8.71 / **26.92** | 8.69 / **26.83** | 8.66 / **26.69** | 8.64 / **26.60** | 8.62 / **26.50** | 8.60 / **26.41** | 8.58 / **26.35** | 8.57 / **26.27** | 8.56 / **26.23** | 8.54 / **26.18** | 8.54 / **26.14** | 8.53 / **26.12** |
| **4** | 7.71 / **21.20** | 6.94 / **18.00** | 6.59 / **16.69** | 6.39 / **15.98** | 6.26 / **15.52** | 6.16 / **15.21** | 6.09 / **14.98** | 6.04 / **14.80** | 6.00 / **14.66** | 5.96 / **14.54** | 5.93 / **14.45** | 5.91 / **14.37** | 5.87 / **14.24** | 5.84 / **14.15** | 5.80 / **14.02** | 5.77 / **13.93** | 5.74 / **13.83** | 5.71 / **13.74** | 5.70 / **13.69** | 5.68 / **13.61** | 5.66 / **13.57** | 5.65 / **13.52** | 5.64 / **13.48** | 5.63 / **13.46** |
| **5** | 6.61 / **16.26** | 5.79 / **13.27** | 5.41 / **12.06** | 5.19 / **11.39** | 5.05 / **10.97** | 4.95 / **10.67** | 4.88 / **10.45** | 4.82 / **10.29** | 4.78 / **10.15** | 4.74 / **10.05** | 4.70 / **9.96** | 4.68 / **9.89** | 4.64 / **9.77** | 4.60 / **9.68** | 4.56 / **9.55** | 4.53 / **9.47** | 4.50 / **9.38** | 4.46 / **9.29** | 4.44 / **9.24** | 4.42 / **9.17** | 4.40 / **9.13** | 4.38 / **9.07** | 4.37 / **9.04** | 4.36 / **9.02** |
| **6** | 5.99 / **13.74** | 5.14 / **10.92** | 4.76 / **9.78** | 4.53 / **9.15** | 4.39 / **8.75** | 4.28 / **8.47** | 4.21 / **8.26** | 4.15 / **8.10** | 4.10 / **7.98** | 4.06 / **7.87** | 4.03 / **7.79** | 4.00 / **7.72** | 3.96 / **7.60** | 3.92 / **7.52** | 3.87 / **7.39** | 3.84 / **7.31** | 3.81 / **7.23** | 3.77 / **7.14** | 3.75 / **7.09** | 3.72 / **7.02** | 3.71 / **6.99** | 3.69 / **6.94** | 3.68 / **6.90** | 3.67 / **6.88** |
| **7** | 5.59 / **12.25** | 4.74 / **9.55** | 4.35 / **8.45** | 4.12 / **7.85** | 3.97 / **7.46** | 3.87 / **7.19** | 3.79 / **7.00** | 3.73 / **6.84** | 3.68 / **6.71** | 3.63 / **6.62** | 3.60 / **6.54** | 3.57 / **6.47** | 3.52 / **6.35** | 3.49 / **6.27** | 3.44 / **6.15** | 3.41 / **6.07** | 3.38 / **5.98** | 3.34 / **5.90** | 3.32 / **5.85** | 3.29 / **5.78** | 3.28 / **5.75** | 3.25 / **5.70** | 3.24 / **5.67** | 3.23 / **5.65** |
| **8** | 5.32 / **11.26** | 4.46 / **8.65** | 4.07 / **7.59** | 3.84 / **7.01** | 3.69 / **6.63** | 3.58 / **6.37** | 3.50 / **6.19** | 3.44 / **6.03** | 3.39 / **5.91** | 3.34 / **5.82** | 3.31 / **5.74** | 3.28 / **5.67** | 3.23 / **5.56** | 3.20 / **5.48** | 3.15 / **5.36** | 3.12 / **5.28** | 3.08 / **5.20** | 3.05 / **5.11** | 3.03 / **5.06** | 3.00 / **5.00** | 2.98 / **4.96** | 2.96 / **4.91** | 2.94 / **4.88** | 2.93 / **4.86** |
| **9** | 5.12 / **10.56** | 4.26 / **8.02** | 3.86 / **6.99** | 3.63 / **6.42** | 3.48 / **6.06** | 3.37 / **5.80** | 3.29 / **5.62** | 3.23 / **5.47** | 3.18 / **5.35** | 3.13 / **5.26** | 3.10 / **5.18** | 3.07 / **5.11** | 3.02 / **5.00** | 2.98 / **4.92** | 2.93 / **4.80** | 2.90 / **4.73** | 2.86 / **4.64** | 2.82 / **4.56** | 2.80 / **4.51** | 2.77 / **4.45** | 2.76 / **4.41** | 2.73 / **4.36** | 2.72 / **4.33** | 2.71 / **4.31** |
| **10** | 4.96 / **10.04** | 4.10 / **7.56** | 3.71 / **6.55** | 3.48 / **5.99** | 3.33 / **5.64** | 3.22 / **5.39** | 3.14 / **5.21** | 3.07 / **5.06** | 3.02 / **4.95** | 2.97 / **4.85** | 2.94 / **4.78** | 2.91 / **4.71** | 2.86 / **4.60** | 2.82 / **4.52** | 2.77 / **4.41** | 2.74 / **4.33** | 2.70 / **4.25** | 2.67 / **4.17** | 2.64 / **4.12** | 2.61 / **4.05** | 2.59 / **4.01** | 2.56 / **3.96** | 2.55 / **3.93** | 2.54 / **3.91** |

*Reproduced with permission from Hoel, P. G.: *Elementary Statistics*, 2nd Ed. New York: John Wiley and Sons, Inc., 1966.

**Table A–4.** *Continued*

$f_1$, Degrees of Freedom (for greater mean square)

| $f_2$ | 1 | 2 | 3 | 4 | 5 | 6 | 7 | 8 | 9 | 10 | 11 | 12 | 14 | 16 | 20 | 24 | 30 | 40 | 50 | 75 | 100 | 200 | 500 | ∞ | $f_2$ |
|---|---|---|---|---|---|---|---|---|---|---|---|---|---|---|---|---|---|---|---|---|---|---|---|---|---|
| 11 | 4.84 / 9.65 | 3.98 / 7.20 | 3.59 / 6.22 | 3.36 / 5.67 | 3.20 / 5.32 | 3.09 / 5.07 | 3.01 / 4.88 | 2.95 / 4.74 | 2.90 / 4.63 | 2.86 / 4.54 | 2.82 / 4.46 | 2.79 / 4.40 | 2.74 / 4.29 | 2.70 / 4.21 | 2.65 / 4.10 | 2.61 / 4.02 | 2.57 / 3.94 | 2.53 / 3.86 | 2.50 / 3.80 | 2.47 / 3.74 | 2.45 / 3.70 | 2.42 / 3.66 | 2.41 / 3.62 | 2.40 / 3.60 | 11 |
| 12 | 4.75 / 9.33 | 3.88 / 6.93 | 3.49 / 5.95 | 3.26 / 5.41 | 3.11 / 5.06 | 3.00 / 4.82 | 2.92 / 4.65 | 2.85 / 4.50 | 2.80 / 4.39 | 2.76 / 4.30 | 2.72 / 4.22 | 2.69 / 4.16 | 2.64 / 4.05 | 2.60 / 3.98 | 2.54 / 3.86 | 2.50 / 3.78 | 2.46 / 3.70 | 2.42 / 3.61 | 2.40 / 3.56 | 2.36 / 3.49 | 2.35 / 3.46 | 2.32 / 3.41 | 2.31 / 3.38 | 2.30 / 3.36 | 12 |
| 13 | 4.67 / 9.07 | 3.80 / 6.70 | 3.41 / 5.74 | 3.18 / 5.20 | 3.02 / 4.86 | 2.92 / 4.62 | 2.84 / 4.44 | 2.77 / 4.30 | 2.72 / 4.19 | 2.67 / 4.10 | 2.63 / 4.02 | 2.60 / 3.96 | 2.55 / 3.85 | 2.51 / 3.78 | 2.46 / 3.67 | 2.42 / 3.59 | 2.38 / 3.51 | 2.34 / 3.42 | 2.32 / 3.37 | 2.28 / 3.30 | 2.26 / 3.27 | 2.24 / 3.21 | 2.22 / 3.18 | 2.21 / 3.16 | 13 |
| 14 | 4.60 / 8.86 | 3.74 / 6.51 | 3.34 / 5.56 | 3.11 / 5.03 | 2.96 / 4.69 | 2.85 / 4.46 | 2.77 / 4.28 | 2.70 / 4.14 | 2.65 / 4.03 | 2.60 / 3.94 | 2.56 / 3.86 | 2.53 / 3.80 | 2.48 / 3.70 | 2.44 / 3.62 | 2.39 / 3.51 | 2.35 / 3.43 | 2.31 / 3.34 | 2.27 / 3.26 | 2.24 / 3.21 | 2.21 / 3.14 | 2.19 / 3.11 | 2.16 / 3.06 | 2.14 / 3.02 | 2.13 / 3.00 | 14 |
| 15 | 4.54 / 8.68 | 3.68 / 6.36 | 3.29 / 5.42 | 3.06 / 4.89 | 2.90 / 4.56 | 2.79 / 4.32 | 2.70 / 4.14 | 2.64 / 4.00 | 2.59 / 3.89 | 2.55 / 3.80 | 2.51 / 3.73 | 2.48 / 3.67 | 2.43 / 3.56 | 2.39 / 3.48 | 2.33 / 3.36 | 2.29 / 3.29 | 2.25 / 3.20 | 2.21 / 3.12 | 2.18 / 3.07 | 2.15 / 3.00 | 2.12 / 2.97 | 2.10 / 2.92 | 2.08 / 2.89 | 2.07 / 2.87 | 15 |
| 16 | 4.49 / 8.53 | 3.63 / 6.23 | 3.24 / 5.29 | 3.01 / 4.77 | 2.85 / 4.44 | 2.74 / 4.20 | 2.66 / 4.03 | 2.59 / 3.89 | 2.54 / 3.78 | 2.49 / 3.69 | 2.45 / 3.61 | 2.42 / 3.55 | 2.37 / 3.45 | 2.33 / 3.37 | 2.28 / 3.25 | 2.24 / 3.18 | 2.20 / 3.10 | 2.16 / 3.01 | 2.13 / 2.96 | 2.09 / 2.89 | 2.07 / 2.86 | 2.04 / 2.80 | 2.02 / 2.77 | 2.01 / 2.75 | 16 |
| 17 | 4.45 / 8.40 | 3.59 / 6.11 | 3.20 / 5.18 | 2.96 / 4.67 | 2.81 / 4.34 | 2.70 / 4.10 | 2.62 / 3.93 | 2.55 / 3.79 | 2.50 / 3.68 | 2.45 / 3.59 | 2.41 / 3.52 | 2.38 / 3.45 | 2.33 / 3.35 | 2.29 / 3.27 | 2.23 / 3.16 | 2.19 / 3.08 | 2.15 / 3.00 | 2.11 / 2.92 | 2.08 / 2.86 | 2.04 / 2.79 | 2.02 / 2.76 | 1.99 / 2.70 | 1.97 / 2.67 | 1.96 / 2.65 | 17 |
| 18 | 4.41 / 8.28 | 3.55 / 6.01 | 3.16 / 5.09 | 2.93 / 4.58 | 2.77 / 4.25 | 2.66 / 4.01 | 2.58 / 3.85 | 2.51 / 3.71 | 2.46 / 3.60 | 2.41 / 3.51 | 2.37 / 3.44 | 2.34 / 3.37 | 2.29 / 3.27 | 2.25 / 3.19 | 2.19 / 3.07 | 2.15 / 3.00 | 2.11 / 2.91 | 2.07 / 2.83 | 2.04 / 2.78 | 2.00 / 2.71 | 1.98 / 2.68 | 1.95 / 2.62 | 1.93 / 2.59 | 1.92 / 2.57 | 18 |
| 19 | 4.38 / 8.18 | 3.52 / 5.93 | 3.13 / 5.01 | 2.90 / 4.50 | 2.74 / 4.17 | 2.63 / 3.94 | 2.55 / 3.77 | 2.48 / 3.63 | 2.43 / 3.52 | 2.38 / 3.43 | 2.34 / 3.36 | 2.31 / 3.30 | 2.26 / 3.19 | 2.21 / 3.12 | 2.15 / 3.00 | 2.11 / 2.92 | 2.07 / 2.84 | 2.02 / 2.76 | 2.00 / 2.70 | 1.96 / 2.63 | 1.94 / 2.60 | 1.91 / 2.54 | 1.90 / 2.51 | 1.88 / 2.49 | 19 |
| 20 | 4.35 / 8.10 | 3.49 / 5.85 | 3.10 / 4.94 | 2.87 / 4.43 | 2.71 / 4.10 | 2.60 / 3.87 | 2.52 / 3.71 | 2.45 / 3.56 | 2.40 / 3.45 | 2.35 / 3.37 | 2.31 / 3.30 | 2.28 / 3.23 | 2.23 / 3.13 | 2.18 / 3.05 | 2.12 / 2.94 | 2.08 / 2.86 | 2.04 / 2.77 | 1.99 / 2.69 | 1.96 / 2.63 | 1.92 / 2.56 | 1.90 / 2.53 | 1.87 / 2.47 | 1.85 / 2.44 | 1.84 / 2.42 | 20 |
| 21 | 4.32 / 8.02 | 3.47 / 5.78 | 3.07 / 4.87 | 2.84 / 4.37 | 2.68 / 4.04 | 2.57 / 3.81 | 2.49 / 3.65 | 2.42 / 3.51 | 2.37 / 3.40 | 2.32 / 3.31 | 2.28 / 3.24 | 2.25 / 3.17 | 2.20 / 3.07 | 2.15 / 2.99 | 2.09 / 2.88 | 2.05 / 2.80 | 2.00 / 2.72 | 1.96 / 2.63 | 1.93 / 2.58 | 1.89 / 2.51 | 1.87 / 2.47 | 1.84 / 2.42 | 1.82 / 2.38 | 1.81 / 2.36 | 21 |
| 22 | 4.30 / 7.94 | 3.44 / 5.72 | 3.05 / 4.82 | 2.82 / 4.31 | 2.66 / 3.99 | 2.55 / 3.76 | 2.47 / 3.59 | 2.40 / 3.45 | 2.35 / 3.35 | 2.30 / 3.26 | 2.26 / 3.18 | 2.23 / 3.12 | 2.18 / 3.02 | 2.13 / 2.94 | 2.07 / 2.83 | 2.03 / 2.75 | 1.98 / 2.67 | 1.93 / 2.58 | 1.91 / 2.53 | 1.87 / 2.46 | 1.84 / 2.42 | 1.81 / 2.37 | 1.80 / 2.33 | 1.78 / 2.31 | 22 |
| 23 | 4.28 / 7.88 | 3.42 / 5.66 | 3.03 / 4.76 | 2.80 / 4.26 | 2.64 / 3.94 | 2.53 / 3.71 | 2.45 / 3.54 | 2.38 / 3.41 | 2.32 / 3.30 | 2.28 / 3.21 | 2.24 / 3.14 | 2.20 / 3.07 | 2.14 / 2.97 | 2.10 / 2.89 | 2.04 / 2.78 | 2.00 / 2.70 | 1.96 / 2.62 | 1.91 / 2.53 | 1.88 / 2.48 | 1.84 / 2.41 | 1.82 / 2.37 | 1.79 / 2.32 | 1.77 / 2.28 | 1.76 / 2.26 | 23 |
| 24 | 4.26 / 7.82 | 3.40 / 5.61 | 3.01 / 4.72 | 2.78 / 4.22 | 2.62 / 3.90 | 2.51 / 3.67 | 2.43 / 3.50 | 2.36 / 3.36 | 2.30 / 3.25 | 2.26 / 3.17 | 2.22 / 3.09 | 2.18 / 3.03 | 2.13 / 2.93 | 2.09 / 2.85 | 2.02 / 2.74 | 1.98 / 2.66 | 1.94 / 2.58 | 1.89 / 2.49 | 1.86 / 2.44 | 1.82 / 2.36 | 1.80 / 2.33 | 1.76 / 2.27 | 1.74 / 2.23 | 1.73 / 2.21 | 24 |
| 25 | 4.24 / 7.77 | 3.38 / 5.57 | 2.99 / 4.68 | 2.76 / 4.18 | 2.60 / 3.86 | 2.49 / 3.63 | 2.41 / 3.46 | 2.34 / 3.32 | 2.28 / 3.21 | 2.24 / 3.13 | 2.20 / 3.05 | 2.16 / 2.99 | 2.11 / 2.89 | 2.06 / 2.81 | 2.00 / 2.70 | 1.96 / 2.62 | 1.92 / 2.54 | 1.87 / 2.45 | 1.84 / 2.40 | 1.80 / 2.32 | 1.77 / 2.29 | 1.74 / 2.23 | 1.72 / 2.19 | 1.71 / 2.17 | 25 |

The function, $F = e$ with exponent $2z$, is computed in part from Fisher's table VI (7). Additional entries are by interpolation, mostly graphical.

*Table continued on the following page*

Table A–4.  *Continued*

$f_1$ Degrees of Freedom (for greater mean square)

| $f_2$ | 1 | 2 | 3 | 4 | 5 | 6 | 7 | 8 | 9 | 10 | 11 | 12 | 14 | 16 | 20 | 24 | 30 | 40 | 50 | 75 | 100 | 200 | 500 | ∞ |
|---|---|---|---|---|---|---|---|---|---|---|---|---|---|---|---|---|---|---|---|---|---|---|---|---|
| 26 | 4.22 / 7.72 | 3.37 / 5.53 | 2.98 / 4.64 | 2.74 / 4.14 | 2.59 / 3.82 | 2.47 / 3.59 | 2.39 / 3.42 | 2.32 / 3.29 | 2.27 / 3.17 | 2.22 / 3.09 | 2.18 / 3.02 | 2.15 / 2.96 | 2.10 / 2.86 | 2.05 / 2.77 | 1.99 / 2.66 | 1.95 / 2.58 | 1.90 / 2.50 | 1.85 / 2.41 | 1.82 / 2.36 | 1.78 / 2.28 | 1.76 / 2.25 | 1.72 / 2.19 | 1.70 / 2.15 | 1.69 / 2.13 |
| 27 | 4.21 / 7.68 | 3.35 / 5.49 | 2.96 / 4.60 | 2.73 / 4.11 | 2.57 / 3.79 | 2.46 / 3.56 | 2.37 / 3.39 | 2.30 / 3.26 | 2.25 / 3.14 | 2.20 / 3.06 | 2.16 / 2.98 | 2.13 / 2.93 | 2.08 / 2.83 | 2.03 / 2.74 | 1.97 / 2.63 | 1.93 / 2.55 | 1.88 / 2.47 | 1.84 / 2.38 | 1.80 / 2.33 | 1.76 / 2.25 | 1.74 / 2.21 | 1.71 / 2.16 | 1.68 / 2.12 | 1.67 / 2.10 |
| 28 | 4.20 / 7.64 | 3.34 / 5.45 | 2.95 / 4.57 | 2.71 / 4.07 | 2.56 / 3.76 | 2.44 / 3.53 | 2.36 / 3.36 | 2.29 / 3.23 | 2.24 / 3.11 | 2.19 / 3.03 | 2.15 / 2.95 | 2.12 / 2.90 | 2.06 / 2.80 | 2.02 / 2.71 | 1.96 / 2.60 | 1.91 / 2.52 | 1.87 / 2.44 | 1.81 / 2.35 | 1.78 / 2.30 | 1.75 / 2.22 | 1.72 / 2.18 | 1.69 / 2.13 | 1.67 / 2.09 | 1.65 / 2.06 |
| 29 | 4.18 / 7.60 | 3.33 / 5.42 | 2.93 / 4.54 | 2.70 / 4.04 | 2.54 / 3.73 | 2.43 / 3.50 | 2.35 / 3.33 | 2.28 / 3.20 | 2.22 / 3.08 | 2.18 / 3.00 | 2.14 / 2.92 | 2.10 / 2.87 | 2.05 / 2.77 | 2.00 / 2.68 | 1.94 / 2.57 | 1.90 / 2.49 | 1.85 / 2.41 | 1.80 / 2.32 | 1.77 / 2.27 | 1.73 / 2.19 | 1.71 / 2.15 | 1.68 / 2.10 | 1.65 / 2.06 | 1.64 / 2.03 |
| 30 | 4.17 / 7.56 | 3.32 / 5.39 | 2.92 / 4.51 | 2.69 / 4.02 | 2.53 / 3.70 | 2.42 / 3.47 | 2.34 / 3.30 | 2.27 / 3.17 | 2.21 / 3.06 | 2.16 / 2.98 | 2.12 / 2.90 | 2.09 / 2.84 | 2.04 / 2.74 | 1.99 / 2.66 | 1.93 / 2.55 | 1.89 / 2.47 | 1.84 / 2.38 | 1.79 / 2.29 | 1.76 / 2.24 | 1.72 / 2.16 | 1.69 / 2.13 | 1.66 / 2.07 | 1.64 / 2.03 | 1.62 / 2.01 |
| 32 | 4.15 / 7.50 | 3.30 / 5.34 | 2.90 / 4.46 | 2.67 / 3.97 | 2.51 / 3.66 | 2.40 / 3.42 | 2.32 / 3.25 | 2.25 / 3.12 | 2.19 / 3.01 | 2.14 / 2.94 | 2.10 / 2.86 | 2.07 / 2.80 | 2.02 / 2.70 | 1.97 / 2.62 | 1.91 / 2.51 | 1.86 / 2.42 | 1.82 / 2.34 | 1.76 / 2.25 | 1.74 / 2.20 | 1.69 / 2.12 | 1.67 / 2.08 | 1.64 / 2.02 | 1.61 / 1.98 | 1.59 / 1.96 |
| 34 | 4.13 / 7.44 | 3.28 / 5.29 | 2.88 / 4.42 | 2.65 / 3.93 | 2.49 / 3.61 | 2.38 / 3.38 | 2.30 / 3.21 | 2.23 / 3.08 | 2.17 / 2.97 | 2.12 / 2.89 | 2.08 / 2.82 | 2.05 / 2.76 | 2.00 / 2.66 | 1.95 / 2.58 | 1.89 / 2.47 | 1.84 / 2.38 | 1.80 / 2.30 | 1.74 / 2.21 | 1.71 / 2.15 | 1.67 / 2.08 | 1.64 / 2.04 | 1.61 / 1.98 | 1.59 / 1.94 | 1.57 / 1.91 |
| 36 | 4.11 / 7.39 | 3.26 / 5.25 | 2.86 / 4.38 | 2.63 / 3.89 | 2.48 / 3.58 | 2.36 / 3.35 | 2.28 / 3.18 | 2.21 / 3.04 | 2.15 / 2.94 | 2.10 / 2.86 | 2.06 / 2.78 | 2.03 / 2.72 | 1.98 / 2.62 | 1.93 / 2.54 | 1.87 / 2.43 | 1.82 / 2.35 | 1.78 / 2.26 | 1.72 / 2.17 | 1.69 / 2.12 | 1.65 / 2.04 | 1.62 / 2.00 | 1.59 / 1.94 | 1.56 / 1.90 | 1.55 / 1.87 |
| 38 | 4.10 / 7.35 | 3.25 / 5.21 | 2.85 / 4.34 | 2.62 / 3.86 | 2.46 / 3.54 | 2.35 / 3.32 | 2.26 / 3.15 | 2.19 / 3.02 | 2.14 / 2.91 | 2.09 / 2.82 | 2.05 / 2.75 | 2.02 / 2.69 | 1.96 / 2.59 | 1.92 / 2.51 | 1.85 / 2.40 | 1.80 / 2.32 | 1.76 / 2.22 | 1.71 / 2.14 | 1.67 / 2.08 | 1.63 / 2.00 | 1.60 / 1.97 | 1.57 / 1.90 | 1.54 / 1.86 | 1.53 / 1.84 |
| 40 | 4.08 / 7.31 | 3.23 / 5.18 | 2.84 / 4.31 | 2.61 / 3.83 | 2.45 / 3.51 | 2.34 / 3.29 | 2.25 / 3.12 | 2.18 / 2.99 | 2.12 / 2.88 | 2.07 / 2.80 | 2.04 / 2.73 | 2.00 / 2.66 | 1.95 / 2.56 | 1.90 / 2.49 | 1.84 / 2.37 | 1.79 / 2.29 | 1.74 / 2.20 | 1.69 / 2.11 | 1.66 / 2.05 | 1.61 / 1.97 | 1.59 / 1.94 | 1.55 / 1.88 | 1.53 / 1.84 | 1.51 / 1.81 |
| 42 | 4.07 / 7.27 | 3.22 / 5.15 | 2.83 / 4.29 | 2.59 / 3.80 | 2.44 / 3.49 | 2.32 / 3.26 | 2.24 / 3.10 | 2.17 / 2.96 | 2.11 / 2.86 | 2.06 / 2.77 | 2.02 / 2.70 | 1.99 / 2.64 | 1.94 / 2.54 | 1.89 / 2.46 | 1.82 / 2.35 | 1.78 / 2.26 | 1.73 / 2.17 | 1.68 / 2.08 | 1.64 / 2.02 | 1.60 / 1.94 | 1.57 / 1.91 | 1.54 / 1.85 | 1.51 / 1.80 | 1.49 / 1.78 |
| 44 | 4.06 / 7.24 | 3.21 / 5.12 | 2.82 / 4.26 | 2.58 / 3.78 | 2.43 / 3.46 | 2.31 / 3.24 | 2.23 / 3.07 | 2.16 / 2.94 | 2.10 / 2.84 | 2.05 / 2.75 | 2.01 / 2.68 | 1.98 / 2.62 | 1.92 / 2.52 | 1.88 / 2.44 | 1.81 / 2.32 | 1.76 / 2.24 | 1.72 / 2.15 | 1.66 / 2.06 | 1.63 / 2.00 | 1.58 / 1.92 | 1.56 / 1.88 | 1.52 / 1.82 | 1.50 / 1.78 | 1.48 / 1.75 |
| 46 | 4.05 / 7.21 | 3.20 / 5.10 | 2.81 / 4.24 | 2.57 / 3.76 | 2.42 / 3.44 | 2.30 / 3.22 | 2.22 / 3.05 | 2.14 / 2.92 | 2.09 / 2.82 | 2.04 / 2.73 | 2.00 / 2.66 | 1.97 / 2.60 | 1.91 / 2.50 | 1.87 / 2.42 | 1.80 / 2.30 | 1.75 / 2.22 | 1.71 / 2.13 | 1.65 / 2.04 | 1.62 / 1.98 | 1.57 / 1.90 | 1.54 / 1.86 | 1.51 / 1.80 | 1.48 / 1.76 | 1.46 / 1.72 |
| 48 | 4.04 / 7.19 | 3.19 / 5.08 | 2.80 / 4.22 | 2.56 / 3.74 | 2.41 / 3.42 | 2.30 / 3.20 | 2.21 / 3.04 | 2.14 / 2.90 | 2.08 / 2.80 | 2.03 / 2.71 | 1.99 / 2.64 | 1.96 / 2.58 | 1.90 / 2.48 | 1.86 / 2.40 | 1.79 / 2.28 | 1.74 / 2.20 | 1.70 / 2.11 | 1.64 / 2.02 | 1.61 / 1.96 | 1.56 / 1.88 | 1.53 / 1.84 | 1.50 / 1.78 | 1.47 / 1.73 | 1.45 / 1.70 |

Table A–4. *Continued*

$f_1$ Degrees of Freedom (for greater mean square)

| $f_2$ | 1 | 2 | 3 | 4 | 5 | 6 | 7 | 8 | 9 | 10 | 11 | 12 | 14 | 16 | 20 | 24 | 30 | 40 | 50 | 75 | 100 | 200 | 500 | ∞ | $f_2$ |
|---|---|---|---|---|---|---|---|---|---|---|---|---|---|---|---|---|---|---|---|---|---|---|---|---|---|
| 50 | 4.03<br>7.17 | 3.18<br>5.06 | 2.79<br>4.20 | 2.56<br>3.72 | 2.40<br>3.41 | 2.29<br>3.18 | 2.20<br>3.02 | 2.13<br>2.88 | 2.07<br>2.78 | 2.02<br>2.70 | 1.98<br>2.62 | 1.95<br>2.56 | 1.90<br>2.46 | 1.85<br>2.39 | 1.78<br>2.26 | 1.74<br>2.18 | 1.69<br>2.10 | 1.63<br>2.00 | 1.60<br>1.94 | 1.55<br>1.86 | 1.52<br>1.82 | 1.48<br>1.76 | 1.46<br>1.71 | 1.44<br>1.68 | 50 |
| 55 | 4.02<br>7.12 | 3.17<br>5.01 | 2.78<br>4.16 | 2.54<br>3.68 | 2.38<br>3.37 | 2.27<br>3.15 | 2.18<br>2.98 | 2.11<br>2.85 | 2.05<br>2.75 | 2.00<br>2.66 | 1.97<br>2.59 | 1.93<br>2.53 | 1.88<br>2.43 | 1.83<br>2.35 | 1.76<br>2.23 | 1.72<br>2.15 | 1.67<br>2.06 | 1.61<br>1.96 | 1.58<br>1.90 | 1.52<br>1.82 | 1.50<br>1.78 | 1.46<br>1.71 | 1.43<br>1.66 | 1.41<br>1.64 | 55 |
| 60 | 4.00<br>7.08 | 3.15<br>4.98 | 2.76<br>4.13 | 2.52<br>3.65 | 2.37<br>3.34 | 2.25<br>3.12 | 2.17<br>2.95 | 2.10<br>2.82 | 2.04<br>2.72 | 1.99<br>2.63 | 1.95<br>2.56 | 1.92<br>2.50 | 1.86<br>2.40 | 1.81<br>2.32 | 1.75<br>2.20 | 1.70<br>2.12 | 1.65<br>2.03 | 1.59<br>1.93 | 1.56<br>1.87 | 1.50<br>1.79 | 1.48<br>1.74 | 1.44<br>1.68 | 1.41<br>1.63 | 1.39<br>1.60 | 60 |
| 65 | 3.99<br>7.04 | 3.14<br>4.95 | 2.75<br>4.10 | 2.51<br>3.62 | 2.36<br>3.31 | 2.24<br>3.09 | 2.15<br>2.93 | 2.08<br>2.79 | 2.02<br>2.70 | 1.98<br>2.61 | 1.94<br>2.54 | 1.90<br>2.47 | 1.85<br>2.37 | 1.80<br>2.30 | 1.73<br>2.18 | 1.68<br>2.09 | 1.63<br>2.00 | 1.57<br>1.90 | 1.54<br>1.84 | 1.49<br>1.76 | 1.46<br>1.71 | 1.42<br>1.64 | 1.39<br>1.60 | 1.37<br>1.56 | 65 |
| 70 | 3.98<br>7.01 | 3.13<br>4.92 | 2.74<br>4.08 | 2.50<br>3.60 | 2.35<br>3.29 | 2.23<br>3.07 | 2.14<br>2.91 | 2.07<br>2.77 | 2.01<br>2.67 | 1.97<br>2.59 | 1.93<br>2.51 | 1.89<br>2.45 | 1.84<br>2.35 | 1.79<br>2.28 | 1.72<br>2.15 | 1.67<br>2.07 | 1.62<br>1.98 | 1.56<br>1.88 | 1.53<br>1.82 | 1.47<br>1.74 | 1.45<br>1.69 | 1.40<br>1.62 | 1.37<br>1.56 | 1.35<br>1.53 | 70 |
| 80 | 3.96<br>6.96 | 3.11<br>4.88 | 2.72<br>4.04 | 2.48<br>3.56 | 2.33<br>3.25 | 2.21<br>3.04 | 2.12<br>2.87 | 2.05<br>2.74 | 1.99<br>2.64 | 1.95<br>2.55 | 1.91<br>2.48 | 1.88<br>2.41 | 1.82<br>2.32 | 1.77<br>2.24 | 1.70<br>2.11 | 1.65<br>2.03 | 1.60<br>1.94 | 1.54<br>1.84 | 1.51<br>1.78 | 1.45<br>1.70 | 1.42<br>1.65 | 1.38<br>1.57 | 1.35<br>1.52 | 1.32<br>1.49 | 80 |
| 100 | 3.94<br>6.90 | 3.09<br>4.82 | 2.70<br>3.98 | 2.46<br>3.51 | 2.30<br>3.20 | 2.19<br>2.99 | 2.10<br>2.82 | 2.03<br>2.69 | 1.97<br>2.59 | 1.92<br>2.51 | 1.88<br>2.43 | 1.85<br>2.36 | 1.79<br>2.26 | 1.75<br>2.19 | 1.68<br>2.06 | 1.63<br>1.98 | 1.57<br>1.89 | 1.51<br>1.79 | 1.48<br>1.73 | 1.42<br>1.64 | 1.39<br>1.59 | 1.34<br>1.51 | 1.30<br>1.46 | 1.28<br>1.43 | 100 |
| 125 | 3.92<br>6.84 | 3.07<br>4.78 | 2.68<br>3.94 | 2.44<br>3.47 | 2.29<br>3.17 | 2.17<br>2.95 | 2.08<br>2.79 | 2.01<br>2.65 | 1.95<br>2.56 | 1.90<br>2.47 | 1.86<br>2.40 | 1.83<br>2.33 | 1.77<br>2.23 | 1.72<br>2.15 | 1.65<br>2.03 | 1.60<br>1.94 | 1.55<br>1.85 | 1.49<br>1.75 | 1.45<br>1.68 | 1.39<br>1.59 | 1.36<br>1.54 | 1.31<br>1.46 | 1.27<br>1.40 | 1.25<br>1.37 | 125 |
| 150 | 3.91<br>6.81 | 3.06<br>4.75 | 2.67<br>3.91 | 2.43<br>3.44 | 2.27<br>3.14 | 2.16<br>2.92 | 2.07<br>2.76 | 2.00<br>2.62 | 1.94<br>2.53 | 1.89<br>2.44 | 1.85<br>2.37 | 1.82<br>2.30 | 1.76<br>2.20 | 1.71<br>2.12 | 1.64<br>2.00 | 1.59<br>1.91 | 1.54<br>1.83 | 1.47<br>1.72 | 1.44<br>1.66 | 1.37<br>1.56 | 1.34<br>1.51 | 1.29<br>1.43 | 1.25<br>1.37 | 1.22<br>1.33 | 150 |
| 200 | 3.89<br>6.76 | 3.04<br>4.71 | 2.65<br>3.88 | 2.41<br>3.41 | 2.26<br>3.11 | 2.14<br>2.90 | 2.05<br>2.73 | 1.98<br>2.60 | 1.92<br>2.50 | 1.87<br>2.41 | 1.83<br>2.34 | 1.80<br>2.28 | 1.74<br>2.17 | 1.69<br>2.09 | 1.62<br>1.97 | 1.57<br>1.88 | 1.52<br>1.79 | 1.45<br>1.69 | 1.42<br>1.62 | 1.35<br>1.53 | 1.32<br>1.48 | 1.26<br>1.39 | 1.22<br>1.33 | 1.19<br>1.28 | 200 |
| 400 | 3.86<br>6.70 | 3.02<br>4.66 | 2.62<br>3.83 | 2.39<br>3.36 | 2.23<br>3.06 | 2.12<br>2.85 | 2.03<br>2.69 | 1.96<br>2.55 | 1.90<br>2.46 | 1.85<br>2.37 | 1.81<br>2.29 | 1.78<br>2.23 | 1.72<br>2.12 | 1.67<br>2.04 | 1.60<br>1.92 | 1.54<br>1.84 | 1.49<br>1.74 | 1.42<br>1.64 | 1.38<br>1.57 | 1.32<br>1.47 | 1.28<br>1.42 | 1.22<br>1.32 | 1.16<br>1.24 | 1.13<br>1.19 | 400 |
| 1000 | 3.85<br>6.66 | 3.00<br>4.62 | 2.61<br>3.80 | 2.38<br>3.34 | 2.22<br>3.04 | 2.10<br>2.82 | 2.02<br>2.66 | 1.95<br>2.53 | 1.89<br>2.43 | 1.84<br>2.34 | 1.80<br>2.26 | 1.76<br>2.20 | 1.70<br>2.09 | 1.65<br>2.01 | 1.58<br>1.89 | 1.53<br>1.81 | 1.47<br>1.71 | 1.41<br>1.61 | 1.36<br>1.54 | 1.30<br>1.44 | 1.26<br>1.38 | 1.19<br>1.28 | 1.13<br>1.19 | 1.08<br>1.11 | 1000 |
| ∞ | 3.84<br>6.64 | 2.99<br>4.60 | 2.60<br>3.78 | 2.37<br>3.32 | 2.21<br>3.02 | 2.09<br>2.80 | 2.01<br>2.64 | 1.94<br>2.51 | 1.88<br>2.41 | 1.83<br>2.32 | 1.79<br>2.24 | 1.75<br>2.18 | 1.69<br>2.07 | 1.64<br>1.99 | 1.57<br>1.87 | 1.52<br>1.79 | 1.46<br>1.69 | 1.40<br>1.59 | 1.35<br>1.52 | 1.28<br>1.41 | 1.24<br>1.36 | 1.17<br>1.25 | 1.11<br>1.15 | 1.00<br>1.00 | ∞ |

Table A-5. DISTRIBUTION OF $\chi^2$*

The first column contains the number of degrees of freedom (see page 157). The values in the body of the table are the values of $\chi^2$ required for the listed probability levels. For example, a $\chi^2$ of 4.22 with 1 df exceeds the tabled value of 3.84 for 1 df at the .05 level and would be judged significant at that level.

| df | P = .99 | .98 | .95 | .90 | .80 | .70 | .50 |
|----|---------|-----|-----|-----|-----|-----|-----|
| 1  | .00016 | .00063 | .0039 | .016 | .064 | .15 | .46 |
| 2  | .02 | .04 | .10 | .21 | .45 | .71 | 1.39 |
| 3  | .12 | .18 | .35 | .58 | 1.00 | 1.42 | 2.37 |
| 4  | .30 | .43 | .71 | 1.06 | 1.65 | 2.20 | 3.36 |
| 5  | .55 | .75 | 1.14 | 1.61 | 2.34 | 3.00 | 4.35 |
| 6  | .87 | 1.13 | 1.64 | 2.20 | 3.07 | 3.83 | 5.35 |
| 7  | 1.24 | 1.56 | 2.17 | 2.83 | 3.82 | 4.67 | 6.35 |
| 8  | 1.65 | 2.03 | 2.73 | 3.49 | 4.59 | 5.53 | 7.34 |
| 9  | 2.09 | 2.53 | 3.32 | 4.17 | 5.38 | 6.39 | 8.34 |
| 10 | 2.56 | 3.06 | 3.94 | 4.86 | 6.18 | 7.27 | 9.34 |
| 11 | 3.05 | 3.61 | 4.58 | 5.58 | 6.99 | 8.15 | 10.34 |
| 12 | 3.57 | 4.18 | 5.23 | 6.30 | 7.81 | 9.03 | 11.34 |
| 13 | 4.11 | 4.76 | 5.89 | 7.04 | 8.63 | 9.93 | 12.34 |
| 14 | 4.66 | 5.37 | 6.57 | 7.79 | 9.47 | 10.82 | 13.34 |
| 15 | 5.23 | 5.98 | 7.26 | 8.55 | 10.31 | 11.72 | 14.34 |
| 16 | 5.81 | 6.61 | 7.96 | 9.31 | 11.15 | 12.62 | 15.34 |
| 17 | 6.41 | 7.26 | 8.67 | 10.08 | 12.00 | 13.53 | 16.34 |
| 18 | 7.02 | 7.91 | 9.39 | 10.86 | 12.86 | 14.44 | 17.34 |
| 19 | 7.63 | 8.57 | 10.12 | 11.65 | 13.72 | 15.35 | 18.34 |
| 20 | 8.26 | 9.24 | 10.85 | 12.44 | 14.58 | 16.27 | 19.34 |
| 21 | 8.90 | 9.92 | 11.59 | 13.24 | 15.44 | 17.18 | 20.34 |
| 22 | 9.54 | 10.60 | 12.34 | 14.04 | 16.31 | 18.10 | 21.34 |
| 23 | 10.20 | 11.29 | 13.09 | 14.85 | 17.19 | 19.02 | 22.34 |
| 24 | 10.86 | 11.99 | 13.85 | 15.66 | 18.06 | 19.94 | 23.34 |
| 25 | 11.52 | 12.70 | 14.61 | 16.47 | 18.94 | 20.87 | 24.34 |
| 26 | 12.20 | 13.41 | 15.38 | 17.29 | 19.82 | 21.79 | 25.34 |
| 27 | 12.88 | 14.12 | 16.15 | 18.11 | 20.70 | 22.72 | 26.34 |
| 28 | 13.56 | 14.85 | 16.93 | 18.94 | 21.59 | 23.65 | 27.34 |
| 29 | 14.26 | 15.57 | 17.71 | 19.77 | 22.48 | 24.58 | 28.34 |
| 30 | 14.95 | 16.31 | 18.49 | 20.60 | 23.36 | 25.51 | 29.34 |

*Reproduced with permission from McNemar, Q.: *Psychological Statistics*, 3rd Ed. New York: John Wiley and Sons, Inc. 1962.

**Table A–5.** *Continued*

| df | .30 | .20 | .10 | .05 | .02 | .01 | .001 |
|----|-----|-----|-----|-----|-----|-----|------|
| 1 | 1.07 | 1.64 | 2.71 | 3.84 | 5.41 | 6.64 | 10.83 |
| 2 | 2.41 | 3.22 | 4.60 | 5.99 | 7.82 | 9.21 | 13.82 |
| 3 | 3.66 | 4.64 | 6.25 | 7.82 | 9.84 | 11.34 | 16.27 |
| 4 | 4.88 | 5.99 | 7.78 | 9.49 | 11.67 | 13.28 | 18.46 |
| 5 | 6.06 | 7.29 | 9.24 | 11.07 | 13.39 | 15.09 | 20.52 |
| 6 | 7.23 | 8.56 | 10.64 | 12.59 | 15.03 | 16.81 | 22.46 |
| 7 | 8.38 | 9.80 | 12.02 | 14.07 | 16.62 | 18.48 | 24.32 |
| 8 | 9.52 | 11.03 | 13.36 | 15.51 | 18.17 | 20.09 | 26.12 |
| 9 | 10.66 | 12.24 | 14.68 | 16.92 | 19.68 | 21.67 | 27.88 |
| 10 | 11.78 | 13.44 | 15.99 | 18.31 | 21.16 | 23.21 | 29.59 |
| 11 | 12.90 | 14.63 | 17.28 | 19.68 | 22.62 | 24.72 | 31.26 |
| 12 | 14.01 | 15.81 | 18.55 | 21.03 | 24.05 | 26.22 | 32.91 |
| 13 | 15.12 | 16.98 | 19.81 | 22.36 | 25.47 | 27.69 | 34.53 |
| 14 | 16.22 | 18.15 | 21.06 | 23.68 | 26.87 | 29.14 | 36.12 |
| 15 | 17.32 | 19.31 | 22.31 | 25.00 | 28.26 | 30.58 | 37.70 |
| 16 | 18.42 | 20.46 | 23.54 | 26.30 | 29.63 | 32.00 | 39.25 |
| 17 | 19.51 | 21.62 | 24.77 | 27.59 | 31.00 | 33.41 | 40.79 |
| 18 | 20.60 | 22.76 | 25.99 | 28.87 | 32.35 | 34.80 | 42.31 |
| 19 | 21.69 | 23.90 | 27.20 | 30.14 | 33.69 | 36.19 | 43.82 |
| 20 | 22.78 | 25.04 | 28.41 | 31.41 | 35.02 | 37.57 | 45.32 |
| 21 | 23.86 | 26.17 | 29.62 | 32.67 | 36.34 | 38.93 | 46.80 |
| 22 | 24.94 | 27.30 | 30.81 | 33.92 | 37.66 | 40.29 | 48.27 |
| 23 | 26.02 | 28.43 | 32.01 | 35.17 | 38.97 | 41.64 | 49.73 |
| 24 | 27.10 | 29.55 | 33.20 | 36.42 | 40.27 | 42.98 | 51.18 |
| 25 | 28.17 | 30.68 | 34.38 | 37.65 | 41.57 | 44.31 | 52.62 |
| 26 | 29.25 | 31.80 | 35.56 | 38.88 | 42.86 | 45.64 | 54.05 |
| 27 | 30.32 | 32.91 | 36.74 | 40.11 | 44.14 | 46.96 | 55.48 |
| 28 | 31.39 | 34.03 | 37.92 | 41.34 | 45.42 | 48.28 | 56.89 |
| 29 | 32.46 | 35.14 | 39.09 | 42.56 | 46.69 | 49.59 | 58.30 |
| 30 | 33.53 | 36.25 | 40.26 | 43.77 | 47.96 | 50.89 | 59.70 |

**Table A–6.** Critical Values of $r$ for the Sign Test

The number of signs with the smaller number of occurrences is counted (ignoring zero differences), and this number is called $r$. Values of $r$ are contained in the body of the table. The column headed "$N$" indicates the total number of observations disregarding the zero differences. For 12 observations with two zero differences, the value of $N$ used would be 10 and $r$ may be no larger than 1 for a difference to be judged significant at the .05 level.

**Table A-6.** CRITICAL VALUES OF $r$ FOR THE SIGN TEST*

| N | 1% | 5% | 10% | 25% | N | 1% | 5% | 10% | 25% |
|---|---|---|---|---|---|---|---|---|---|
| 1 | | | | | 46 | 13 | 15 | 16 | 18 |
| 2 | | | | | 47 | 14 | 16 | 17 | 19 |
| 3 | | | | 0 | 48 | 14 | 16 | 17 | 19 |
| 4 | | | | 0 | 49 | 15 | 17 | 18 | 19 |
| 5 | | | 0 | 0 | 50 | 15 | 17 | 18 | 20 |
| 6 | | 0 | 0 | 1 | 51 | 15 | 18 | 19 | 20 |
| 7 | | 0 | 0 | 1 | 52 | 16 | 18 | 19 | 21 |
| 8 | 0 | 0 | 1 | 1 | 53 | 16 | 18 | 20 | 21 |
| 9 | 0 | 1 | 1 | 2 | 54 | 17 | 19 | 20 | 22 |
| 10 | 0 | 1 | 1 | 2 | 55 | 17 | 19 | 20 | 22 |
| 11 | 0 | 1 | 2 | 3 | 56 | 17 | 20 | 21 | 23 |
| 12 | 1 | 2 | 2 | 3 | 57 | 18 | 20 | 21 | 23 |
| 13 | 1 | 2 | 3 | 3 | 58 | 18 | 21 | 22 | 24 |
| 14 | 1 | 2 | 3 | 4 | 59 | 19 | 21 | 22 | 24 |
| 15 | 2 | 3 | 3 | 4 | 60 | 19 | 21 | 23 | 25 |
| 16 | 2 | 3 | 4 | 5 | 61 | 20 | 22 | 23 | 25 |
| 17 | 2 | 4 | 4 | 5 | 62 | 20 | 22 | 24 | 25 |
| 18 | 3 | 4 | 5 | 6 | 63 | 20 | 23 | 24 | 26 |
| 19 | 3 | 4 | 5 | 6 | 64 | 21 | 23 | 24 | 26 |
| 20 | 3 | 5 | 5 | 6 | 65 | 21 | 24 | 25 | 27 |
| 21 | 4 | 5 | 6 | 7 | 66 | 22 | 24 | 25 | 27 |
| 22 | 4 | 5 | 6 | 7 | 67 | 22 | 25 | 26 | 28 |
| 23 | 4 | 6 | 7 | 8 | 68 | 22 | 25 | 26 | 28 |
| 24 | 5 | 6 | 7 | 8 | 69 | 23 | 25 | 27 | 29 |
| 25 | 5 | 7 | 7 | 9 | 70 | 23 | 26 | 27 | 29 |
| 26 | 6 | 7 | 8 | 9 | 71 | 24 | 26 | 28 | 30 |
| 27 | 6 | 7 | 8 | 10 | 72 | 24 | 27 | 28 | 30 |
| 28 | 6 | 8 | 9 | 10 | 73 | 25 | 27 | 28 | 31 |
| 29 | 7 | 8 | 9 | 10 | 74 | 25 | 28 | 29 | 31 |
| 30 | 7 | 9 | 10 | 11 | 75 | 25 | 28 | 29 | 32 |
| 31 | 7 | 9 | 10 | 11 | 76 | 26 | 28 | 30 | 32 |
| 32 | 8 | 9 | 10 | 12 | 77 | 26 | 29 | 30 | 32 |
| 33 | 8 | 10 | 11 | 12 | 78 | 27 | 29 | 31 | 33 |
| 34 | 9 | 10 | 11 | 13 | 79 | 27 | 30 | 31 | 33 |
| 35 | 9 | 11 | 12 | 13 | 80 | 28 | 30 | 32 | 34 |
| 36 | 9 | 11 | 12 | 14 | 81 | 28 | 31 | 32 | 34 |
| 37 | 10 | 12 | 13 | 14 | 82 | 28 | 31 | 33 | 35 |
| 38 | 10 | 12 | 13 | 14 | 83 | 29 | 32 | 33 | 35 |
| 39 | 11 | 12 | 13 | 15 | 84 | 29 | 32 | 33 | 36 |
| 40 | 11 | 13 | 14 | 15 | 85 | 30 | 32 | 34 | 36 |
| 41 | 11 | 13 | 14 | 16 | 86 | 30 | 33 | 34 | 37 |
| 42 | 12 | 14 | 15 | 16 | 87 | 31 | 33 | 35 | 37 |
| 43 | 12 | 14 | 15 | 17 | 88 | 31 | 34 | 35 | 38 |
| 44 | 13 | 15 | 16 | 17 | 89 | 31 | 34 | 36 | 38 |
| 45 | 13 | 15 | 16 | 18 | 90 | 32 | 35 | 36 | 39 |

For values of $N$ larger than 90, approximate values of $r$ may be found by taking the nearest integer less than $(N - 1)/2 - k \sqrt{N + 1}$, where $k$ is 1.2879, 0.9800, 0.8224, 0.5752 for the 1, 5, 10, 25% values, respectively.

*Reproduced with permission from Dixon, W. J., and Massey, F. J., Jr.: *Introduction to Statistical Analysis*, 2nd Ed. New York: McGraw-Hill, 1957.

**Table A–7.** SIGNIFICANT VALUES OF $U$

The value at the top of each column is the number of observations in the larger sample ($N_2$). The value along the left hand column is the number of observations in the smaller sample. The body of the table contains values of $U$. For example a $U$ of 4 with $N_1 = 4$ and $N_2 = 11$ is smaller than the tabled value of $U(6)$ at the .05 level and is judged to be significant at the .05 level.

**Table A–7.** SIGNIFICANT VALUES OF $U^*$

Two-Tailed Test, $\alpha = .05$

| $N_1$ \ $N_2$ | 3 | 4 | 5 | 6 | 7 | 8 | 9 | 10 | 11 | 12 | 13 | 14 | 15 | 16 | 17 | 18 | 19 | 20 |
|---|---|---|---|---|---|---|---|---|---|---|---|---|---|---|---|---|---|---|
| 1 | – | – | – | – | –. | – | – | – | – | – | – | – | – | – | – | – | – | – |
| 2 | – | – | – | – | – | 0 | 0 | 0 | 0 | 1 | 1 | 1 | 1 | 1 | 2 | 2 | 2 | 2 |
| 3 | – | – | 0 | 1 | 1 | 2 | 2 | 3 | 3 | 4 | 4 | 5 | 5 | 6 | 6 | 7 | 7 | 8 |
| 4 | | 0 | 1 | 2 | 3 | 4 | 4 | 5 | 6 | 7 | 8 | 9 | 10 | 11 | 11 | 12 | 13 | 13 |
| 5 | | | 2 | 3 | 5 | 6 | 7 | 8 | 9 | 11 | 12 | 13 | 14 | 15 | 17 | 18 | 19 | 20 |
| 6 | | | | 5 | 6 | 8 | 10 | 11 | 13 | 14 | 16 | 17 | 19 | 21 | 22 | 24 | 25 | 27 |
| 7 | | | | | 8 | 10 | 12 | 14 | 16 | 18 | 20 | 22 | 24 | 26 | 28 | 30 | 32 | 34 |
| 8 | | | | | | 13 | 15 | 17 | 19 | 22 | 24 | 26 | 29 | 31 | 34 | 36 | 38 | 41 |
| 9 | | | | | | | 17 | 20 | 23 | 26 | 28 | 31 | 34 | 37 | 39 | 42 | 45 | 48 |
| 10 | | | | | | | | 23 | 26 | 29 | 33 | 36 | 39 | 42 | 45 | 48 | 52 | 55 |
| 11 | | | | | | | | | 30 | 33 | 37 | 40 | 44 | 47 | 51 | 55 | 58 | 62 |
| 12 | | | | | | | | | | 37 | 41 | 45 | 49 | 53 | 57 | 61 | 65 | 69 |
| 13 | | | | | | | | | | | 45 | 50 | 54 | 59 | 63 | 67 | 72 | 76 |
| 14 | | | | | | | | | | | | 55 | 59 | 64 | 67 | 74 | 78 | 83 |
| 15 | | | | | | | | | | | | | 64 | 70 | 75 | 80 | 85 | 90 |
| 16 | | | | | | | | | | | | | | 75 | 81 | 86 | 92 | 98 |
| 17 | | | | | | | | | | | | | | | 87 | 93 | 99 | 105 |
| 18 | | | | | | | | | | | | | | | | 99 | 106 | 112 |
| 19 | | | | | | | | | | | | | | | | | 113 | 119 |
| 20 | | | | | | | | | | | | | | | | | | 127 |

$z = 1.960$

Two-Tailed Test, $\alpha = .01$

| $N_1$ \ $N_2$ | 3 | 4 | 5 | 6 | 7 | 8 | 9 | 10 | 11 | 12 | 13 | 14 | 15 | 16 | 17 | 18 | 19 | 20 |
|---|---|---|---|---|---|---|---|---|---|---|---|---|---|---|---|---|---|---|
| 1 | – | – | – | – | – | – | – | – | – | – | – | – | – | – | – | – | – | – |
| 2 | – | – | – | – | – | – | – | – | – | – | – | – | – | – | – | – | 0 | 0 |
| 3 | – | – | – | – | – | – | 0 | 0 | 0 | 1 | 1 | 1 | 2 | 2 | 2 | 2 | 3 | 3 |
| 4 | | – | – | 0 | 0 | 1 | 1 | 2 | 2 | 3 | 4 | 4 | 5 | 5 | 6 | 6 | 7 | 8 |
| 5 | | | 0 | 1 | 2 | 3 | 3 | 4 | 5 | 6 | 7 | 7 | 8 | 9 | 10 | 11 | 12 | 13 |
| 6 | | | | 2 | 3 | 4 | 5 | 6 | 7 | 9 | 10 | 11 | 12 | 13 | 15 | 16 | 17 | 18 |
| 7 | | | | | 4 | 6 | 7 | 9 | 10 | 12 | 13 | 15 | 16 | 18 | 19 | 21 | 22 | 24 |
| 8 | | | | | | 8 | 10 | 12 | 14 | 16 | 18 | 19 | 21 | 23 | 25 | 27 | 29 | 31 |
| 9 | | | | | | | 11 | 13 | 16 | 18 | 20 | 22 | 24 | 27 | 29 | 31 | 33 | 36 |
| 10 | | | | | | | | 16 | 18 | 21 | 24 | 26 | 29 | 31 | 34 | 37 | 39 | 42 |
| 11 | | | | | | | | | 21 | 24 | 27 | 30 | 33 | 36 | 39 | 42 | 45 | 48 |
| 12 | | | | | | | | | | 27 | 31 | 34 | 37 | 41 | 44 | 47 | 51 | 54 |
| 13 | | | | | | | | | | | 34 | 38 | 42 | 45 | 49 | 53 | 56 | 60 |
| 14 | | | | | | | | | | | | 42 | 46 | 50 | 54 | 58 | 63 | 67 |
| 15 | | | | | | | | | | | | | 51 | 55 | 60 | 64 | 69 | 73 |
| 16 | | | | | | | | | | | | | | 60 | 65 | 70 | 74 | 79 |
| 17 | | | | | | | | | | | | | | | 70 | 75 | 81 | 86 |
| 18 | | | | | | | | | | | | | | | | 81 | 87 | 92 |
| 19 | | | | | | | | | | | | | | | | | 93 | 99 |
| 20 | | | | | | | | | | | | | | | | | | 105 |

$z = 2.576$

* Reproduced with permission from Freeman, L. C.: Elementary Applied Statistics. New York, Wiley, 1965.

**Table A–8.** VALUES OF $H$ FOR THREE SAMPLES SIGNIFICANT AT THE 10, 5, AND 1 PER CENT SIGNIFICANCE LEVELS

Locate the combination of sample sizes in the left hand columns. The values of $H$ are in the body of the table. To be significant, a value of $H$ must be equal to or larger than the tabled value. For example, with sample sizes of 5, 2, and 1 the value of $H$ must be equal to or greater than the tabled value of 5.00 to be judged significant at the .05 level.

**Table A–8.** VALUES OF $H$ FOR THREE SAMPLES SIGNIFICANT AT THE 10, 5, AND 1 PER CENT SIGNIFICANCE LEVELS*

| Sample Sizes | | | Significance Level | | |
|---|---|---|---|---|---|
| $N_1$ | $N_2$ | $N_3$ | .10 | .05 | .01 |
| 2 | 2 | 2 | 4.57 | | |
| 3 | 2 | 1 | 4.29 | | |
| 3 | 2 | 2 | 4.50 | 4.71 | |
| 3 | 3 | 1 | 4.57 | 5.14 | |
| 3 | 3 | 2 | 4.56 | 5.36 | 6.25 |
| 3 | 3 | 3 | 4.62 | 5.60 | 6.49 |
| 4 | 2 | 1 | 4.50 | | |
| 4 | 2 | 2 | 4.46 | 5.33 | |
| 4 | 3 | 1 | 4.06 | 5.21 | |
| 4 | 3 | 2 | 4.51 | 5.44 | 6.30 |
| 4 | 3 | 3 | 4.70 | 5.73 | 6.75 |
| 4 | 4 | 1 | 4.17 | 4.97 | 6.67 |
| 4 | 4 | 2 | 4.55 | 5.45 | 6.87 |
| 4 | 4 | 3 | 4.55 | 5.60 | 7.14 |
| 4 | 4 | 4 | 4.65 | 5.69 | 7.54 |
| 5 | 2 | 1 | 4.20 | 5.00 | |
| 5 | 2 | 2 | 4.37 | 5.16 | 6.53 |
| 5 | 3 | 1 | 4.02 | 4.96 | |
| 5 | 3 | 2 | 4.49 | 5.25 | 6.82 |
| 5 | 3 | 3 | 4.53 | 5.44 | 6.98 |
| 5 | 4 | 1 | 3.99 | 4.99 | 6.84 |
| 5 | 4 | 2 | 4.52 | 5.27 | 7.12 |
| 5 | 4 | 3 | 4.55 | 5.63 | 7.40 |
| 5 | 4 | 4 | 4.62 | 5.62 | 7.74 |
| 5 | 5 | 1 | 4.11 | 5.13 | 6.84 |
| 5 | 5 | 2 | 4.51 | 5.25 | 7.27 |
| 5 | 5 | 3 | 4.55 | 5.63 | 7.54 |
| 5 | 5 | 4 | 4.52 | 5.64 | 7.79 |
| 5 | 5 | 5 | 4.56 | 5.66 | 7.98 |

*Reproduced with permission from Tate, M. W., and Clelland, R. C.: *Nonparametric and Shortcut Statistics.* Danville, Ill.: Interstate, 1957.

**Table A–9.** CRITICAL VALUES OF THE CORRELATION COEFFICIENT*

The number of degrees of freedom are given in the left-hand column. An obtained correlation coefficient must be as large as or larger than the value in the body of the table to be significant at the level of significance stated for the column. For example, an obtained $r$ with $N = 20$ would have a $df$ of 18 and must exceed the tabled value of .444 to be judged significant at the .05 level.

| $df$ | Level of significance for two-tailed test | | | |
|---|---|---|---|---|
| | .10 | .05 | .02 | .01 |
| 1 | .988 | .997 | .9995 | .9999 |
| 2 | .900 | .950 | .980 | .990 |
| 3 | .805 | .878 | .934 | .959 |
| 4 | .729 | .811 | .882 | .917 |
| 5 | .669 | .754 | .833 | .874 |
| 6 | .622 | .707 | .789 | .834 |
| 7 | .582 | .666 | .750 | .798 |
| 8 | .549 | .632 | .716 | .765 |
| 9 | .521 | .602 | .685 | .735 |
| 10 | .497 | .576 | .658 | .708 |
| 11 | .476 | .553 | .634 | .684 |
| 12 | .458 | .532 | .612 | .661 |
| 13 | .441 | .514 | .592 | .641 |
| 14 | .426 | .497 | .574 | .623 |
| 15 | .412 | .482 | .558 | .606 |
| 16 | .400 | .468 | .542 | .590 |
| 17 | .389 | .456 | .528 | .575 |
| 18 | .378 | .444 | .516 | .561 |
| 19 | .369 | .433 | .503 | .549 |
| 20 | .360 | .423 | .492 | .537 |
| 21 | .352 | .413 | .482 | .526 |
| 22 | .344 | .404 | .472 | .515 |
| 23 | .337 | .396 | .462 | .505 |
| 24 | .330 | .388 | .453 | .496 |
| 25 | .323 | .381 | .445 | .487 |
| 26 | .317 | .374 | .437 | .479 |
| 27 | .311 | .367 | .430 | .471 |
| 28 | .306 | .361 | .423 | .463 |
| 29 | .301 | .355 | .416 | .456 |
| 30 | .296 | .349 | .409 | .449 |
| 35 | .275 | .325 | .381 | .418 |
| 40 | .257 | .304 | .358 | .393 |
| 45 | .243 | .288 | .338 | .372 |
| 50 | .231 | .273 | .322 | .354 |
| 60 | .211 | .250 | .295 | .325 |
| 70 | .195 | .232 | .274 | .303 |
| 80 | .183 | .217 | .256 | .283 |
| 90 | .173 | .205 | .242 | .267 |
| 100 | .164 | .195 | .230 | .254 |

*Abridged from Fisher, R. A., and Yates, F.: *Statistical Tables for Biological, Agricultural, and Medical Research,* Oliver & Boyd, Ltd., Edinburgh, by permission of the authors and publisher. Reproduced with permission from Ferguson, G. A.: *Statistical Analysis in Psychology and Education.* New York: McGraw-Hill, 1959.

**Table A–10.** ABSOLUTE VALUES OF THE RANK-CORRELATION COEFFICIENT SIGNIFICANT AT THE 20, 10, 5, 2, AND 1 PER CENT LEVELS*

The column headed "$N$" contains the number of observations. A rank-correlation coefficient must exceed the tabled value to be significant at the level stated for the column. For an $N$ of 20, the obtained rank correlation must exceed .45 to be judged significant at the .05 level.

| | Level of Significance $\alpha$† | | | | |
|---|---|---|---|---|---|
| $N$ | .20 | .10 | .05 | .02 | .01 |
| 4 | | 1.00 | | | |
| 5 | .80 | .90 | | 1.00 | |
| 6 | .66 | .83 | .89 | .94 | 1.00 |
| 7 | .57 | .71 | .79 | .89 | .93 |
| 8 | .52 | .64 | .74 | .83 | .88 |
| 9 | .48 | .60 | .68 | .78 | .83 |
| 10 | .45 | .56 | .65 | .73 | .79 |
| 11 | .41 | .52 | .61 | .71 | .77 |
| 12 | .39 | .50 | .59 | .68 | .75 |
| 13 | .37 | .47 | .56 | .65 | .71 |
| 14 | .36 | .46 | .54 | .63 | .69 |
| 15 | .34 | .44 | .52 | .60 | .66 |
| 16 | .33 | .42 | .51 | .58 | .64 |
| 17 | .32 | .41 | .49 | .57 | .62 |
| 18 | .31 | .40 | .48 | .55 | .61 |
| 19 | .30 | .39 | .46 | .54 | .60 |
| 20 | .29 | .38 | .45 | .53 | .58 |
| 21 | .29 | .37 | .44 | .51 | .56 |
| 22 | .28 | .36 | .43 | .50 | .55 |
| 23 | .27 | .35 | .42 | .49 | .54 |
| 24 | .27 | .34 | .41 | .48 | .53 |
| 25 | .26 | .34 | .40 | .47 | .52 |
| 26 | .26 | .33 | .39 | .46 | .51 |
| 27 | .25 | .32 | .38 | .45 | .50 |
| 28 | .25 | .32 | .38 | .44 | .49 |
| 29 | .24 | .31 | .37 | .44 | .48 |
| 30 | .24 | .31 | .36 | .43 | .47 |

*Reproduced with permission from Tate, M. W., and Clelland, R. C.: *Nonparametric and Shortcut Statistics.* Danville, Ill.: Interstate, 1957.
†$\alpha$ is halved for a one-sided test.

### Table A–11. SQUARES AND SQUARE ROOTS

The squares and square roots of numbers ranging from 1 to 1000 may be read from the table. The second column contains the square of the number contained in the first column. Hence, the square of 1.03 is 1.0609; the square of 3.49 is 12.1801, and so forth. In order to obtain the square of numbers larger than 10.00 it is necessary to move the decimals appropriately. Hence, the square of 10.3 is 106.09; the square of 34.9 is 1218.01; the square of 349 is 121,801.

The third column contains the square root of the number listed in the first column. Thus, the square root of 1.03 is 1.01489; the square root of 3.49 is 1.86815. The last column contains the square root of ten times the number listed in the first column. Hence, the square root of 10.3 is 3.20936; the square root of 34.9 is 5.90762. To find the square root of 103 look in the $\sqrt{10N}$ column for 1.03 and multiply the listed number by ten. You find the number 3.20936: ten times that number is 32.0936. Using these principles you can find the square root of any number between 1 and 1000.

Table A–11. SQUARES AND SQUARE ROOTS*

| N | N² | √N | √10N | N | N² | √N | √10N |
|---|---|---|---|---|---|---|---|
| 1.00 | 1.0000 | 1.00000 | 3.16228 | 1.50 | 2.2500 | 1.22474 | 3.87298 |
| 1.01 | 1.0201 | 1.00499 | 3.17805 | 1.51 | 2.2801 | 1.22882 | 3.88587 |
| 1.02 | 1.0404 | 1.00995 | 3.19374 | 1.52 | 2.3104 | 1.23288 | 3.89872 |
| 1.03 | 1.0609 | 1.01489 | 3.20936 | 1.53 | 2.3409 | 1.23693 | 3.91152 |
| 1.04 | 1.0816 | 1.01980 | 3.22490 | 1.54 | 2.3716 | 1.24097 | 3.92428 |
| 1.05 | 1.1025 | 1.02470 | 3.24037 | 1.55 | 2.4025 | 1.24499 | 3.93700 |
| 1.06 | 1.1236 | 1.02956 | 3.25576 | 1.56 | 2.4336 | 1.24900 | 3.94968 |
| 1.07 | 1.1449 | 1.03441 | 3.27109 | 1.57 | 2.4649 | 1.25300 | 3.96232 |
| 1.08 | 1.1664 | 1.03923 | 3.28634 | 1.58 | 2.4964 | 1.25698 | 3.97492 |
| 1.09 | 1.1881 | 1.04403 | 3.30151 | 1.59 | 2.5281 | 1.26095 | 3.98748 |
| 1.10 | 1.2100 | 1.04881 | 3.31662 | 1.60 | 2.5600 | 1.26491 | 4.00000 |
| 1.11 | 1.2321 | 1.05357 | 3.33167 | 1.61 | 2.5921 | 1.26886 | 4.01248 |
| 1.12 | 1.2544 | 1.05830 | 3.34664 | 1.62 | 2.6244 | 1.27279 | 4.02492 |
| 1.13 | 1.2769 | 1.06301 | 3.36155 | 1.63 | 2.6569 | 1.27671 | 4.03733 |
| 1.14 | 1.2996 | 1.06771 | 3.37639 | 1.64 | 2.6896 | 1.28062 | 4.04969 |
| 1.15 | 1.3225 | 1.07238 | 3.39116 | 1.65 | 2.7225 | 1.28452 | 4.06202 |
| 1.16 | 1.3456 | 1.07703 | 3.40588 | 1.66 | 2.7556 | 1.28841 | 4.07431 |
| 1.17 | 1.3689 | 1.08167 | 3.42053 | 1.67 | 2.7889 | 1.29228 | 4.08656 |
| 1.18 | 1.3924 | 1.08628 | 3.43511 | 1.68 | 2.8224 | 1.29615 | 4.09878 |
| 1.19 | 1.4161 | 1.09087 | 3.44964 | 1.69 | 2.8561 | 1.30000 | 4.11096 |
| 1.20 | 1.4400 | 1.09545 | 3.46410 | 1.70 | 2.8900 | 1.30384 | 4.12311 |
| 1.21 | 1.4641 | 1.10000 | 3.47851 | 1.71 | 2.9241 | 1.30767 | 4.13521 |
| 1.22 | 1.4884 | 1.10454 | 3.49285 | 1.72 | 2.9584 | 1.31149 | 4.14729 |
| 1.23 | 1.5129 | 1.10905 | 3.50714 | 1.73 | 2.9929 | 1.31529 | 4.15933 |
| 1.24 | 1.5376 | 1.11355 | 3.52136 | 1.74 | 3.0276 | 1.31909 | 4.17133 |
| 1.25 | 1.5625 | 1.11803 | 3.53553 | 1.75 | 3.0625 | 1.32288 | 4.18330 |
| 1.26 | 1.5876 | 1.12250 | 3.54965 | 1.76 | 3.0976 | 1.32665 | 4.19524 |
| 1.27 | 1.6129 | 1.12694 | 3.56371 | 1.77 | 3.1329 | 1.33041 | 4.20714 |
| 1.28 | 1.6384 | 1.13137 | 3.57771 | 1.78 | 3.1684 | 1.33417 | 4.21900 |
| 1.29 | 1.6641 | 1.13578 | 3.59166 | 1.79 | 3.2041 | 1.33791 | 4.23084 |
| 1.30 | 1.6900 | 1.14018 | 3.60555 | 1.80 | 3.2400 | 1.34164 | 4.24264 |
| 1.31 | 1.7161 | 1.14455 | 3.61939 | 1.81 | 3.2761 | 1.34536 | 4.25441 |
| 1.32 | 1.7424 | 1.14891 | 3.63318 | 1.82 | 3.3124 | 1.34907 | 4.26615 |
| 1.33 | 1.7689 | 1.15326 | 3.64692 | 1.83 | 3.3489 | 1.35277 | 4.27785 |
| 1.34 | 1.7956 | 1.15758 | 3.66060 | 1.84 | 3.3856 | 1.35647 | 4.28952 |
| 1.35 | 1.8225 | 1.16190 | 3.67423 | 1.85 | 3.4225 | 1.36015 | 4.30116 |
| 1.36 | 1.8496 | 1.16619 | 3.68782 | 1.86 | 3.4596 | 1.36382 | 4.31277 |
| 1.37 | 1.8769 | 1.17047 | 3.70135 | 1.87 | 3.4969 | 1.36748 | 4.32435 |
| 1.38 | 1.9044 | 1.17473 | 3.71484 | 1.88 | 3.5344 | 1.37113 | 4.33590 |
| 1.39 | 1.9321 | 1.17898 | 3.72827 | 1.89 | 3.5721 | 1.37477 | 4.34741 |
| 1.40 | 1.9600 | 1.18322 | 3.74166 | 1.90 | 3.6100 | 1.37840 | 4.35890 |
| 1.41 | 1.9881 | 1.18743 | 3.75500 | 1.91 | 3.6481 | 1.38203 | 4.37035 |
| 1.42 | 2.0164 | 1.19164 | 3.76829 | 1.92 | 3.6864 | 1.38564 | 4.38178 |
| 1.43 | 2.0449 | 1.19583 | 3.78153 | 1.93 | 3.7249 | 1.38924 | 4.39318 |
| 1.44 | 2.0736 | 1.20000 | 3.79473 | 1.94 | 3.7636 | 1.39284 | 4.40454 |
| 1.45 | 2.1025 | 1.20416 | 3.80789 | 1.95 | 3.8025 | 1.39642 | 4.41588 |
| 1.46 | 2.1316 | 1.20830 | 3.82099 | 1.96 | 3.8416 | 1.40000 | 4.42719 |
| 1.47 | 2.1609 | 1.21244 | 3.83406 | 1.97 | 3.8809 | 1.40357 | 4.43847 |
| 1.48 | 2.1904 | 1.21655 | 3.84708 | 1.98 | 3.9204 | 1.40712 | 4.44972 |
| 1.49 | 2.2201 | 1.22066 | 3.86005 | 1.99 | 3.9601 | 1.41067 | 4.46094 |
| 1.50 | 2.2500 | 1.22474 | 3.87298 | 2.00 | 4.0000 | 1.41421 | 4.47214 |
| N | N² | √N | √10N | N | N² | √N | √10N |

*Reproduced with permission from McNemar, Q.: *Psychological Statistics*, 3rd Ed. New York: John Wiley and Sons, Inc., 1962.

*Table continued on the following page*

**Table A–11.** *Continued*

| N | N² | √N | √10N | N | N² | √N | √10N |
|------|--------|---------|---------|------|--------|---------|---------|
| **2.00** | 4.0000 | 1.41421 | 4.47214 | **2.50** | 6.2500 | 1.58114 | 5.00000 |
| 2.01 | 4.0401 | 1.41774 | 4.48330 | 2.51 | 6.3001 | 1.58430 | 5.00999 |
| 2.02 | 4.0804 | 1.42127 | 4.49444 | 2.52 | 6.3504 | 1.58745 | 5.01996 |
| 2.03 | 4.1209 | 1.42478 | 4.50555 | 2.53 | 6.4009 | 1.59060 | 5.02991 |
| 2.04 | 4.1616 | 1.42829 | 4.51664 | 2.54 | 6.4516 | 1.59374 | 5.03984 |
| 2.05 | 4.2025 | 1.43178 | 4.52769 | 2.55 | 6.5025 | 1.59687 | 5.04975 |
| 2.06 | 4.2436 | 1.43527 | 4.53872 | 2.56 | 6.5536 | 1.60000 | 5.05964 |
| 2.07 | 4.2849 | 1.43875 | 4.54973 | 2.57 | 6.6049 | 1.60312 | 5.06952 |
| 2.08 | 4.3264 | 1.44222 | 4.56070 | 2.58 | 6.6564 | 1.60624 | 5.07937 |
| 2.09 | 4.3681 | 1.44568 | 4.57165 | 2.59 | 6.7081 | 1.60935 | 5.08920 |
| **2.10** | 4.4100 | 1.44914 | 4.58258 | **2.60** | 6.7600 | 1.61245 | 5.09902 |
| 2.11 | 4.4521 | 1.45258 | 4.59347 | 2.61 | 6.8121 | 1.61555 | 5.10882 |
| 2.12 | 4.4944 | 1.45602 | 4.60435 | 2.62 | 6.8644 | 1.61864 | 5.11859 |
| 2.13 | 4.5369 | 1.45945 | 4.61519 | 2.63 | 6.9169 | 1.62173 | 5.12835 |
| 2.14 | 4.5796 | 1.46287 | 4.62601 | 2.64 | 6.9696 | 1.62481 | 5.13809 |
| 2.15 | 4.6225 | 1.46629 | 4.63681 | 2.65 | 7.0225 | 1.62788 | 5.14782 |
| 2.16 | 4.6656 | 1.46969 | 4.64758 | 2.66 | 7.0756 | 1.63095 | 5.15752 |
| 2.17 | 4.7089 | 1.47309 | 4.65833 | 2.67 | 7.1289 | 1.63401 | 5.16720 |
| 2.18 | 4.7524 | 1.47648 | 4.66905 | 2.68 | 7.1824 | 1.63707 | 5.17687 |
| 2.19 | 4.7961 | 1.47986 | 4.67974 | 2.69 | 7.2361 | 1.64012 | 5.18652 |
| **2.20** | 4.8400 | 1.48324 | 4.69042 | **2.70** | 7.2900 | 1.64317 | 5.19615 |
| 2.21 | 4.8841 | 1.48661 | 4.70106 | 2.71 | 7.3441 | 1.64621 | 5.20577 |
| 2.22 | 4.9284 | 1.48997 | 4.71169 | 2.72 | 7.3984 | 1.64924 | 5.21536 |
| 2.23 | 4.9729 | 1.49332 | 4.72229 | 2.73 | 7.4529 | 1.65227 | 5.22494 |
| 2.24 | 5.0176 | 1.49666 | 4.73286 | 2.74 | 7.5076 | 1.65529 | 5.23450 |
| 2.25 | 5.0625 | 1.50000 | 4.74342 | 2.75 | 7.5625 | 1.65831 | 5.24404 |
| 2.26 | 5.1076 | 1.50333 | 4.75395 | 2.76 | 7.6176 | 1.66132 | 5.25357 |
| 2.27 | 5.1529 | 1.50665 | 4.76445 | 2.77 | 7.6729 | 1.66433 | 5.26308 |
| 2.28 | 5.1984 | 1.50997 | 4.77493 | 2.78 | 7.7284 | 1.66733 | 5.27257 |
| 2.29 | 5.2441 | 1.51327 | 4.78539 | 2.79 | 7.7841 | 1.67033 | 5.28205 |
| **2.30** | 5.2900 | 1.51658 | 4.79583 | **2.80** | 7.8400 | 1.67332 | 5.29150 |
| 2.31 | 5.3361 | 1.51987 | 4.80625 | 2.81 | 7.8961 | 1.67631 | 5.30094 |
| 2.32 | 5.3824 | 1.52315 | 4.81664 | 2.82 | 7.9524 | 1.67929 | 5.31037 |
| 2.33 | 5.4289 | 1.52643 | 4.82701 | 2.83 | 8.0089 | 1.68226 | 5.31977 |
| 2.34 | 5.4756 | 1.52971 | 4.83735 | 2.84 | 8.0656 | 1.68523 | 5.32917 |
| 2.35 | 5.5225 | 1.53297 | 4.84768 | 2.85 | 8.1225 | 1.68819 | 5.33854 |
| 2.36 | 5.5696 | 1.53623 | 4.85798 | 2.86 | 8.1796 | 1.69115 | 5.34790 |
| 2.37 | 5.6169 | 1.53948 | 4.86826 | 2.87 | 8.2369 | 1.69411 | 5.35724 |
| 2.38 | 5.6644 | 1.54272 | 4.87852 | 2.88 | 8.2944 | 1.69706 | 5.36656 |
| 2.39 | 5.7121 | 1.54596 | 4.88876 | 2.89 | 8.3521 | 1.70000 | 5.37587 |
| **2.40** | 5.7600 | 1.54919 | 4.89898 | **2.90** | 8.4100 | 1.70294 | 5.38516 |
| 2.41 | 5.8081 | 1.55242 | 4.90918 | 2.91 | 8.4681 | 1.70587 | 5.39444 |
| 2.42 | 5.8564 | 1.55563 | 4.91935 | 2.92 | 8.5264 | 1.70880 | 5.40370 |
| 2.43 | 5.9049 | 1.55885 | 4.92950 | 2.93 | 8.5849 | 1.71172 | 5.41295 |
| 2.44 | 5.9536 | 1.56205 | 4.93964 | 2.94 | 8.6436 | 1.71464 | 5.42218 |
| 2.45 | 6.0025 | 1.56525 | 4.94975 | 2.95 | 8.7025 | 1.71756 | 5.43139 |
| 2.46 | 6.0516 | 1.56844 | 4.95984 | 2.96 | 8.7616 | 1.72047 | 5.44059 |
| 2.47 | 6.1009 | 1.57162 | 4.96991 | 2.97 | 8.8209 | 1.72337 | 5.44977 |
| 2.48 | 6.1504 | 1.57480 | 4.97996 | 2.98 | 8.8804 | 1.72627 | 5.45894 |
| 2.49 | 6.2001 | 1.57797 | 4.98999 | 2.99 | 8.9401 | 1.72916 | 5.46809 |
| **2.50** | 6.2500 | 1.58114 | 5.00000 | **3.00** | 9.0000 | 1.73205 | 5.47723 |
| N | N² | √N | √10N | N | N² | √N | √10N |

**Table A-11.** *Continued*

| N | N² | √N̄ | √10N̄ | N | N² | √N̄ | √10N̄ |
|---|---|---|---|---|---|---|---|
| **3.00** | 9.0000 | 1.73205 | 5.47723 | **3.50** | 12.2500 | 1.87083 | 5.91608 |
| 3.01 | 9.0601 | 1.73494 | 5.48635 | 3.51 | 12.3201 | 1.87350 | 5.92453 |
| 3.02 | 9.1204 | 1.73781 | 5.49545 | 3.52 | 12.3904 | 1.87617 | 5.93296 |
| 3.03 | 9.1809 | 1.74069 | 5.50454 | 3.53 | 12.4609 | 1.87883 | 5.94138 |
| 3.04 | 9.2416 | 1.74356 | 5.51362 | 3.54 | 12.5316 | 1.88149 | 5.94979 |
| 3.05 | 9.3025 | 1.74642 | 5.52268 | 3.55 | 12.6025 | 1.88414 | 5.95819 |
| 3.06 | 9.3636 | 1.74929 | 5.53173 | 3.56 | 12.6736 | 1.88680 | 5.96657 |
| 3.07 | 9.4249 | 1.75214 | 5.54076 | 3.57 | 12.7449 | 1.88944 | 5.97495 |
| 3.08 | 9.4864 | 1.75499 | 5.54977 | 3.58 | 12.8164 | 1.89209 | 5.98331 |
| 3.09 | 9.5481 | 1.75784 | 5.55878 | 3.59 | 12.8881 | 1.89473 | 5.99166 |
| **3.10** | 9.6100 | 1.76068 | 5.56776 | **3.60** | 12.9600 | 1.89737 | 6.00000 |
| 3.11 | 9.6721 | 1.76352 | 5.57674 | 3.61 | 13.0321 | 1.90000 | 6.00833 |
| 3.12 | 9.7344 | 1.76636 | 5.58570 | 3.62 | 13.1044 | 1.90263 | 6.01664 |
| 3.13 | 9.7969 | 1.76918 | 5.59464 | 3.63 | 13.1769 | 1.90526 | 6.02495 |
| 3.14 | 9.8596 | 1.77200 | 5.60357 | 3.64 | 13.2496 | 1.90788 | 6.03324 |
| 3.15 | 9.9225 | 1.77482 | 5.61249 | 3.65 | 13.3225 | 1.91050 | 6.04152 |
| 3.16 | 9.9856 | 1.77764 | 5.62139 | 3.66 | 13.3956 | 1.91311 | 6.04979 |
| 3.17 | 10.0489 | 1.78045 | 5.63028 | 3.67 | 13.4689 | 1.91572 | 6.05805 |
| 3.18 | 10.1124 | 1.78326 | 5.63915 | 3.68 | 13.5424 | 1.91833 | 6.06630 |
| 3.19 | 10.1761 | 1.78606 | 5.64801 | 3.69 | 13.6161 | 1.92094 | 6.07454 |
| **3.20** | 10.2400 | 1.78885 | 5.65685 | **3.70** | 13.6900 | 1.92354 | 6.08276 |
| 3.21 | 10.3041 | 1.79165 | 5.66569 | 3.71 | 13.7641 | 1.92614 | 6.09098 |
| 3.22 | 10.3684 | 1.79444 | 5.67450 | 3.72 | 13.8384 | 1.92873 | 6.09918 |
| 3.23 | 10.4329 | 1.79722 | 5.68331 | 3.73 | 13.9129 | 1.93132 | 6.10737 |
| 3.24 | 10.4976 | 1.80000 | 5.69210 | 3.74 | 13.9876 | 1.93391 | 6.11555 |
| 3.25 | 10.5625 | 1.80278 | 5.70088 | 3.75 | 14.0625 | 1.93649 | 6.12372 |
| 3.26 | 10.6276 | 1.80555 | 5.70964 | 3.76 | 14.1376 | 1.93907 | 6.13188 |
| 3.27 | 10.6929 | 1.80831 | 5.71839 | 3.77 | 14.2129 | 1.94165 | 6.14003 |
| 3.28 | 10.7584 | 1.81108 | 5.72713 | 3.78 | 14.2884 | 1.94422 | 6.14817 |
| 3.29 | 10.8241 | 1.81384 | 5.73585 | 3.79 | 14.3641 | 1.94679 | 6.15630 |
| **3.30** | 10.8900 | 1.81659 | 5.74456 | **3.80** | 14.4400 | 1.94936 | 6.16441 |
| 3.31 | 10.9561 | 1.81934 | 5.75326 | 3.81 | 14.5161 | 1.95192 | 6.17252 |
| 3.32 | 11.0224 | 1.82209 | 5.76194 | 3.82 | 14.5924 | 1.95448 | 6.18061 |
| 3.33 | 11.0889 | 1.82483 | 5.77062 | 3.83 | 14.6689 | 1.95704 | 6.18870 |
| 3.34 | 11.1556 | 1.82757 | 5.77927 | 3.84 | 14.7456 | 1.95959 | 6.19677 |
| 3.35 | 11.2225 | 1.83030 | 5.78792 | 3.85 | 14.8225 | 1.96214 | 6.20484 |
| 3.36 | 11.2896 | 1.83303 | 5.79655 | 3.86 | 14.8996 | 1.96469 | 6.21289 |
| 3.37 | 11.3569 | 1.83576 | 5.80517 | 3.87 | 14.9769 | 1.96723 | 6.22093 |
| 3.38 | 11.4244 | 1.83848 | 5.81378 | 3.88 | 15.0544 | 1.96977 | 6.22896 |
| 3.39 | 11.4921 | 1.84120 | 5.82237 | 3.89 | 15.1321 | 1.97231 | 6.23699 |
| **3.40** | 11.5600 | 1.84391 | 5.83095 | **3.90** | 15.2100 | 1.97484 | 6.24500 |
| 3.41 | 11.6281 | 1.84662 | 5.83952 | 3.91 | 15.2881 | 1.97737 | 6.25300 |
| 3.42 | 11.6964 | 1.84932 | 5.84808 | 3.92 | 15.3664 | 1.97990 | 6.26099 |
| 3.43 | 11.7649 | 1.85203 | 5.85662 | 3.93 | 15.4449 | 1.98242 | 6.26897 |
| 3.44 | 11.8336 | 1.85472 | 5.86515 | 3.94 | 15.5236 | 1.98494 | 6.27694 |
| 3.45 | 11.9025 | 1.85742 | 5.87367 | 3.95 | 15.6025 | 1.98746 | 6.28490 |
| 3.46 | 11.9716 | 1.86011 | 5.88218 | 3.96 | 15.6816 | 1.98997 | 6.29285 |
| 3.47 | 12.0409 | 1.86279 | 5.89067 | 3.97 | 15.7609 | 1.99249 | 6.30079 |
| 3.48 | 12.1104 | 1.86548 | 5.89915 | 3.98 | 15.8404 | 1.99499 | 6.30872 |
| 3.49 | 12.1801 | 1.86815 | 5.90762 | 3.99 | 15.9201 | 1.99750 | 6.31664 |
| **3.50** | 12.2500 | 1.87083 | 5.91608 | **4.00** | 16.0000 | 2.00000 | 6.32456 |
| N | N² | √N̄ | √10N̄ | N | N² | √N̄ | √10N̄ |

*Table continued on the following page*

**Table A–11.** *Continued*

| N | N² | √N | √10N | N | N² | √N | √10N |
|---|---|---|---|---|---|---|---|
| 4.00 | 16.0000 | 2.00000 | 6.32456 | 4.50 | 20.2500 | 2.12132 | 6.70820 |
| 4.01 | 16.0801 | 2.00250 | 6.33246 | 4.51 | 20.3401 | 2.12368 | 6.71565 |
| 4.02 | 16.1604 | 2.00499 | 6.34035 | 4.52 | 20.4304 | 2.12603 | 6.72309 |
| 4.03 | 16.2409 | 2.00749 | 6.34823 | 4.53 | 20.5209 | 2.12838 | 6.73053 |
| 4.04 | 16.3216 | 2.00998 | 6.35610 | 4.54 | 20.6116 | 2.13073 | 6.73795 |
| 4.05 | 16.4025 | 2.01246 | 6.36396 | 4.55 | 20.7025 | 2.13307 | 6.74537 |
| 4.06 | 16.4836 | 2.01494 | 6.37181 | 4.56 | 20.7936 | 2.13542 | 6.75278 |
| 4.07 | 16.5649 | 2.01742 | 6.37966 | 4.57 | 20.8849 | 2.13776 | 6.76018 |
| 4.08 | 16.6464 | 2.01990 | 6.38749 | 4.58 | 20.9764 | 2.14009 | 6.76757 |
| 4.09 | 16.7281 | 2.02237 | 6.39531 | 4.59 | 21.0681 | 2.14243 | 6.77495 |
| 4.10 | 16.8100 | 2.02485 | 6.40312 | 4.60 | 21.1600 | 2.14476 | 6.78233 |
| 4.11 | 16.8921 | 2.02731 | 6.41093 | 4.61 | 21.2521 | 2.14709 | 6.78970 |
| 4.12 | 16.9744 | 2.02978 | 6.41872 | 4.62 | 21.3444 | 2.14942 | 6.79706 |
| 4.13 | 17.0569 | 2.03224 | 6.42651 | 4.63 | 21.4369 | 2.15174 | 6.80441 |
| 4.14 | 17.1396 | 2.03470 | 6.43428 | 4.64 | 21.5296 | 2.15407 | 6.81175 |
| 4.15 | 17.2225 | 2.03715 | 6.44205 | 4.65 | 21.6225 | 2.15639 | 6.81909 |
| 4.16 | 17.3056 | 2.03961 | 6.44981 | 4.66 | 21.7156 | 2.15870 | 6.82642 |
| 4.17 | 17.3889 | 2.04206 | 6.45755 | 4.67 | 21.8089 | 2.16102 | 6.83374 |
| 4.18 | 17.4724 | 2.04450 | 6.46529 | 4.68 | 21.9024 | 2.16333 | 6.84105 |
| 4.19 | 17.5561 | 2.04695 | 6.47302 | 4.69 | 21.9961 | 2.16564 | 6.84836 |
| 4.20 | 17.6400 | 2.04939 | 6.48074 | 4.70 | 22.0900 | 2.16795 | 6.85565 |
| 4.21 | 17.7241 | 2.05183 | 6.48845 | 4.71 | 22.1841 | 2.17025 | 6.86294 |
| 4.22 | 17.8084 | 2.05426 | 6.49615 | 4.72 | 22.2784 | 2.17256 | 6.87023 |
| 4.23 | 17.8929 | 2.05670 | 6.50384 | 4.73 | 22.3729 | 2.17486 | 6.87750 |
| 4.24 | 17.9776 | 2.05913 | 6.51153 | 4.74 | 22.4676 | 2.17715 | 6.88477 |
| 4.25 | 18.0625 | 2.06155 | 6.51920 | 4.75 | 22.5625 | 2.17945 | 6.89202 |
| 4.26 | 18.1476 | 2.06398 | 6.52687 | 4.76 | 22.6576 | 2.18174 | 6.89928 |
| 4.27 | 18.2329 | 2.06640 | 6.53452 | 4.77 | 22.7529 | 2.18403 | 6.90652 |
| 4.28 | 18.3184 | 2.06882 | 6.54217 | 4.78 | 22.8484 | 2.18632 | 6.91375 |
| 4.29 | 18.4041 | 2.07123 | 6.54981 | 4.79 | 22.9441 | 2.18861 | 6.92098 |
| 4.30 | 18.4900 | 2.07364 | 6.55744 | 4.80 | 23.0400 | 2.19089 | 6.92820 |
| 4.31 | 18.5761 | 2.07605 | 6.56506 | 4.81 | 23.1361 | 2.19317 | 6.93542 |
| 4.32 | 18.6624 | 2.07846 | 6.57267 | 4.82 | 23.2324 | 2.19545 | 6.94262 |
| 4.33 | 18.7489 | 2.08087 | 6.58027 | 4.83 | 23.3289 | 2.19773 | 6.94982 |
| 4.34 | 18.8356 | 2.08327 | 6.58787 | 4.84 | 23.4256 | 2.20000 | 6.95701 |
| 4.35 | 18.9225 | 2.08567 | 6.59545 | 4.85 | 23.5225 | 2.20227 | 6.96419 |
| 4.36 | 19.0096 | 2.08806 | 6.60303 | 4.86 | 23.6196 | 2.20454 | 6.97137 |
| 4,37 | 19.0969 | 2.09045 | 6.61060 | 4.87 | 23.7169 | 2.20681 | 6.97854 |
| 4.38 | 19.1844 | 2.09284 | 6.61816 | 4.88 | 23.8144 | 2.20907 | 6.98570 |
| 4.39 | 19.2721 | 2.09523 | 6.62571 | 4.89 | 23.9121 | 2.21133 | 6.99285 |
| 4.40 | 19.3600 | 2.09762 | 6.63325 | 4.90 | 24.0100 | 2.21359 | 7.00000 |
| 4.41 | 19.4481 | 2.10000 | 6.64078 | 4.91 | 24.1081 | 2.21585 | 7.00714 |
| 4.42 | 19.5364 | 2.10238 | 6.64831 | 4.92 | 24.2064 | 2.21811 | 7.01427 |
| 4.43 | 19.6249 | 2.10476 | 6.65582 | 4.93 | 24.3049 | 2.22036 | 7.02140 |
| 4.44 | 19.7136 | 2.10713 | 6.66333 | 4.94 | 24.4036 | 2.22261 | 7.02851 |
| 4.45 | 19.8025 | 2.10950 | 6.67083 | 4.95 | 24.5025 | 2.22486 | 7.03562 |
| 4.46 | 19.8916 | 2.11187 | 6.67832 | 4.96 | 24.6016 | 2.22711 | 7.04273 |
| 4.47 | 19.9809 | 2.11424 | 6.68581 | 4.97 | 24.7009 | 2.22935 | 7.04982 |
| 4.48 | 20.0704 | 2.11660 | 6.69328 | 4.98 | 24.8004 | 2.23159 | 7.05691 |
| 4.49 | 20.1601 | 2.11896 | 6.70075 | 4.99 | 24.9001 | 2.23383 | 7.06399 |
| 4.50 | 20.2500 | 2.12132 | 6.70820 | 5.00 | 25.0000 | 2.23607 | 7.07107 |
| N | N² | √N | √10N | N | N² | √N | √10N |

**Table A–11.** *Continued*

| N | N² | √N | √10N | N | N² | √N | √10N |
|---|---|---|---|---|---|---|---|
| **5.00** | 25.0000 | 2.23607 | 7.07107 | **5.50** | 30.2500 | 2.34521 | 7.41620 |
| 5.01 | 25.1001 | 2.23830 | 7.07814 | 5.51 | 30.3601 | 2.34734 | 7.42294 |
| 5.02 | 25.2004 | 2.24054 | 7.08520 | 5.52 | 30.4704 | 2.34947 | 7.42967 |
| 5.03 | 25.3009 | 2.24277 | 7.09225 | 5.53 | 30.5809 | 2.35160 | 7.43640 |
| 5.04 | 25.4016 | 2.24499 | 7.09930 | 5.54 | 30.6916 | 2.35372 | 7.44312 |
| 5.05 | 25.5025 | 2.24722 | 7.10634 | 5.55 | 30.8025 | 2.35584 | 7.44983 |
| 5.06 | 25.6036 | 2.24944 | 7.11337 | 5.56 | 30.9136 | 2.35797 | 7.45654 |
| 5.07 | 25.7049 | 2.25167 | 7.12039 | 5.57 | 31.0249 | 2.36008 | 7.46324 |
| 5.08 | 25.8064 | 2.25389 | 7.12741 | 5.58 | 31.1364 | 2.36220 | 7.46994 |
| 5.09 | 25.9081 | 2.25610 | 7.13442 | 5.59 | 31.2481 | 2.36432 | 7.47663 |
| **5.10** | 26.0100 | 2.25832 | 7.14143 | **5.60** | 31.3600 | 2.36643 | 7.48331 |
| 5.11 | 26.1121 | 2.26053 | 7.14843 | 5.61 | 31.4721 | 2.36854 | 7.48999 |
| 5.12 | 26.2144 | 2.26274 | 7.15542 | 5.62 | 31.5844 | 2.37065 | 7.49667 |
| 5.13 | 26.3169 | 2.26495 | 7.16240 | 5.63 | 31.6969 | 2.37276 | 7.50333 |
| 5.14 | 26.4196 | 2.26716 | 7.16938 | 5.64 | 31.8096 | 2.37487 | 7.50999 |
| 5.15 | 26.5225 | 2.26936 | 7.17635 | 5.65 | 31.9225 | 2.37697 | 7.51665 |
| 5.16 | 26.6256 | 2.27156 | 7.18331 | 5.66 | 32.0356 | 2.37908 | 7.52330 |
| 5.17 | 26.7289 | 2.27376 | 7.19027 | 5.67 | 32.1489 | 2.38118 | 7.52994 |
| 5.18 | 26.8324 | 2.27596 | 7.19722 | 5.68 | 32.2624 | 2.38328 | 7.53658 |
| 5.19 | 26.9361 | 2.27816 | 7.20417 | 5.69 | 32.3761 | 2.38537 | 7.54321 |
| **5.20** | 27.0400 | 2.28035 | 7.21110 | **5.70** | 32.4900 | 2.38747 | 7.54983 |
| 5.21 | 27.1441 | 2.28254 | 7.21803 | 5.71 | 32.6041 | 2.38956 | 7.55645 |
| 5.22 | 27.2484 | 2.28473 | 7.22496 | 5.72 | 32.7184 | 2.39165 | 7.56307 |
| 5.23 | 27.3529 | 2.28692 | 7.23187 | 5.73 | 32.8329 | 2.39374 | 7.56968 |
| 5.24 | 27.4576 | 2.28910 | 7.23878 | 5.74 | 32.9476 | 2.39583 | 7.57628 |
| 5.25 | 27.5625 | 2.29129 | 7.24569 | 5.75 | 33.0625 | 2.39792 | 7.58288 |
| 5.26 | 27.6676 | 2.29347 | 7.25259 | 5.76 | 33.1776 | 2.40000 | 7.58947 |
| 5.27 | 27.7729 | 2.29565 | 7.25948 | 5.77 | 33.2929 | 2.40208 | 7.59605 |
| 5.28 | 27.8784 | 2.29783 | 7.26636 | 5.78 | 33.4084 | 2.40416 | 7.60263 |
| 5.29 | 27.9841 | 2.30000 | 7.27324 | 5.79 | 33.5241 | 2.40624 | 7.60920 |
| **5.30** | 28.0900 | 2.30217 | 7.28011 | **5.80** | 33.6400 | 2.40832 | 7.61577 |
| 5.31 | 28.1961 | 2.30434 | 7.28697 | 5.81 | 33.7561 | 2.41039 | 7.62234 |
| 5.32 | 28.3024 | 2.30651 | 7.29383 | 5.82 | 33.8724 | 2.41247 | 7.62889 |
| 5.33 | 28.4089 | 2.30868 | 7.30068 | 5.83 | 33.9889 | 2.41454 | 7.63544 |
| 5.34 | 28.5156 | 2.31084 | 7.30753 | 5.84 | 34.1056 | 2.41661 | 7.64199 |
| 5.35 | 28.6225 | 2.31301 | 7.31437 | 5.85 | 34.2225 | 2.41868 | 7.64853 |
| 5.36 | 28.7296 | 2.31517 | 7.32120 | 5.86 | 34.3396 | 2.42074 | 7.65506 |
| 5.37 | 28.8369 | 2.31733 | 7.32803 | 5.87 | 34.4569 | 2.42281 | 7.66159 |
| 5.38 | 28.9444 | 2.31948 | 7.33485 | 5.88 | 34.5744 | 2.42487 | 7.66812 |
| 5.39 | 29.0521 | 2.32164 | 7.34166 | 5.89 | 34.6921 | 2.42693 | 7.67463 |
| **5.40** | 29.1600 | 2.32379 | 7.34847 | **5.90** | 34.8100 | 2.42899 | 7.68115 |
| 5.41 | 29.2681 | 2.32594 | 7.35527 | 5.91 | 34.9281 | 2.43105 | 7.68765 |
| 5.42 | 29.3764 | 2.32809 | 7.36206 | 5.92 | 35.0464 | 2.43311 | 7.69415 |
| 5.43 | 29.4849 | 2.33024 | 7.36885 | 5.93 | 35.1649 | 2.43516 | 7.70065 |
| 5.44 | 29.5936 | 2.33238 | 7.37564 | 5.94 | 35.2836 | 2.43721 | 7.70714 |
| 5.45 | 29.7025 | 2.33452 | 7.38241 | 5.95 | 35.4025 | 2.43926 | 7.71362 |
| 5.46 | 29.8116 | 2.33666 | 7.38918 | 5.96 | 35.5216 | 2.44131 | 7.72010 |
| 5.47 | 29.9209 | 2.33880 | 7.39594 | 5.97 | 35.6409 | 2.44336 | 7.72658 |
| 5.48 | 30.0304 | 2.34094 | 7.40270 | 5.98 | 35.7604 | 2.44540 | 7.73305 |
| 5.49 | 30.1401 | 2.34307 | 7.40945 | 5.99 | 35.8801 | 2.44745 | 7.73951 |
| **5.50** | 30.2500 | 2.34521 | 7.41620 | **6.00** | 36.0000 | 2.44949 | 7.74597 |
| N | N² | √N | √10N | N | N² | √N | √10N |

*Table continued on the following page*

**Table A–11.** *Continued*

| N | N² | √N | √10N | N | N² | √N | √10N |
|---|---|---|---|---|---|---|---|
| **6.00** | 36.0000 | 2.44949 | 7.74597 | **6.50** | 42.2500 | 2.54951 | 8.06226 |
| 6.01 | 36.1201 | 2.45153 | 7.75242 | 6.51 | 42.3801 | 2.55147 | 8.06846 |
| 6.02 | 36.2404 | 2.45357 | 7.75887 | 6.52 | 42.5104 | 2.55343 | 8.07465 |
| 6.03 | 36.3609 | 2.45561 | 7.76531 | 6.53 | 42.6409 | 2.55539 | 8.08084 |
| 6.04 | 36.4816 | 2.45764 | 7.77174 | 6.54 | 42.7716 | 2.55734 | 8.08703 |
| 6.05 | 36.6025 | 2.45967 | 7.77817 | 6.55 | 42.9025 | 2.55930 | 8.09321 |
| 6.06 | 36.7236 | 2.46171 | 7.78460 | 6.56 | 43.0336 | 2.56125 | 8.09938 |
| 6.07 | 36.8449 | 2.46374 | 7.79102 | 6.57 | 43.1649 | 2.56320 | 8.10555 |
| 6.08 | 36.9664 | 2.46577 | 7.79744 | 6.58 | 43.2964 | 2.56515 | 8.11172 |
| 6.09 | 37.0881 | 2.46779 | 7.80385 | 6.59 | 43.4281 | 2.56710 | 8.11788 |
| **6.10** | 37.2100 | 2.46982 | 7.81025 | **6.60** | 43.5600 | 2.56905 | 8.12404 |
| 6.11 | 37.3321 | 2.47184 | 7.81665 | 6.61 | 43.6921 | 2.57099 | 8.13019 |
| 6.12 | 37.4544 | 2.47386 | 7.82304 | 6.62 | 43.8244 | 2.57294 | 8.13634 |
| 6.13 | 37.5769 | 2.47588 | 7.82943 | 6.63 | 43.9569 | 2.57488 | 8.14248 |
| 6.14 | 37.6996 | 2.47790 | 7.83582 | 6.64 | 44.0896 | 2.57682 | 8.14862 |
| 6.15 | 37.8225 | 2.47992 | 7.84219 | 6.65 | 44.2225 | 2.57876 | 8.15475 |
| 6.16 | 37.9456 | 2.48193 | 7.84857 | 6.66 | 44.3556 | 2.58070 | 8.16088 |
| 6.17 | 38.0689 | 2.48395 | 7.85493 | 6.67 | 44.4889 | 2.58263 | 8.16701 |
| 6.18 | 38.1924 | 2.48596 | 7.86130 | 6.68 | 44.6224 | 2.58457 | 8.17313 |
| 6.19 | 38.3161 | 2.48797 | 7.86766 | 6.69 | 44.7561 | 2.58650 | 8.17924 |
| **6.20** | 38.4400 | 2.48998 | 7.87401 | **6.70** | 44.8900 | 2.58844 | 8.18535 |
| 6.21 | 38.5641 | 2.49199 | 7.88036 | 6.71 | 45.0241 | 2.59037 | 8.19146 |
| 6.22 | 38.6884 | 2.49399 | 7.88670 | 6.72 | 45.1584 | 2.59230 | 8.19756 |
| 6.23 | 38.8129 | 2.49600 | 7.89303 | 6.73 | 45.2929 | 2.59422 | 8.20366 |
| 6.24 | 38.9376 | 2.49800 | 7.89937 | 6.74 | 45.4276 | 2.59615 | 8.20975 |
| 6.25 | 39.0625 | 2.50000 | 7.90569 | 6.75 | 45.5625 | 2.59808 | 8.21584 |
| 6.26 | 39.1876 | 2.50200 | 7.91202 | 6.76 | 45.6976 | 2.60000 | 8.22192 |
| 6.27 | 39.3129 | 2.50400 | 7.91833 | 6.77 | 45.8329 | 2.60192 | 8.22800 |
| 6.28 | 39.4384 | 2.50599 | 7.92465 | 6.78 | 45.9684 | 2.60384 | 8.23408 |
| 6.29 | 39.5641 | 2.50799 | 7.93095 | 6.79 | 46.1041 | 2.60576 | 8.24015 |
| **6.30** | 39.6900 | 2.50998 | 7.93725 | **6.80** | 46.2400 | 2.60768 | 8.24621 |
| 6.31 | 39.8161 | 2.51197 | 7.94355 | 6.81 | 46.3761 | 2.60960 | 8.25227 |
| 6.32 | 39.9424 | 2.51396 | 7.94984 | 6.82 | 46.5124 | 2.61151 | 8.25833 |
| 6.33 | 40.0689 | 2.51595 | 7.95613 | 6.83 | 46.6489 | 2.61343 | 8.26438 |
| 6.34 | 40.1956 | 2.51794 | 7.96241 | 6.84 | 46.7856 | 2.61534 | 8.27043 |
| 6.35 | 40.3225 | 2.51992 | 7.96869 | 6.85 | 46.9225 | 2.61725 | 8.27647 |
| 6.36 | 40.4496 | 2.52190 | 7.97496 | 6.86 | 47.0596 | 2.61916 | 8.28251 |
| 6.37 | 40.5769 | 2.52389 | 7.98123 | 6.87 | 47.1969 | 2.62107 | 8.28855 |
| 6.38 | 40.7044 | 2.52587 | 7.98749 | 6.88 | 47.3344 | 2.62298 | 8.29458 |
| 6.39 | 40.8321 | 2.52784 | 7.99375 | 6.89 | 47.4721 | 2.62488 | 8.30060 |
| **6.40** | 40.9600 | 2.52982 | 8.00000 | **6.90** | 47.6100 | 2.62679 | 8.30662 |
| 6.41 | 41.0881 | 2.53180 | 8.00625 | 6.91 | 47.7481 | 2.62869 | 8.31264 |
| 6.42 | 41.2164 | 2.53377 | 8.01249 | 6.92 | 47.8864 | 2.63059 | 8.31865 |
| 6.43 | 41.3449 | 2.53574 | 8.01873 | 6.93 | 48.0249 | 2.63249 | 8.32466 |
| 6.44 | 41.4736 | 2.53772 | 8.02496 | 6.94 | 48.1636 | 2.63439 | 8.33067 |
| 6.45 | 41.6025 | 2.53969 | 8.03119 | 6.95 | 48.3025 | 2.63629 | 8.33667 |
| 6.46 | 41.7316 | 2.54165 | 8.03741 | 6.96 | 48.4416 | 2.63818 | 8.34266 |
| 6.47 | 41.8609 | 2.54362 | 8.04363 | 6.97 | 48.5809 | 2.64008 | 8.34865 |
| 6.48 | 41.9904 | 2.54558 | 8.04984 | 6.98 | 48.7204 | 2.64197 | 8.35464 |
| 6.49 | 42.1201 | 2.54755 | 8.05605 | 6.99 | 48.8601 | 2.64386 | 8.36062 |
| **6.50** | 42.2500 | 2.54951 | 8.06226 | **7.00** | 49.0000 | 2.64575 | 8.36660 |
| **N** | **N²** | **√N** | **√10N** | **N** | **N²** | **√N** | **√10N** |

**Table A–11.** *Continued*

| N | N² | √N̄ | √10N̄ | N | N² | √N̄ | √10N̄ |
|---|----|----|-----|---|----|----|-----|
| **7.00** | 49.0000 | 2.64575 | 8.36660 | **7.50** | 56.2500 | 2.73861 | 8.66025 |
| 7.01 | 49.1401 | 2.64764 | 8.37257 | 7.51 | 56.4001 | 2.74044 | 8.66603 |
| 7.02 | 49.2804 | 2.64953 | 8.37854 | 7.52 | 56.5504 | 2.74226 | 8.67179 |
| 7.03 | 49.4209 | 2.65141 | 8.38451 | 7.53 | 56.7009 | 2.74408 | 8.67756 |
| 7.04 | 49.5616 | 2.65330 | 8.39047 | 7.54 | 56.8516 | 2.74591 | 8.68332 |
| 7.05 | 49.7025 | 2.65518 | 8.39643 | 7.55 | 57.0025 | 2.74773 | 8.68907 |
| 7.06 | 49.8436 | 2.65707 | 8.40238 | 7.56 | 57.1536 | 2.74955 | 8.69483 |
| 7.07 | 49.9849 | 2.65895 | 8.40833 | 7.57 | 57.3049 | 2.75136 | 8.70057 |
| 7.08 | 50.1264 | 2.66083 | 8.41427 | 7.58 | 57.4564 | 2.75318 | 8.70632 |
| 7.09 | 50.2681 | 2.66271 | 8.42021 | 7.59 | 57.6081 | 2.75500 | 8.71206 |
| **7.10** | 50.4100 | 2.66458 | 8.42615 | **7.60** | 57.7600 | 2.75681 | 8.71780 |
| 7.11 | 50.5521 | 2.66646 | 8.43208 | 7.61 | 57.9121 | 2.75862 | 8.72353 |
| 7.12 | 50.6944 | 2.66833 | 8.43801 | 7.62 | 58.0644 | 2.76043 | 8.72926 |
| 7.13 | 50.8369 | 2.67021 | 8.44393 | 7.63 | 58.2169 | 2.76225 | 8.73499 |
| 7.14 | 50.9796 | 2.67208 | 8.44985 | 7.64 | 58.3696 | 2.76405 | 8.74071 |
| 7.15 | 51.1225 | 2.67395 | 8.45577 | 7.65 | 58.5225 | 2.76586 | 8.74643 |
| 7.16 | 51.2656 | 2.67582 | 8.46168 | 7.66 | 58.6756 | 2.76767 | 8.75214 |
| 7.17 | 51.4089 | 2.67769 | 8.46759 | 7.67 | 58.8289 | 2.76948 | 8.75785 |
| 7.18 | 51.5524 | 2.67955 | 8.47349 | 7.68 | 58.9824 | 2.77128 | 8.76356 |
| 7.19 | 51.6961 | 2.68142 | 8.47939 | 7.69 | 59.1361 | 2.77308 | 8.76926 |
| **7.20** | 51.8400 | 2.68328 | 8.48528 | **7.70** | 59.2900 | 2.77489 | 8.77496 |
| 7.21 | 51.9841 | 2.68514 | 8.49117 | 7.71 | 59.4441 | 2.77669 | 8.78066 |
| 7.22 | 52.1284 | 2.68701 | 8.49706 | 7.72 | 59.5984 | 2.77849 | 8.78635 |
| 7.23 | 52.2729 | 2.68887 | 8.50294 | 7.73 | 59.7529 | 2.78029 | 8.79204 |
| 7.24 | 52.4176 | 2.69072 | 8.50882 | 7.74 | 59.9076 | 2.78209 | 8.79773 |
| 7.25 | 52.5625 | 2.69258 | 8.51469 | 7.75 | 60.0625 | 2.78388 | 8.80341 |
| 7.26 | 52.7076 | 2.69444 | 8.52056 | 7.76 | 60.2176 | 2.78568 | 8.80909 |
| 7.27 | 52.8529 | 2.69629 | 8.52643 | 7.77 | 60.3729 | 2.78747 | 8.81476 |
| 7.28 | 52.9984 | 2.69815 | 8.53229 | 7.78 | 60.5284 | 2.78927 | 8.82043 |
| 7.29 | 53.1441 | 2.70000 | 8.53815 | 7.79 | 60.6841 | 2.79106 | 8.82610 |
| **7.30** | 53.2900 | 2.70185 | 8.54400 | **7.80** | 60.8400 | 2.79285 | 8.83176 |
| 7.31 | 53.4361 | 2.70370 | 8.54985 | 7.81 | 60.9961 | 2.79464 | 8.83742 |
| 7.32 | 53.5824 | 2.70555 | 8.55570 | 7.82 | 61.1524 | 2.79643 | 8.84308 |
| 7.33 | 53.7289 | 2.70740 | 8.56154 | 7.83 | 61.3089 | 2.79821 | 8.84873 |
| 7.34 | 53.8756 | 2.70924 | 8.56738 | 7.84 | 61.4656 | 2.80000 | 8.85438 |
| 7.35 | 54.0225 | 2.71109 | 8.57321 | 7.85 | 61.6225 | 2.80179 | 8.86002 |
| 7.36 | 54.1696 | 2.71293 | 8.57904 | 7.86 | 61.7796 | 2.80357 | 8.86566 |
| 7.37 | 54.3169 | 2.71477 | 8.58487 | 7.87 | 61.9369 | 2.80535 | 8.87130 |
| 7.38 | 54.4644 | 2.71662 | 8.59069 | 7.88 | 62.0944 | 2.80713 | 8.87694 |
| 7.39 | 54.6121 | 2.71846 | 8.59651 | 7.89 | 62.2521 | 2.80891 | 8.88257 |
| **7.40** | 54.7600 | 2.72029 | 8.60233 | **7.90** | 62.4100 | 2.81069 | 8.88819 |
| 7.41 | 54.9081 | 2.72213 | 8.60814 | 7.91 | 62.5681 | 2.81247 | 8.89382 |
| 7.42 | 55.0564 | 2.72397 | 8.61394 | 7.92 | 62.7264 | 2.81425 | 8.89944 |
| 7.43 | 55.2049 | 2.72580 | 8.61974 | 7.93 | 62.8849 | 2.81603 | 8.90505 |
| 7.44 | 55.3536 | 2.72764 | 8.62554 | 7.94 | 63.0436 | 2.81780 | 8.91067 |
| 7.45 | 55.5025 | 2.72947 | 8.63134 | 7.95 | 63.2025 | 2.81957 | 8.91628 |
| 7.46 | 55.6516 | 2.73130 | 8.63713 | 7.96 | 63.3616 | 2.82135 | 8.92188 |
| 7.47 | 55.8009 | 2.73313 | 8.64292 | 7.97 | 63.5209 | 2.82312 | 8.92749 |
| 7.48 | 55.9504 | 2.73496 | 8.64870 | 7.98 | 63.6804 | 2.82489 | 8.93308 |
| 7.49 | 56.1001 | 2.73679 | 8.65448 | 7.99 | 63.8401 | 2.82666 | 8.93868 |
| **7.50** | 56.2500 | 2.73861 | 8.66025 | **8.00** | 64.0000 | 2.82843 | 8.94427 |
| N | N² | √N̄ | √10N̄ | N | N² | √N̄ | √10N̄ |

*Table continued on the following page*

**Table A–11.** *Continued*

| N | N² | √N | √10N | N | N² | √N | √10N |
|---|---|---|---|---|---|---|---|
| **8.00** | 64.0000 | 2.82843 | 8.94427 | **8.50** | 72.2500 | 2.91548 | 9.21954 |
| 8.01 | 64.1601 | 2.83019 | 8.94986 | 8.51 | 72.4201 | 2.91719 | 9.22497 |
| 8.02 | 64.3204 | 2.83196 | 8.95545 | 8.52 | 72.5904 | 2.91890 | 9.23038 |
| 8.03 | 64.4809 | 2.83373 | 8.96103 | 8.53 | 72.7609 | 2.92062 | 9.23580 |
| 8.04 | 64.6416 | 2.83549 | 8.96660 | 8.54 | 72.9316 | 2.92233 | 9.24121 |
| 8.05 | 64.8025 | 2.83725 | 8.97218 | 8.55 | 73.1025 | 2.92404 | 9.24662 |
| 8.06 | 64.9636 | 2.83901 | 8.97775 | 8.56 | 73.2736 | 2.92575 | 9.25203 |
| 8.07 | 65.1249 | 2.84077 | 8.98332 | 8.57 | 73.4449 | 2.92746 | 9.25743 |
| 8.08 | 65.2864 | 2.84253 | 8.98888 | 8.58 | 73.6164 | 2.92916 | 9.26283 |
| 8.09 | 65.4481 | 2.84429 | 8.99444 | 8.59 | 73.7881 | 2.93087 | 9.26823 |
| **8.10** | 65.6100 | 2.84605 | 9.00000 | **8.60** | 73.9600 | 2.93258 | 9.27362 |
| 8.11 | 65.7721 | 2.84781 | 9.00555 | 8.61 | 74.1321 | 2.93428 | 9.27901 |
| 8.12 | 65.9344 | 2.84956 | 9.01110 | 8.62 | 74.3044 | 2.93598 | 9.28440 |
| 8.13 | 66.0969 | 2.85132 | 9.01665 | 8.63 | 74.4769 | 2.93769 | 9.28978 |
| 8.14 | 66.2596 | 2.85307 | 9.02219 | 8.64 | 74.6496 | 2.93939 | 9.29516 |
| 8.15 | 66.4225 | 2.85482 | 9.02774 | 8.65 | 74.8225 | 2.94109 | 9.30054 |
| 8.16 | 66.5856 | 2.85657 | 9.03327 | 8.66 | 74.9956 | 2.94279 | 9.30591 |
| 8.17 | 66.7489 | 2.85832 | 9.03881 | 8.67 | 75.1689 | 2.94449 | 9.31128 |
| 8.18 | 66.9124 | 2.86007 | 9.04434 | 8.68 | 75.3424 | 2.94618 | 9.31665 |
| 8.19 | 67.0761 | 2.86182 | 9.04986 | 8.69 | 75.5161 | 2.94788 | 9.32202 |
| **8.20** | 67.2400 | 2.86356 | 9.05539 | **8.70** | 75.6900 | 2.94958 | 9.32738 |
| 8.21 | 67.4041 | 2.86531 | 9.06091 | 8.71 | 75.8641 | 2.95127 | 9.33274 |
| 8.22 | 67.5684 | 2.86705 | 9.06642 | 8.72 | 76.0384 | 2.95296 | 9.33809 |
| 8.23 | 67.7329 | 2.86880 | 9.07193 | 8.73 | 76.2129 | 2.95466 | 9.34345 |
| 8.24 | 67.8976 | 2.87054 | 9.07744 | 8.74 | 76.3876 | 2.95635 | 9.34880 |
| 8.25 | 68.0625 | 2.87228 | 9.08295 | 8.75 | 76.5625 | 2.95804 | 9.35414 |
| 8.26 | 68.2276 | 2.87402 | 9.08845 | 8.76 | 76.7376 | 2.95973 | 9.35949 |
| 8.27 | 68.3929 | 2.87576 | 9.09395 | 8.77 | 76.9129 | 2.96142 | 9.36483 |
| 8.28 | 68.5584 | 2.87750 | 9.09945 | 8.78 | 77.0884 | 2.96311 | 9.37017 |
| 8.29 | 68.7241 | 2.87924 | 9.10494 | 8.79 | 77.2641 | 2.96479 | 9.37550 |
| **8.30** | 68.8900 | 2.88097 | 9.11043 | **8.80** | 77.4400 | 2.96648 | 9.38083 |
| 8.31 | 69.0561 | 2.88271 | 9.11592 | 8.81 | 77.6161 | 2.96816 | 9.38616 |
| 8.32 | 69.2224 | 2.88444 | 9.12140 | 8.82 | 77.7924 | 2.96985 | 9.39149 |
| 8.33 | 69.3889 | 2.88617 | 9.12688 | 8.83 | 77.9689 | 2.97153 | 9.39681 |
| 8.34 | 69.5556 | 2.88791 | 9.13236 | 8.84 | 78.1456 | 2.97321 | 9.40213 |
| 8.35 | 69.7225 | 2.88964 | 9.13783 | 8.85 | 78.3225 | 2.97489 | 9.40744 |
| 8.36 | 69.8896 | 2.89137 | 9.14330 | 8.86 | 78.4996 | 2.97658 | 9.41276 |
| 8.37 | 70.0569 | 2.89310 | 9.14877 | 8.87 | 78.6769 | 2.97825 | 9.41807 |
| 8.38 | 70.2244 | 2.89482 | 9.15423 | 8.88 | 78.8544 | 2.97993 | 9.42338 |
| 8.39 | 70.3921 | 2.89655 | 9.15969 | 8.89 | 79.0321 | 2.98161 | 9.42868 |
| **8.40** | 70.5600 | 2.89828 | 9.16515 | **8.90** | 79.2100 | 2.98329 | 9.43398 |
| 8.41 | 70.7281 | 2.90000 | 9.17061 | 8.91 | 79.3881 | 2.98496 | 9.43928 |
| 8.42 | 70.8964 | 2.90172 | 9.17606 | 8.92 | 79.5664 | 2.98664 | 9.44458 |
| 8.43 | 71.0649 | 2.90345 | 9.18150 | 8.93 | 79.7449 | 2.98831 | 9.44987 |
| 8.44 | 71.2336 | 2.90517 | 9.18695 | 8.94 | 79.9236 | 2.98998 | 9.45516 |
| 8.45 | 71.4025 | 2.90689 | 9.19239 | 8.95 | 80.1025 | 2.99166 | 9.46044 |
| 8.46 | 71.5716 | 2.90861 | 9.19783 | 8.96 | 80.2816 | 2.99333 | 9.46573 |
| 8.47 | 71.7409 | 2.91033 | 9.20326 | 8.97 | 80.4609 | 2.99500 | 9.47101 |
| 8.48 | 71.9104 | 2.91204 | 9.20869 | 8.98 | 80.6404 | 2.99666 | 9.47629 |
| 8.49 | 72.0801 | 2.91376 | 9.21412 | 8.99 | 80.8201 | 2.99833 | 9.48156 |
| **8.50** | 72.2500 | 2.91548 | 9.21954 | **9.00** | 81.0000 | 3.00000 | 9.48683 |
| N | N² | √N | √10N | N | N² | √N | √10N |

Table A–11. *Continued*

| N | N² | √N | √10N | N | N² | √N | √10N |
|---|---|---|---|---|---|---|---|
| **9.00** | 81.0000 | 3.00000 | 9.48683 | **9.50** | 90.2500 | 3.08221 | 9.74679 |
| 9.01 | 81.1801 | 3.00167 | 9.49210 | 9.51 | 90.4401 | 3.08383 | 9.75192 |
| 9.02 | 81.3604 | 3.00333 | 9.49737 | 9.52 | 90.6304 | 3.08545 | 9.75705 |
| 9.03 | 81.5409 | 3.00500 | 9.50263 | 9.53 | 90.8209 | 3.08707 | 9.76217 |
| 9.04 | 81.7216 | 3.00666 | 9.50789 | 9.54 | 91.0116 | 3.08869 | 9.76729 |
| 9.05 | 81.9025 | 3.00832 | 9.51315 | 9.55 | 91.2025 | 3.09031 | 9.77241 |
| 9.06 | 82.0836 | 3.00998 | 9.51840 | 9.56 | 91.3936 | 3.09192 | 9.77753 |
| 9.07 | 82.2649 | 3.01164 | 9.52365 | 9.57 | 91.5849 | 3.09354 | 9.78264 |
| 9.08 | 82.4464 | 3.01330 | 9.52890 | 9.58 | 91.7764 | 3.09516 | 9.78775 |
| 9.09 | 82.6281 | 3.01496 | 9.53415 | 9.59 | 91.9681 | 3.09677 | 9.79285 |
| **9.10** | 82.8100 | 3.01662 | 9.53939 | **9.60** | 92.1600 | 3.09839 | 9.79796 |
| 9.11 | 82.9921 | 3.01828 | 9.54463 | 9.61 | 92.3521 | 3.10000 | 9.80306 |
| 9.12 | 83.1744 | 3.01993 | 9.54987 | 9.62 | 92.5444 | 3.10161 | 9.80816 |
| 9.13 | 83.3569 | 3.02159 | 9.55510 | 9.63 | 92.7369 | 3.10322 | 9.81326 |
| 9.14 | 83.5396 | 3.02324 | 9.56033 | 9.64 | 92.9296 | 3.10483 | 9.81835 |
| 9.15 | 83.7225 | 3.02490 | 9.56556 | 9.65 | 93.1225 | 3.10644 | 9.82344 |
| 9.16 | 83.9056 | 3.02655 | 9.57079 | 9.66 | 93.3156 | 3.10805 | 9.82853 |
| 9.17 | 84.0889 | 3.02820 | 9.57601 | 9.67 | 93.5089 | 3.10966 | 9.83362 |
| 9.18 | 84.2724 | 3.02985 | 9.58123 | 9.68 | 93.7024 | 3.11127 | 9.83870 |
| 9.19 | 84.4561 | 3.03150 | 9.58645 | 9.69 | 93.8961 | 3.11288 | 9.84378 |
| **9.20** | 84.6400 | 3.03315 | 9.59166 | **9.70** | 94.0900 | 3.11448 | 9.84886 |
| 9.21 | 84.8241 | 3.03480 | 9.59687 | 9.71 | 94.2841 | 3.11609 | 9.85393 |
| 9.22 | 85.0084 | 3.03645 | 9.60208 | 9.72 | 94.4784 | 3.11769 | 9.85901 |
| 9.23 | 85.1929 | 3.03809 | 9.60729 | 9.73 | 94.6729 | 3.11929 | 9.86408 |
| 9.24 | 85.3776 | 3.03974 | 9.61249 | 9.74 | 94.8676 | 3.12090 | 9.86914 |
| 9.25 | 85.5625 | 3.04138 | 9.61769 | 9.75 | 95.0625 | 3.12250 | 9.87421 |
| 9.26 | 85.7476 | 3.04302 | 9.62289 | 9.76 | 95.2576 | 3.12410 | 9.87927 |
| 9.27 | 85.9329 | 3.04467 | 9.62808 | 9.77 | 95.4529 | 3.12570 | 9.88433 |
| 9.28 | 86.1184 | 3.04631 | 9.63328 | 9.78 | 95.6484 | 3.12730 | 9.88939 |
| 9.29 | 86.3041 | 3.04795 | 9.63846 | 9.79 | 95.8441 | 3.12890 | 9.89444 |
| **9.30** | 86.4900 | 3.04959 | 9.64365 | **9.80** | 96.0400 | 3.13050 | 9.89949 |
| 9.31 | 86.6761 | 3.05123 | 9.64883 | 9.81 | 96.2361 | 3.13209 | 9.90454 |
| 9.32 | 86.8624 | 3.05287 | 9.65401 | 9.82 | 96.4324 | 3.13369 | 9.90959 |
| 9.33 | 87.0489 | 3.05450 | 9.65919 | 9.83 | 96.6289 | 3.13528 | 9.91464 |
| 9.34 | 87.2356 | 3.05614 | 9.66437 | 9.84 | 96.8256 | 3.13688 | 9.91968 |
| 9.35 | 87.4225 | 3.05778 | 9.66954 | 9.85 | 97.0225 | 3.13847 | 9.92472 |
| 9.36 | 87.6096 | 3.05941 | 9.67471 | 9.86 | 97.2196 | 3.14006 | 9.92975 |
| 9.37 | 87.7969 | 3.06105 | 9.67988 | 9.87 | 97.4169 | 3.14166 | 9.93479 |
| 9.38 | 87.9844 | 3.06268 | 9.68504 | 9.88 | 97.6144 | 3.14325 | 9.93982 |
| 9.39 | 88.1721 | 3.06431 | 9.69020 | 9.89 | 97.8121 | 3.14484 | 9.94485 |
| **9.40** | 88.3600 | 3.06594 | 9.69536 | **9.90** | 98.0100 | 3.14643 | 9.94987 |
| 9.41 | 88.5481 | 3.06757 | 9.70052 | 9.91 | 98.2081 | 3.14802 | 9.95490 |
| 9.42 | 88.7364 | 3.06920 | 9.70567 | 9.92 | 98.4064 | 3.14960 | 9.95992 |
| 9.43 | 88.9249 | 3.07083 | 9.71082 | 9.93 | 98.6049 | 3.15119 | 9.96494 |
| 9.44 | 89.1136 | 3.07246 | 9.71597 | 9.94 | 98.8036 | 3.15278 | 9.96995 |
| 9.45 | 89.3025 | 3.07409 | 9.72111 | 9.95 | 99.0025 | 3.15436 | 9.97497 |
| 9.46 | 89.4916 | 3.07571 | 9.72625 | 9.96 | 99.2016 | 3.15595 | 9.97998 |
| 9.47 | 89.6809 | 3.07734 | 9.73139 | 9.97 | 99.4009 | 3.15753 | 9.98499 |
| 9.48 | 89.8704 | 3.07896 | 9.73653 | 9.98 | 99.6004 | 3.15911 | 9.98999 |
| 9.49 | 90.0601 | 3.08058 | 9.74166 | 9.99 | 99.8001 | 3.16070 | 9.99500 |
| **9.50** | 90.2500 | 3.08221 | 9.74679 | **10.00** | 100.000 | 3.16228 | 10.0000 |
| N | N² | √N | √10N | N | N² | √N | √10N |

**Table A–12.** Reciprocals

The reciprocal of any number between 1.00 and 9.99 may be found in the table. For larger and smaller numbers use the following guide to determine placement of the decimal point.

| $N$ | Reciprocal $\dfrac{1}{N}$ |
|---|---|
| 3160 | .00031646 |
| 316 | .0031646 |
| 31.6 | .031646 |
| 3.16 | .31646 |
| .316 | 3.1646 |

Table A-12. RECIPROCALS*

| | 0 | 1 | 2 | 3 | 4 | 5 | 6 | 7 | 8 | 9 |
|---|---|---|---|---|---|---|---|---|---|---|
| 1.00 | 1.00000 | .99900 | .99800 | .99701 | .99602 | .99502 | .99404 | .99305 | .99206 | .99108 |
| 1.01 | .99010 | .98912 | .98814 | .98717 | .98619 | .98522 | .98425 | .98328 | .98232 | .98135 |
| 1.02 | .98039 | .97943 | .97847 | .97752 | .97656 | .97561 | .97466 | .97371 | .97276 | .97182 |
| 1.03 | .97087 | .96993 | .96899 | .96805 | .96712 | .96618 | .96525 | .96432 | .96339 | .96246 |
| 1.04 | .96154 | .96061 | .95969 | .95877 | .95785 | .95694 | .95602 | .95511 | .95420 | .95329 |
| 1.05 | .95238 | .95147 | .95057 | .94967 | .94877 | .94787 | .94697 | .94607 | .94518 | .94429 |
| 1.06 | .94340 | .94251 | .94162 | .94073 | .93985 | .93897 | .93809 | .93721 | .93633 | .93545 |
| 1.07 | .93458 | .93371 | .93284 | .93197 | .93110 | .93023 | .92937 | .92851 | .92764 | .92678 |
| 1.08 | .92593 | .92507 | .92421 | .92336 | .92251 | .92166 | .92081 | .91996 | .91912 | .91827 |
| 1.09 | .91743 | .91659 | .91575 | .91491 | .91408 | .91324 | .91241 | .91158 | .91075 | .90992 |
| 1.1 | .90909 | .90090 | .89286 | .88496 | .87719 | .86957 | .86207 | .85470 | .84746 | .84034 |
| 1.2 | .83333 | .82645 | .81967 | .81301 | .80645 | .80000 | .79365 | .78740 | .78125 | .77519 |
| 1.3 | .76923 | .76336 | .75758 | .75188 | .74627 | .74074 | .73529 | .72993 | .72464 | .71942 |
| 1.4 | .71429 | .70922 | .70423 | .69930 | .69444 | .68966 | .68493 | .68027 | .67568 | .67114 |
| 1.5 | .66667 | .66225 | .65789 | .65359 | .64935 | .64516 | .64103 | .63694 | .63291 | .62893 |
| 1.6 | .62500 | .62112 | .61728 | .61350 | .60976 | .60606 | .60241 | .59880 | .59524 | .59172 |
| 1.7 | .58824 | .58480 | .58140 | .57803 | .57471 | .57143 | .56818 | .56497 | .56180 | .55866 |
| 1.8 | .55556 | .55249 | .54945 | .54645 | .54348 | .54054 | .53763 | .53476 | .53191 | .52910 |
| 1.9 | .52632 | .52356 | .52083 | .51813 | .51546 | .51282 | .51020 | .50761 | .50505 | .50251 |
| 2.0 | .50000 | .49751 | .49505 | .49261 | .49020 | .48780 | .48544 | .48309 | .48077 | .47847 |
| 2.1 | .47619 | .47393 | .47170 | .46948 | .46729 | .46512 | .46296 | .46083 | .45872 | .45662 |
| 2.2 | .45455 | .45249 | .45045 | .44843 | .44643 | .44444 | .44248 | .44053 | .43860 | .43668 |
| 2.3 | .43478 | .43290 | .43103 | .42918 | .42735 | .42553 | .42373 | .42194 | .42017 | .41841 |
| 2.4 | .41667 | .41494 | .41322 | .41152 | .40984 | .40816 | .40650 | .40486 | .40323 | .40161 |
| 2.5 | .40000 | .39841 | .39683 | .39526 | .39370 | .39216 | .39063 | .38911 | .38760 | .38610 |
| 2.6 | .38462 | .38314 | .38168 | .38023 | .37879 | .37736 | .37594 | .37453 | .37313 | .37175 |
| 2.7 | .37037 | .36900 | .36765 | .36630 | .36496 | .36364 | .36232 | .36101 | .35971 | .35842 |
| 2.8 | .35714 | .35587 | .35461 | .35336 | .35211 | .35088 | .34965 | .34843 | .34722 | .34602 |
| 2.9 | .34483 | .34364 | .34247 | .34130 | .34014 | .33898 | .33784 | .33670 | .33557 | .33445 |
| 3.0 | .33333 | .33223 | .33113 | .33003 | .32895 | .32787 | .32680 | .32573 | .32468 | .32362 |
| 3.1 | .32258 | .32154 | .32051 | .31949 | .31847 | .31746 | .31646 | .31546 | .31447 | .31348 |
| 3.2 | .31250 | .31153 | .31056 | .30960 | .30864 | .30769 | .30675 | .30581 | .30488 | .30395 |
| 3.3 | .30303 | .30211 | .30120 | .30030 | .29940 | .29851 | .29762 | .29674 | .29586 | .29499 |
| 3.4 | .29412 | .29326 | .29240 | .29155 | .29070 | .28986 | .28902 | .28818 | .28736 | .28653 |
| 3.5 | .28571 | .28490 | .28409 | .28329 | .28249 | .28169 | .28090 | .28011 | .27933 | .27855 |
| 3.6 | .27778 | .27701 | .27624 | .27548 | .27473 | .27397 | .27322 | .27248 | .27174 | .27100 |
| 3.7 | .27027 | .26954 | .26882 | .26810 | .26738 | .26667 | .26596 | .26525 | .26455 | .26385 |
| 3.8 | .26316 | .26247 | .26178 | .26110 | .26042 | .25974 | .25907 | .25840 | .25773 | .25707 |
| 3.9 | .25641 | .25575 | .25510 | .25445 | .25381 | .25316 | .25253 | .25189 | .25126 | .25063 |
| 4.0 | .25000 | .24938 | .24876 | .24814 | .24752 | .24691 | .24631 | .24570 | .24510 | .24450 |
| 4.1 | .24390 | .24331 | .24272 | .24213 | .24155 | .24096 | .24038 | .23981 | .23923 | .23866 |
| 4.2 | .23810 | .23753 | .23697 | .23641 | .23585 | .23529 | .23474 | .23419 | .23364 | .23310 |
| 4.3 | .23256 | .23202 | .23148 | .23095 | .23041 | .22989 | .22936 | .22883 | .22831 | .22779 |
| 4.4 | .22727 | .22676 | .22624 | .22573 | .22523 | .22472 | .22422 | .22371 | .22321 | .22272 |
| 4.5 | .22222 | .22173 | .22124 | .22075 | .22026 | .21978 | .21930 | .21882 | .21834 | .21786 |
| 4.6 | .21739 | .21692 | .21645 | .21598 | .21552 | .21505 | .21459 | .21413 | .21368 | .21322 |
| 4.7 | .21277 | .21231 | .21186 | .21142 | .21097 | .21053 | .21008 | .20964 | .20921 | .20877 |
| 4.8 | .20833 | .20790 | .20747 | .20704 | .20661 | .20619 | .20576 | .20534 | .20492 | .20450 |
| 4.9 | .20408 | .20367 | .20325 | .20284 | .20243 | .20202 | .20161 | .20121 | .20080 | .20040 |

*Reproduced with permission from Dixon, W. J., and Massey, F. J., Jr.: *Introduction to Statistical Analysis*, 2nd Ed. New York: McGraw-Hill, 1957.

*Table continued on the following page*

**Table A–12.** Reciprocals. *Continued*

| | 0 | 1 | 2 | 3 | 4 | 5 | 6 | 7 | 8 | 9 |
|---|---|---|---|---|---|---|---|---|---|---|
| 5.0 | .20000 | .19960 | .19920 | .19881 | .19841 | .19802 | .19763 | .19724 | .19685 | .19646 |
| 5.1 | .19608 | .19569 | .19531 | .19493 | .19455 | .19417 | .19380 | .19342 | .19305 | .19268 |
| 5.2 | .19231 | .19194 | .19157 | .19120 | .19084 | .19048 | .19011 | .18975 | .18939 | .18904 |
| 5.3 | .18868 | .18832 | .18797 | .18762 | .18727 | .18692 | .18657 | .18622 | .18587 | .18553 |
| 5.4 | .18519 | .18484 | .18450 | .18416 | .18382 | .18349 | .18315 | .18282 | .18248 | .18215 |
| 5.5 | .18182 | .18149 | .18116 | .18083 | .18051 | .18018 | .17986 | .17953 | .17921 | .17889 |
| 5.6 | .17857 | .17825 | .17794 | .17762 | .17731 | .17699 | .17668 | .17637 | .17606 | .17575 |
| 5.7 | .17544 | .17513 | .17483 | .17452 | .17422 | .17391 | .17361 | .17331 | .17301 | .17271 |
| 5.8 | .17241 | .17212 | .17182 | .17153 | .17123 | .17094 | .17065 | .17036 | .17007 | .16978 |
| 5.9 | .16949 | .16920 | .16892 | .16863 | .16835 | .16807 | .16779 | .16750 | .16722 | .16694 |
| 6.0 | .16667 | .16639 | .16611 | .16584 | .16556 | .16529 | .16502 | .16474 | .16447 | .16420 |
| 6.1 | .16393 | .16367 | .16340 | .16313 | .16287 | .16260 | .16234 | .16207 | .16181 | .16155 |
| 6.2 | .16129 | .16103 | .16077 | .16051 | .16026 | .16000 | .15974 | .15949 | .15924 | .15898 |
| 6.3 | .15873 | .15848 | .15823 | .15798 | .15773 | .15748 | .15723 | .15699 | .15674 | .15649 |
| 6.4 | .15625 | .15601 | .15576 | .15552 | .15528 | .15504 | .15480 | .15456 | .15432 | .15408 |
| 6.5 | .15385 | .15361 | .15337 | .15314 | .15291 | .15267 | .15244 | .15221 | .15198 | .15175 |
| 6.6 | .15152 | .15129 | .15106 | .15083 | .15060 | .15038 | .15015 | .14993 | .14970 | .14948 |
| 6.7 | .14925 | .14903 | .14881 | .14859 | .14837 | .14815 | .14793 | .14771 | .14749 | .14728 |
| 6.8 | .14706 | .14684 | .14663 | .14641 | .14620 | .14599 | .14577 | .14556 | .14535 | .14514 |
| 6.9 | .14493 | .14472 | .14451 | .14430 | .14409 | .14388 | .14368 | .14347 | .14327 | .14306 |
| 7.0 | .14286 | .14265 | .14245 | .14225 | .14205 | .14184 | .14164 | .14144 | .14124 | .14104 |
| 7.1 | .14085 | .14065 | .14045 | .14025 | .14006 | .13986 | .13966 | .13947 | .13928 | .13908 |
| 7.2 | .13889 | .13870 | .13850 | .13831 | .13812 | .13793 | .13774 | .13755 | .13736 | .13717 |
| 7.3 | .13699 | .13680 | .13661 | .13643 | .13624 | .13605 | .13587 | .13569 | .13550 | .13532 |
| 7.4 | .13514 | .13495 | .13477 | .13459 | .13441 | .13423 | .13405 | .13387 | .13369 | .13351 |
| 7.5 | .13333 | .13316 | .13298 | .13280 | .13263 | .13245 | .13228 | .13210 | .13193 | .13175 |
| 7.6 | .13158 | .13141 | .13123 | .13106 | .13089 | .13072 | .13055 | .13038 | .13021 | .13004 |
| 7.7 | .12987 | .12970 | .12953 | .12937 | .12920 | .12903 | .12887 | .12870 | .12853 | .12837 |
| 7.8 | .12821 | .12804 | .12788 | .12771 | .12755 | .12739 | .12723 | .12706 | .12690 | .12674 |
| 7.9 | .12658 | .12642 | .12626 | .12610 | .12594 | .12579 | .12563 | .12547 | .12531 | .12516 |
| 8.0 | .12500 | .12484 | .12469 | .12453 | .12438 | .12422 | .12407 | .12392 | .12376 | .12361 |
| 8.1 | .12346 | .12330 | .12315 | .12300 | .12285 | .12270 | .12255 | .12240 | .12225 | .12210 |
| 8.2 | .12195 | .12180 | .12165 | .12151 | .12136 | .12121 | .12107 | .12092 | .12077 | .12063 |
| 8.3 | .12048 | .12034 | .12019 | .12005 | .11990 | .11976 | .11962 | .11947 | .11933 | .11919 |
| 8.4 | .11905 | .11891 | .11876 | .11862 | .11848 | .11834 | .11820 | .11806 | .11792 | .11779 |
| 8.5 | .11765 | .11751 | .11737 | .11723 | .11710 | .11696 | .11682 | .11669 | .11655 | .11641 |
| 8.6 | .11628 | .11614 | .11601 | .11587 | .11574 | .11561 | .11547 | .11534 | .11521 | .11507 |
| 8.7 | .11494 | .11481 | .11468 | .11455 | .11442 | .11429 | .11416 | .11403 | .11390 | .11377 |
| 8.8 | .11364 | .11351 | .11338 | .11325 | .11312 | .11299 | .11287 | .11274 | .11261 | .11249 |
| 8.9 | .11236 | .11223 | .11211 | .11198 | .11186 | .11173 | .11161 | .11148 | .11136 | .11123 |
| 9.0 | .11111 | .11099 | .11086 | .11074 | .11062 | .11050 | .11038 | .11025 | .11013 | .11001 |
| 9.1 | .10989 | .10977 | .10965 | .10953 | .10941 | .10929 | .10917 | .10905 | .10893 | .10881 |
| 9.2 | .10870 | .10858 | .10846 | .10834 | .10823 | .10811 | .10799 | .10787 | .10776 | .10764 |
| 9.3 | .10753 | .10741 | .10730 | .10718 | .10707 | .10695 | .10684 | .10672 | .10661 | .10650 |
| 9.4 | .10638 | .10627 | .10616 | .10604 | .10593 | .10582 | .10571 | .10560 | .10549 | .10537 |
| 9.5 | .10526 | .10515 | .10504 | .10493 | .10482 | .10471 | .10460 | .10449 | .10438 | .10428 |
| 9.6 | .10417 | .10406 | .10395 | .10384 | .10373 | .10363 | .10352 | .10341 | .10331 | .10320 |
| 9.7 | .10309 | .10299 | .10288 | .10277 | .10267 | .10256 | .10246 | .10235 | .10225 | .10215 |
| 9.8 | .10204 | .10194 | .10183 | .10173 | .10163 | .10152 | .10142 | .10132 | .10121 | .10111 |
| 9.9 | .10101 | .10091 | .10081 | .10070 | .10060 | .10050 | .10040 | .10030 | .10020 | .10010 |

# ANSWERS TO EXERCISES

**Chapter 3**

1. 17.67.
2. (a) $\bar{X} = 9.12$; Median $= 5$; Mode $= 5$.
   (b) Yes. Positively skewed.
3. (a) $\bar{X} = 17.4$; Median $= 13.5$.
   (b) Median. The distribution is positively skewed. As a result, the mean is located considerably above the center of the distribution.
4. (a) Mean. Each extreme observation contributes its algebraic weight to the mean, but influences the median and the mode as only one frequency.
   (b) Mode. Its value depends on the density of measures at the modal point only, and thus is relatively unaffected by the location of scores at the extremes of the distribution.
5. Zero. $\Sigma x = 0$.
6. 50th. It is the point above which 50% of the cases occur and below which 50% of the cases occur.
7. Mean; Median; Mode.
8. $11.5\ (8) = 92$.
9. 22.0.
10. 76.55.

**Chapter 4**

1. (a) 51.33.
   (b) $\Sigma x^2 = 458.9$; $s^2 = 65.55$; $s = 8.10$.
2. No. The variances of the two distributions might be different.
3. 61.
4. $A: Q_1 = 38.2, Q_3 = 45.3, Q = 3.55$; Negatively skewed.
   $B: Q_1 = 74.64, Q_3 = 89.85, Q = 7.60$; Positively skewed.
   $C: Q_1 = 14.5, Q_3 = 23.5, Q = 4.50$; Positively skewed.
5. A.D. $= 6.2$.
6. 51.
7. 83.2.
8. 55; 65; 25; 100; 120; 100.
9. 70.24 and 49.76.

### Chapter 5

1. .0156.
2. 30240.
3. 252.
4. 53.29 and 66.71.
5. About 7.
6. The values in the triangle represent the number of ways a yes-no event can happen. For example, in coin tossing, there is only one way that the result of 5 heads and 0 tails can occur; five ways that 4 heads and 1 tail can occur, etc. The sum refers to the total number of ways that the events can occur.
7. (a) 44.52.
   (b) 52.68.
8. .6826.

### Chapter 6

1. 70.66 and 79.34.
2. 23.32 and 26.68.
3. (a) 0.2.
   (b) 90.8 and 93.2.
   (c) 91.8 and 92.2.
4. $s_{\bar{x}} = 2.37$.
5. (a) .40.
   (b) 20.31 and 21.89.
   (c) 20.07 and 22.13.
6. $s_{\bar{x}} = .91$.
   $UL_{95} = 21.1 + 2.13\,(.91) = 23.04$.
   $LL_{95} = 21.1 - 2.13\,(.91) = 19.16$.
   $UL_{99} = 21.1 + 2.95\,(.91) = 23.78$.
   $LL_{99} = 21.1 - 2.95\,(.91) = 18.42$.
7. .678.
8. $UL_{95} = 97 + 1.96\,(10) = 116.6$.
   $LL_{95} = 97 - 1.96\,(10) = 77.4$.
9. 74.4 and 119.6.

### Chapter 7

1. $t = 1.87$; 8 $df$; $p > .05$; No.
2. 1.) The samples are randomly selected.
   2.) There is zero difference between the groups prior to treatment.
   3.) That a null hypothesis can be stated.
3. $t = 4.22$.
4. $t = 4.55$; $p < .01$. The difference is significant.
5. $t = 2.08$; 9 $df$; $p > .05$; No.
6. $\Sigma D = -2.7$; $\bar{D} = -.27$; $\Sigma D^2 = 3.41$; $s_D = .547$; $s_{\bar{D}} = .173$; $t = 1.59$.
   There is no significant effect on attitude.
7. (a) No.
   (b) That $\mu = 50$.
   (c) .05.
   (d) .9004.
   (e) .0996.

## Chapter 8

| 1. | Source | $\Sigma x^2$ | df | Mean Sq. | F | p |
|---|---|---|---|---|---|---|
| | Between groups | 103.97 | 2 | 51.98 | 13.36 | <.01 |
| | Within groups | 38.95 | 10 | 3.89 | | |
| | Total | 142.92 | 12 | | | |
| 2. | Source | $\Sigma x^2$ | df | Mean Sq. | F | p |
| | Between groups | 50.08 | 2 | 25.04 | 6.05 | <.01 |
| | Within groups | 86.88 | 21 | 4.14 | | |
| | Total | 136.96 | 23 | | | |
| 3. | Source | $\Sigma x^2$ | df | Mean Sq. | F | p |
| | Between groups | 662.27 | 4 | 165.57 | 15.62 | <.01 |
| | Within groups | 275.67 | 26 | 10.60 | | |
| | Total | 937.94 | 30 | | | |

That the five methods differ.

## Chapter 9

1. $\chi^2 = 4.60$; 5 $df$; $p > .30$; Yes. We would conclude that the die is evenly balanced.
2. $\chi^2 = 5.33$; 1 $df$; $p < .05$; No.
3. $\chi^2 = 7.64$; 1 $df$; $p < .01$; No. Strictly speaking, however, the problem requires two answers: a one-way classification $\chi^2$ for men, and another for women. When this is done, the answer for men (with Yates' Correction) is $\chi^2 = 4.50$; $p < .05$: For women (with Yates' Correction) $\chi^2 = 1.69$; $p > .05$. Therefore, we cannot accept the claim for men, but can accept it for women.
4. $\chi^2 = 57.4$; 9 $df$; $p < .001$; Yes.
5. $\chi^2 = 4.71$; $p < .05$; No.
   $z = 2.17$; $p < .05$; No.

## Chapter 10

1. $N = 9$; $r = 2$; $p = .25$; No.
2. $\chi^2 = 1.8$; 1 $df$; $p > .05$; No.
3. $\chi^2 = .20$; 1 $df$; $p > .05$; No.
4. $r = 3$; $p > .25$; No.
5. $U = 4$; $p < .05$; Yes.
6. (a) $t = 3.59$; 11 $df$; $p < .005$; Yes.
   (b) The Mann-Whitney would be preferred here since it requires significantly less computational labor.
7. $H = 7.09$; $p < .05$; Yes. (corrected $H$).

## Chapter 11

1. $b = \dfrac{846.97 - \dfrac{[(183)(144)]}{35}}{1119 - \dfrac{183^2}{35}}$

$= .580.$
$a = 4.114 - (.580)(5.23)$
$= 1.08;$
$Y' = 1.08 + .580\,X.$

2. $Y' = 1.08 + .580 \,(25)$
   $Y' = 15.58$.
3. $Y' = 1.08 + .580 \,(-1.877)$;
   $Y' = -0.009$.
4. $b = \dfrac{1356.87 - \dfrac{(97)\,(87)}{25}}{1732 - \dfrac{7569}{25}} = \dfrac{1356.87 - 337.56}{1732 - 302.76} = \dfrac{1019.31}{1429.24}$

   $= .713$;
   $a = 3.88 - (.713)\,(3.48)$
   $= 1.40$;
   $Y' = 1.40 + .713 \, X$.
5. $Y' = 1.40 + (.713)\,(3.48)$
   $= 3.88$.
6. $Y' = 4.85$.

## Chapter 12

1. $r = 19.71/54 = .365$.
2. Yes, at .01.

3a. $r = \dfrac{864.97 - \dfrac{(183)\,(144)}{35}}{\sqrt{\left[1119 - \dfrac{33489}{35}\right]\left[962 - \dfrac{20736}{35}\right]}}$

   $= .46$.

3b. $s_y = 3.30$; $s_{y \cdot x} = 3.30 \sqrt{1 - .46^2} = 2.93$

4. No, it is not significant.

5.

| | X rank | Y rank | $d$ | $d^2$ |
|---|---|---|---|---|
| 1. | 10 | 8 | 2 | 4 |
| 2. | 9 | 10 | 1 | 1 |
| 3. | 8 | 7 | 1 | 1 |
| 4. | 7 | 3 | 4 | 16 |
| 5. | 6 | 5 | 1 | 1 |
| 6. | 5 | 9 | −4 | 16 |
| 7. | 4 | 4 | 0 | 0 |
| 8. | 3 | 6 | −3 | 9 |
| 9. | 2 | 1 | 1 | 1 |
| 10. | 1 | 2 | −1 | 1 |

$\text{rho} = 1 - \dfrac{6(50)}{10(99)}$

$= 1 - \dfrac{300}{990}$

$= 1 - .303$

$= .697$

6. A rho of .697 is significant at the .05 level.

7. (a) $r = \dfrac{(10)\,(288) - (60)\,(40)}{\sqrt{[10(494) - 3600]\,[10(212) - 1600]}} = \dfrac{480}{834.75} = .575$

   (b) $\Sigma y^2 = 212 - \dfrac{1600}{40} = 172$;

   $sy^2 = \dfrac{172}{40} = 4.30$;

   $s = 2.08$;

   $s_{y \cdot x} = 2.08 \sqrt{1 - (.575)^2} = 2.08 \, \sqrt{1 - .331} = 2.08 \sqrt{.669}$

   $= 2.08\,(.817) = 1.70$.

8.  #7 is significant at the .05 level.

9.  

$$\Sigma X = 1553 \qquad\qquad \Sigma Y = 1559$$

$$\Sigma X^2 = 166913 \qquad\qquad \Sigma Y^2 = 167657$$

$$(\Sigma X)^2 = 2411809 \qquad\qquad (\Sigma Y)^2 = 2430481$$

$$N = 15 \qquad\qquad \Sigma XY = 167140$$

$$r = \frac{167140 - \dfrac{(1553)(1559)}{15}}{\sqrt{\left[166913 - \dfrac{2411809}{15}\right]\left[167657 - \dfrac{2430481}{15}\right]}} = \frac{5731.53}{5869.64} = .976$$

10.  

$$\Sigma X = 1553 \qquad\qquad \Sigma Y = 1547$$

$$\Sigma X^2 = 166913 \qquad\qquad \Sigma Y^2 = 165391$$

$$(\Sigma X)^2 = 2411809 \qquad\qquad (\Sigma Y)^2 = 2393209$$

$$N = 15 \qquad\qquad \Sigma XY = 166049$$

$$r = \frac{166049 - \dfrac{(1553)(1547)}{15}}{\sqrt{\left[166913 - \dfrac{2411809}{15}\right]\left[165391 - \dfrac{2393209}{15}\right]}}$$

$$= \frac{5882.93}{5983.07}$$

$$= .983.$$

# SUMMARY OF ARITHMETICAL RULES

## A. Signed numbers

1. *Addition:* To add numbers with different signs, add all the numbers with the same signs, find the difference of the sums, and assign the difference to the sign of the larger sum.

$$
\begin{array}{r}
-4 \\
-8 \\
-3 \\
\hline
-15
\end{array}
\qquad
\begin{array}{r}
+2 \\
+6 \\
+1 \\
\hline
+9
\end{array}
$$

Difference = 6 and the larger sum has a minus sign, so the total is −6.

2. *Multiplication:* The multiplication of numbers with the same sign results in a positive product; multiplying numbers with different signs results in a negative product.

$$
\begin{array}{r}
-2 \\
-3 \\
\hline
+6
\end{array}
\qquad
\begin{array}{r}
-2 \\
+3 \\
\hline
-6
\end{array}
$$

3. *Division:* A signed number divided by another with the same sign results in a positive number; a signed number divided by another with an unlike sign results in a negative number.

$$
-2\overline{)\,\,-6\,\,}^{\,3}
\qquad\qquad
-2\overline{)\,\,6\,\,}^{\,-3}
$$

## B. Decimals

1. *Addition and subtraction:* To add or subtract numbers with

decimals, keep the decimal points in line. The decimal point in the result should be in line with the figures being added or subtracted.

$$
\begin{array}{r}
1.34 \\
+2.07 \\
\hline
3.41
\end{array}
\qquad
\begin{array}{r}
1.47049 \\
-0.00032 \\
\hline
1.47017
\end{array}
$$

2. *Multiplication:* The number of decimal places in the product of the two numbers multiplied together is equal to sum of the decimal places in the two numbers.

$$
\begin{array}{r}
1.20 \\
1.14 \\
\hline
480 \\
120 \\
120 \\
\hline
1.3680
\end{array}
$$

3. *Division:* The number of decimal places in the result of a number divided by another is equal to the number of decimal places in the dividend minus the number of places in the divisor.

$$
.2\overline{)\,.04\phantom{}}^{\,.2}
$$

## C. Proportions

1. *Finding a proportion of a number:* To find the proportion of a total for a number, divide the number by the total.

Example: Find what proportion 27 is of 60.

$$
60\overline{)\,27\phantom{}}^{\,.4500}
$$

2. *Changing a proportion to a number:* To find the number for a proportion of a total, multiply the total by the proportion.

$$
.45 \times 75 = 33.75
$$

## D. Reciprocals

1. The reciprocal of a number is the value obtained by dividing one by that number.

2.   Multiplication of a number (A) by the reciprocal of another number (B) is equivalent to dividing A by B.

Example:

$$A \div B \qquad A = 8$$

$$
\begin{array}{r}
8 \\
.25000 \\
\hline
\end{array}
$$

$$B = 4 \qquad 1/B = .2500 \qquad \overline{40000}$$

$$16$$

$$\overline{2.00000}$$

## E.   Operations

1.   In any sequence of operations involving addition, subtraction, multiplication, and division, multiplication and division are performed first.

Example:   $2 \times 4 + 3 - 1 + 8/2 = 8 + 3 - 1 + 4 = 14$

2.   Terms inside parentheses, brackets, or square root signs are treated as single terms.

$$
\begin{aligned}
\text{Example:} \quad & (3 + 1) - [(6 + 2) - (3 + 1) + \sqrt{3 + 6}] \\
= & (4) - [(8) - (4) + \sqrt{9}] \\
= & (4) - [(8) - (4) + 3] \\
= & (4) - [7] \\
= & -3
\end{aligned}
$$

# INDEX